C000128880

CRISIS
MANAGEMENT
for managers
and executives

CRISIS
MANAGEMENT
for managers
and executives

Business crises –
the definitive handbook to
reduction, readiness, response
and recovery

ROBERT HEATH

FINANCIAL TIMES
PITMAN PUBLISHING

FINANCIAL TIMES
MANAGEMENT

LONDON · SAN FRANCISCO
KUALA LUMPUR · JOHANNESBURG

Financial Times Management delivers the knowledge,
skills and understanding that enable students,
managers and organizations to achieve their ambitions,
whatever their needs, wherever they are.

London Office:
128 Long Acre, London WC2E 9AN
Tel: +44 (0)171 447 2000
Fax: +44 (0)171 240 5771
Website: www.ftmanagement.com

A Division of Financial Times Professional Limited

First published in Great Britain 1998

© Financial Times Professional Limited 1998

The right of Robert Heath to be identified as
Author of this Work has been asserted by him in accordance
with the Copyright, Designs, and Patents Act 1988.

ISBN 0 273 63168 3

British Library Cataloguing in Publication Data
A CIP catalogue record for this book can be obtained
from the British Library.

1 3 5 7 9 10 8 6 4 2

Typeset by Northern Phototypesetting Co Ltd, Bolton
Printed and bound in Great Britain by
Biddles Ltd, Guildford & King's Lynn

The Publishers' policy is to use paper manufactured
from sustainable forests.

About the Author

Dr Robert Heath is a counselling, organizational and managerial psychologist who has consulted in management and communication issues since 1982 and in crisis management since 1986.

At Queensland University, he developed the first undergraduate management course in Australia involving crisis management. In 1990, he provided expert evidence on crisis management issues for the New South Wales State Coronial Inquest into the Newcastle Earthquake of 1989.

In 1993, Dr Heath was recruited to help develop and implement Australia's newest Master of Business Administration programme at La Trobe University (Melbourne). This became a skills-based management degree which included course work in corporate crisis management – covering risk assessment, crisis audits, planning, training, conducting exercises and business recovery and resumption planning.

In June 1995, Dr Heath became full-time consultant and moved to London (England) to help establish *Crisis Corp Ltd*. This company is a crisis management consultancy that provides advice, skills training and management consultations across the full range of crisis management for government and business organizations – from planning and assessment through response and recovery management to evaluation of crisis situations. Under Dr Heath, *Crisis Corp Ltd* seeks to improve services for international clients, particularly among the Global 1000 businesses.

Dr Heath is a Fellow of the Business Continuity Institute. He is an Inaugural Member of the International Executive Board for Local Authorities Confronting Disasters and Emergencies (LACDE), and is currently (1996–98) Chairman of the LACDE International Scientific Committee. He has presented and published numerous papers on various aspects of crisis management.

Dr Heath may be contacted at:

Crisis Corp Ltd
Chesham House, 150 Regent Street, London W1R 5FA
Telephone: [+44] (0)171 432 0386
Fax: [+44] (0)171 432 0516
Email: robert.heath@crisiscorp.com

Acknowledgements

I would like to thank my parents for their continued support and encouragement, and to thank Helen for her love and her patience and assistance during the writing of this book.

Contents

Introduction

This *may* be the most important book you ever read. Thoughtful use of the principles and techniques contained in this book can literally save any organization to which you belong, and even your job and your career.

Maybe even more important than this, applying the principles and skills in this book can save your life and the lives of your family, friends and those around you. The same principles and skills in crisis management apply at work or at home, in a natural disaster or in a car accident, or in a building fire. The principles and techniques apply whenever things suddenly go wrong.

The skills and techniques outlined in this book can improve your ability to operate in day-to-day activities at work or at play.

This can be the most important book you ever read.

Everyone on this planet will have at least one crisis situation arise in his or her life. Houses will suffer structural damage from wind, earthquake, fire and flood. Cars, aircraft and ships will be involved in accidents. Businesses will suffer from natural disasters, deliberate damage, accidents and commercial situations. Communities will face fire, storms, earthquake, floods, large-scale accidents, terrorism, disease and environmental hardship. As individuals we will face birth, loss of loved ones, accidents, crime and death. All of these situations form the stimulus that can lead to the conditions that make a crisis. All of us thus need to learn the skills necessary to deal with all sorts of disasters.

Often we do not face crisis situations on our own. Communities face natural disasters and businesses face a wide range of sudden events that threaten their existence. Many of us consequently need to organize ourselves and others to handle these situations. Managers and executives need to acquire the concepts and capabilities of crisis management and then need to incorporate such skills within their everyday responsibilities and activities so that their organizations and their own jobs have a chance to survive when things go wrong. They also need to gain these skills and develop the necessary support activities to satisfy an increasing demand for resilience and preparedness by external auditors, insurance companies and shareholders.

Executives and managers need to better manage crisis situations. In a 1997 Survey of Fortune 1000 companies undertaken by The Corporate Response Group, 45 per cent of responding managers felt interest was increasing at corporate headquarters and that senior management maintained a high interest in dealing with potential crisis situations. This survey identified some potential crisis situations as being workplace violence (55 per cent), kidnap (53 per cent), terrorist action (51 per cent), fraud (35 per cent), product tampering/recall (34 per cent), ethics (30 per cent), CEO succession (28 per cent), racism-sexism litigation (26 per cent) and takeovers (20 per cent). Those responding to the survey identified a number of areas they thought needed to be improved in organizations. These areas for improvement included internal awareness (50 per cent), communications (45 per cent), drills and training (37 per cent), vulnerability/risk analysis (35 per cent), information technology (32 per cent), planning (31 per cent) and business continuity (24 per cent).

Crisis management for managers and executives helps the reader come to grips with how to manage these situations and how to improve their own capacity to effectively manage crisis situations. The book also helps managers develop effective crisis management practices for any organization – business, home, community, industrial or national.

So what is a crisis exactly?

Perhaps the best way to commence our understanding of crisis management is to look at a brief example of an actual crisis. This example is one of many used throughout this book to illustrate and reinforce points made in the specialized chapters and to bring a touchstone of reality. These examples are called Reality Bites. As most crisis situations are complex mixtures of actions and behaviours that happen before, during and after a crisis situation, the Reality Bites provide succinct background details and highlight specific points or details using common headings:

- *Background* – a quick outline of dates, places or events that lead into the example.
- *Incident* – a brief outline of the onset of the crisis.
- *Response* – time tracks or headline elements illustrating the main impact management used in the crisis event.
- *Statistics* – summary statistics on size, scale or impact data drawn from the crisis.
- *Comment* – specific observations about the general onset, impact and recovery lessons that can be deduced from the example.
- *Management perspective* – more specific observations on crisis management from an executive and managerial point of view.

Many of the Reality Bites presented in this book have had numerous lengthy articles and books written on the events leading up to, during and after the crisis situation. Readers may find the reference sections contain one or more works that provide further details. Do read these where possible. For *Crisis management for managers and executives* these case studies are deliberately made 'bite'-sized for ease of reading and to focus on one or more learning issues which can be drawn from the study. The 'bites' are presented to help readers reconnect with 'reality' after passages of theory and practice have been outlined. The opening example happened on the London Underground in 1987.

REALITY BITE

King's Cross Railway Station, London, 1987

Background

King's Cross underground railway station covers an area ancient in history, being placed on (and under) a ridge believed to be where Boadicea defeated a Roman Legion. The station handles around 250 000 passengers a day.

Safety and fire protection has been a recurrent topic for railways and London Underground management. In 1985, a fire at Oxford Circus killed one person and increased public concerns about safety management in railway systems. The resulting inquiry recommended that smoking be banned in Underground facilities and noted with alarm the lack of staff in attendance over the working day.

Incident

On Wednesday, 18 November 1987, a fire started beneath an elevator that conveyed people from the Underground platforms to the ticketing area and exits from the station. This fire began just after the evening rush-hour had ended (around 7.30 pm). By 7.53 pm, fire had reached flashpoint and exploded, leading to a flashfire across the ceiling around the ticketing office in the station.

Response

At 6.30 pm, a commuter, John Hickson, noticed smoke and a smell of burning rubber and notified a booking clerk in the ticketing office at King's Cross Station about the smoke and smell.

At 7.35 pm, fire exploded around the upward escalators at the station.

At 7.36 pm (and at 7.42 pm) calls about a possible fire at King's Cross were logged in the London Fire Brigade Control Centre.

On site, initial response from available Underground staff was disbelieving and casual. One managerial-level employee investigated the source of the small fire but was unable to operate the fire-sprinkler system.

Early response (even from subway users) seemed low key. One witness commented that 'Everyone was calm. There was no sign of a fire, no bells going, no one shouting fire, no people running away.'

At 7.42 pm an attempt was made to evacuate the passengers. The prevailing plan determined that evacuations should be by train. This attempt failed because:

● too few officials were available to fully assist in implementing the plan;

- people tried to get out by going up to ground level (not only to get away from the fire but also because of the need to escape a claustrophobic sense of being entombed); and
- the Transport Police decided that trains should not stop at the station.

At 7.43 pm, the first fire units arrived.

At 7.45 pm, the flashover explosion of fire occurred around the ticketing office. Most casualties were caused by this occurrence.

At 7.46 pm, the first ambulance arrived on site. Within a minute 13 more ambulances arrived.

At 7.50 pm, train drivers were ordered not to stop at the King's Cross station. Staff at the University College Hospital were alerted that a major accident had happened.

At 7.53 pm, the fire was defined as a major incident and more units were requested to attend the site.

Around 8.00 pm, Divisional Officer Shore requested a further 12 units to attend.

At 8.09 pm, the ambulance service declared the event a 'major incident', called in reinforcements and advised the University College Hospital and St Bartholomew's Hospital to go to Red Alert.

By 8.20 pm, 20 fire units were at King's Cross, while plastic surgeons began to treat patients with intensive flashburns at the hospitals.

At 8.22 pm, the Ambulance Incident Officer informed control that all patients had been located.

At 8.42 pm, Station Officer Colin Townley (the first fire brigade officer on site) was found dead in the site.

By 9.42 pm, all apparent casualties had been removed to hospitals.

At 11.32 pm, first public announcement of 32 deaths was made.

At 12.12 am, the University College Hospital informed site controllers that it was unable accept any more patients.

At 1.30 am, the official death count was confirmed at 30 with 20 people seriously injured.

At 1.42 am, the fire was officially extinguished.

At midnight, British Prime Minister Margaret Thatcher visited victims at the University College Hospital. She made the visit to offer comfort to victims and because the media and opposition spokespeople would attack non-attendance as being uncaring. The visit irritated health workers who felt that reductions in the financial budgets for the National Health Service restricted their ability to respond to the demands of the crisis.

Long-term response

Under Desmond Fennell (1988), an inquiry into causes and response to the fire lasted 91 days and heard evidence from over 140 witnesses. The report made 157 recommendations, including fitting escalators with heat detectors, provision of automatic sprinklers, availability of up-to-date plans of the stations, removal of wooden escalators, staff undertaking refresher courses in safety and emergency response management, more vigorous inspections by Inspectorate staff, and improvements in communication equipment and public address systems.

London Transport made an offer of £2500 compensation per injured and deceased passenger. This was perceived as a mean offer, and several victims filed claims against London Transport.

Statistics
Some 31 people were killed in this fire, including Fire Station Officer Colin Townley, and 20 people were seriously injured.

Comment
Some significant issues emerge from this example. The low-key, almost dilatory response often indicates an organizational culture in which response to non-normal events has a low priority. This is supported by evidence at the Fennel Inquiry, which showed safety priorities were financially pruned and training in emergency management and response was infrequent and patchy.

The rapid shift from normal to emergency or non-normal situations is a principal concern in crisis management. The numbers of victims involved can overwhelm many professional staff as demand for limited resources rapidly escalates. Due to constrained budgets and poor estimations of potential crisis demands, resources needed to respond to the crisis quickly become scarce. People need to quickly shift from normal thinking and behaviours to non-normal approaches to dealing with a threatening situation. In many cases, people need confirmatory signals and time to adjust to the non-normal situation.

At the time of the fire, King's Cross Station had reduced numbers of staff. At set times some of these were absent on meal breaks. The staff that were available, however, appeared to be unfamiliar with the fire control and suppression equipment. When professional firefighting respondents arrived they were hampered by a lack of knowledge about the layout of the station until 8.45 pm, an hour after the crucial flashover fire erupted.

An intentionality study of 24 victims by Donald and Cantor (1992) suggests that people who died in the King's Cross fire behaved in similar ways to those that escaped and survived. In general, people caught in fire events tend to continue along their intended routes or try to leave by the way they came into the site. The implications of this are obvious. If the routes habitually used by people are the most likely routes they will use under threat then any planning for mass evacuation needs to take this into account.

Management perspective
The death of Colin Townley illustrates the fragility of reaction when even professional respondents fail to undertake appropriate safety measures due to the perceived demands of the situation. By hastening to make an on-the-spot appreciation of what needed to be done, Townley apparently failed to take the extra time to put on breathing apparatus which undoubtedly contributed to his loss of life. While accepting that he worked heroically to save life and assess the situation, we need to remember that the first duty of managers is to manage. Responding to the immediate needs of one or two people can put more people at risk, as managers who become involved in a specific tactical task can fail to provide overall attention to the management of the incident and members of the response team.

As emerges in post-event evaluation of many corporate and people-caused crises, a trail of warning signs emerged during the Fennel Inquiry. The wooden escalator that was the initiating site of the fire had caught fire around 18 times over the 45 years it had been used. The chief fire inspector of London Transport claimed that the same fire hazards could be found year after year at most stations. In defence of London Transport, operating budgets from the national government were being cut back each year.

Crisis situations

Quite a few points about crisis management are present in this example. The first point is that *crises happen suddenly* but may have a trail of signals that became apparent in post-event review. The evidence given at the Fennel Inquiry, for example, included indications of such signals. These indications included an impression that smouldering fires were part of the everyday organizational environment, a critical safety report from the chief fire inspector and a statistic that there had been 18 fires in 45 years at the site. Effective and rapid signal detection and action triggers are an essential part of good crisis management practice.

The crisis example also illustrates a chronological shape that we call a linear progression, as shown in the Response section's time track. In broad terms we can discuss the crisis as an event that has a start and a finish. The period of time between the first indications of a threatened crisis to the time the crisis begins to cause damage can be called the *crisis onset*. This is where work is done to prevent the crisis from happening and reduce or minimize the likely impact(s) of that crisis. The effort spent in handling the onset of crisis event – how it was dealt with, what was done and what happened – is called *crisis onset management*.

The impact or effect the crisis event had on the surrounding environment and the people therein is called *crisis impact*. What was done to deal with the crisis impact is termed *crisis impact management*. Here, we work to resolve the damage caused by a crisis event.

Differentiation between crisis event and crisis impact is important because in most cases different people, resources and even situations are likely to be involved in each case. The easiest way to see how these components arise is to imagine an aircraft that suddenly loses its engine power. The efforts by the pilots, air traffic controllers, engineers and company experts to keep the aircraft from crashing form the crisis onset management. Should these efforts fail, then the resulting crash, fire, impact damage, victim and victim family support, organizational reputation and clean-up form part of the crisis impact management. Both components are part of crisis management.

In the King's Cross fire, the crisis onset occupied a very short space of time – from the unrecorded moment in which conditions for ignition of fire came together until the fire started. In some cases the crisis onset management period is longer. In businesses, the first time a crisis threat is properly apprehended is usually long after signals about that potential crisis have been emitted. Onset management appears to occupy a short space of time before impact management begins. Given that the onset management period may be very short, executives and managers need to develop better pre-crisis management in terms of risk (*see* Chapter 2), risk reduction (*see* Chapter 4) and implementing early warning systems (*see* Chapter 5).

Crisis impact management in the King's Cross fire lasted from the 6.30 pm alarm by John Hickson until the official statement that the fire was extinguished at 1.42 am.

Almost as soon as the crisis impact management is started, a parallel set of activities aimed at recovering the people, resources and structures in the affected environment may commence. Here, the emphasis is on re-normalizing the affected environment. Re-normalization means returning the structures, systems and people to a functional state that equals or improves upon (but is unlikely to mirror) the normal state that existed in the environment prior to the onset of the crisis. This is termed *impact recovery management* and may take a far longer period of time – from the moment the first casualties are being treated, through physical reconstruction and repair, to rehabilitation and litigation procedures. The impact recovery period has not fully finished in the case of the King's Cross fire. While the station was quickly repaired and returned to full operational state, some of those impacted by the crisis were still being treated and undertaking legal action for damages in 1997.

For convenience we can combine crisis onset and crisis impact periods into a response-based entity called the *crisis event*. This enables us to more easily discuss the three important features of crisis management and of crisis evaluation (*see* Chapter 17): pre-event, event and post-event. We explore the pre-event period for cause-and-effect links that may lead to the onset of a crisis. Likewise we look at the post-event period for ways to improve recovery. In both cases we need to seek ways in which we may reduce the onset and impact of crisis situations (*see* Chapters 3 and 4) and to become more resilient and crisis-resistant (Chapter 18).

The King's Cross example highlights other significant features about crisis situations. Quite early we see that a crisis usually contains a threat to resources and people. This threat is increased by the apparent lack of time in which to respond and resolve the event. In the King's Cross fire there was a very short onset period, followed by an impact management period of just over seven hours – from 6.30 pm to 1.42 am. The apparent threat is also increased by missing or uncertain information. In the King's Cross fire, the firefighters gained information about the station layout around 8.45 pm, just over an hour after the fire became serious. Transport Police decided not to stop trains even through this was the official evacuation procedure. Information under the stresses and demands of a crisis event may appear fuzzy, vague or distant.

Three key elements that indicate the presence of a crisis situation can be deduced. These three elements are:

- *little time in which to act (or respond);*
- *missing or uncertain (unreliable) information;*

- *a threat to resources and/or people.*

We will be returning to these three basic elements throughout this book, particularly in Chapter 13.

As noted earlier, most crisis situations have three major response initiating problems. These initiating problems are:

- signal transmission;
- signal recognition;
- signal translation into response action.

These issues are discussed in more detail in Chapter 5. Three important issues are illustrated in the King's Cross example. First, managers and executives need to consider what constitutes meaningful early warning and what messages should be conveyed with such warnings. There were few automatic fire warning systems in action in the King's Cross event. Given the thick smoke, maze-like twists and corridors in the underground station, and the confused intention to evacuate or not evacuate by train, early warnings and passenger warnings were non-optimal.

Fire evacuation needs to take into account the most likely actions undertaken by those trying to leave the crisis environment and the conditions under which these may be attempted. Even less transient and more static sites (such as multi-storey office blocks and high-rise buildings) are likely to have only rudimentary evacuation plans – such as 'Get out of here and meet at...' rather than more planned and prepared responses (*see* ACCCE in Chapter 4).

Second, people generally react slowly and poorly to non-normal signals. Evidence at the Fennel Inquiry into the King's Cross fire found casual and disbelieving reactions by staff, a time lag of an hour between John Hickson reporting the presence of smoke and the fire alerts received by the firefighting services and an indifferent response from the passengers. People continued to use the upward moving escalators even as flames became apparent.

Third, people usually perform two non-optimal behaviours on receiving an alert. The first behaviour is to await further information or a supporting signal. The other behaviour is to confirm the warning by their senses (sight, feeling, hearing and smell). These behaviours arise because we desire confirmatory support for the non-normal signal. In the King's Cross case, the manager who checked the physical existence of the crisis was unable to operate the fire suppression equipment.

This example also illustrates that one crisis event can often lead to other crisis situations. Just after midnight, for example, the University College Hospital could take no more casualties. This overload situation can create resource failures that may precipitate other crisis situations such as failure to treat other critical non-King's Cross fire emergencies. Other critical issues may arise from the congestion in traffic caused by commuters finding alternative travel during and long after the crisis event was over. Such changes can lead to other crisis events from road accidents to crowd crushing situations. Long-term crisis implications may include the cost to families and communities in supporting families who lost income-earners and people who are hospitalized for long periods of time.

The ability of a crisis to cause other crisis situations is termed a *ripple effect* because these crises seem to fan outward like ripples after a stone is thrown into a pool of water. The initiating crisis may be the stone striking the water. Subsequent impact damage may include the stone striking the bottom of the pool, the impact of the splashes of water on the pool surface and surrounds, and the damage caused by the ripples on the pool shoreline. Mitroff and Pearson (1993) note this ripple effect as a chain reaction that may be caused by poor management of the original crisis situation.

Crisis events can cause ripple effects in organizations and communities. An industrial plant that is destroyed or badly damaged drains money from an organization, puts people out of work and may cause further damage to the surrounding community system through loss of resources or pollution. In Seveso (Italy, 1971), the accidental release of dangerous chemicals from a factory led to long-term pollution of surrounding farming land and communities. This necessitated the relocation of those living in the area. Likewise, the meltdown accident at the Chernobyl nuclear power station (USSR/Ukraine, 1986) devastated large areas of land through radioactive fallout.

A graphic example of a ripple effect can be seen in Switzerland in 1978 when a fire in a chemical plant run by Sandoz in Zug was a crisis event that was relatively quickly controlled. One consequence, however, was that over 30 tons of toxic sludge from putting out the fire entered the Rhine river. During the next ten days a chemical slick 40 kilometres (25 miles) long flowed to the sea, causing damage to river ecosystems and industries in a number of countries. The Swiss government and Sandoz had to pay compensation for this pollution.

Some of these ripple effects may cause crisis situations that are larger than the initiating crisis. Before wild fires struck communities in Oakland, California (1982) or in the state of Victoria (Australia, 1989), the initial crisis onset management was the prevention of fire. Once the fires ignited, impact management consisted of trying to prevent greater loss of resources and life until the fires were brought under control or were extinguished. After the fires were out, further crises on personal and community levels emerged. Family structures disintegrated and communities found recovery difficult. In Oakland, half the residents and businesses did not return to the community. This subsequently caused a critical impact on the ability of that community to repair and recover its infrastructure through the collection of local taxes. In large community crisis situations such as fire, major flood, catastrophic windstorms (tornadoes and hurricanes) and earthquakes, just over one-in-four small businesses (around 29 per cent) will still exist within two years (Stuart, 1992).

Another feature of crisis management that is illustrated in the King's Cross example is the need for communications management (*see* Chapter 6). Communication is perhaps the most important task in crisis management. Not only do we need to manage communications effectively within the crisis event and within an organization involved in onset and impact management, but also we need to manage how we communicate to the outside world. How we are seen to manage a crisis can be as critical to survival and successful resolution of that crisis as how we actually manage that crisis. This 'how we are seen' effort is called *image management* (*see* Chapter 8). In fact, many managers and people ignore image management. In doing so, they can appear to have performed ineffectively (or even suspiciously as if covering something up) although the crisis situation was brought under control and resolved.

In the King's Cross fire, a number of communication and image management issues include the transmission of warnings and evacuation procedures as well as informing respondents about the nature and specifications of the affected environment. Image management concerns are also apparent. The offer of £2500 in compensation for seriously hurt and dead victims by London Transport was seen as 'mean'. Sections of the community (including railway staff and health care workers) saw the visit by Margaret Thatcher as a hypocritical act because they blamed her actions to cut their budgets as contributory to the fire at the station and the overload on hospital resources. On the other hand, advisers to Margaret Thatcher would have pointed out the equally negative image of an uncaring person that would have been created had she not visited hospitalized victims and expressed her sorrow at the event.

Scale or size of a crisis

For an individual a simple house fire or car accident may produce a crisis event. A death in a family has the same impact whether the cause is from a car accident or from a major earthquake. The individual or small group crisis event may have little impact on a community. As the size of the event increases, however, the resources available to respond and recover may be less than the demand for those resources. This excess of demand over supply creates a complicated impact and recovery management position. As the size or scale of the crisis situation increases, management of response and recovery is likely to become more complicated with the need to assign priorities and offset gains with losses.

In the King's Cross example, the small size of the initial fire seemed non-threatening, and yet the fire grew from just visible flames (7.35 pm) to a flashover (7.45 pm) and a major declared incident (7.53 pm). More and more resources were required to resolve the impacts of the crisis, which meant increased demands on site management of resources and personnel.

Size and scale are also reflected in commercial or business and industrial crisis situations. The destruction of one computer out of a hundred is less likely to be critical than the loss of all computers. Similarly, one small bad debt may not create a crisis in terms of liquidity and cash flow, but cumulative small bad debts or a very large bad debt may cripple a company. Barings Bank (UK, 1995) and Yamaichi Securities (Japan, 1997) failed because of hidden bad debts that overwhelmed the immediate ability to cover liabilities and daily cash flows.

Visibility of a crisis

In the King's Cross example, the limited access to the fire site below ground combined with the thick outpouring smoke to create a physically invisible situation. Victims and respondents became disoriented and distracted by smoke. Incident managers saw less and gained less accurate reports about the progress and threat of the situation. In this case physical invisibility heightened the sense of threat and loss of control and made management decision making more difficult.

Crisis events may be invisible due to the nature of the situation. Reputation assaults become more difficult to manage because the crisis is invisible until the impacts emerge. Likewise, collapse of a share market or hostile takeovers leave next to no time for crisis onset management and little time in which to respond.

One important issue that emerges from the degree of visibility or tangibility of a crisis threat is the effect on those who may have to face that threat. The more the crisis situation is invisible or intangible then the more communities and organizational members will feel threatened by (and give salience or greater emphasis to) the possible crisis situation. The threat of nuclear contamination to communities, for example, is perceived to be far greater than the most pessimistic of 'objective' assessments.

In general, the less visible the mechanics of a crisis situation, the more complicated will become the management of that crisis.

Complexity level of a crisis

One result of this brief outline of the King's Cross Underground Rail Station fire is the deduction that crisis situations can become complex management situations. This complexity is due to the knock-on effects of ripple-type consequential crisis situations, the increasing size and/or scale of the event, and the increasing invisibility or intangibility of the event. A crisis situation is likely to become complex in nature should any of the following criteria be present:

- There are *insufficient resources* to resolve the crisis.
- The numbers of people and/or resources under threat mean that *choices concerning priorities in response actions need to be made.*
- The threat occurs when and where *specialized resources and skills may not be readily available.*
- The impact of the initial crisis is likely to generate a large number of different effects, each of which may lead to *a need for specialized resources for effective management.*

11

One outcome of increasingly complex crisis situations is that the costs in resources and time to resolve that crisis will increase, as will the cost in time and resources to recover from the impacts from that event.

What is involved in crisis management

In its most comprehensive form crisis management involves managing all aspects of the before, during and after of a crisis situation. In conventional forms crisis management has a strong emphasis on response management and pays little attention to the antecedents and the aftermath of crisis situations. Most planning and thinking about crisis management – whether called contingency, emergency or disaster management, or business recovery or business continuity management – has been reactive management – putting out fires and healing and repairing the injured and damaged. Such a narrow emphasis reduces the chance of effective management. We need only to consider the King's Cross fire example and the previous comments to realize that effective management needs to seek to reduce the size and scale of damage before a crisis happens and to establish early warning systems. Had the combustible material under the wooden escalators been removed or not permitted to accumulate and had there been effective warning and fire suppression systems, the cost in resources and human life is likely to have been significantly reduced. By seeking the sources and nature or shape of crisis situations and by analysing the impacts caused by such crises, we can work toward better crisis management through risk reduction and mitigation management.

Effective crisis management involves seeking ways in which:

- the sources, size and impacts of a crisis are mitigated or reduced;
- onset management may be enhanced;
- response management of the impacts of the crisis event can be improved; and
- recovery management can effectively and rapidly resolve the damage caused by the impacts of a crisis.

Defining a crisis

So far we have been using a real example of a crisis to generate an understanding of aspects of crisis management and to help us establish a universal terminology that can be used for any crisis situation in any culture. By establishing some understanding of crisis situations and of the needs of crisis management, we can move to consider aspects presented by other observers, analysts and practitioners. Note that this sample of sources uses different terminology to describe the same concepts – emergencies, disasters or crises. This variation of terminology contributes to ambiguity and poor communication and is a key reason for us to move toward specific yet encompassing universal terminology. Disasters and emergencies involve the same thoughts and concepts as the use of the term crisis, although some users may argue the terms specify a specific accent or subset of elements within the crisis concept. In most cases the words appear interchangeable, and we will use crisis and crisis management as our universal terms in *Crisis management for managers and executives.*

- Foster (1980, p. 217) finds that *'emergencies are characterized by four distinguishing features, an urgent need for rapid decisions, accompanied by acute shortages of the necessary trained personnel, materials, and time to carry them out effectively'.* As a working definition of a crisis, the ideas of 'an urgent need for decisions', 'acute shortages of personnel', 'acute shortages of material' and 'acute shortages of time' point to fundamental aspects of a crisis situation.
- Rosenthal and Pijnenburg (1991, p. 3) outline a broader concept of crisis in that *'the concept of crisis relates to situations featuring severe threat, uncertainty, and sense of urgency.'* Crises can be threatening situations that stress urgency in response and which are uncertain in the nature and impact of the crisis.
- Barton (1993, p. 2) finds a crisis to be *'a major, unpredictable event that has potentially negative results. The event and its aftermath may significantly damage an organization and its employees, products, services, financial condition, and reputation'.* Barton extends the impact of a crisis to include the reputations of people and organizations, supporting the need to manage communication and image.
- Green (1992) notes that a characteristic of crisis management is that *'one starts from a position in which control of events has been lost'* (p. 67). Once in crisis mode, he states that *'damage limitation will be the major concern and time is critical'* (p. 91). For Green, the mission of crisis managers is to prevent loss of control when and where possible, to limit the damage during the crisis event, and to regain control when loss of control happens.
- Mitroff and Pearson (1993) find that gathering, analysis and dissemination of information is the immediate effort for crisis managers. The first few hours (or days for crises that may last for long periods of time) are used to simultaneously perform a number of activities associated with the critical responsibilities of crisis managers. These responsibilities are those of *'fact finding, analysis, damage control, and communication'* (p. 101).

We may now develop a fairly comprehensive technical picture of what is involved in a crisis situation and thus in crisis management.

A crisis situation involves:
- **a threat to resources and people**
- **a loss of control**
- **visible and/or invisible effects on people, resources and organizations.**

From a management perspective the threats, loss of control and potential damage to people and resources place a pressure for resolution of the crisis situation that also defines a crisis. From the management perspective a crisis is a crisis because:

- there is very limited time in which to respond (or such time appears very limited);
- decisions have to be made rapidly (given the constraints of limited time);
- available information appears unreliable or missing;
- the demands of the response in terms of people and equipment may (or appear to) exceed the available people and resources.

Crisis situations thus generate a need to find more time, gather more reliable information, and protect and effectively deploy available resources. The feelings of pressure felt by those involved in a crisis situation need to be managed. These feelings can be eased by using stimulus–response circuit breakers (often called 'stoppers' in psychology) such as the simple PBR (Pause–Breathe–Relax) technique that is presented in Chapter 14. Managers can also use the pressure they feel to get more time, more information, and to preserve and efficiently use resources to focus their decision making. One technique that helps this focus is *CrisisThink* (*see* Chapter 13) which involves mentally re-cycling three key questions while operating in a crisis situation:

- *How can I (or we) gain more time?*
- *How can I (or we) gain more information?*
- *How can I (or we) reduce the loss or cost of resources?*

These three questions allow a manager to focus on the means to reduce the feelings of pressure and resolve the crisis situation. As a bonus, the focus on preserving or reducing the costs and losses in resources will help present a positive image – particularly with other senior managers in the affected organization or organizations.

Crisis management consequently involves five main activity clusters:

1 Crisis managers work to *prevent crisis situations from arising and to minimize crisis impacts.*
2 Before crisis situations arise, crisis managers *plan response and recovery activities and rehearse organizational members in doing those activities* so that organizations and communities are prepared in some way to deal with future crisis situations and crisis impacts.
3 When a crisis situation arises, crisis managers *deal with the crisis onset* in the available time.
4 When the crisis threat or threats begin to affect the situation, crisis managers *deal with any crisis impacts.* This may mean using different resources, personnel and management approaches from those used in dealing with the crisis onset period.
5 After a crisis, crisis managers can be involved in managing *recovery and restoration* programmes. This may mean using different resources, personnel and management approaches from those used in dealing with the crisis onset and crisis impact periods.

The human side of crisis situations

So far we have considered technical aspects about crisis situations and crisis management. In a sense, crisis situations do not happen unless any threat or likely impact from a crisis is against humans or resources valued by humans. Many managers assigned business continuity tasks tend to overlook this perspective because of the ease with which objective approaches lull users into complacency. Few crisis or business continuity plans give people more than task-driven recognition, yet people are the buyers, sellers, communicators and consumers that enable an organization to exist and function. We overlook the management of people (and of their fears, hurt and points of view) at our own cost.

Because people are threatened by a crisis, they become participants within the situation. Traditionally, participants included *victims* (those affected by the crisis), *respondents* (those who respond to the crisis) and *bystanders* (those who observe the crisis from nearby but do not get directly involved). Victims were those who were physically injured during a crisis. Respondents were those who had jobs that involved dealing with crisis situations. Bystanders were those who were physically unaffected but quite physically close to (or within) the environment surrounding the crisis event. With the growth of knowledge and technology, these definitions have blurred.

Victims

Victims are people directly or indirectly affected by a crisis event. Respondents, bystanders, family members of those hurt or killed and friends of those directly affected by the crisis event may also become victims. In the King's Cross Underground Railway Station fire, passengers on passing trains that did not stop who saw those trapped by the fire also became victims. Victims can include those who vicariously observe the event, even from a great physical distance. When a terrorist bombing campaign recommenced in Israel in 1994 and 1995, those affected by similar incidents many years earlier were reaffected. The spree killing of schoolchildren in Dunblane (United Kingdom, 1996) refreshed the hurt for parents and survivors of the Aberfan landslip event (1966). The survivors and parents of the dead schoolchildren at Dunblane were themselves affected by the television and media coverage of a spree shooting at Port Arthur in Australia (1997). Most of us will become victims in some form as details of crisis events are quickly and graphically broadcast to anywhere in the world. Sounds and pictures bring us up close to the physical and tangible evidence of a crisis.

The term victim need not imply 'must be cured' or 'needs counselling'. Many people re-normalize themselves after emotional impacts from crisis events, particularly if their role was that of a spectator or observer. We do need to use this encompassing classification of victim to remind us that all of those involved *can be* sufficiently harmed psychologically that they begin to disrupt their own lives and the lives of those around them.

Not all news coverage need have negative impacts on people. Graphic depiction of the famine in Africa in the 1980s produced a world-wide Live Aid event in which people contributed millions of dollars to help alleviate the suffering. Equally graphic coverage of major incidents such as the *Exxon Valdez* grounding and leakage of petroleum products in Alaskan waters makes us more conscious of the effects of pollution.

Respondents

Respondents include those untrained people (bystanders and victims) who are present when the crisis situation arises. In community crisis situations, these amateurs are soon replaced by professional respondents (law enforcement agents, paramedics and medical staff, firefighters and personnel from armed services) who are usually more trained and disciplined, enabling them to function more effectively under conditions of stress found in the crisis situation.

In major disasters, professional respondents are too few in number or too far away to provide immediate assistance. Those at the scene then need to cope on their own. Major crisis situations such as earthquakes and floods in urban and city areas usually result in humans having to look out for themselves and those around them with little or no professional assistance at any specific time. Non-professional bystanders undertook over 90 per cent of the rescues of people trapped by impact damage to structures in the Northridge earthquake (California, USA, 1994).

The term 'respondent' covers volunteer assistance from bystanders and from those outside the crisis situation. Most community planning for natural disasters needs to allow for outside volunteer assistance and must consider how such assistance may be used to optimal benefits. Two benefits from outside assistance (be it from outside professional bodies or from volunteers) are that:

1 the assistance frees local professional respondents for other response tasks; and
2 humans from outside the affected area are more likely to be less emotionally affected by the crisis event and more able to think clearly.

The arrival of outside law enforcement personnel in the Northridge earthquake allowed local law enforcement personnel to focus on specific problem areas. Two counterbalancing negatives against the use of outside assistance are that:

1 the presence of outside personnel can add a drain on scarce resources such as accommodation and supplies; and
2 too many personnel in one site can get in each other's way and impede the response activity.

Bystanders

Bystanders can be divided into two groups – those who were actually present (real bystanders) and those who were able to see the event as spectators (virtual bystanders). Both sets of people may believe they have witnessed the event. This belief has three important implications:

- While each of the sub-group members believes they have witnessed the event, they actually have seen only distorted parts of the event (and of the management of that event).
- The greater numbers of 'witnesses' means that greater public pressure for outcome resolution will be felt. This pressure results in more legal inquiries, increased pressure to assign blame and greater media attention.
- Beliefs about the event held by members of both sub-groups will converge resulting in rationalized facts that can differ from the actual course of actions that each 'witness' did not see or experience (*see* Chapter 17). One important point to note from this convergence of belief is that evidence from actual witnesses needs to be gained as soon as possible.

Human involvement – psychological and physiological perspectives

People are affected by the impacts of a crisis upon themselves and their surrounding environment. Public perception of crisis situations has changed as some causes have become less mysterious (e.g. natural disasters) and as other threats (radioactive and chemical contamination) have become less tangible and thus more perceptually threatening.

Early crises were either *people-sourced* (tribal raids) or *environment-sourced* (natural disasters, attacks by wild animals and hazards). Until around two hundred years ago, solutions to these crises were also very simple. One either *fought* the raiders or *ran away* and either *fought* the wild animals or *ran away*. One further *avoided* the natural hazards such as quicksand and falling rock. The actions of fighting or fleeing are two basic human responses to sudden events such as crises, and are colloquially termed the *fight or flight response* (*see* Chapter 6).

Natural disasters were another matter for our ancestors. With little understanding of the structure of the earth and its atmosphere, volcanic activity, earthquakes, floods, droughts and huge storms were seen as beyond human control. In most cases these events were attributed to the anger of some specific god. Given such manifest anger from the gods, primitive crisis management actions tended to be placatory in nature – god worship, gift-giving and sacrifice of living animals or humans.

After a natural disaster communities often sought for people to blame for displeasing the god or gods. New actions or behaviours (such as farming new lands, killing particular sacred animals, changing the physical structure of a community, failing to properly observe the placatory worship rituals) or people who were different (strangers, those physically different from the community, outcasts) were often identified as offending the god or gods and were thus ritually eliminated. Given the sporadic nature of such events any move to appease the gods would be seen as successful as the natural disaster usually did not immediately reoccur.

Today we understand more about the formation of major storms, the effects of floods and drought, and what causes volcanoes and earthquakes. On a personal level, however, many of us still react superstitiously to events that happen. We experience guilt at having survived. We express beliefs about our sins catching up with us because of some negative impact. We express dismay at how small and defenceless we may be in the event of a major crisis.

These feelings of discomfort and guilt still direct us to seek ways in which we can appease our disquiet. We cannot stop a passenger aircraft from crashing, a ship from sinking or land vehicles from crashing. We still cannot predict or manage volcanic activity or earthquakes, and while our understanding of large storms is better we can do little to prevent the damage caused by violent windstorms like tornadoes or hurricanes. Feeling powerless, we still seek to identify guilty people and we often seek someone to blame for our own collective inadequacy.

Such behaviour promotes further interest in crisis management. Not only does the general community seek more knowledge in order to know what community leaders and managers *should have done*, but people also feel a need to increase their personal level of safety *when a threat or crisis has happened*.

The effects of a crisis may not only be the physical impact-related ones. People can be mentally affected and are increasingly seeking compensation for those effects. This is illustrated in the Buffalo Dam situation.

REALITY BITE

Buffalo Creek Dam-burst, West Virginia, USA, 1972

Background

In the United States of America, the coal industry has exerted a long and dominant influence in local and state governments such as that of the state of West Virginia. As a consequence, coal companies ran 'company towns' and undertook operational actions as they saw fit. In this case, the Buffalo Mining Company used what turned out to be an unsafe (and probably illegally built) slag waste dumping dam for tailings.

Incident

On the night of 26 February 1972, the slag waste dam ruptured and sent a torrent of slag and black water down a valley, inundating a number of small housing sites (virtually small towns) used by local miners.

Response

Most rescue operations were undertaken by victims and bystanders, and essentially remained a local initiative.

Survivors were distributed randomly around makeshift refugee centres, causing dislocation among close-knit communities and increasing the difficulty of establishing who were dead and what members of families remained intact.

Statistics
Around 125 people were killed and 600 were injured. Over 654 victims sued the Buffalo Mining Company for damages. Successful litigants received between US$7500 and US$10 000 each.

Comment
This incident was probably the first in which psychological assessment of victims and litigation over mental trauma was seriously undertaken. The defending company tried to minimize the effect, evade blame and deter litigation. Settlement was made out of court (including over US$6 000 000 in psychological damages).

Research ordered by the court assessing the 654 claimants suggested that 90 per cent of the litigants had symptoms of psychological disability. These symptoms included sleeplessness, a feeling about the 'flatness' of life after the event, increased irritability, psychological withdrawal, phobias about wind and water, hyper-anxiety when exposed to reminders about the disaster and loss of interest in their work. Survivors also evinced lack of cognitive concentration (forgetting names and addresses or the errand for which they had set out) and survivor guilt. Other measures of community disturbance were also uncovered. There appeared more delinquency, theft, divorce and marital difficulties after the event. The volume and impact of the research was such that the *American Journal of Psychiatry* devoted a whole issue (April 1976) to the disaster.

Related research found that many survivors felt a rage against the helplessness linked to their inability to prevent the man-made disaster and to their experiences of the disaster. This rage has two probable dominant sources:

1 beliefs that had the survivors acted differently and thus not allowed the event to happen, the disaster could have been stopped; and
2 the loss of control, not only of the situation but of their lives long after the event had ceased to be.

This sense of survivor guilt arises not only in large disaster situations or in sharp accident situations (transportation accidents, structure fires), but even in less physical crisis situations.

Managerial perspective
This example provides three important issues for our consideration. First, company managers tend to contest compensation payments for at least two fundamental reasons – the legal liability and the cost to an organization. Any attempts at early (and often fair but cheaper) compensation tend to be restrained by the legal advisers to an organization who are primarily concerned with the compensation being an admission of liability. In more general terms, managers and executives tend to resist compensation claims because of the cost to the organization (and possibly because of the potential loss of their own positions). The long-term effects commonly increase costs (if only in court and legal representation costs) and inflated compensation decisions, and a negative public image of the organi-

zation (as being uncaring, remote or even criminal). Only governments of large countries, large public service bureaucracies and large multinational companies seem immune to the immediate resource costs of negative organizational image – although we do not really know what results continued negative images may have over very long periods of time.

Second, people who experience trauma are affected by that trauma. Survivor guilt and rage are natural responses to traumatic events and how we respond to these. The period in which the mental disturbance lingers and physically disrupts a survivor depends on each person involved. For many, a period of days or years may be needed before the displacement in their thinking and behaviour fades away. For some, the change in self-perception and in their interpretation of their surrounding world is so displaced that they experience various levels of post-traumatic stress disorder (see Chapter 16) that may permanently remain.

Third, a workforce that is experiencing heightened sensitivity to environmental stimuli or is traumatized is likely to be less than optimal in workplace performance. Many organizations often face loss of members after a major crisis due to one or more of four factors:

- loss of stimulation after the crisis situation;
- burn out;
- increased fear of the environment surrounding the organization; or
- dissatisfaction with the treatment received during or after the crisis situation.

While organizations are unable to address each of these in full for each member, managers and executives can be more sensitive to the likely psychological effects a crisis may have on staff (see Chapter 16).

Putting it all together – the big picture

We have looked at what we can gain from considering an example of a real crisis, at definitions from theorists and practitioners of crisis management, and at the human aspect of crisis situations. Now we can begin to put together a big picture that integrates these aspects and around which *Crisis management for managers and executives* is structured.

First we can explore our perceptions about resources, people, response, recovery and communication. A simple means of doing this is to use a geometric shape – in this case, a circle. As a result we can depict an integrated management in terms of a *crisis management sphere* (see Figure 1.1).

In the crisis management sphere in Figure 1.1, the two left-hand quadrants represent the communications activities of crisis management while the two right-hand quadrants represent the action elements of crisis management. The top two quadrants reflect the onset to the clean-up phase of the crisis event, while the bottom two quadrants reflect the recovery management period. Physical (and visible) impacts dominate in the onset to clean-up

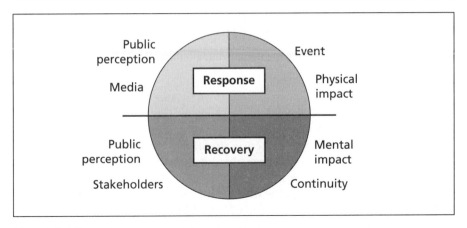

Fig. 1.1 The crisis management sphere

phases and the mental impacts emerge more dominantly in the recovery phase. Do note the strong emphasis given public perception in both response and in recovery management. Finally note the term *stakeholders*. We will use this term consistently to cover all of those people who have a direct or indirect investment in an organization. These groupings may include (in no particular ranking or order) customers, creditors, staff, suppliers, product users, shareholders, owners and government regulatory agencies. Each of these groupings needs careful management during response and recovery periods should we wish to accomplish a positive and effective crisis management.

Unhappily most organizations pay too much attention to resource management (structures, facilities and processes) and insufficient attention to people and communication. For many organizations the effort put into the left-hand side of the sphere is so small as to be invisible, with the consequent outcomes of appearing non-communicative, uncaring and even unprepared to interact with stakeholders and the outside world. Media interactions and interactions with pressure groups and the general public (*see* Chapters 7 and 8) take on either an almost *ad hoc* and fumbling appearance or are presented so slickly and so content-constrained as to appear a transparent cover-up or a dismissive gesture to the audiences involved.

The crisis management sphere can help managers focus on an overall approach to crisis management. Managers and executives need to consider reducing exposure to crisis situations and getting their organization prepared to manage crisis situations, as well as planning and training to respond to (and recover from) a crisis situation. These four elements form the basis of crisis management and can be defined in many ways. Conventional usage talks in terms of Prevention, Preparation, Response, and Recovery (PPRR), while the Federal Emergency Management Agency (USA) uses a modification: Mitigation, Preparation, Response and Recovery.

In *Crisis management for managers and executives* we use a more active set of terms to focus on what managers need to do to be effective. These terms are:

- **Reduction**
- **Readiness**
- **Response**
- **Recovery.**

Managers actively need to cover the tasks in all four groups of the RRRR model – reduce the onset and impact of crisis situations, get the organization ready to handle crisis situations and provide the capability to respond to – and recover from – those crisis situations that arise.

Each of these groupings can be divided into important task characteristics, as illustrated in Figure 1.2. Consequently, the RRRR model is used to shape the central structure of Crisis management for managers and executives. Effective crisis management starts before any crisis arises through an evaluation of the risks (Chapter 2) of a crisis situation happening and a consequent assessment of how impacts from a crisis may damage an organization and the surrounding environment (Chapter 3). These evaluations and assessments then enable decisions on each of the four Rs to be made.

The first R, Reduction (Chapter 4), is often treated lightly by many organizations yet can dramatically reduce costs and impact damage. Effective crisis

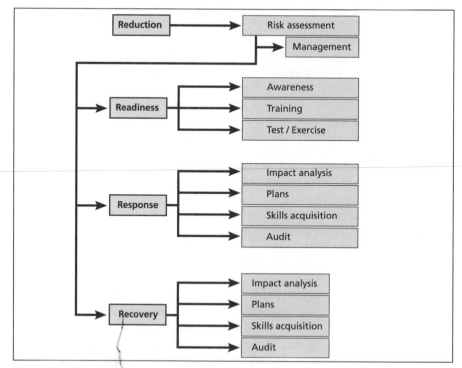

Fig. 1.2 The crisis management modules

management involves a synthesis of all four R modules and so comments about reduction (and readiness, response and recovery activities) arise throughout the book. An immediate example of this interactive synthesis can be seen in developing better warning strategies (Chapter 5), communications skills (Chapter 6), media management skills (Chapter 7) and image management skills (Chapter 8). Improvements in these can reduce the effects of a crisis situation, can improve the level of Readiness, and can lead to better Response and Recovery management.

Similarly managers can identify approaches to management in general (Chapter 9) and crisis management in particular (Chapter 10) that influence Readiness preparations, Response management and how Recovery efforts may be better managed. From these background chapters managers can begin to develop more effective Response and Recovery plans (Chapter 11) and approaches that foster and enhance Readiness (Chapter 12) that include training and conducting exercises.

Having established strategies for reducing crisis risks and impacts and for preparing people and organizations for responding to (and recovering from) crisis situations, managers need to identify ways in which situations (Chapter 13) and people (Chapter 14) can be better managed. Similarly approaches for managing Recovery (Chapter 15) can be explored in greater detail, and the psychological impact from crisis situations on people (Chapter 16) can be looked at from both a responding management perspective and in terms of dealing with stress and psychological impairment.

This approach helps executives and managers to move sequentially through a dynamic and interactive process. Given this dynamic and interactive nature of crisis management, expect reference to ideas and principles across chapters. Executives and managers are also given an introduction to evaluating crisis management (Chapter 17). The book concludes with the pragmatic goal of effective crisis management – that of the fifth R that is the outcome of the RRRR model (R+R+R+R = R) which is Resilience (Chapter 18).

References

Barton, L. (1993) *Crisis in organizations: Managing and Communicating in the Heat of Chaos*. Cincinnati, Ohio: South-Western.

Donald, I. and Cantor, D. (1992) 'Intentionality and fatality during the King's Cross fire', *European Journal of Social Psychology*, 22, 203–18.

Fennell, D. (1988) *Investigation into the King's Cross Underground Fire*. London: HMSO.

Foster, H. D. (1980) *Disaster Planning: The Preservation of Life and Property*. New York: Springer-Verlag.

Green, P. S. (1992) *Reputation Risk Management*. London: Pitman/Financial Times.

Mitroff, I. I. and Pearson C. M. (1993). *Crisis Management: A Diagnostic Guide for improving Your Organization's Crisis-Preparedness*. San Francisco: Jossey-Bass.

Rosenthal, U. and Pijnenburg, B. (1991) 'Simulation-oriented scenarios', in U. Rosenthal and B. Pijnenburg (eds), *Crisis Management and Decision Making: Simulation Oriented Scenarios*. Dordrecht: Kluwer, pp. 1–6.

Stuart, H. (1992) 'The Newcastle earthquake: local government response', *Macedon Digest*, 7(4), 17–21.

2

Assessing and managing risk

The obvious starting point in our quest to be effective crisis managers is to identify sources of crisis situations. Thus we assess what risks or threats or hazards may exist for ourselves and our organizations. This is called risk assessment. If we have enough time and resources we can use the list of threats, risks and hazards to begin our management of these risks. Time and resources, however, are often limited, and we need to establish some form of priority of attention. Such priorities are usually determined by weighing up the magnitude and frequency of each hazard, risk and threat. This process is termed risk evaluation. Once we have identified all – or established a list of priority-ranked – risks, threats and hazards we can consider how we may best manage each of these sources. This management process is risk management (and can be termed risk treatment because we try to fix the causes of problems before the problems arise).

Risks, threats and hazards are words used to describe very similar sources of problems and crises, but can also be used to denote specific concepts. The work *risk* comes mainly from financial management activities and contains strong elements of quantification – calculations that estimate gains and losses through exposure to various sources of risks. The word *threat* is more often used in social science research that seeks some understanding of how people perceive situations that could threaten their safety and existence. This approach also discusses threat perception in terms of how exposed or vulnerable people feel to these situations (and thus uses the term vulnerability). The term *hazard* is generally used by engineers and scientists to describe physical risks such as dangerous chemicals and threats from the world around us (earthquakes, fire, floods, windstorms and war).

In *Crisis management for managers and executives* the term risk will mostly be used to cover all these meanings.

This chapter follows the natural divisions of looking at risk assessment and issues about risk evaluation and then moves on to simple risk management techniques. Before dealing with these areas we need to consider the strengths and weaknesses in current approaches to risk assessment and evaluation.

Points to remember about the concept of risk

Risk

In the context of crisis management, the term *risk* tends to be a technical estimate of likely failure or negative outcome that is usually deduced from statistical reviews of past data or from 'objectively' inferred estimates from experts about the likelihood of a situation actually happening. Problems with this approach are that:

- historical data is often incomplete or inaccurately measured;
- the qualifications and selection of *experts* may be inexact; and
- the objectivity of experts may also be questioned.

Looking at historical data to generate probability statistics for an industry, for example, can lead to our overlooking specific vulnerabilities within a specific region. Even concerns over apparent global warming may be based upon our inability to deduce cycles or patterns of global weather spanning thousands of years.

Likewise, the quality and substance of expertness is likely to be a variable. Some experts are simply people with academic certificates that seem relevant. Other experts have hands-on experience but little training in assessing situations beyond an intuitive reliance on remembered past experience. Moreover, once expert opinion operates more as an art than as a measurable science the possibility of subjectivity rather than objectivity is raised.

Such issues are countered by trying to collect large samples of outcome data or large numbers of expert opinions.

Accuracy of risk estimates

The issue of accuracy is important for those planning for, or financing, crisis management activities. Governments and insurance companies, for example, often use estimates of the frequency of event occurrences in terms of once-in-fifty or once-in-a-hundred-year events. Emergency service resources, on the other hand, are often based on a combination of economic priorities and common demand (such as yearly forecasts of demand and use) and thus fall short of the larger cycle of resources needed in a hundred-year or fifty-year situation. The Kobe earthquake (1994) and Sydney/New South Wales wildfires (1996) are examples of such events. Crises in these situations can arise because the frequency of the event occurrence (and thus the scale of resources needed) may be miscalculated and because the resources made available to response agencies are limited by economic considerations.

Use of computer-based software

There are many computer software programs that can help managers identify sources of crisis situations and assess the impact of these sources, and which help generate standardized plans for risk, response and recovery management. Many of these are quite good tools to assist organizations plan to cope with crisis situations in terms of physical asset management and resource deployment. Most current software applications, however, do not provide sufficient emphasis on human management, communication processes and areas such as reputation and image management. Moreover, many software applications may not be flexible in terms of identifying the unique features and vulnerabilities that exist in each organization. Use these applications as tools to help develop a crisis management programme, not as the only source for management planning and conduct.

Fatal attraction of technical risk assessments

Because of the ease and apparent scientific accuracy of technical and objective measures of risk, we often become too dependent on frequency and probability estimates of a situation arising. We lose sight of how *threatened or vulnerable people feel by various sources of crisis*. Crisis management is as much about dealing with human perceptions about the crisis and the management of a crisis as it is about physically resolving the crisis situation. Objective assessments are often technical and mathematical in nature and are thus difficult to fully comprehend. Should we use only objective assessments, we may fail to deal with those people likely to behave before (protests), during (inappropriate response behaviours and actions) and after (expensive litigation and pressure for formal and legal inquiries) a crisis situation. While experts may have confidence in scientific data and process engineering management, the perceptions of people who may be affected by a crisis situation need to be assessed as well. This is particularly true for impact management (*see* Chapter 3).

The reason for including perceived risk information is that the perception of risk held by individuals and groups usually differs from any objective evaluation of that risk. The risk of being a victim of an aircraft accident is often perceived as being higher than that of being a victim of a car accident – yet the statistical probability of being involved in a car accident is much higher than that of being involved in an aircraft accident. People fear being infected by AIDS far more than by influenza, yet more people die per year from influenza than from AIDS.

Three fundamental psychological elements that need to be incorporated into any examination of risk are that people:

- behave according to their perceptions;
- often respond to a crisis situation only when they sensorily encounter that situation;
- after experiencing a crisis event, behave according to how vividly they per-

ceived that event (called *salience*) rather than the likely occurrence of that event.

By allowing for, and responding appropriately to, these perceptions of threat we may reduce anxiety, post-traumatic disorders and litigation. Likewise, by working toward sensitively identifying and attending to the fears held by our stakeholders and surrounding community groups, we can reduce many obstructions and much resistance to our crisis management activities – particularly to risk and impact management.

Four possible reasons help explain this dependence on our own internal perceptions and beliefs rather than upon expert and external information. These reasons are:

1 We grow up as first-principles experimenters. What we see, feel, taste, touch, cause to happen are accepted as true facts. What others report to us is regarded as unverified and therefore suspect.
2 We are victims of the recency and salience of other sources of information. Graphic pictures of major accidents and disasters have greater impact than figures or common reports, provided that such pictures are infrequent in presentation. We become over-familiar, for example, with pictures and stories about car accidents to the point that we filter out the salience of these. On the other hand, community tension and over-alertness is almost always triggered by a serious sex crime (particularly against children) or terrorist act even though these happen far less frequently than car accidents.
3 We are victims of partial reinforcement wherein crisis events happen infrequently and at apparently random times and thus fix our learning of the 'threat'. The high frequency of reports on street violence and car accidents again implies a filtering and over-familiarity which would degrade the level of impact each report has on each of us – until the event happens to us. The low frequency of major crisis events (passenger aircraft crashes, finance company failures, major earthquakes and floods) in most regions of the world often leads to greater media coverage and thus more prominent experiences for us to use as risk assessment data.
4 We are becoming used to being misled or misinformed by authoritative sources, and so tend to rely on our own judgements. Such misinformation may be accidental. The number of false alarms, for example, in broadcasting warnings about oncoming violent weather or spurious alarm signals of burglary, fire or car theft tend to make us doubt the validity of any subsequent warning or alarm. Some misinformation appears more deliberate and deceitful. Scientific facts and surveys that are found to be unreliable or are selectively distorted lead to cynical disregard for information provided by organizational sources (particularly from government organizations and from large national or multinational companies).

We can quickly understand how risk items may be seen as more or less risky when we realize that all of us cope better when we feel we have the ability to see and control the risk. Moreover, we generally cope poorly when the risk is invisible and we feel unable to exert control over that risk.

Risks are seen as less risky when the risks are one or more of the following:

- voluntarily undertaken;
- over-familiar to a person;
- seen as controllable;
- undertaken by the percipient of the risk;
- fairly apportioned according to outcomes;
- seem unlikely or not memorable;
- hold little fear;
- seen as long term and chronic;
- either spread thinly all over the geophysical space or arise everywhere;
- brief in length of exposure;
- non-lethal;
- seen as part of nature;
- seen as able to be acted against;
- tactile (able to be seen, tasted, smelled, touched and/or heard).

Risks are seen as more risky when the risks are one or more of the following:

- involuntarily done;
- unfamiliar or new;
- beyond control;
- managed by others;
- have benefits and costs that seem unequal in distribution;
- graphic and very memorable;
- very frightening;
- sudden or surprising in onset;
- fixed and focused;
- have a long-term exposure (and consequential impact takes a long time to become manifest);
- lethal;
- introduced by people;
- beyond managed action;
- beyond tactile sensory awareness.

The perceptions of risk held by stakeholders and the people in the community surrounding an organization generate two points that managers, politicians and business executives ignore at their own cost. These two points are:

1 If the risk is invisible but the damage is potentially horrific, people are unwilling to accept much of that risk.
2 People are increasingly likely to resist risks to their safety and lifestyle.

People will resist imposition or acceptance of risks from governments and industry by direct campaign and through pressure groups, often forming specifically local single-issue groups called NIMBY ('Not In My Back Yard') groups – *see* Chapter 8. There is a growing trend for individuals and groups to legally sue for suspected damage, for the stress caused by any crisis event and for the effects of living under that threat.

Risk analysis

Risk analysis and management can be a simple task for crisis management. The process is quite straightforward:

1 Identify the risks – what are the threats, hazards and things that could go wrong?
2 Identify how these risks may best be managed.
3 Do it.

To a great extent this is all we need to do to reduce the crisis exposure for any organization.

This activity becomes complicated should we find ourselves subject to limited availability of resources. This limitation may take one or more forms, including:

● budget
● staff
● response capacity.

Once an organization's ability to deal with the identified threats is limited, or the number of threats is so large that the organization cannot deal with all threat sources at once, managers need to develop a sequential set of priorities.

Sources of risk are often poorly identified. Many managers tend to focus too closely on a set of obvious threats that arise within the organization or within the structure or site in which the organization is placed. Risks, hazards and threats come from four core groups:

● internal sources from within the organization and the physical site or structure in which the organization exists;
● adjacent or neighbouring sources from organizations and sites or structures that immediately surround the organization;
● external or regional sources from organizations or structures within the surrounding community or geophysical area;
● remote or over-the-horizon sources from organizations or structures beyond the community or region (including national and international sources).

By examining each of these groups for sources of threat and risk, managers can develop policies and plans to deal with risk and threats at appropriate levels within the organization. Notice that as the groupings move from internal to external, the capacity of the organization to manage the size, nature and impact of the threat diminishes.

Risks, threats and hazards can be quantified. So we will first look at simple risk analysis (called *risk identification*) then move into weighting and quantifying these risks (called *risk evaluation*).

Risk identification

Risk identification involves generating lists of possible risks and sources of risk. This process can include some sorting of risk sources into groups of similar origins or of similar impacts. Thus floods, storm damage, dam bursts, tsunamis and cyclonic windstorms may be grouped together as having a similar origin (water and bad weather), or earthquakes, war, bomb blasts, fires and landslides may be grouped together in terms of sources that generate similar impacts (structural failure and loss of organization).

Sufficient information can generally be gathered by combining information from a number of different sources. These sources may provide the information in different forms, from qualitative (verbal descriptions, such as vulnerability assessments from people) to numeric descriptions (frequencies and probabilities of occurrence). Four key approaches for undertaking risk identification are:

- brainstorming
- statistical review
- cued analysis
- walking around.

These four need to be used in this sequence so that as many elements of data as possible are uncovered. Brainstorming needs to be done before statistical reviews because the statistical review procedure is likely to narrow the range of thinking of the users. Likewise, cued analysis may distort the reality of what has happened in the surrounding environment and previously in the organization space. Once the three 'cerebral' processes have been attempted a walk around the organizational space often elicits other sources of risks.

Brainstorming

Of the four approaches, brainstorming is the most fun and most creative. By bringing a group of people together to generate possible sources of risk, we can quickly produce a large list of most sources. For a given environment or organization, groups of around 30 people can generate 50 to 70 sources of risk in 30 minutes.

Brainstorming made easy

Brainstorming encourages creative and original thinking while combining a number of insights from a group.

The object is to create a process in which people generate ideas and thoughts without the usual immediate accompaniment of critical comment.

The basic process is as follows:

- Assemble a group of people in a quiet room that is isolated from interruption.
- Ensure that the room has tables, chairs, pen and paper for each member of the group, and facilities for writing lists of items that can be viewed by all present (overhead projector with overheads, whiteboard, blackboard or flipcharts).
- A facilitator then outlines any ground rules on time use and makes the following rule clear to all members: *'Generate as many ideas on the following topic as they can without any consideration as to the validity or feasibility of each idea.'*

Get each member to contemplate the topic and jot down as clearly as possible all potential concepts or ideas possible for that topic. In risk identification, this means all possible sources of risk each person can think of for a given environment or organization.

Next, the facilitator collects the ideas from all participants using either a two-stage or three-stage process.

The two-stage approach

The facilitator collects everyone's ideas either by collating all of the lists into one list or by having each person read out their list of ideas and writing these on a medium capable of being seen by all participants at the same time (overhead transparency, blackboard, flipchart, whiteboard or networked computer screens). The facilitator needs to ensure that no critical comment is made by anyone present until all ideas are collected.

The three-stage process

The facilitator has members form small groups of no more than four people once each person has conducted their own idea generation. The small groups then discuss the topic and draw up a list of ideas from their individual ideas that is agreed upon by the group. This helps stimulate further ideas and often helps people think. A handicap of this approach is that a group-view is likely to prevail and will eliminate eccentric or apparently silly ideas. Facilitators need to ensure that all ideas (individual or group) are collected. After the small group discussion the group lists (and any individual's further additions) are collected in the same way as for the two-stage approach.

Once the list is displayed we have a choice of three actions:

- simply determine how all items may be managed;
- sort the list into groups of similar items and then determine how each group may be managed; or
- given lack of resources, time or funding, seek to develop some order of priority with which the most significant items or groups of items can be handled – risk evaluation.

Statistical review

Two main sources of statistical information for risk identification are the historical records of risk-sourced events within an organization (or of an association or institute representing kindred organizations) and statistical summaries generated by government statisticians and insurance organizations. Sources of historical records can include internal (accident reports, equipment failure reports, variations on labour and production figures) and external (local newspaper reports, local government records, public information on industry and business incidents). Insurance groups and government statistics offices can provide information on types of incidents, size of impacts and on statistical probabilities of the incident occurring. Internet sites also are beginning to provide information on crisis situations.

Cued analysis

Three main sources for cued analysis are software programs, expert assessment and checklist questionnaires. At this point outside prompts help extend the coverage by sequentially prompting risk identification. Software programs are good at supplying easily accessible questions that quickly enable risk summaries to be made. Outside experts can be used to facilitate the whole process and to provide an outside point of view that often proves most useful. Checklist questionnaires help supply a cheaper springboard from which risk identification may be made. Remember to check that any computer software used does adequately cover the unique as well as the common elements of any specific organization, or add such information at the appropriate time.

Walking around

One final sweep for sources of risks (and very useful for generating impact information – *see* Chapter 3) is done by physically surveying the given organization space or environment. By actually seeing the site and the operations (or by asking the people involved) other sources of threat and risk may be uncovered. This process also allows users to talk with various stakeholder groups – staff, users, suppliers, creditors, customers and shareholders.

The 'walking around' technique is an approach that is underused by managers and consultants. Walking around enables managers to view the daily activities and get to know both environment and stakeholders more closely. One means we may use to assess the likely utility of advice from a consultant is to see how quickly that consultant indicates a desire to walk around the space occupied by an organization. The value of walking around an organization cannot be overstated for crisis managers. Stakeholders see that the issues are being taken seriously (and begin to invest in the process when those walking around ask the stakeholders for their opinion). Similarly, walking around enables crisis managers to see the organization. Security issues, unsafe practices, the build-up of combustible rubbish, the obstruction of evacuation paths and new structures or facilities that were not identified in the other processes are often quickly uncovered.

Risk evaluation

In many cases we are unable to address all identified crisis-source items at once. In these situations we need to determine which items should be handled before others. Brainstorming processes can be used to evaluate any compiled list of risks.

Evaluating identified risks

Everyone can develop his or her own assessment measures and dimensions. The basic ones would be:

- likelihood of situation arising;
- size or scale of the situation;
- perceived scale of the situation by stakeholders; and
- impact upon organization.

Each of these can be assigned a rating that is as simple or as precise as desired by the crisis assessment team. As a default measure we can use small, moderate and large to cover these values and assign each verbal rating a numeric scale for ease of establishing the priority rank. These numeric values are called *weights* because the value contributes to the overall assessment (or weights that assessment). Conventionally we tend to value large numbers over small numbers (except those who play golf) and so we normally assign high weights to large ratings and small weights to those ratings of less size:

Large   = 3
Moderate = 2
Small   = 1

▶

▶
> We also need to determine how we will combine the weights. We can simply add up the assigned weights (the *additive* model) or multiply the weights with each other (the *compound* or *multiplicative* model). Either approach produces the same rank-order of risk, although the compound approach can make high priorities more readily identifiable than the additive model (e.g. 3 + 2 + 2 + 1 = 8 versus 3 x 2 x 2 x 1 = 12).
>
> We can gain a consensus-driven assessment of what verbal rating (and thus what numeric weight to use) by getting each participant to vote for their best estimate. If, for example, we had 20 participants and we were assessing the risk of an earthquake for a specific area we may have 2 members voting for large likelihood, 6 members voting for moderate likelihood, and 12 members voting for small likelihood. The assigned weight in this case would be 1 (reflecting the majority assessment of small likelihood).

Of course, the information gathered from other procedures used to generate sources of risk can help assign such weights. Governmental and insurance statistics, for example, can provide likelihood and size weight estimates, while comments gained from any stakeholder research can lead to useful threat perception weights.

Problems with quantifying risk assessments

A number of problems exist with using quantified risk assessment. Kloman (1992) finds that users tend to forget that:

● complex human behaviour is difficult to reduce to numbers;
● numbers reflecting real life are oversimplifications;
● lack of applicable data means dishonest guessing;
● decision makers may substitute numbers for reasoning;
● risk trade-offs against benefit can be unrealistic when relying solely on numbers.

Any risk assessment needs to balance a quantitative process with a qualitative process that explores the sources and nature of risks as viewed by stakeholders (those groups of people who interact with the organization – including organization members, users, investors, suppliers, customers, consumers and those affected by the organization's activities). Any risk assessment without a qualitative people approach runs the risk of not only beginning to believe guesstimates and statistics, but of losing touch with the image and perceptions of the organization (the left-hand half of the *crisis management sphere* shown in Chapter 1).

Moreover, risk assessed only in probabilistic terms can be misleading. Research on the presence of cognitive biases and the less than accurate calculation of probabilities suggests that expert and layperson assessment of subjective risk can be flawed (Kahneman, Slovic and Tversky, 1982; Yates and Stone, 1992). People tend to over-assess threats which appear vivid, very dangerous or very recent in their experience.

Expert assessments can be incorrect. As one example, several statistical assessments of natural disasters are inaccurate. These inaccuracies may have arisen through incomplete or inaccurate historical information or because the pattern being assessed is incomplete through lack of specific knowledge about the complete picture. Assessments of frequency of occurrence of an event (particularly of major natural disasters) need to be treated conservatively. Expect more frequent major occurrences than the expert assessment indicates.

Managers can ensure greater reliability in statistically inferred events by checking that:

- the question that generates the frequency or probability assessment is the one for which they need the statistical measure;
- all units or items or cases or occurrences are counted; and
- users realize that any probability estimates are only accurate when used against very large numbers.

Consider the following brief notes.

Check that the question is the one for which you need the measure

Derived statistics only reflect the question used to establish the frequencies involved. When the context of a question is changed the figures or statistics are also likely to change. The context of the question is often termed the frame of the question. An example of the effect of a frame can be seen in the ensuing example. An outbreak of a plague threatens a city population of 10 million people. An available vaccine can save 99.9 per cent of the population but may be fatal to 0.1 per cent. Would the vaccination be acceptable? The risk seems acceptable because the crucial figure (0.1 per cent) seems small – an acceptable risk. When the question is rephrased, however, experiments tend to show that fewer people choose the vaccination option. An outbreak of a plague threatens a city population of 10 million people. An available vaccine may kill 10 000 people through complications. Would the vaccination be acceptable?

Without due care, a manager can elicit the wrong risk assessment. Take a possible experiment to assess the effect of dangerous versus safe tasks being undertaken in drug-using and drug-free environments. If the assessment question was 'What conditions produce the fewest accidents and what conditions produce the most accidents?' then the likely predictions would be that safe tasks undertaken when drug-free should prove to have fewer accidents than when tasks are dangerous and done under the influence of drugs. Average daily samples from the same production lines may appear to produce confounding findings. If the total number of accidents was 300 in a sample of

30 000 tasks performed then there is a 1 per cent chance of an accident or 1 in 100 chance of having an accident. The number of accidents for all four conditions could be as follows:

	Drug free	Drug using	Total
Safe task	80	80	160
Dangerous task	75	65	140
Total	155	145	300

On inspection these figures suggest that more accidents happen when drugs are not taken and that more accidents happen when tasks are safe. Each of the four conditions produces fairly similar numbers of accidents (a range of 65 to 80) and the fewest number of accidents occurs when drugs are taken and dangerous tasks are performed. Theories would emerge – people are more careless when doing safe tasks, people take more care when tasks are dangerous. Were managers not cautious, policies enforcing the taking of drugs may be implemented and tasks made more dangerous in the interests of worker health and safety.

The answers appear to contradict the predictions made. A different picture would have been produced had the question asked 'How frequent were the accidents under each condition (expressed per hundred tasks)?'

	Drug free	Drug using	Total
Safe	80 in 12 000 = 0.67	80 in 8000 = 1	160 in 20 000 = 0.8
Dangerous	75 in 6500 = 1.15	65 in 3500 = 1.85	140 in 10 000 = 1.4
Total	155 in 18 500 = 0.83	145 in 11 500 = 1.26	300 in 30 000 = 1

The frequencies show outcomes that support the initial predictions. The fewest accidents per hundred tasks occur when workers are drug-free and doing safe tasks (0.67) and the most accidents per hundred tasks arise when drugs are used while performing dangerous tasks (1.85). What changed was the type of question asked – frequency of accident per condition. This shifted the comparison of counted accidents and any comparison with the total number of tasks counted in the total study to checks against the baseline for each condition. The risk statistics then reflect a more accurate picture of the frequency of accidents.

Count all units or items or cases

When cases that should be counted are excluded or cases that should not be counted are included the resulting statistics are likely to be inaccurate. Managers need to establish some clear rules for inclusion and exclusion of cases. Similarly they need to identify an appropriate baseline measure. Validate the rules and baseline by checking these with some experienced researchers.

The *Challenger* space shuttle disaster (USA, 1986) was a possible case where the right baseline information was overlooked. Just after being launched on 28 January the *Challenger* space shuttle exploded (killing all seven crew). Putting to one side political pressures to launch a delayed mission and any desire to protect the public image of NASA as an on-time service deliverer, an apparent decision was made to discount advice not to launch made by engineers from Thiokol by both NASA managers and the senior management of Thiokol.

The engineers from Thiokol were mainly concerned with the possible failure of the rubber O-rings used to seal off sections of the booster rockets when temperatures were cold. The O-rings appeared to provide less effective seals to the rocket fuel at lower temperatures. On 28 January 1986, the shuttle launch was assessed to be at temperatures below 30 degrees Fahrenheit. The engineers said that the greatest amount of erosion in the O-rings was found when a shuttle had been launched at 53 degrees Fahrenheit, which was the previous lowest temperature at a shuttle launch. The NASA managers pointed out that temperature seemed not to be correlated with incidents of significant erosion as there were more cases of erosion at higher temperatures than at the lower temperatures.

Each group had overlooked the need to include the cases where little or no erosion of O-rings had been recorded on other flights. The baseline count needed to include all space shuttle flights to January 1986 and the issue of concern – in this case O-ring damage at specified temperatures. Had this been done, the apparent risk of launching at low temperatures may have been more obvious. If the question was framed as 'What is the risk of damage to the O-rings at cool to hot temperatures?' then the ratios of damage per launch would have been higher for low temperatures and much lower for higher temperatures.

Probabilities are only accurate when used for very large numbers

When probabilities are used as a basis for risk management decisions, managers need to be cautious. A probability of five per cent (5%), for example, means that over a very large number of times, a particular type of outcome generally will happen five in a hundred times. The previous discussion of baseline measures and the way questions are framed show that these frequency and probability measures may not be completely reliable. While geophysical analysis and supportive historical information may expand the measures to 1000 years or more, the sample size may not be large enough to avoid errors that distort subsequent frequency of occurrence estimates.

Another problem often arises when managers (and their superiors) use probabilities to make a decision. Managers often appear to use a positive frame to decide on preparedness and reduction strategies. A '1 in 20 years' probability can be seen in terms of a more positive '19 in 20 years' of that outcome not occurring. The consequence is often a decision to reduce resource expenditure or to defer action to a later date.

Even when used cautiously, probabilities can lead to false confidence when used to predict what will happen over small periods of time or during relatively small repetitions of industrial and business activities. People (including managers) often act under an assumption that the occurrence of an event is a uniform outcome of the assessed frequency of that event happening. In doing this, decision makers can become trapped into two states of false confidence. The first of these states is the conclusion that 'this particular event happens so infrequently that it will not happen this time'. The second state of false confidence takes place when a risk event occurs and leads many people to believe that 'now the big event has happened, this event will not happen until the number of times it should not happen is exceeded'. Both states of mind lead to poor risk acceptance and risk management decisions.

A 2000-year simulation of the occurrence of a 1 in 100 year event can be modelled on a computer relatively easily. Under the assumption of a regular and stable occurrence there should be 20 such events roughly 100 years apart. One simulation provides the following occurrences:

Century	Year of incidence	Century	Year of incidence
1	17	11	1066
2	126, 183, 196	12	1124, 1157, 1158
3	307	13	–
4	–	14	–
5	564	15	–
6	–	16	1575, 1594
7	–	17	1620, 1622
8	–	18	1770, 1776
9	–	19	1804, 1815, 1848
10	–	20	1901, 1918, 1939

Such regularity does not arise. In this simulation run the event occurs 22 times rather than the 20 times expected from an assumption of a regular and uniform occurrence. The 1 in 100 year event happens in the first, second (three times), third, sixth, eleventh, twelfth (three times), sixteenth (twice), seventeenth, eighteenth (twice), nineteenth (three times) and twentieth (three times) centuries. In the hundred years from 1740 to 1840 the event happened four times. This would appear to be a 1 in 25 year event for these people. If the full 2000 year period were used, the frequency would appear to be 22 in 2000 or 1 in 90 years.

Frequency of outcome thus does not occur in a uniform distribution over small samples. Infrequent events may occur close together, as shown in this example – 183 and 196; 1124, 1157, 1158; 1575, 1594, 1620 and 1622; 1804 and 1815; 1901, 1918 and 1939. Such events may also not happen for long periods of time – 307 to 564; 564 to 1066; 1158 to 1575. In reality, preparation for probabilistic events needs to be based on the fact that the event will happen – rather than using the mental traps of 'won't happen for a long time' or 'just happened so won't happen for another long period of time'.

After the risk lists are completed

The lists of risks (weighted or not) can be used in three ways:

- Risks can be grouped according to type of common effect or by common response activity. This helps generate response planning procedures. Note that risk items may fit into more than one group.
- Risks can be assessed according to the effect or impact the risks have upon operations (traditional business impact analysis) and stakeholders (stakeholder impact analysis). These analyses are developed in more detail in Chapter 3.
- Risks can be considered in terms of *risk management*.

Why seek to manage risk rather than wait for a crisis to arise?

The obvious reason is that the cost of crisis events is rapidly increasing. In 1995, for example, the cost of natural disasters around the world was $US180 billion (£120 billion) according to Munich Re (*Financial Times*, 28.12.95, p. 11). Over 600 natural disasters were recorded along with a death toll exceeding 18000. Yet the cost to insurers was down in 1995 simply because much of the community, commercial and private cost of the Kobe (Japan, 1994) earthquake was absorbed by the Japanese government. Private insurance covered only around $US3 billion (£2 billion) of the estimated $US100 billion (£66 billion) cost of this earthquake. Add the costs to taxpayers and insurers (and thus all of us who pay insurance premiums) of the more prevalent costs of accidents and non-natural disasters and we all need to become more interested in managing crises. Moreover, we need to become interested in managing these events before they arise.

For business and community organizations the need for risk management is also strengthened by a growing demand from insurance companies, external auditors and shareholders for greater resistance to the impacts of crisis events and improved preparedness. Some regions in the world have prohibitive insurance because of the frequency of natural disasters. In many cases, however, insurance premiums are being reduced or increased according to an insurance company's perception of the level of readiness and resilience held by a client organization. External auditors are increasingly providing qualified audits should the auditors be unhappy with the existing preparedness of a commercial organization for dealing with crisis situations.

One further reason for working at risk management (and improving our ability to manage crisis events) is the growing readiness of individuals and groups to sue for damages due to the negligence or mistakes committed by an organization. An organization that establishes an acceptable level of readiness and planning (and risk reduction) is less likely to be assessed with punitive damages.

Some legal perspectives

In England, *Cambridge Water Co.* v *Eastern Counties Leather plc* was a case in which a chemical leak from a tannery had seeped underground into the plaintiff's water supply. The chemical had escaped many years earlier. The possibility of damage was unknown to the tannery operator. The House of Lords found that the pollution of the water supply was not foreseeable. As a consequence, the plaintiff lost the case.

Currently there would be more strict liability over the pollution of water by escaped substances.

Managers need to have good advice about the prevailing legislation covering worker health and safety, site safety, environment, trading laws and product safety.

Where does risk assessment fit in most legal situations? This involves the question of 'duty of care'. In many cases there is no such duty, however, unless there is a relationship of what is called proximity between the plaintiff and defendant, and unless it is reasonably foreseeable to the defendant that there is relevant risk of injury to the plaintiff. 'Duty of care' arises only when the injury could have been avoided or minimized.

Sometimes organizations gain an extra benefit from conducting risk assessments, particularly if acceptable experts from outside the organization conduct such assessments. Outside experts often gain a clearer picture of an organization than do insiders who have daily preoccupations with specific elements within that organization. When NatWest Bank in the United Kingdom requested a risk assessment of their London headquarters, the motivating factor at the time was the threat of terrorist bombing (particularly from the Irish Republican Army). The risk assessors, however, found that a greater risk was the effects of flooding on below-ground-level data storage and computer operations.

Risk management

As part of crisis management, risk management begins with four basic questions:

1 *What could need managing?*
2 *What is needed to manage these risks?*

3 *What are the likely outcomes from (a) successfully managing and (b) failing to manage the risks?*
4 *How can the risks be best managed?*

What could need managing?

The initial response to this question appears to be *'everything'*. Once we think about what may be done (without any regard for resources and time limits) an infinite list may be generated. Such a list can seem too threatening and require too much effort to manage. In this case we need to sort the items into groups of similar risks and into a perceived ranking on how easy to hard it will be to manage these risks. The approaches used in risk identification can be used to establish how easily we assess each risk may be managed and we can again weight each risk according to ease of management (for example: easy = 3, moderately easy = 2, hard = 1).

What is needed to manage these risks?

We can also use the evaluation approaches to determine the likely costs in resources and time to try to manage each risk. Such consideration can give rise to a new set of priority rankings based on capacity to manage, as well as the resource needs (for example: high capacity = 3, moderate capacity = 2, low capacity = 1).

What are the likely outcomes from (a) successfully managing and (b) failing to manage the risks?

Our view of costs to our organization may also help determine priorities – this time in terms of possible outcomes (in gains and costs) should we succeed or fail in managing each identified risk. We can again use some form of weight to rank the risks numerically (even our high, moderate, low scale). Should we do so, however, note that we need to separate the question into its two independent elements of successful management and failure to manage.

How can the risks be best managed?

While assessing each risk on the list and determining a workable set of these should we be constrained by resources and time, we can begin to identify how each risk may be managed.

Managing or controlling risks is becoming known as *risk treatment*. Treatment involves identifying the options for control or management that are available, evaluating each of these, selecting the most appropriate option, then planning for and implementing that control or management. Conventionally, four options are often explored:

41

- elimination
- reduction
- transfer
- acceptance.

Elimination means that the risk is removed. Organization managers, for example, may eliminate causes of fire by removing rubbish. They can reduce the risk of fire by properly housing flammable material and undertaking regular maintenance of the premises, as well as by installing fire-suppression equipment. They may transfer the risk by either assigning responsibility to another party (fuel stored by fuel retailers rather than by fuel users) or by 'covering' the assessed risk with another party (insurance). Finally, they may decide that a level of risk needs to be accepted because the work performed within the organization involves equipment and material that is flammable.

Traditional risk management can be altered to reflect four basic mitigation and four basic response strategies. This altered approach would appear as:

- **eliminate or reduce the risk;**
- **modify or transfer the risk;**
- **counter or insure against the occurrence of the risk;**
- **develop impact response and recovery strategies.**

In this approach, risk elimination and reduction can be done by following the ABC mitigation principles (*see* Chapter 4). In applying these principles, executives and managers consider 'building':

- *Away* – removing the source of risk from the environment or removing the environment from the source of risk;
- *Better* – better environments through stronger and safer designs and structural materials;
- *Compatible* – designing and constructing materials that meet the demands of the environment and thus reduce risks.

Risk elimination and reduction can involve strategies other than simply 'building' things better or stronger or safer.

In general terms, risk elimination involves any activities undertaken to remove a risk, from designing flaws out of systems and products to removing hazards from the environment. Often these activities are straightforward. Removing unnecessary stockpiles of hazardous chemicals is easily achieved once the problems of 'to where?' and 'with what access?' are resolved. Placing the organization in a safe environment and thus not building where floods, earthquakes or tidal surges happen is one way to eliminate risks. Similarly many exposures to risk can be eliminated by establishing rules for stopping tasks or activities – for example, ruling in what weather aircraft will not be flown.

Risk reduction reduces risk through redesigning products or structures. In earthquake and bomb threatened environments, managers could have unsupported building facades removed or strengthened, walls and facilities reinforced, and lifelines made more flexible, redundant and secure. Many reduction activities may change the environment as well. The real difference between risk reduction and risk modification depends on whether the incidence of the risk is changed (reduction) or the source of risk is changed (modification).

Strategies that transfer risk are used when the product or feature introducing the risk is used in organizational activities. Should an organization need to use areas that can flood, such as waterways and harbours, then the risks could be transferred to a third party by outsourcing the operations involved. Sometimes advantages of risk transfer may introduce other risks. Transferring storage of hazardous chemicals (including petroleum products) to a third party reduces storage risks but may introduce other risks such as increased resupply traffic for those products and an increased risk of loss of supply due to problems that arise at that third-party source.

Once mitigation approaches have been undertaken, managers then develop defences and response strategies to regain control over a crisis situation or to reduce the impact(s) of the crisis on the organization and environment surrounding the organization.

Defence strategies confront the risk-induced crisis situation and aim to contain any impacts when the risk leads to a crisis situation. Fundamental sets of defence strategies are containment strategies which stop or limit the impact(s) from a crisis. Walls or bunds to contain leaks of dangerous chemicals are examples of containment as these keep the impact of a leak to a specified area. Containment may also mean environmental modification. For example, areas prone to surges from cyclonic storms or from tsunamis may become green spaces that slow the force of these events and buildings may be designed to resist such impacts or to allow water to surge through open space under the buildings.

Insuring against the risk is a passive response measure. There are some regions in which insurance is nearly impossible or in which the premiums are excessive because these regions are susceptible to specific repeated risks. Earthquakes in California or floods along the Mississippi River are areas in which commercial insurance is excessive or unavailable. Many insurers are also moving to require proof of mitigation actions and of response and recovery preparedness before accepting such risks.

Most managers are familiar with the need to plan and develop response and recovery management. Currently, such strategies probably are done at the expense of the more permanent mitigation and elimination aspects of risk management. Managers often do not regularly update and audit existing plans, resulting in unworkable measures that may even contribute to the costs and losses of the crisis situation.

Risk acceptability strategies

There are four main risk accepting strategies executives and managers can use. These are:

- *risk aversion*, which means developing ways in which the risk may be avoided (from elimination to isolation procedures);
- *risk balancing*, which means offsetting the benefits of living with the risk with the costs implied by the risk;
- *cost effectiveness*, which means establishing a scale of accepted costs within the organization or community that determine expenditure in risk management;
- *cost benefit analysis*, which involves an economic assessment of costs and benefits in order to establish how much of the risk is acceptable.

The overall process is quite simple. We identify risk, evaluate that risk, then seek ways to best manage each risk element that we have identified – *see* Figure 2.1. As shown by the feedback loop in this figure, the process is dynamic and ongoing. This simple figure may be expanded (*see* Standards Australia, 1995) to outline the management structure for an organization.

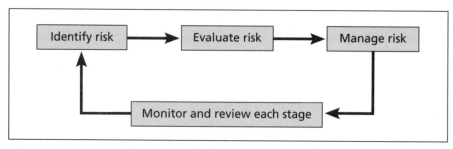

Fig. 2.1 A simple risk management process model

Risk communication

No approach to risk management is worth much unless the outcomes are effectively communicated to those who handle the risk-inducing systems or processes and those put at risk. Effective communication of risk is both simple to achieve and difficult to do. Obviously telling people in simple language what inherent risks are present is simple to do. The difficulty exists in translating abstract terms of reference (frequencies, probabilities and technical terms) into easily grasped frames of reference. A 'once in a hundred years' flood, for example, may mean nothing until someone makes a simpler and more tangible statement such as 'floods bigger than the one we had in 1992'. One problem in simplifying risk forecasts in this way is that environments (and situation impacts) are subject to so many moderating variables that the statements may still lead to overconfidence. Among those with properties not flooded in 1992, for example, floods may still happen. At the same time, those with properties that were flooded in 1992 may be given a threat that is not valid in this case.

Risk communication can be divided into two central treatments – internal (within the organization) and external (to those outside the organization).

Internal communication

Internal information needs to be factual, show clearly how to avoid or mitigate the risk, state what to do if things go wrong, and be seen to be firmly supported by all senior and middle management. New members and those promoted internally need to be educated in the risks involved and how to manage these risks. Organizational policies need to reflect the ongoing nature of risk evaluation and assessment, employee risk education and risk management.

External communication

Risk communication to the world outside an organization traditionally has been minimal and poorly done. Commercial and industrial organizations react defensively about profit-making systems and operations and government bureaucracies 'do not want to unduly panic' the public. Done properly and consistently, however, risk communication can reduce pressures on organizations to halt their operations and ease fears within the surrounding community over the nature and likelihood of the risks involved.

Managers and executives can undertake twelve steps to effectively communicate risk to those outside the organization.

1 Undertake a detailed evaluation of the risks to the public that may be caused by any processes or systems

Most risk assessments conducted by organizations focus only on that organization's exposure to these risks. Consequently further risk evaluation may be needed to analyze the risks to the surrounding community.

2 Determine who the stakeholders are and how these stakeholders may view the risks

Risk communication cannot successfully operate as a shotgun approach to the whole community. By determining who are the stakeholders (those exposed to potential risks, including those inside the organization), communication can be shaped to meet their needs and their capacity to understand what the risks are and what the risks may mean to them. Consequently, stakeholders may include families, education institutions, homes for the elderly or incapacitated, health service institutions and other similar organizations. NIMBY (*see* Chapter 7) and protest groups are also likely to exert community pressure about possible risks to which communities are being exposed.

45

3 Open communication with the outside world – listening to and addressing the emotions involved

The first action is to find out what the community and the stakeholders are seeing as the likely risks involved. So *listen* to these groups and people. Deal with their emotional responses before trying to communicate rational facts and figures.

This is an area in which many managers pay lip service. Questionnaires can be sent out, collated and ignored. Public meetings may produce signs of listening but fail to change the perceived wisdom of the managers involved in controlling or creating the risk under discussion.

This attitude arises from two internal attitudes:

- managers are under internal pressure to accomplish an organization's objectives; and
- managers seem to believe that cloaks of invisibility descend upon them because the decision is a corporate or organizational one.

Many managers perceive the public as alarmist and ignorant, and believe that dialogue is pointless if not dangerous. Petts (1994) found a number of fallacies about risk communication from managers to general public groups. These mistaken ideas included:

- the public perceives risks while experts understand risks;
- the public is and will be irrational;
- more information will overcome irrationality; and
- risk comparisons provide perspective.

In particular many business, government and community organizations tend to flood audiences with information that is based more on 'listen to our arguments' than upon 'let us talk together about what you feel threatens you'.

4 Make any pertinent information available in an open and honest style

Risk communication depends on source credibility. If people suspect the credibility of the organization, then whatever is done and said will be considered as manipulative and concealing. Ensure that the assessed facts are openly and freely available.

5 Gain independent evaluations, seeking support from other credible organizations

One means of increasing credibility and acceptance of the information about risk is to get other independent and appropriate organizations to conduct a risk assessment for the community – or at least get them to review and/or monitor the research and assessments undertaken by the organization. We already do this when we use auditors in organizational financial management and accounting.

6 Ensure the needs of the media are addressed

Remember that the media is the prime vehicle for shaping community thought and educating members of the community. Ensure that extra effort is made in co-operation with the media, so that useful and appropriate information is broadcast into the surrounding community. Local media are particularly useful for these efforts.

7 Communicate clearly and in simple language – avoid jargon and too many scientific and compressed terminologies

Ensure that any scientific and professional advice used is presented in simple forms. Where possible, this information needs to avoid any in-house, professional or technical abbreviations and terms. Define those terms that are used, so that the target audience can comprehend what is being said.

8 Avoid conflict and aggressive case presentation

While remaining polite, non-aggressive and non-defensive, spokespeople need to communicate the notions of risk exposure, what will be (is being) done to reduce and protect against the risk, what will be done should the risk become real, and what the community can do should the risk become real.

9 Involve the public – particularly potential NIMBY groups

Having listened to the various stakeholders in the community and presented the organizational assessment of the risk faced by the community, the most important stage can begin: *involvement in the process by the community*. Have representatives of the community work with the organization to assess and evaluate the risks involved, how to manage so the risks do not become crisis situations, and what to do if the risk becomes a crisis. In doing so, the community attitude toward the risk and the organization is more likely to change.

10 Commence a joint evaluation of the risk exposure faced by the community, and get the joint evaluation team to publicly announce the findings

Use the community and stakeholder involvement to conduct either a new study of the risks or a re-evaluation of past assessments. Get a joint report written and publicly available so that the community becomes more informed, and the organization is seen as being more positive and competent in its operations.

11 Develop education and information strategies within the surrounding community

Seek to develop information and education programmes that meet the needs and understanding of the community. These programmes could include an outline of the risks, some explanation of what the organization (and other

47

organizations will do) to reduce and manage these risks, and key steps stake-holders may take to reduce their exposure to the risks should these become real.

12 Get feedback: find out if the message and understanding is getting through

Do not undertake Steps 1 to 11 without using a feedback loop that informs those in the organization and the joint evaluation participants on community perceptions of what is going on (including how well the risk communication is being absorbed).

Using risk in dealing with crisis situations

So far risk and risk management have been viewed from a relatively static perspective. Risk identification and assessment is the important first step in developing effective crisis management strategies. After all, people need to know what crisis situations may arise. As we see in Chapter 3, the same approach will work to assess the effects we feel from the crisis situation – the impact. When risk and impact analysis are combined, a useful tool (often called a methodology) is formed that helps preparation for crisis management.

Risk assessment approaches can also be used to shape organizational health and safety and task management approaches. This means shifting from rela-tively static risk identification usage (pre-crisis) to using the approach to help prepare for (pre-crisis), handle (during crisis) and recover (post-crisis) from a crisis situation. The approaches can be used across these crisis management stages because the methodology enables checklists to be developed that are easy and quick to use and which can be readily tailored to any unique needs of an organization.

The use of risk management as a crisis management driver (or starting point) also leads to a different emphasis of resource allocation and task man-agement. Where traditional crisis management tends to take the form of a stimulus–response reaction to a situation (*see* Figure 2.2), risk management shifts emphasis toward reduction and mitigation of risk as a primary task rather than a secondary post-crisis learning phase (*see* Figure 2.3).

The emphasis on risk management (elimination, reduction, onset manage-ment, impact management) means that primary emphasis is evenly shared between crisis elimination and reduction and event management (onset and impact management, recovery management). Such an approach can reduce the costs of onset and impact damage, and enable us to invest more efficiently in response and recovery resources when our budgets are constrained.

Risk assessments can be used in specific pre-event planning and in response and recovery management. These assessments are used to produce checklist procedures or to determine weights for decision evaluation in the field. Prac-tical crisis management has two levels in which risk assessment can particu-larly improve management. These levels are:

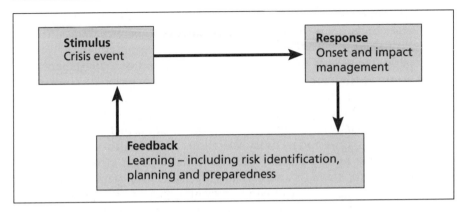

Fig. 2.2 Traditional crisis management

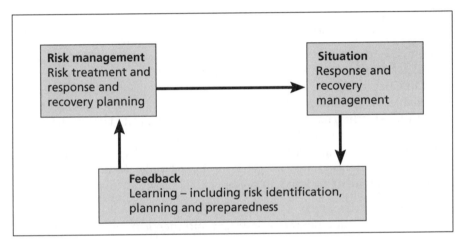

Fig. 2.3 Risk management approach to crisis management

- as a check of facilities and personnel equipment and safety procedures;
- as a component of operational task management (e.g. as RPP or OMT tools – *see* Chapter 13).

By doing so, a thorough means of ensuring optimal conditions for crisis management is established in what can be chaotic and dangerous environments.

Facilities and personnel equipment and safety procedures

Risk management in combination with impact assessments allows users to generate checklists of the equipment and safety gear necessary for operating in specific hazardous conditions. Loflin and Kipp (1995a and 1995b) outline a risk management model that provides pre-crisis checklist procedures for inspecting equipment and safety gear as well as training and fitness of personnel. They also find a need for emergency incident risk management that elevates the juncture of risk-based assessments of the prevailing situation and environment, safety requirements and incident management.

In general this level of risk management-based resource management consists of ensuring the acquisition and maintenance of appropriate equipment, training in the safe use of that equipment (pre-crisis) and monitoring the supply and use of the equipment on site (crisis management). Risk management approaches may also help assess the status of personnel in terms of stress and fatigue in response and recovery operations. Here, health and stress issues can be measured by the exposure of personnel during a crisis situation in terms of duration, stressors and activity. More effective personnel management is thus provided and health and safety management is improved, which is an issue gaining political and legislative attention in most Western countries.

Operational management triage

In most cases risk assessments make useful weights in making field decisions on priority of attention. This decision-making approach is outlined in more detail in Chapter 13. For example, we can develop a priority-based checklist that enables crisis managers to rapidly establish where impact damage exists within the crisis impact environment while systematically checking areas or structures or organizational priorities for damage.

By using assessments of risk of impact, risk to survival, risk to organization, and need for attention we can generate a rank order of areas, structures, processes, equipment and human presence that allows us to quickly:

- check what is damaged;
- provide preliminary damage assessment and therefore response needs estimates;
- identify areas or groups who need little or no attention at that point in time.

For communities this allows a fluent reconnaissance that enables priority attention to critical structures (hospitals, evacuation and holding centres, lifelines such as power, water, gas and communications) and to critical human concentration centres (schools, shopping centres, high-rise complexes, sports stadia). For business and industrial organizations, risk-based priority reconnaissance enables a quick check of core and essential components of the organization, again with a joint focus on stakeholders (especially customers, visitors and staff) and processes (value-adding and outcome-producing systems and equipment).

Response and recovery management decisions can also benefit by incorporating assessments of risks. In many situations, demand for resources exceeds the available resources and so a priority-based approach is needed to deploy the available resources most effectively. Onset and impact management task decisions may reflect assessments of ease of access, amount of resources required, urgency of need for attention, number of people and/or amount of resources that may be saved and threat to respondents. By combining these factors field managers and team supervisors can make a decision that is rational and capable of being presented in any subsequent inquiry or litigation in court. As outlined in more detail in Chapter 13, such approaches reduce the stress on the user, prompt more rational decisions in a stressful environment, and generally should lead to more efficient use of resources.

This chapter has presented a brief overview of risk management. There are several books and journals readers may use for more detailed information. Books include *Risk* (Adams, 1995), *Acceptable Risk* (Fischhoff et al., 1981), *Theories of Risk* (Golding and Krimsky, 1992), and *Effective Risk Communication* (Covello, McCallum and Pavlova, 1989). Journals include *Risk Management* and *Risk Analysis*.

Twelve quick tips to effective risk assessment and management

1 Undertake the risk analysis.
2 Remember to consult all parties exposed to the identified risks.
3 Do not let quantitative estimates appear as reality statements.
4 Explore risk management approaches.
5 Remember to look first for ways of reducing risk exposure before examining response and recovery measures.
6 Examine existing security, control and response and recovery measures.
7 Remember to look for inadequacies in existing risk management practices.
8 Determine new and improved risk management strategies.
9 Implement the selected risk management strategies.
10 Remember to check that strategies are implemented.
11 Communicate risk management to the stakeholders of the organization.
12 Establish a management process for regular review and audit of risk exposure and risk management practices.

References

Adams, J. (1995) *Risk*. London: UCL Press.

Covello, V. T., McCallum, D. B. and Pavlova, M. (eds) (1989) *Effective Risk Communication*. New York: Plenum.

Fischhoff, B., Lichtenstein, S., Slovic, P., Derby, S. and Keeney, R. (1981) *Acceptable Risk*. Cambridge: Cambridge University Press.

Golding, D. and Krimsky, S. (1992) *Theories of Risk*. London: Praeger.

Kahneman, D., Slovic, P. and Tversky, A. (eds) (1982) *Judgement under Uncertainty: Heuristics and Biases*. Cambridge: Cambridge University Press.

Kloman, H. F. (1992) 'Rethinking risk management', *Geneva Papers on Risk and Insurance*, 17(64), 299–313.

Loflin, M. and Kipp, J. (1995a) 'Risk management for emergency medical services: Part one', *The Times*, 2 July, pp. 10–13.

Loflin, M. and Kipp, J. (1995b) 'Risk management for emergency medical services: Part two', *The Times*, 3 September, pp. 10–13.

Petts, J. (1994) 'Risk communication and environmental risk assessment', *Nuclear Energy*, 33(2), 95–102.

Standards Australia (1995) *Risk Management*, AS/NZS 4360:1995. Homebush, NSW: Standards Australia.

Yates, J. F. and Stone, E. (1992) 'The risk construct', in Yates, J. F. (ed.), *Risk-Taking Behavior*. Chichester: Wiley, pp.1–26.

chapter 2
EXERCISE

See how many risk types you can generate. If you are working in a group you may wish to try the brainstorming process so take time to reread that section.

Take no more than 15 to 20 minutes for the first round of idea generation.

See pp. 446–7, Appendix 2, for a guide to risk types.

To gain further insight into the risk assessment process after you have done the task and checked through the suggestions in Appendix 2, try to:

1 identify the various sources of impact for each risk type; and

2 identify whether these risks may have to be considered on a more detailed scale (per work group or per person).

c h a p t e r

Assessing the impact of a crisis

Once risk exposures have been considered and risk management programmes have been initiated, analysis shifts from 'what could happen' to 'what damage could each source of risk do'. To some extent this analysis happens as sources of risk are identified, but now the amount and nature of the risk needs to be determined in greater detail. In particular, damage to any equipment, facilities, processes or people directly involved in achieving the objectives or output of an organization is seen as 'critical' and is closely assessed. This process is conventionally known as *business impact analysis (BIA)*.

Benefits of undertaking business impact analysis

Benefits of undertaking a business impact analysis can include:

- reduced potential costs of losses;
- reduced exposure to risks and impacts;
- reduced operational disruptions;
- reduced insurance premiums or loadings;
- reduced decision-making structure building during response and recovery;
- reduced response and recovery times;
- increased response and recovery capabilities;
- increased protection of assets and organizational members;
- increased image of resilience and management in the public perception;
- increased likelihood of meeting legal liability requirements;
- increased capacity to co-operate in multi-agency response and recovery operations;
- increased integration of organizational effort and objectives during response and recovery operation.

These benefits can be used to help clarify and sell a project and subsequent programme(s) to organizational members and management.

Beginning business impact analysis

We take the risks and risk sources identified in our risk analysis (*see* Chapter 2) and seek to identify how these may impact upon the organization. Many experts (especially in the USA) may term this as 'outage assessment'. What is done now is to identify what gets affected and then establish the key (also called core) elements of what is affected in terms of the organization continuing to deliver its output or objectives. This means searching for the key process operations, and thus the key equipment, personnel, data, facilities and materials required to perform those operations.

Many organizations may produce a scale of operational performance – such as 'necessary', 'meet all commitments' and 'optimal' so response and recovery teams can identify the requirements for particular levels of recovery. This scale allows some flexibility in responding to the amount of damage and the amount of resources able to be deployed.

Essentially, BIA helps identify what will happen to an organization when something goes critically wrong. The approach means users identify the critical elements (from processes and equipment to people and data management) that sustain the operations vital for organizational continuity, and then develop strategies for meeting and even reducing the impacts crisis situations may have on these critical elements.

Functional analysis

The basic process of BIA is to get each section in each department in each division of the organization to clearly define their critical operations, the equipment needs for these operations, and the likely costs should these operations not be undertaken. Care should be taken here that respondents report accurately upon what processes and equipment are deemed critical – and that this level of data gathering is not used for purposes other than identifying impact. Otherwise, respondents tend to report everything they do as being critical.

The data is gathered under three general headings and can be shaped into a unique organization-shaped questionnaire that can be completed via pen and paper, spreadsheets or even Intranet access. The three headings are:

- Business
- Impact
- Remedies.

These form the BIR model for undertaking BIA. This model will be modified to reflect a more accurate impact picture by involving stakeholder impact analysis later in this chapter. The BIR questionnaire needs responses from all identifiable units or workgroups in the organization – organization-wide, by site or office, by division, department or section. This sequential analysis leads to a cost-efficient and reliable BIA and is conducted from the overall organization down to the next major subsection, down to the next major subsection and so on until the smallest unit is covered. One benefit of this top-down approach is that any conflicts or differences between the 'big picture' from the larger section to which a sub-group belongs and the 'local or small picture' can be resolved.

Business

This section asks respondents to describe the business function involved in their area of operation. Questions cover:

- size (including where relevant revenue, number of employees, number of customers);
- primary purpose or function of the unit;
- other purpose(s) or function(s) of the unit;
- critical processes or work undertaken.
- critical systems, equipment, facilities, material needed for the critical processes to be accomplished;
- dependencies on other units for continued operations;
- other units depending on the described unit for output.

This data helps define critical processes and critical interdependencies, thus allowing us to identify linked critical processes and potential choke points. We can also use this data to help shape likely priorities for attention and resource deployment, and consequently begin to define an integrated organization-wide response and recovery strategy or set of strategies.

Impact

The data generated in the business description now helps respondents supply specific data to enable assessment of impact costs. Most of the questions require a time estimate or a monetary cost estimate and are all focused upon the critical processes or work the respondents defined in the business description. Questions cover:

- an estimate of the *minimum* acceptable outage (loss of operation, downtime) for each identified process or work activity;
- an estimate of the *maximum* acceptable outage (loss of operation, downtime) for each identified process or work activity;
- impacts upon each identified critical work activity or process (including loss of control, potential choke points or bottlenecks, likely points where the activity or process may be stopped);

- impact costs in terms of money value and action by an organization other than the host organization. These may include:
  - impact on revenue (losses);
  - costs of not meeting existing contracts;
  - legal implications in terms of governmental regulations;
  - implications from existing insurance contracts;
  - loss of business (and loss of reputation, where relevant);
  - other penalties for being non-operational;
  - costs of continuing supply of materials from other parties;
  - increased operating costs (including idle machinery and staff);
  - impact on public and customers;
  - impact on share value (where relevant);
  - other organization-unique impact costs.

This data helps refine the likely resource deployment strategies and also highlights public relations or legal situations that may have a bearing on how management is seen to respond and recover the situation.

Remedies

This section covers existing and proposed strategies according to the RRRR model – indicating clearly what exists and what could be done. Questions include:

- potential reduction activities (including costs in resources and personnel and suggested implementation time frames, where relevant and able to be assessed);
- insurance cover, including what is specifically covered and what qualifiers or restraints exist;
- response measures that may contain or reduce impacts;
- existing response and recovery strategies involving internal and external party assistance, including vendor names, estimated costs and expected delivery times (and whether these are service level agreements (SLAs), standing arrangements or informal/provisional agreements);
- recovery strategies, including available redundancy in facilities, equipment, personnel or other resources;
- recovery strategies that may involve alternative actions to the normal method for conducting each process or work activity.

This section helps the assessment team identify the current situation, while encouraging those most likely to be affected by any impact to own the response and recovery processes involved by sharing the planning and creative thinking. At the same time, the data collected in this section helps shape the response and recovery strategies required from senior management – making them aware of the likely resource deployments they can derive under certain circumstances.

Two important points about undertaking BIA need to be remembered. First, as with risk assessment, business impact assessment needs to be conducted regularly – at least once a year and after each major reorganization, site modification or change in processes, systems or material. Organizations undergoing rapidly changing operational situations may need to undertake fairly regular risk assessments and BIA.

The second point is that the conventional BIA programme outlined above tends to place a little too much emphasis on the physical components and the internal operational activities of an organization. There is little benefit in having brilliant strategies for getting processes, systems and work activities back into action if there is no supply of input material, no cash investment to keep the organization in action, no demand from customers and no staff to run the processes, systems and work activities. What is needed is a parallel evaluation of the impact on these groups of people that can be integrated into a BIA.

Stakeholder impact analysis

Luckily, only the frame of reference needs to be changed to develop a parallel assessment that easily integrates with the BIA to form a business and stakeholder impact assessment (or BASIA). First, however, we need to identify what is meant by a 'stakeholder', as this concept is not only central to this enhanced approach to impact analysis but also equally important in dealing with crisis situations.

A stakeholder is literally 'one who holds a stake' or investment in or an interaction with a given organization. Executives and managers may be surprised by who belong to some stakeholder groups because these groups are so obvious that they are often overlooked in planning. The following list includes most of the key groupings:

- customers, clients or consumers;
- users (people who may not acquire the output of an organization but use the output in some way);
- organization members (managers, staff and associated contractors);
- investors (shareholders, financial services);
- creditors and debtors;
- suppliers;
- access services (transportation, advertising, accountants);
- government organizations;
- neighbours to the site (where relevant).

Two other groups often make themselves interactive with the organization in terms of owning a piece of a crisis (or potential crisis) situation. These are:

- media representatives; and
- pressure group members.

Probably other organization-specific stakeholder groups can be identified. For assessment and programme purposes, some organizations may find it useful to subsection some of the groups where it appears relevant to do so. Customers, for example, may be defined in terms of size of purchase (big or small), continuity of interaction (ongoing or one-off) and importance. Be wary of judgemental classifications (such as friendly media versus unfriendly media) and keep the utility of and the strategies involving any subsectioned group confidential.

Once the stakeholder groups are identified many of the prompt questions used in the BIR approach can be used to gather stakeholder impact data. The use of the same or similar questions enables both frames of reference to be easily integrated. As a consequence, the final product can identify priorities of action, acceptable response and recovery strategies, and estimates of likely costs in terms of personnel, resources, time and money. We also gain a second valid and independent opinion on our core revenue operations.

Undertaking stakeholder impact analysis

The BIR questions can mostly be quickly adapted for the SIA data-gathering activity.

Business

This section asks respondents to describe the business function from the point of view of each identified stakeholder group for an organization. Questions cover:

- type of stakeholder group and size;
- primary purpose or function of the unit for each stakeholder group;
- other purpose(s) or function(s) of the unit for each stakeholder group;
- critical interaction(s) with each stakeholder group;
- critical systems, equipment, facilities, material needed for the critical inter-actions for each stakeholder group;
- other units depending on the described unit for output.

Impact

The data generated in the business description now helps respondents supply specific data to enable assessment of impact costs. Most of the questions require a time estimate or a monetary cost estimate and are all focused upon the defined critical processes or work the respondents defined in the business description. Questions cover:

- an estimate of the *minimum* acceptable outage (loss of operation, down-time) for each stakeholder group;

- an estimate of the *maximum* acceptable outage (loss of operation, down-time) for each stakeholder group;
- impacts upon each identified critical interaction for each stakeholder group;
- impact costs in terms of money value and action for each stakeholder group. These may include:
  - impact on revenue (losses);
  - costs of not meeting existing contracts;
  - legal implications in terms of governmental regulations;
  - implications from existing insurance contracts;
  - loss of business (and loss of reputation, where relevant);
  - other penalties for being non-operational;
  - costs of continuing supply of materials from other parties;
  - increased operating costs (including idle machinery and staff);
  - impact on public and customers;
  - impact on share value (where relevant);
  - other organization-unique impact costs.

Remedies

This section covers existing and proposed strategies according to the RRRR model – indicating clearly what exists and what could be done. Questions include:

- potential reduction activities (including costs in resources and personnel and suggested implementation time frames, where relevant and able to be assessed) for each stakeholder group;
- insurance cover, including what is specifically covered and what qualifiers or restraints exist for each stakeholder group;
- response measures that may contain or reduce impacts for each stakeholder group;
- existing response and recovery strategies involving internal and external party assistance, including vendor names, estimated costs and expected delivery times (and whether these are service level agreements (SLAs), standing arrangements, or informal/provisional agreements) for each stakeholder group;
- recovery strategies, including available redundancy in facilities, equipment, personnel or other resources for each stakeholder group;
- recovery strategies that may involve alternative actions to a normal method of conducting each process or work activity for each stakeholder group.

The obvious and easy design for the SIA questionnaire is a matrix with the stakeholder groups listed across the top and the questions running down the page. The consequent boxes will enable quick evaluation.

When integrating the two approaches into the BASIA, managers may find coherency improved by placing the answers for the nearly identical questions side-by-side rather than under each other. From this the BASIA report can be written with details and recommendations being drawn from both assessment questionnaires.

While most section leaders or managers feel able to draw upon their knowledge and the collective knowledge of their subordinates to respond to the BIA, some feel less able to respond to the SIA. Many respondents, however, have some understanding of client needs and requirements, and such data can be supplemented by casual inquiry or by direct request. The organization's senior executives tend to worry about doing SIA because they perceive that their stakeholders may become alarmed at a suggestion that something may go wrong in the work arrangements. In most cases the opposite is most likely. Stakeholders feel more valued when asked about their needs and opinions and are likely to become more loyal to the organization. Moreover, many stakeholders are only too aware that crisis situations can happen, and feel more confident about interacting with organizations who appear to be capable of successfully dealing with such situations.

There exists a third valuable benefit for organizations using any form of an SIA approach. Managers of organizations who take the trouble to evaluate such information will increase their insight into (and understanding of) groups of people who can have a substantial effect on the degree of success and profit – however calculated. By knowing more about the needs and desires of stakeholders (especially staff, shareholders and customers) organizations can improve their services, products and stakeholder relationships and thus establish greater stakeholder loyalty and support. Such loyalty and support can be reflected in day-to-day operations, and is vital when things begin to go critically wrong.

Conceptual analysis

Analysis needs to involve *event analysis* and *response analysis*. In many cases, governments and organizations focus on analysis of potential events and fail to adequately analyze the response capacity and requirements involved in handling crisis situations. Event analysis involves an active and multi-level search for potential crises that may be faced by a community or organization. Response analysis explores the requirements needed for a response to crisis situations and an exploration of management approaches that may be used.

Both analysis approaches hold important sub-sets of analysis, each of which preconditions the eventual outcomes. In event analysis, two methods of dealing with missing and probabilistic information aid analysts and planners in determining (1) a *likely* or *probable* level of event occurrence, and (2) the most acceptable *means of offsetting costs and crisis risk* for a community or organization. The first of these methods assigns probabilities of occurrence to each determined event. The second method is a specialized risk analysis approach

61

that considers the intermix of available resources, willingness to accept risk and potential end-costs of the crisis event.

Once the likelihood of an event is determined and the risk analysis undertaken, a more detailed *incident analysis* is undertaken. Incident analysis is used to determine how a crisis situation may arise, how the crisis situation may impact on the organization and environment, and what sub-components of incidents may have parallel or similar means of management. This search for common means of management not only leads to efficiencies in planning and response management, but also allows general priorities of response management (and any specialized response agency management) to be assigned.

Response analysis is used to determine ways in which a crisis can be handled and the resources required to undertake such management and handling. This analysis enables a more concrete understanding of the capability of an organization to respond, which should be a reality check on what can be done as against what may be done in an ideal world. *Capability analysis* enables analysts and trainers to maintain a realistic grasp on the deployment of finite organizational resources, while also enforcing considerations of strategic management in terms of priorities and reserve options.

Undertaking BIA or BASIA reports

The BIA or BASIA reports provide summaries of the three questionnaire sections (business, impact, remedies) followed by a review that then determines:

- priority assignment;
- improvements to, or additional, remedy programmes;
- process administration (how these will be implemented).

These latter three sections are at first likely to be recommendations requiring review by the sections to which the report or reports apply, and then agreement from the relevant senior management involved. Once all appropriate acceptance and support is gained, an implementation workgroup may require more specific instructions or further section-specific planning to convert the proposals into operational actions.

Co-ordinating personnel (such as working groups or project teams) and senior organizational management need to spend some time ensuring that:

- section or unit plans can be integrated with the other sections or units around them – too many plans involving the use of the same exits, transports and suppliers are likely to fail if the situation impacts on more than one section or unit;
- core, support and non-essential processes and work activities are carefully identified for each section or unit;
- the BASIAs or BIAs are updated regularly, as equipment, facilities and resources regularly change.

Remember that BIA itself assesses impact (usually in terms of money values) which is then used to determine priorities or response and expenditure estimates for responding to, and recovering from, impacts from crisis situations. These are estimates and probably need to be increased (and should not become treated as inflexible and unchanging).

Moving toward developing RRRR programmes

So far we have looked at risk assessment and business impact analysis. In small businesses or business departments one to three people with direct access to the department manager or small business owner (if these persons are not already included) can readily undertake these activities and develop the overall crisis management programme. The small team is likely to become enthusiastic and this can help the team accomplish the planning for crisis management and training programmes for getting the workforce ready for managing crisis situations with little more formal management than regular team meetings.

In larger organizations, however, there is less likelihood of direct involvement by key staff and the senior executives. The chief executive officer or senior departmental executive may be several levels removed from those undertaking each department or business unit effort. Other personnel and managers will appear to have more important organizational objectives and heavy day-to-day task priorities, and the working group or project team can quickly feel isolated and ignored. As a consequence, there is a greater need to formalize the process within the organization and establish clear and organizationally visible links to senior management and the chief executive officer or the senior departmental executive so that the crisis planning and preparedness project is supported and becomes reality.

How can this be achieved?

Every organization may hold different cultural values and different ways of doing things. However, a number of steps that help formalize and maintain support for the project can be identified. From the start, four main elements are needed to achieve any satisfactory outcome. These elements are:

1 direct support and demand for action from the person in charge of the organization;
2 the establishment of a strategic (senior management) crisis resolution committee;
3 a senior manager as sponsor of each section or unit effort;
4 access to the appropriate knowledge (which means participation by those who hold the knowledge that enables risk and impact assessments to be made).

These four elements are only the start. Most executives and managers of organizations and departments will quickly realize that there is a need for three interlocked but separate action groups – co-ordination, response management and recovery management. This structure emerges over five primary action stages that take the project from conception to operational status:

- *Stage 1.* Establish criteria for the project. Undertake risk and impact analyses and define the strategies involved. An initial broad-based project team may do this with input from all sections or units within the organization.
- *Stage 2.* Identify the most appropriate plan development strategy or strategies (bottom-up, top-down, mix of both; holistic or compartmentalized to each section or unit). The initial project team may devolve into section or department-specific working groups, with a senior co-ordinating committee or group providing direction and common purpose. Most likely, some general needs analysis and functional design will be undertaken by both co-ordinators and the teams in the sections or units as strategies are considered.
- *Stage 3.* Determine the policies (often a top-down direction activity) and action plans (often a bottom-up activity) that aligns field or site needs, skills and tasks with the strategic policies determined by the senior management co-ordination committee or group. Toward the end of this stage, a transformation of working groups into action teams may occur. Members of the planning groups may still be required to continue ongoing assessment (audits) of risks, impacts and plans.
- *Stage 4.* Implement the plans and policies through training and skill acquisition. In this stage, most organizations need to refine the plans in terms of the unique needs of each section or unit within the organization. At this point, many managers will add some form of corrective and monitoring process to control changes to the plans and make this monitoring and corrective process part of someone's regular job-related activities.
- *Stage 5.* Begin training and exercises. This is the stage in which the plans and action-tasks are normalized into being part of the job.

A common representation of the first four stages is shown in Figure 3.1. Here, the steering senior management co-ordination team, the project team, and the subdivision into whatever unit level is deemed appropriate for the organization (division, department, business unit or site, or site by division, department or business unit) is illustrated.

The transformation from working group or project to user structure may mean changes in leaders and members of the groups, although the basic structure stays the same as shown in Figure 3.2. In this structure the working group names change into a linked and co-ordinated structure that retains senior management involvement.

Differentiation may still be made between response and recovery action tasks. The separation into these action tasks depends on how the managers of the organization view the crisis. Should the crisis situation take a non-

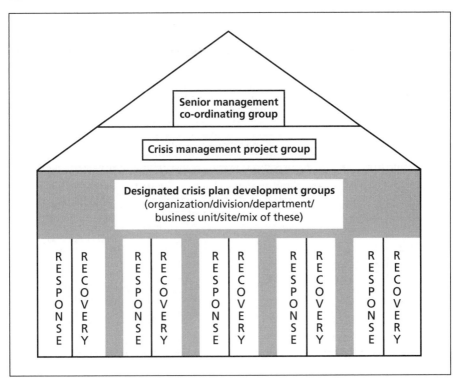

Fig. 3.1 Establishing the crisis management project

physical form (rumour, takeover, image assault, for example) or be managed before impact damage arises, then the action tasks are likely to be response in nature. On the other hand, should the crisis situation lead to physical damage, or should the organization management be limited to waiting for others to deal with the crisis event (partial management) then the action tasks are more likely to be recovery in nature.

Senior management and planners need to ensure that the groups or teams developed throughout the five stages continue to place at least equal emphasis upon the prevention, mitigation or reduction activities of crisis management. Too often, people planning for crisis management (or more narrowly for business continuity) become trapped into focusing only upon the reactive and 'band-aid' strategies of dealing with the crisis situation and the impacts of that situation after the event has happened.

Selling the effort

Probably the first activity undertaken by anyone appointed to a crisis management, business continuity or risk evaluation development role is to 'sell' to

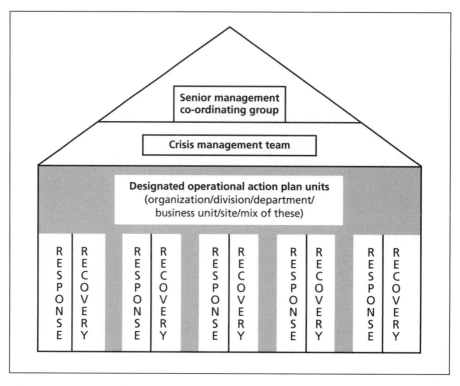

Fig. 3.2 Crisis action management structure

the rank and file of an organization the merits of putting effort into the development and continuation of such programmes. Resistance comes from various sources, including:

- inertia from a 'what's in it for me?' attitude;
- low priority due to the demands of must-do day-to-day work;
- the non-contribution of such programmes to the profit or added-value operation;
- inappropriate placement of staff within the organization;
- lack of support from senior management;
- adoption of a 'won't happen here' or 'not in my time' attitude.

These obstructions are worth considering further.

'What's in it for me?'

The first line of resistance from junior managers, supervisors and many staff is based upon a number of perceptions about their place and ability to contribute to the organization. In many cases, these people see their contribution as one-way with little benefit for themselves. Moreover, these employees may see that they are small cogs in a machine and so their personal efforts are meaningless. Basically the underlying question becomes 'What is in it for me?'

The initiating project team needs to spell out the personal benefits (enhanced safety, increased skills, feelings of greater security, increased protection against loss of employment due to loss of the organization or loss of the organization's place of work) as well as the corporate benefits. Staff members who have been seconded, co-opted and brought into the development of the project need to be encouraged to contribute to the plans through their own knowledge of particular operations and organizational practices.

Demands of must-do day-to-day work

The second line of resistance (and perhaps the hardest line to overcome) is the continued focus on day-to-day activities by participants and associated employees. This often combines with the next line of resistance – a perception that crisis management, business continuity or risk assessment activities do not contribute to profit or income. Managers and staff tend to focus on what they are directly paid to do and on what they are told are the important or core tasks they need to perform.

To overcome this resistance, strong support for these activities is needed from the topmost managers. The activities need to be made an acceptable part of the job or position package, rather than an add-on component to be squeezed in somewhere during the day. Should senior management not feel able to directly support such activities (even to the point of undergoing a task responsibility reorganization) then it is questionable whether the project will become an effectively implemented programme.

Profit or added-value operation

As mentioned before, a central line of resistance that emerges from middle to senior levels of management is that such activities do not contribute to the income or profits of an organization. Many managers see the activities as being costs-only in nature.

In fundamental immediate cash terms this is accurate. Crisis management works toward resolving greater losses that may happen. This is not the complete picture, however. Crisis management can provide three added-value factors to an organization's operations. First, the staff can acquire useful skills through proper training in crisis management approaches – from improved communications to better decision making and time management. Second, the organization can gain cost-reducing benefits from the processes involved in implementing crisis management practices. Risk assessments, for example, may not only lead to risks being reduced and better managed (and thus less frequent crisis situations), but also lead to improved security and safety (with the consequent reduction in costs through loss of goods or lost working time per employee). Third, crisis management can enhance and support other effective management programmes (such as total quality management) through the use of regular risk analyses that include production operations and accident records. Improved safety and quality in task output often reduces the likelihood of some types of crisis situation (industrial and mass transport accidents, for example).

A key proposition to put to managers failing to see the real benefits of spending resources on crisis management activities (which include business continuity programmes) is to focus on costs. Start with the loss in profits and income that results from many types of crisis situations. Many of the Reality Bites and explanatory examples throughout this text illustrate this fact, including the experience of the Canadian Steelco Company (outlined in Chapter 14). Many managers see this as non-substantial because the loss stems from a 'what if things go wrong' proposition. Moreover, many managers (particularly senior and chief executive level managers) tend to see crisis situations as both a negative reflection on their management and a 'not in my time' concept. The easiest action is thus to go into denial and rely on gut-reaction when things go wrong.

A second key proposition is to show the asset values placed at risk in given crisis situations, including some situations other than structural and operational damage caused by natural disasters, human intention and accidents (e.g. loss of value on the stock market, a product recall or an image assault due to local or global pressure group action). Present the figures auditors and internal organizational accountants have produced for brand value and goodwill. Look at the resources being spent on organizational improvement or enlargement, on product improvement or development, and on advertising budgets. All of these can be lost under various crisis situations.

Green (1992) offers a conservative approach to what he terms reputation risk management pricing. He states that a reasonable estimate of insurance plus risk protection programmes would be 6.5 per cent of the total value of the asset (which includes the value assigned the reputation of the asset). Hence an asset with a total worth of 1 000 000 in currency units could be argued to need 65 000 currency units worth of protection and insurance. After subtracting known replacement and income-loss insurance costs and other related assigned costs (public relations, industry monitoring and quality control, for example) the resulting figure could be used to finance risk protection and crisis management activities.

Inappropriate placement within the organization

Assigning the project to a specific department or set of specialists can create an insidious line of resistance. The resulting effect on the rest of the organization is to shrug collective shoulders and state that 'the activity is not our concern, see [name of specialist department or set of people].'

Business organizations, for example, place the main body of crisis management or business continuity operations within either an information technology setting (often because the need for contingency planning for computers marked the first awareness of the need for crisis management within the organization) or within either a public relations or group risk environment. Two problems emerge with these placements. First, as noted above, the rest of the organization tends to shrug off responsibility onto these departments. Second, as a result of the day-to-day focus of these departments (information technology, media and advertising management, financial risk evaluation), the overall approach is likely to be limited in skill application and in action.

The project team and the resulting operational taskforce needs to have membership drawn from all sections within the organization, and be placed close to central management. The point that needs to be stressed is that any crisis management (and thus risk management and business continuity programmes) needs to be part of the overall operational and management structure. Key crisis management executives need to be able to quickly access the top levels of management as well as the bottom of any organization structure.

Lack of senior management support

Yet another line of resistance arises when those on the project team (and any consultants) find lukewarm or little support from key managers up to the chief executive. Many managers often feel that having made the decision to implement some form of crisis management (or business continuity) programme, that is the end of the involvement.

The team needs to gain active and continuing commitment from these people, otherwise the commitment from the rest of the organization will reflect the prevailing attitude and the project and operations will suffer. Note that continuing commitment not only means active emphasis being placed on reading the plans, training and exercises – but also taking part in those exercises. Too often senior managers and chief executive officers (or their top management equivalent, such as the managing director or president of the board of directors) state their support for the programmes but find little time to take part in any planning, training or exercises. This not only clearly signals the low priority given the programmes to the rest of the organization but ultimately leads to chaos when things do go wrong. After all, when things go wrong senior managers often try to take control, whether they know what they should be doing in such situations or not.

'Won't happen here'

A final resistance comes from the feeling that disasters do not happen to the organization. This perception arises from three possible sources. First, crisis situations – by their very definition and incidence – do not happen frequently within a given organization. In the USA, for example, the civil aircraft transportation industry has many companies that have experienced few accidents over a number of years or decades of operation. On the other hand, the

National Transportation Safety Board investigates a major accident every month on average. The second source emerges from both the attitude of denial mentioned earlier and the fact that it is less expensive in resources and energy to do nothing when compared with establishing active crisis management programmes. Because a crisis is seen as unlikely to happen tomorrow a laissez-faire attitude of forgetting about it or leaving it for tomorrow prevails. The third source can come from guesstimations of the relative frequencies of the occurrence of various risks. An estimate of a 1 per cent threat or a one-in-a-hundred chance of a risk causing a crisis situation often is translated into a 99 per cent safety estimate or ninety-nine-chances-in-a-hundred that things will *not* go wrong. The result is a feeling that the risks are so remote that (a) the risks will not become crisis situations, or (b) the risks will not become crisis situations in my time.

Those charged with doing impact and risk assessments face other pressures. Many business and industry organizations having increasingly complex structures. Some activities are even accomplished by virtual business units, or through separate organizations coming together for a brief one-off combined effort or linking to develop a specific product or to present a specific service. Receiving support for and determining who pays for and will undertake the risk assessment, the impact analysis, and the crisis and continuity activities becomes very difficult in such circumstances.

Other pressures include cost cutting and downsizing in organizations. This leads to few staff and resources being available when a crisis happens. Cost-cutting or budgetary economies may also mean that structural and equipment maintenance is less regularly undertaken and that management will continue to use structures, equipment, procedures and facilities that are becoming older and perhaps less resilient.

There are two further pressures on how risk and impact activities are undertaken and how these activities may be shaped. The reliance by many organizations on just-in-time service supply means a reduced tolerance for time lost due to impacts from a crisis. At the same time, many organizations are becoming increasingly customer-focused which means that risk and impact activities need to consider more than just technical or statistical risk analyses of organizational processes. Customer perceptions and needs (stakeholder impacts) also require greater study and analysis.

Executives and managers need to be careful about how risk and impact assessments are presented to people. The basic goal of risk and impact assessments is to indicate what can happen, what impacts will result and thus what needs to be covered in risk reduction, readiness preparation and response and recovery planning.

Reference

Green, P. S. (1992) *Reputation Risk Management*. London: Pitman Publishing/Financial Times.

4

Reducing crises and crisis impacts

Writers and authorities often overlook reduction. There are three probable reasons for this oversight:

- the reactive mindset that comes from most crisis management practice being generated by people from professional response agencies (the military, law enforcement, firefighters and paramedics);
- the fact that most reduction and preparedness activities lack the excitement and the challenge of response and recovery management (for most people, building a racing car would not be as exciting as driving that racing car at high speeds);
- most applications of reduction management are simple and obvious once these have been brought to people's attention and thought through.

The reality is that reduction management seems pedestrian and sometimes like stating the obvious. Yet most organizations barely make the effort to consider what is perhaps the most powerful and effective approach to crisis management. When sources of crisis situations are removed or the impacts of these situations are reduced in potency, then management has accomplished the most effective action possible. The reason for this effectiveness is that crisis management practice needs to be as much about 'managing so that crisis situations are reduced' as about 'managing crises when these happen'.

Theorists and practitioners are increasingly aware of the potential reduction in crisis situations that comes from improving management and organizational communication and quality of effort (e.g. Allinson, 1993; Pastin, 1986; Turner, 1976; Wagenaar, 1996). Some people assume that human error can be eliminated and that education will somehow counterbalance greed, apathy, self-preservation, job-security and expediency. These assumptions are idealistic. Effective crisis management needs to emphasize the goals of being ready to respond and recover from crisis situations as well as promoting education and determined efforts to reduce exposure to crisis situations and sources of risk.

Reduction management involves increased costs when deficiencies or errors are uncovered. This may prove another reason for lack of emphasis on reducing exposure to risk and crisis situations. Moreover, spending on mitigation and crisis reduction can become a somewhat embarrassing action when the effort is retrospective and thus could appear to be a confession of historic poor management. Consequently organization managers may prefer to invest resources elsewhere. The problem in having a fixation with costs is that when a crisis happens the cost to resolve the situation and recover is often far greater than the cost of undertaking crisis reduction management. There is an appealing yet false economy in being reactive, as the investment and effort costs are negligible until a crisis situation actually happens.

Crisis reduction management

Crisis reduction management is central to any effective crisis management programme because by reducing the risks, time wastage and poor resource management, fewer crisis situations will arise and the impacts of those that do arise are likely to be reduced. The approach can be used across the RRRR model. On examining each reduction, readiness, response and recovery activity cluster, four interlocked applications can be identified. These are the:

- *environment* within which the crisis happens;
- *structures* and facilities that produce products or services;
- *systems* that are used to create and maintain the structures, facilities, products and services;
- *people* who come into contact with the systems and structures (managers, workers, users, bystanders, customers, suppliers) who may become involved in a crisis situation and the impacts of that situation.

Not surprisingly these four features are the keys for the effective evaluation of crisis management and of the causes leading to a crisis situation (*see* Chapter 17). This is because these are the significant elements present when a crisis happens. By systematic examination of each feature for (a) what was brought to the crisis situation or was present when the crisis happened, (b) what then happened, and (c) what the result was after the crisis was ended, managers can seek ways in which the situation may be better handled. At the same time, managers can also seek the sources and causal links that led to the crisis in order to establish which of these can be eliminated or modified so that the incidence of the crisis and impact damage can be reduced. In other words, crisis reduction management is an ongoing process that even looks for lessons and improvements from crisis situations that have already arisen.

When the four features are placed within each of the RRRR components, 16 possible reduction management activity clusters can be identified. While most of this chapter focuses on the first R (reduction), reduction strategies and management will be commented upon throughout the rest of this book. Managers and executives need to grasp the simple message of crisis reduction management: *reduce the sources of crisis situations and thus reduce the costs for the organization.*

The environment and the built environment (structures)

Mitigation strategies form the primary approach to reducing crisis situations and crisis impacts. These strategies emphasize eliminating or reducing crisis situations and impacts. This is done so that the organization is more able to operate continuously and safely and so that the output created by the organization (whether seen as a service, profit or lifestyle satisfier) is maintained. Organizations may also need to undertake effort in this area to fulfil the legal requirements and obligations imposed by governments (e.g. the duty of care) or to protect the organization from criminal proceedings (e.g. corporate manslaughter) and other litigation.

A key mitigation strategy that can apply in physical and business contexts is the ABC mitigation principles. ABC stands for 'Away–Better–Compatible', and these terms remind managers that better crisis management practice would be to 'build' structures:

- *Away* from sources of risk or threat;
- *Better* than the level required to resist sources of risk or threat; and
- *Compatible* with the design features that best resist or deflect sources of risk or threat.

The use of these three steps is most obvious in the environments within which organizations exist. By examining the environment in which the organization may be placed (or in which the organization currently resides), managers can identify sites which have fewer risks and sources of crisis. In geophysical terms, sites that resist seismic waves from earthquakes (such as rock stratas) are preferable to areas that amplify such wave motions (clay, sand, landfill areas). Most large cities are built on the latter rather than the former, and thus expose their residents to increased threat of loss of resources and life. Indeed, cities are generally built where natural disasters are more likely to happen. Many cities are built at harbour sites and along rivers and are therefore more vulnerable to earthquakes (rivers follow the line of least resistance on the ground and thus follow potential faults in the earth), flooding and windstorms. Even tornadoes appear to move in directions associated with the lowest ground levels.

As a consequence, many city governments then try to establish stronger ('Better') and more natural ('Compatible') structures. They establish earthquake-resistant building codes, undertake drainage programmes and build dams (which add benefits of hydroelectricity and water supply in some cases). Such actions may not always remove or reduce the sources of risk or threats.

73

Dams, for example, can flood regions behind the point where the dam is built that were never flooded previously. Some dams have even resulted in earthquake activity.

Modifying the environment may have crisis-compounding consequences. Modifications that involve building better increase direct costs because more resources and better quality resources are required. This approach can also lead to indirect increases in costs should the structures still not resist the crisis. Buildings constructed to resist earthquakes, for example, may still be so damaged that they need to be repaired or replaced. Because of the added strength given these buildings, repair or demolition is more costly to undertake.

Stronger and better structures may also contribute to crisis situations. As illustrated repeatedly in floods of the Mississippi River (1992, for example), once the strong containment walls (or riverside levees) are breached, crisis impacts increase. The increase stems from the greater speed of the inrushing water (as with a dam burst) that happens immediately a breech occurs and from the action of the rest of the levee system that then becomes a dam preventing the floodwaters from flowing back into the river.

A prime example of ineffective 'building stronger' policies may be identified in Bangladesh, which occupies the combined delta areas of three major rivers of over 1.55 million square kilometres (11 times the land size of Bangladesh). As a consequence, the country is often flooded. In April 1991, for example, a cyclone was estimated to have killed over 100 000 people.

The conventional response was to build embankments to protect agriculture from normal floods, but the apparent failure of the embankment policy (as occurred in 1988) indicates that this strategy may not reduce the threat of loss of life in extreme events. The 1988 flood affected around 60 per cent of the country and about 30 million people. Given the poverty of the country, assistance from the United Nations and World Bank appeared necessary in order to reduce the costs of this flooding from monsoonal rains and from storm surges due to large cyclonic storms. The government and donor countries (around 26 in number) established Flood Action Plans co-ordinated by the World Bank.

In general the Flood Action Plans were not so much concerned with flood loss mitigation as with increasing agricultural output (Thompson, 1993). As a consequence, the areas where people are most seriously affected by floods and where loss of life is greatest have received relatively less attention. Problems have included a lack of integration with administrative planning and the minimal involvement of local government in the planning of the Flood Action Plans. These plans have also been criticized on environmental grounds. Such large-scale embankment projects near major rivers may introduce a number of environmental impacts, including unanticipated impacts on internal drainage, external floods and on the quantity and quality of fish caught in the coastal regions.

Compatibility strategies involve managers seeking solutions that work with the prevailing sources of risk and the environment so that the impacts of the threats and hazards are reduced. Hilo, a major city in Hawaii, experiences tsunamis from time to time. After the last damaging tsunami (1960, 61 dead) the foreshore of Hilo was turned into a parkland buffer ('Build Away'). The exposed buildings were designed so that the narrow ends of these buildings were perpendicular to the likely surge ('Build Better'), and houses were built high off the ground so that water could surge underneath the buildings ('Build Compatible'). Compatibility strategies thus seek ways in which impact damage may be deflected or avoided by using the shapes and materials naturally occurring in the environment.

So far the environment and threats have been seen in terms of geophysical location and natural disasters. However, the same three principles can be as easily applied within built structures and in less tangible settings. Once the built structure that houses the organization has been evaluated against the surrounding environment, sites within the structure may also be similarly evaluated. Particular sites may be removed from the vicinity of threats to those sites. In the Norwegian offshore oil regions, for example, crew quarters are separated from working areas. Dangerous industries and chemical storage sites are best removed from residential localities. Managers can choose not to occupy structures that have added vulnerabilities – proximity to natural disasters, proximity to airports, proximity to dangerous sites. Hence 'Build Away' strategies still apply, and these strategies can be applied room by room, floor by floor, building by building.

Building Better and Compatible strategies are just as applicable. Better design of sites and of fixtures on sites can improve the resistance of those sites to sources of risk and enhance the safety of people at those sites. Using explosive and fire resistant materials and designing sites for easy flows of goods and people add compatibility strengths to such sites.

Less physical crisis situations may also benefit from the ABC principles. Hostile takeovers, for example, may be less likely if organizations avoid the states in which they become attractive for takeover (usually underperforming and asset rich). The impact of violence and terrorist activities can be reduced by safer designs and by building away from sources of such risk. Product failures and contamination can be reduced by better product design, adding safety features and making the packaging tamper-resistant. Loss of reputation and organizational image can be reduced by avoiding issues and practices that inflame pressure groups, by developing stronger brand acceptance, and by working with the groups in the surrounding community rather than by being seen as indifferent to the desires and needs of those groups.

Systems

Systems are those processes that establish and regulate the operations and work undertaken by the organization. Obvious systems are the communications and information management (computer) systems, and any production line process in industry. These processes can be made crisis resistant and safer by looking at:

- how these systems may cause crisis situations to arise;
- under what conditions these systems may fail;
- what impact damage other features (environment, structures, people) may have on the systems;
- what can be done to eliminate, reduce or counter the causes, failure modes and damage of the previous three points.

The approach is similar to the analyses outlined in risk analysis and management (Chapter 2) and in impact analysis (Chapter 3). Essentially the same identification and impact assessment processes are likely to be used.

Systems can be made more crisis resistant and sources of risk and threat can be reduced or eliminated when the design, implementation and maintenance of the systems incorporate a number of features. These features include:

- Keep the process or system simple and direct. Where possible, use dedicated single-issue systems rather than complex multi-function systems.
- Keep personnel properly trained and using correct system-user practices.
- Where feasible ensure system redundancy (more capacity to function and more than one way of undertaking the process).
- Ensure the environment and built structures do not reduce system efficiency and system work practices.

By observing these core principles and developing other principles that reflect the specific operations of an organization, managers can eliminate and reduce the sources of crisis that may reside in (or threaten) systems.

People

Crisis reduction management can effectively seek ways of reducing the incidence and impact of crisis situations by examining how people who interact with the organization or who are members of the organization can be trained and assisted in their tasks. As with systems and structures, managers use approaches similar to stakeholder impact analysis to identify then manage these factors.

Four core areas for action are:

- work practices;
- skills acquisition;
- protection and safety measures;
- group interaction training for task management.

While other areas may emerge in a given organization, managerial effort in these areas can reduce the incidence and nature of many crisis situations.

Work practices

By ensuring that work practices are regularly audited for safety and for efficient output management, managers can reduce losses not only in terms of reduced incidence of crisis situations but also in terms of lost work hours, imperfect products and resource losses in damaged facilities and materials. Audits help establish safe practices and can be used to determine whether the facilities and structures can be better designed to meet task and operator needs.

Part of this approach means that staff are appropriately trained, that all those on site are protected from risk, and that vulnerable sites within the organization are suitably secured from intrusion.

Skills acquisition

People need proper training not only in undertaking work practices but also in associated skills. This can include survival skills (lifeboat drills, immersion practice, first-aid courses) and interaction skills (dealing with threatening situations and with aggressive people). Managers need to ensure that skills required by the industry and legislation are maintained at the certified or regulated standard and that all skill acquisition is regularly refreshed.

Protection and safety measures

Organizations need stakeholders to maintain safe work practices and to undertake appropriate tasks using appropriate tools and wearing or employing the required safety equipment. Managers need to seek crisis resistant facilities and structures and to develop and use impact-reducing action skills for people belonging to and interacting with the organization.

One basic measure is to have a site evacuation procedure that is more detailed than the everyone-out-now policies that are often in place. One approach is to adopt a staged process, as is outlined in ACCCE.

ACCCE – an improved evacuation procedure

- *Attend* the alarm.
- *Close* down equipment where this is feasible.
- *Cover* any idle electrical equipment (e.g. computers) and clear papers into covers (e.g. desk drawers where applicable).
- *Collect* appropriate personal items (e.g. car keys, purses, coats) so long as these are within outstretched arm's reach.
- *Evacuate* site on instruction.

By following such simple rules the cost of a physical disaster can be reduced dramatically, as less smoke and water damage may result from these precautions and security of environment is enhanced.

Group interaction training for task management

Many organizations rely on people working in teams to achieve complex and potentially dangerous outcomes or goals. Flight crews on aircraft, workers on oil rigs and personnel involved in nuclear power projects are examples of these teams. Similarly professional response agencies and crisis management teams can also benefit from group interaction training.

In considering any such training, managers need to carefully consider:

- the objectives of the training;
- who undertakes the training; and
- the uses to which the training is applied (beyond team improvement).

Care needs to be taken otherwise those required to undertake such training may resist or simply 'go through the motions' due to distrust and disregard of what is often considered a warm and fuzzy concept.

Training needs to focus on how to better perform the given task (especially in crisis situations) using all available resources and using the team to everyone's capabilities. Trainers should be qualified in understanding the principles involved and have an understanding of the realities of people interacting under stress and within organizations. Holding academic or organization-specific knowledge may not be sufficient. Managers need to ensure that the training is used only for teamwork and personal enhancement and not for work performance evaluations (promotions, job exclusions). To allow other uses of the evaluation measures from such courses will increase resistance from some people, lead others to cynically pay lip-service to the process, and decrease any learning through trying out different behaviours and approaches.

One approach is that of CRM (crew resource management), also modified into TRM (team resource management).

Crew resource management/team resource management

Crew resource management (CRM) or team resource management (TRM) looks at increasing teamwork through trust, understanding and assisting each team member to monitor their tasks at work. By increasing support and vigilance, errors from oversight or precipitate action may be reduced and efficiency and safety increased.

CRM is currently being used in the oil industry, particularly in the offshore industry of the United Kingdom (Flin, 1996) and in the aviation industry

(Helmreich, 1997; Job, 1996). Lauber (1984) defined cockpit resource management (the forerunner of CRM) as 'using all the available resources – information, equipment and people'. Research conducted by NASA also confirmed the need for non-technical training that concentrated upon the leadership, command, decision making, communication and teamwork promoted by the pilot.

Many major international airlines use some variant of CRM involving initial three-day courses, ongoing training, and monitoring of skills in crew-based evaluation situations such as line oriented flight training (LOFT). In a LOFT session, the flight crew undertakes a complete flight – from doing the necessary paperwork and pre-flight briefings to flying the time in a flight simulator. During the flight the facilitating instructor (who has been trained in analyzing group interactions) introduces a problem and the crew are free to try different strategies in managing the situation. An overly authoritative pilot, for example, may try to ask for, and listen to, advice from the rest of the flight crew. The most important element of LOFT, according to Helmreich (1997), is the post-simulation debriefing. The importance of thorough debriefing and learning from the findings of that debriefing is reiterated in Chapter 12.

Job (1996) illustrated the need for people interaction training in a review of the crash of United Airlines Flight 173 on 28 December 1978. The DC8 aircraft was about to land at Portland airport when instead of the normal sound of the wheel bays opening and the wheels descending and locking in place with their normal moderate thump, a much larger shudder and thump was felt. Only the green light for the nosewheel came on, and the cockpit crew became preoccupied for 23 minutes with ascertaining whether the main undercarriage was locked for landing. The crew then turned toward preparing themselves and the passengers for a possible emergency landing, and began calculating landing angles and speeds, barely registering warnings from indicators that the fuel level was very low. When Engine No. 4 stopped, then No. 3, the crew tried cross-feeding fuel – with the flight engineer remarking that the 'fuel sure went to hell all of a sudden'. Six miles short of the Portland airport the aircraft crashed. Given the gradual descent and the lack of fuel to cause fire, 156 of the 189 occupants were able to scramble to safety on the ground.

The lack of significance placed upon the remaining fuel was an obvious problem. Job finds that 'although a captain is in command and responsible for the performance of his crew, the first officer's and the flight engineer's inputs are important because they provide backup for his decision' (p. 46). The primary responsibility of the first officer, according to Job, is to monitor the captain. Herein lies the need for all crew members to be able to communicate and give attention to feedback. Certainly, the aircrash investigating agency – the National Transportation Safety Board – found that such communication and assertiveness needed to be improved, and recommended that some form of crew interaction training needed to be part of the standard curriculum of all airline flight and cabin crew.

The basic British Airways CRM course covers six major issues of decision-shaping interaction skills:

- Choosing behaviour
- Communications
- Decision taking
- Feedback
- Medical
- Self-awareness.

While some of these issues have some credence, experience suggests that self-awareness and feedback aspects are likely to be treated somewhat rapturously or with cynical superficiality.

Flin and others have transferred this approach to control-room operations in the UK offshore oil industry. Theoretic constructs (models of decision making, assertiveness and effective communication techniques) are linked with role-play exercises and simulated incidents that reflect actual situations that have happened. To establish whether positive outcomes are gained from CRM-type training, pen-and-paper tests are used, commonly using a five-point disagreement-to-agreement scale. These tests (such as the cockpit management attitudes questionnaire or CMAQ – *see* Gregorich, Helmreich and Wilhelm, 1990) take around ten minutes to fill out and are presented before and after a training programme.

One problem with such testing is that many career-minded participants may consciously or unconsciously feed back what the course and trainers seem to value. The reported value of the participant's CRM skill thus may differ from the value placed on CRM by that participant when involved in a crisis situation. One further problem any user needs to consider is the stability of teams being formed. While any CRM-type training can offer an overall positive effect, the effect is lessened if team membership changes regularly.

Helmreich (1997) claims that a major goal of CRM training is to get the crew to work as a team to reduce errors. He also is aware of the cultural inhibitors that reduce efficient management under stress. Pilots, for example, tend to be strong individualists with great professional pride, are likely to deny susceptibility to stress, and generally will express a sense of invulnerability – especially to fatigue. These characteristics can also be found in many professional response agency personnel and among many senior managers and executives. A CRM programme can help reduce such attitudes by emphasizing the limits each person has and the inevitability of error as a consequence if these limits are not corrected and reduced through mutual interaction.

Programmes using CRM models can be developed for most types of work that involve intensive team activities. Law enforcement, firefighting, paramedic and medical organizations can use CRM models. In Basel, Switzerland, for example, CRM programmes have been developed for surgical teams.

CRM-type programmes that focus on human interaction and personality issues can be dismissed by some as 'touchy-feely' stuff that is not really relevant. Faith (1996) reports some airline insiders as stating that one in five pilots find the CRM concept nonsensical, irrelevant and a waste of their time. He further reports that CRM programmes may enable airline executives to say that problems associated with aircraft accidents were the result of emotional defects in the crew and thus avoid any executive responsibility. A modified approach called Command Leadership Resource Management moves away from sensitivity training toward pilots making synergistic use of all available resources in managing a situation. United Airlines uses this approach.

Likewise, receiving feedback from others about personality and performance negatives can be hard to accept. Many may resort to denial and defensive attitudes rather than accept the perceived characteristics as part of their personality that they either note and work with or try to modify. Should the trainers not be skilled and able, programmes may degenerate into personality slanging matches and the consolidation of extreme positions. Another danger is that organizations may unintentionally or intentionally hijack the training process by incorporating the existing corporate culture and mindset into the programme (rather than letting the programme modify what may be dangerous attitudes), and by using scores and negative descriptions of participants to sift out undesirable non-team players. While this latter point is acceptable in an ideal world, in practical terms the sifting is likely to shift from bringing in the CRM-appropriate types to shutting out corporate culture misfits.

So what can make a reasonably useful CRM? Ten points worth considering in detail would be as follows:

- Ensure the programme is committed to CRM objectives and does not become a corporate approval tool.
- Ensure those providing the training (and those who train the trainers) have appropriate intellectual knowledge and pragmatic skill in applying that knowledge.
- Undertake a rigorous examination of the tasks for which CRM is being considered to connect the CRM improvements with task efficiency improvement expectations (and regularly recheck these).
- Ensure that the programme is not used for promotion or other career-based corporate decisions, as participants will modify their involvement if this is seen to be the case. They may pay lip-service and not rock the boat rather than take the opportunity to enhance their interaction abilities.
- Ensure the programme reflects sensitivity to cultures. People from some cultures are more likely to accept CRM than others.
- Ensure the focus of such programmes is on the gains from the awareness rather than on the 'how bad am I' aspects.
- Ensure the points learned are made clearly and simply and that these points are reinforced by examples and experiential exercises.
- Ensure that participants have time to assimilate the findings on their own as well as within the group.
- Ensure that there exists ongoing training so that the principles are reinforced.

- Ensure that changes measured by ratings used to assess the training programme are reflected in task management situations – seek actual rather than espoused (rating only) confirmation of the effectiveness of the programme.

Reduction strategies and the readiness module

Environment

Readiness implies a state of preparedness among people to meet crisis situations. Consequently, reduction strategies are used to ensure that warning signals appropriate to the environment are constructed and maintained. These strategies may also focus on developing environmentally friendly ('Compatible') management procedures.

Structures

Reduction strategies involve ensuring that the right equipment is in place and that users are able to operate that equipment. In certain circumstances equipment may need to be modified or specially developed to meet the requirements of the site. Reduction management also needs to ensure that correct labels and appropriate, easily read and understood instructions are securely placed with the equipment. This latter action conforms to principles outlined in ISO proclamations (4000 and 9000 series).

Systems

Besides having the right systems in place and system redundancy (where possible), managers can use reduction strategies to establish where readiness enhancing systems (warning systems, mobilization and deployment systems) may fail and modify or strengthen these accordingly.

People

A key element in reducing crisis incidence and impact emerges when response and recovery staff have a high capacity to operate effectively. This capacity is gained through training and exercises that increase people's ability to predict events, make them feel familiar with the crisis situation and provide them with the skill capability to resolve the situation successfully (*see* the FPC model in Chapter 12). Note that reduction strategies include constructive debriefings to determine how response and recovery operations could be improved, and even to uncover ways in which sources of risk and threat may be eliminated or reduced.

Reduction strategies and the response module

Environment

Reduction strategies include identifying ways in which the environment can help the response. By designing plans and tasks to meet the nature of the environment managers can speed up response times and equipment resilience.

Structures

Managers need to ensure that the right response equipment is available. Reduction strategies also include establishing commonality in equipment (and systems) so that the response effort is more likely to be uniform and consistent between different teams of respondents. One example of this is the decision by the State of California Emergency Management for all firefighting units to either have the same hose couplings or to have readily available adaptors. This means response units from across the state are able to respond to large fire emergencies.

Systems

As with equipment, reduction strategies need to focus on having the right systems to support the response management (including where possible system redundancy). In this way communications and task achievements are enhanced and made more efficient, choke points may be reduced and impact damage minimized by the timeliness with which the response is co-ordinated and delivered.

People

Staff holding appropriate skills and knowledge reduce possible impact damage through timely and appropriate action. Executives and managers also need to consider staff support and safety as these extend the duration and capacity of response and recovery operations, and reduce injury and mistakes.

Reduction strategies and the recovery module

Environment

In recovery management, reduction strategies start with proactive recovery planning that includes working with the nature of the environment rather than against it. Reduction of time loss and inefficient resource allocation can be made through proactively developing recovery wishlists (*see* Chapter 15).

Remember that recovery situations can be used to reduce future exposure to risks and threats (by using ABC mitigation principles, for example).

Structures

Resource costs can be reduced by having the right equipment in the right place. By proactively considering possible options and choices, costs and time losses can be reduced and injuries and damage to equipment minimized. Not many building site or community plans have considered the disposal of debris, yet this may act as the moderating factor in a full-scale recovery programme.

Systems

Reduction in recovery management systems has two core features. First, managers need to ensure that the systems used to control and process recovery are robust and able to be co-ordinated. Quick communication and timely outputs mean less time and resource wastage. Second, those systems being recovered (as with environments and structures) can be assessed for ways in which the systems can be improved (operational efficiency) and made more crisis-resistant.

People

As with systems, crisis incidence and impact reduction has two core perspectives. First, managers need to ensure that the right people have the right skills, equipment, support and protection to enable speedy and efficient recovery management. Second, managers need to focus on the human perspective which also has two core elements. The first of these is to help people recover from any emotional and cognitive trauma the crisis may have induced. The second element is to look for ways in which crisis incidence and impact may be reduced through improving psychological resilience. By improving readiness and response management (and increasing the capacity of people to be able to meet the impacts of crisis situations) recovery processes are enhanced.

Reduction management

A consistent theme can be seen emerging. Good management, and especially good effective crisis management, starts from the moment the organization commences to exist. This good management involves evaluating risk exposure and the likely impacts of this exposure so that:

- crisis reduction management is built into the surrounding environment, the structures, systems and people;

- where the environment, structures, systems and people already exist, crisis reduction becomes part of the renewal and change process;
- crisis management and reduction become core activities within the organization.

By doing these as part of ongoing operations and management, an organization reduces exposure to risks and threats, reduces costs in impact damage, and increases the chances of continuing to function and even flourishing.

REALITY BITE

Sioux City

This example illustrates some of the effects of reduction management approaches.

Background
United Airlines DC10 Flight UA 232 operated between the cities of Denver, Chicago and Philidelphia in the USA. On 19 July 1989, Flight 232 was cruising at 37 000 feet (approximately 11 300 metres) with the Captain (Alfred Haynes), First Officer (William Records) and Second Officer (Dudley Dvorak) as the cabin crew. Over the last three months these three had crewed together on six previous flights. Records was in control at 3.10 pm (Central USA time) with the autopilot switched on and cruising at 270 knots (around 299 miles per hour or 539 kilometres per hour).

Incident
As the aircraft changed course to Chicago a loud cracking explosive sound came from the rear of the aircraft and the aircraft frame shuddered. While flight attendants on their own initiative advised passengers to fasten their seatbelts, the crew in the cockpit found that Engine No. 2 (mounted in the tail of a DC10) had failed. Haynes immediately called for the engine failure procedure. While this process was conducted, Dvorak (working as flight engineer) noted that gauges measuring the pressure and quantity of hydraulic fluid for all three independent control systems on board the aircraft were falling. The aircraft continued to swing to the right and adjusting the autopilot made no difference. Records found that the aircraft would not respond to the controls when the autopilot was disconnected.

Onset response
Haynes immediately took control, found that he could get no response and adjusted power on No. 1 engine to return the aircraft to level flight. He ordered the emergency air driven pump be switched on to give pressure to the hydraulic fluid system. This pump had no effect.

At 3.20 pm the aircraft continued to slowly descend and pitch slightly. The crew reported their plight to air traffic control and requested an emergency landing at the nearest airport. They also sent a coded aircraft communication to United Airlines seeking further advice on what more the crew could do. The aircraft was diverted to Des Moines but became uncontrollable, swinging to the northwest, and was directed toward Sioux City airport. Haynes then informed passengers over the public address system that the No. 2 engine had ceased and they might be late in arriving at Chicago. He requested the senior flight attendant to report to the flightdeck and there she was told to prepare the cabin and passengers for an emergency landing.

The only means of controlling the aircraft was through throttle adjustments to the two remaining engines. At 3.27 pm, the crew reported their problem at length to United Airlines maintenance engineers in San Francisco. An off-duty DC10 Captain (Dennis Fitch) was on board the flight and joined the flight crew in the cockpit. Fitch was requested to go to the rear of the aircraft to visually assess the situation. He returned to report that there was no movement on the primary control surfaces, that the air spoilers were locked down, and that the inboard ailerons were in a slightly upright position. Fitch asked what he could do and was asked to attempt manipulating the two engine throttles to gain control over the flight. This enabled the other three to monitor the aircraft progress, communicate with ground control and their airline's engineers, and continue to seek solutions to the problem. Fitch knelt on the floor and experimented in trying to flatten out the slight pitch and roll of the aircraft but was never able to gain satisfactory stability.

Haynes contacted Sioux City airport and informed them of the situation. Given Fitch's rising frustration at not achieving reasonable control, Haynes determined that the aircraft had to be landed in minimum time. Accordingly he asked Records to obtain the V speeds for landing with no flaps and no slats. The aircraft underwent two erratic descending orbits before heading due north. Haynes instructed Dvorak to dump fuel, then requested Fitch to try to veer the aircraft some 10 degrees. Records determined that the no flaps, no slats landing speed would be around 200 knots (220 miles per hour or just over 350 kilometres per hour).

At 3.40 pm United Airlines' San Francisco maintenance centre contacted the air crew to inform them that further advice may be available in five minutes from the airline's operational engineering department. Haynes recalled the senior flight attendant to check that the cabin was secure and passengers were prepared for a crash landing. He told her that precise landing was impossible given the poorly controlled motion of the aircraft. The warning 'brace, brace, brace' over the public address system would indicate that the landing was imminent.

The crew used the alternative system to lower the undercarriage as the lack of hydraulic fluid meant the normal system was inoperative. Approach Control requested that they widen their turn to the left and Haynes agreed, stating 'What ever you do, keep us away from the city.' Fitch had difficulty in maintaining the left bank using throttle adjustments and Haynes decided to use a direct approach. This was cleared by Sioux City Approach Control. Haynes instructed Records to inform the passengers via the public address system that there was about four minutes to landing.

Around 3.55 pm Haynes reported they were roughly on the right heading, having allowed the aircraft to make a near 360 degree turn to the right. Given the angle of approach Haynes decided to land on Runway 22 rather than Runway 31, which required a last minute rearrangement of the response vehicles, which were aligned for Runway 31.

Around five miles from Runway 22, Records gave the 'brace' warning to the passengers and cabin crew. Some 16 seconds later the ground proximity warning sounded and 14 seconds later the aircraft was roughly 100 feet (around 30 metres) above the runway when Haynes ordered the throttles closed. Fitch warned that closing the throttles would cause the aircraft to turn and dip. The aircraft swung left, the nose pitched down and then the starboard wing dropped rapidly. Despite corrective efforts by Fitch the right wing clipped the ground and the aircraft disintegrated into five main sections. The tail and rear sections slid some distance down Runway 22, while the main body and nose veered to the right and crossed the diagonal Runway 17 before coming to rest deep in a two-metre high corn crop that grew some 50 metres from the runway. Some aircraft sections had slid over a kilometre. The crumpled nose section came to rest at the junction of Runway 22 and Runway 17.

Impact response

A Casevac helicopter was in the air and a number of airport, air force and civil response units were on standby. Once the aircraft impacted, disintegrated and began burning, response personnel were sure there could be no survivors. Units moved to the initial points of impact and then to the cornfield from which some disoriented survivors emerged. The crash was a crash in three parts. Survivors came from the strong midsection forward of the wings and nine rows back from the front. The dead scattered along the path of the crash came from rows 1 to 5 and 31 to 38. Around 35 badly injured and trapped passengers died of smoke inhalation in a section where the wings joined the aircraft.

The senior fire officer first checked the tail section then ordered all fire units to concentrate on the cornfield area, leaving the wreckage strewn along and beside Runway 22 to ambulance and paramedic teams. The first fire tender arriving at the cornfield site spread a heavy layer of foam over the inverted centre section from which most survivors emerged. This unit exhausted its capacity in three minutes and was replaced by a second unit that deployed a hose to deal with a burning section covered by the fragmented right wing. The second fire unit exhausted its water and foam supplies. A third unit – a water tanker – tried to connect with both fire units but mechanical failures prevented any water resupply. By the time civil fire units arrived, the fire had intensified and led to death by smoke inhalation of around 35 survivors.

Statistics

The aircraft carried 285 passengers (including four infants seated on the laps of their parents) and 11 crew. Of these, 111 died (110 passengers, 1 flight attendant). All four flight crew survived. Of the survivors 47 sustained serious injuries, 125 had slight to minor injuries and 13 were uninjured.

Comment

This example clearly illustrates the different set of response management tasks that can arise in onset (where effort is placed on attempting to control and resolve the crisis trigger or incident) as opposed to crisis impact (where effort is directed toward dealing with impact damage). Where the cabin crew, air traffic control and Sioux City Approach Control dealt with tasks in onset management, a different set of managers (airfield, military and civilian response agencies) dealt with the impact damage.

All four lap-sitting children were held on the floor as instructed by the cabin crew. One was successfully held and sustained only minor injuries. The three others were jolted loose on impact although one was grabbed by his mother and was uninjured. One disappeared into an overhead luggage locker and was found by a passenger who re-entered the wreckage on hearing his cries. One died of smoke inhalation. There was a call for greater safety measures for infants. Airline executives pointed out that having to pay for extra seats for infants could cause low-income families not to fly (with loss of income and profit) but to drive to destinations (thus becoming more likely to die in the more frequent road accidents).

Three months after the accident key engine components were found on the ground near where the trouble started. Detailed examination revealed that an undetected flaw in the metal of the engine's fan disk led to an explosive failure. The explosive failure severed each of three independent hydraulic systems and this loss of hydraulic systems led to loss of aircraft control. The fan disk had operated safely for 17 years.

Pilots attempting reconstruction of Flight 232 on flight simulators failed to reach the airport. That the crew brought the aircraft to the airport and saved over half of the passengers showed what may be accomplished when a crew uses effective teamwork to resolve a problem. The fact that the crew knew each other and had recently flown on duty together six times over the previous three months undoubtedly led to increased familiarity and trust between them. Their interactions and ready acceptance of Captain Fitch has been used to emphasize the benefits of CRM or TRM. Their ability to remain relatively calm, to stay focused on resolving the situation by retrieving some aircraft control then attempt a landing at Sioux City, and to work as a team illustrates some of the benefits.

Management perspective

Reduction management can be proactive and reactive. The proactive component includes reducing risks through quality control, better design management, better training and better provision of support aids (from warning instruments to alternative task procedures). The reactive process involves carefully analyzing the crisis situation in terms of pre-existing and post-derived outcomes for environment, structures, systems and people (see Chapter 17 for more of this in detail). Safer and better designs, construction, systems and management approaches can be developed by trying to establish how each of these elements contributed to:

- the onset of crisis;
- impact damage; and
- the response management of the impact damage.

This helps reduce exposure to risks and threats as well as decreasing impact damage and increasing response management.

The reactive outcomes from the crash of Flight 232 illustrate how crisis reduction management processes work. The manufacturers redesigned a safer tail section that protected systems and limited the amount of fluid that can be lost in a similar event. This meant that aircraft control surfaces would retain at least half performance should a hydraulic system be ruptured. Further emphasis was given to the positive aspects of well-trained crews.

The investigators also determined that while the flaw in the fan disk probably occurred when it was being forged and not when it was machined, there were automated inspection approaches (ultrasonic, fluorescent penetrant inspection) that could improve on human inspection.

The investigators also suggested that major unit exercises for response agencies might uncover mechanical failures as well as prepare personnel for response actions. The investigators also recommended a review on permitting farming so close to the airport.

References

Allinson, R. E. (1993) *Global Disasters: Inquiries into Management Ethics*. New York: Prentice-Hall.

Faith, N. (1996) *Black Box: Why Air Safety Is No Accident*. London: Boxtree.

Flin, R. (1996) *Sitting in the Hot Seat: Leaders and Teams for Critical Incident Management*. Chichester, England: Wiley.

Gregorich, S., Helmreich, R. and Wilhelm, J. (1990) 'The structure of cockpit management attitudes', *Journal of Applied Psychology*, 75, 682–90.

Helmreich, R. L. (1997) 'Managing human error in aviation', *Scientific American*, 276 (5), 40–5.

Job, M. (1996) *Air Disaster: Volume 2*. Weston Creek, ACT, Australia: Aerospace Publications.

Lauber, J. (1984) 'Resource management in the cockpit', *Air Line Pilot*, 53, 20–3.

Pastin, M. (1986) *The Hard Problems of Management: Gaining the Ethics Edge*. San Francisco: Jossey Bass.

Thompson, P. M. (1993) 'The Bangladesh Flood Action Plan – a view', *Macedon Digest*, 8 (2), 27–30.

Turner, B. A. (1976) 'The organizational and interorganizational development of disasters', *Administrative Science Quarterly*, 21, 380–1.

Wagenaar, W. A. (1996) 'Profiling crisis management', *Journal of Contingencies and Crisis Management*, 4 (3), 169–74.

Warning systems

Once executives and managers have undertaken risk and impact analysis and commenced crisis and risk reduction programmes, they need to help organization members become ready to deal with any crisis situations. This readiness emerges from developing response and recovery plans, ensuring members become familiar with these plans, and from mental preparedness that involves experience from skills training and from simulated crisis situations. The objective of this readiness is to limit the damage (physical, verbal and perceptual) and to recover the situation to a more normal state of function.

The key to quick restoration to a more normal situation is to limit the damage caused by the crisis and crisis impact. Speedy damage limitation comes from getting the appropriate response to the right site as soon as possible. One way of gaining this speedy response is to have effective surveillance and warning systems in place and training people in responding appropriately to those warnings. Hence warning or alert systems form the first line of defences that limit the damage when sources of risk cause crisis situations.

Warning systems

Warning and monitoring systems are an integral part of any crisis management. These systems oversee a given environment so that specified adverse changes within that environment are signalled to other systems or to people who are responsible for maintaining that environment. Warning systems enable:

- faster response to a crisis onset (adverse changes are noted and communicated);
- protection of personnel and assets (through signalling evacuation and through triggering containment systems);
- activation of active response systems (such as suppression systems).

Thus fire alarms may lead to early evacuation, automatic closure of fire screens and activation of water or chemical fire suppression systems.

As with any system-driven process, however, there are disadvantages to using automated systems. These disadvantages include:

- failure of system;
- false alarms;
- over-dependence from people.

Automated systems can themselves malfunction or fail (or be switched off). Likewise, automated systems can give repeated false alarms due to triggering sensors eliciting a false reading. Car theft alarms, for example, simply operate on sensors that seek changes in pressure or electromagnetic waves. Consequently the swift and close passage of a large vehicle or the close proximity of a pedestrian can trigger a false alarm. Given the number of cars fitted with alarms in urban areas, few people react to a car theft alarm sounding, beyond desiring to remonstrate with the owner.

Perhaps the most insidious and the most important factor is the over-dependence of humans upon the equipment they operate. While users begin by actively monitoring the operation of a machine, they eventually relax and tend to rely on the machine and not their own senses and judgement. Consequently many warning systems are used as automated systems, rather than as the combination of machine and human surveillance for which the systems were designed. This means the alerts and warnings then depend on:

- the limitations of the equipment or system;
- the level of maintenance of the equipment or system;
- the degree to which the operators correctly use the equipment or system.

Managers thus need to ensure that warning systems are properly maintained and operated. As a safeguard, systems need to overlay each other so that they act as both confirmatory and support systems.

Types of system

Warning systems can be divided into five basic types using two dimensions. Systems can be either dynamic or static and either mobile or stationary. The fifth group is a combination of systems that include elements of all four types.

Dynamic mobile systems are the most expensive to acquire and maintain. The chief advantages are that:

- the systems are dynamic and thus actively interrogate the environment or respond to the adverse change through activating containment or suppression systems;
- the systems can be shifted from site to site or randomly relocated in sites for greater security.

There are a number of major disadvantages. These include:

- the mobility of systems may leave parts of the site unmonitored;
- active interrogation may lead to a focus on part of the site at the expense of other parts;
- activated containment and suppression systems may cause damage and losses;
- the added complexity of dynamic mobile systems means that there are more components and sub-systems that may fail.

Spy satellites and reconnaissance aircraft are examples of this type of system.

Dynamic stationary systems are cheaper than dynamic mobile systems while retaining the advantage of being so designed that site coverage is complete. The system has the capacity for dynamic interrogation and/or response system triggering. Disadvantages may include:

- cost;
- the loss of coverage of all parts of the site through a 'close-up' focus on one part;
- the complexity of the dynamic sub-systems leading to more system failures;
- losses due to inappropriate activation of suppression and containment systems.

In some circumstances, the immobility of the system can be a disadvantage as crisis impact damage can eliminate the system. Additionally, those wishing to counter the system can identify the weak points more easily. Examples of dynamic stationary systems include surveillance cameras operated by people and modern fire-warning systems that link warnings with suppression systems.

Static mobile systems are generally cheaper than the previous two types. The advantages of this type are that:

- the warning system is usually easy to operate;
- mobility means that the system can be relocated, which increases security and effectiveness.

Disadvantages include:

- the potential loss of complete site coverage when systems are shifted around;
- the increased likelihood of system failure due to failures in mobility;
- the lack of close checking or response activation available in interrogative dynamic systems.

Examples of static mobile systems include police radar traps for speeding motorists, mobile aircraft radar systems and air pollution scanners on aircraft or cars.

Static stationary systems are the cheapest as these systems simply respond to specified adverse changes on a given site. Disadvantages include:

- the lack of capacity to do more than emit a warning signal when encountering an adverse change of state;
- an increased likelihood of being put out of action through crisis impact damage or deliberate action by those wishing to counter the system.

While each static stationary system will have a higher operational reliability than the other system types (due to lack of complexity), use of large numbers of static stationary systems will mean that system failure and false alarms will still seem prevalent. This is likely to lead to diminished responses to alarms. Examples of static stationary alarms include car theft alarms, most burglar alarms and many residential smoke or heat detector alarms.

Mixed systems are likely to be most used by organizations, as these appear to be a comprehensive yet cheaper approach to warning systems. Many industrial and business organizations may have armed security personnel who 'randomly' patrol the site (dynamic mobile systems), wall-mounted video cameras (dynamic or static stationary devices), fire alarms linked to suppression and containment systems (dynamic stationary systems) and forced-entry or burglar alarms (static stationary). Disadvantages in using mixed systems include patchy coverage, increased likelihood of system failure, and probable relaxation of maintenance and attention until the seemingly most potent system becomes the system most relied upon (and most used).

As managers determine the type or types of system that best suit the needs of their organizations, one further system feature is worth considering: whether the system is made visible or invisible. The advantages with visible systems is that these can offer reassurance to those working or living around the site, or can be used as 'warnings' to others to stay out of the site. The disadvantages include the visibility of the systems and the loss of deterrence due to people knowing where the system is. Invisible systems often provide less interference in day-to-day operations as the systems are out of sight. Some invisible systems (e.g. electrified fences or hidden explosives) breach the laws in many countries.

A realistic approach to designing warning systems is to start from the desired outcome and work back to the types of system likely to produce that outcome. In many cases, the primary mission may be to warn those within a given site or area that an adverse change has arisen and that they had better (a) deal with it, or (b) evacuate. This means we need also to consider how best to communicate warnings to people.

Problems with warning systems

One important problem with warning and alert systems is how people adjust to the presence of the systems. Most of these systems signal an alert or warning when a change in the surrounding environment registers on the sensor or sensors of the system. Given that the normal level of operation for the system is silence until something goes wrong, people are likely to disbelieve the initial warning signal. This disbelief can lead to a suspension of action that can be damaging when action selection is both situation-critical and time-critical.

What is most likely is that those receiving warnings tend to question signals that are rare in occurrence or non-normal from the expected behaviour of the system. Similarly, non-response is likely when there are many warning signals over a period of time, with many false alarms. Those receiving warnings or alerts may often physically freeze for some seconds then furtively check what other people are doing, or move to explore reasons for failure of the system and thus confirm the signal. One common example of the effect of false alarms is seen in the reaction of people who hear a car theft alarm. The normal state for this system is to be unheard. Over time, people learn that car theft alarms often do not signal theft.

A non-response to warnings can be due to:

- disbelief that the non-normal signal is signalling an actual adverse change in the system; or
- a learned disposition to expect a non-normal or outlier signal due to false alarms.

Non-normal signals can be rejected until people receiving the warnings gain further *confirmatory information*. There are many reasons for this rejection. Key reasons are that people:

- become familiar with false alarms;
- are punished for responding to false alarms;
- recognize the non-normality of the signal but await further confirmation;
- find the signal is too vague for specific action;
- find that they need to see and sense a crisis situation before acting; or
- conform their behaviour to those around them.

The problem remains that non-response to vague or over-familiar signals can endanger those receiving the alarm.

Drabek (1986) points out that vague signals tend to be further disbelieved or unheeded. People are likely to wait for a more specific signal. Thus when a simple sound warning is made people may choose to believe that the signal is for somewhere else or covers a different issue (burglar alarm as opposed to fire alarm, for example). At best, recipients of vague signals await or seek confirmatory signals before undertaking a course of action (such as evacuating or securing the surrounding site).

Even when an alarm is received, the message may not make sense to recipients who do not know the codes or terminologies used. On responding to the Clapham rail crash (12 December 1988) the London Ambulance Service issued a cascaded alarm that declared a 'Yellow Alert'. The switchboard workers at St George's Hospital that would handle most of the injured did not know what a Yellow Alert meant. As a result, staff at St George's did not realize the size of the required response until accident and emergency teams considered the incoming data and the number of casualties being brought in.

The human response to warnings needs to be remembered when planning for response actions in crisis situations and when evaluating what happened during a crisis situation (*see* Chapter 17). In the *Challenger* disaster, for example, trails of warnings and danger signals can be found, *but only with hindsight* – when the big picture of events up to, and past, the crisis situation is considered. Indeed, concerns about the sifting of information as decisional information was passed up the management chain were expressed after the disaster of the *Challenger* launch. These actions often emerge as part either of guilty confessions or position protection *only after a disaster happens*. The problem is that people react poorly to warnings, particularly when the warnings are surrounded by the noise of day-to-day work.

Just before the tornado struck Andover in the USA (*see* the Reality Bite in this chapter), a police car was driven through many of the streets of the community with its siren sounding. Those hearing the siren did not associate the signal with a tornado warning (lack of specificity). They thought that the police were chasing a speeding car or en route to an emergency. Some of those who did hear the warning over radio or television or registered the import of the police siren did not react because their previous experience suggested that the warning would turn out to be another false alarm.

During the Chernobyl nuclear reactor failure, critical minutes were lost as key personnel sought to confirm the signals of their monitors that a crisis situation had arisen (*see* Chapter 6). Others continued to disbelieve the warning signals and the subsequent impact signals (muffled explosion, shaking structures, smoke). In the *Herald of Free Enterprise* disaster where a cross-Channel ferry capsized just after leaving the port of Zeebrugge in Belgium (1987), the port admiralty began a cascade contact alert of the coastal emergency services and fire brigade. The alert message was ambiguous, however, as it only mentioned a ferry being adrift. The response services that were contacted waited for clarification and confirmation messages.

The lack of response to warnings can also result from the effects of organizational culture and structures.

The inertia of structures and organizations

If individuals react poorly to warnings, then groups of people are likely to react even more slowly. Groups are more likely to:

- wait for leaders (or organizational management) to instruct them on what to do; and
- watch each other to see what other people are doing.

This problem is more critical when the group or organization is a professional response or support agency or when the organization is one affected by crisis impact damage.

The tendency to move sluggishly or resist sudden changes may arise from a number of sources, including:

- the size of the organization;
- the degree of rigidity and formality implanted within the culture of the organization;
- the degree to which administrative staff and managers fear post-crisis evaluation of their actions and behaviours.

Other sources of inertia are inadequate communication systems and the absence of link persons within communication systems (*see* Chapter 6), and the absence of key decision makers and resource allocators when the crisis happens.

Inertia also may arise because of the unexpectedness and unpredictabilty of the alert and early communications. Drabek (1986) and Perry (1985) find that a sudden and unexpected message (especially indicating a threat to resources or people) tends to create a reaction of disbelief. Given such disbelief, decision makers and communication 'gatekeepers' (those who receive and pass on messages) tend to avoid action choices. They tend to ignore the communication or to wait or seek confirmation of the warning. When Pearl Harbor was bombed in the Second World War warning messages from radar and watch posts were ignored because these messages were seen as contradictory to the ongoing state of affairs (which was that nothing was happening).

Warnings to the public

Warning messages need to be simple, direct and redundant (repeated in different ways). 'Precise' jargon and in-house terminologies need to be changed into simple, often short, declarative sentences.

Public warnings need to be as simple as possible so that all listeners get as clear an understanding of the oncoming threat as possible. As a working heuristic (rule of thumb), use the *three-finger method*:

1 Say what the warning is about.
2 Say what this means to the listener.
3 Say what the listener needs to do in the time available.

Warnings need to get the attention of recipients from the beginning of the message. Australian cyclone warnings, for example, begin with several seconds of modulated sounds that get attention. Attention-getting is important because:

- the extraneous and competing noise in most 'listening' environments can block the warning;
- the attention-getting effort allows the recipients to focus on the ensuing content of the warning message.

With repeated use of the attention-getter and education in what the attention-getter heralds, recipients can identify the type of message being presented.

The content of the warning message needs to state:

- the name of the source authority, the date and the time of the message;
- the area or site being alerted;
- the nature of the threat;
- the likely impact of the threat;
- the forecast time range for the threat;
- the impact of the threat;
- the immediate basic actions those being warned in the areas likely to be affected need to undertake.

These points need to be repeated and then summarized so that recipients can fill in details they missed the first time and check their understanding of the message. Finally, the message needs to inform the listener of the next likely information broadcast, particularly when updated information will be transmitted.

Note that a number of broadcast media are available, including radio, television, facsimile networks, computer networks (including e-mail and Internet), public address systems, mobile vans and citizen band radio. While these are effective means of communication, managers need to realize that most potential recipients will not necessarily receive the warning – even if all media are used simultaneously. Consequently, warnings need to be repeated.

Remember that media time is valuable. Media organizations like to reduce messages into 'bites' of between 15 and 45 seconds. If longer times are available, personalize the import of the message and ensure major points are repeated to ensure retention by the audience. Where the message is uncertain, use simple words to convey the uncertainty: 'may', 'could', 'potential', 'if ... then'. Where uncertainty is present, include simple means by which listeners may confirm information where possible – direction of threat, signs or symptoms to seek, or levels of performance or behaviour to expect.

Variables that influence reception of a warning

Just how well recipients respond to a warning often depends upon the experience and beliefs of each recipient and on the content variables in the warning. Research (Drabek, 1986; Fischer and Harr, 1994; Foster, 1980; Perry, Lindell and Greene, 1982) suggests that key variables are:

- the *clarity* of the message (how *specific* is it?);
- the *consistency* of the message (do other sources report the same message?);
- the *frequency* of the message;
- the *source of authority* of the message;
- the *accuracy* of past warnings;
- the *frequency of occurrence* of the crisis or disaster event.

When recipients find that the message is clear and specific, other sources say the same things, the message is repeated, the source of authority is appropriate, past warnings have generally been accurate and the crisis has happened before, then they are likely to respond quickly. Their actions may still be less than desired as they have forgotten, not received or not understood any educational material.

Should recipients find that the key variables are not present, then they are likely to ignore the warning or search for more information. In either case, time for selecting and undertaking an appropriate response action is lost, and recipients may well increase the likelihood of asset damage and personal injury.

Warnings and the 80–20 rule

Field experience suggests that as many as one in five of those in the area or site being warned will do the opposite to the advice given in the warning. This 20 per cent will include people who:

- claim not to have heard the warning;
- need to confirm things for themselves;
- were afraid of consequences;
- had other concerns (e.g. leaving valuable documents or assets behind in an evacuation);
- believe they know better than the advice given in the warning.

Managers need to incorporate strategies for handling these people and potentially for having to add rescue operations in physical crisis situations.

REALITY BITE

Tornado at Andover, Kansas, USA, 1991

Background
Every year a number of tornadoes cause damage, death and injuries in the United States of America. Tornadoes are hard to predict and consequently many tornado warnings are 'false alarms'. While tornadoes happen all over the world, around 30 per cent strike along a strip of mid-America that runs from the Great Lakes to the Gulf of Mexico.

Andover, Kansas, is a town of 4000 residents located within this area of tornado threat.

Incident
On Friday, 26 April 1991, a tornado watch was declared for an area that included Andover. By 6.00 pm the watch had become a warning. At 6.39 pm a tornado struck the town of Andover, particularly ravaging the Golden Spur Mobile Home Park.

Before impact, an attempt to provide a local alert via a civil defence siren failed as the siren did not work. A police car was used to enter the area with its siren switched on as a last-minute warning of the impact from the tornado. Some residents were at work, others were out dining or shopping, and around 200 to 300 Park residents heeded the warning and evacuated to a centrally located underground shelter.

Response
After the tornado had moved on, response personnel moved in. Search and rescue operations shifted some debris, especially material obstructing streets and access to the Park, and helped dazed residents and bystanders deal with the dead and injured.

An emergency operation centre (EOC) was established in an empty store in the small shopping mall near to the Golden Spur Mobile Home Park. The community had no emergency plan, so the mayor acted as a de facto co-ordinator. Other local politicians formed an advisory committee, and community, church and other volunteer organizations began to arrive in order to help clean up the devastated area. Virtually all equipment and facilities were donated by local businesses within hours of the event.

The five members of the Andover law enforcement organization supplied security at the EOC. The site also eventually had a Red Cross canteen in the parking lot and a communications vehicle directly in front of the store. On site at the Golden Spur Mobile Home Park, National Guard personnel maintained security. Their mission was to prevent looting and assist in traffic control. As the number of sightseers increased, emergency respondents found they were obstructed in their work and residents trying to return to their homes were impeded. A system of security badges was in place at the EOC within 36 hours.

The EOC managers had to decide when a complete removal of debris should commence. Aid volunteered by businesses and community groups was likely to fade if not used quickly and owners of destroyed property would not be able to install replacements until the site was cleared. On the other hand, some survivors needed more time to retrieve personal possessions and valuables. Moreover, some absentee victims of property losses were still sorting themselves out and wanted a few more days to recover their personal property. Some local television and newspaper reportage criticized an initial decision to clean the site up immediately, and this prompted a rethink by the committee. The clean-up was deferred to allow residents more time to retrieve their valuables.

Statistics
The tornado killed 13 people and injured 175. Around 840 residents of the town of Andover (population of 4047) lost their homes.

Comment
Four interesting points emerge from this example:

- the reaction to warning systems by those around the system;
- how the response management took shape;
- the problem of sightseers;
- the stimulus–response effects that can arise from media reports and speculation surrounding a crisis situation.

Reaction to warnings

The primary warning system (the civil defence siren) failed, probably as a result of second-hand parts having been used in a cost-saving measure in maintaining the siren. Many people claimed not to be listening to radio or watching television.

An obvious factor in the use of alarm systems is that familiarity with the signal can lead to the signal being ignored. Use of a siren from a police car and even a civil defence area siren may prove to have less than optimal outcomes as these may not provide a sufficiently specific warning of the nature of the threat. Only some of the population of Andover (including around half of the Mobile Park population) took evacuation or refuge-seeking action.

Town officials claimed that a final tornado warning involving the siren of a police car was standard operating procedure that had been described in public service announcements. Some residents said that police sirens simply indicated that the police were after criminals or rushing to the scene of a crime. Warnings need to be simple, specific and clear to those receiving the warnings. One improvement, for example, would be to use a public address system attached to the patrol car to state clearly that a tornado was approaching.

Response management

For its disaster management, the town relied on an emergent organization structure (see Dynes and Quarantelli, 1977). An emergent organization is one that takes shape as a response to the demands of the surrounding environment – the organization 'emerges' over time. This is a reactive structure and much time and effort is often spent in establishing who does what and what order of priority is assigned tasks. This loss of time can be critical when dealing with threats to life and other assets.

While there is flexibility in the approach, the time wastage, interpersonal friction and misunderstandings that ensue generally lead to non-optimal management. This time wastage, interpersonal friction and misunderstanding also presents a non-optimal image of the management to onlookers and media personnel. Such images lead to criticism from media representatives and from groups of victims and bystanders.

The number of people in the Mobile Home Park provides an insight into crisis management planning. Of the estimated 1000 residents, some 200 to 300 took appropriate action (shelter in the underground facility). Around 500 were absent. Of the non-responders (most of whom contributed to the 188 casualties), some tried to protect valuables, sought significant others or felt movement outside was more dangerous than staying inside. Others did not know what to do, claimed not to hear the alarm or ignored the alarm. Note the ratio of non-responders to those who either responded or were absent from the crisis site – 200 to 800 or 1 in 4. This reinforces the point made about one in five acting contrary to the intentions of the warning.

Crisis planners need to consider the effects of absentees in managing a crisis situation. The effects include:

- uncertainty over who is missing (believed trapped, injured or dead) in the wake of the impact of the event); and
- attempts to return to their home or business location once they re-enter the site.

Failure to identify absentees leads to some paralysis in response actions and aftermath clean-up, as happened in the Andover incident. Moreover, those returning to the affected site tend to want to retrieve personal effects and valuables. Any denial of access can lead to site penetration that adds to fears about looting and increased concern over site safety. If there is no procedure in place for safe admission onto a site by those absent at the moment of impact or who had been removed from the site during the crisis, frustration and criticism will distract managers from their response activities. Restriction on entry by victims can lead to anger, resentment and consequent agitation, as well as generating criticism from media sources. Litigation may also ensue.

Plans that include dealing with the desires of absentees and promoting site access can help raise morale among response personnel. Assisted site access allows respondents to do something positive to assist people. Emergency workers in the Northridge earthquake, for example, expressed improved morale when they were permitted to assist people to recover valuables from their destroyed properties. This effort also fostered a positive perception of the response management from victims and other community members.

Sightseers

In most visible crisis situations (especially major accidents and natural disasters), people management planning includes the need to deal with:

- spontaneous and unsolicited offers of assistance; and
- sightseers.

Both groups can inundate management attention and lead to blockages in critical access routes.

Managers need to consider how to cope with sightseers, particularly in community-based crisis situations. Organization managers need to consider what is best done with personnel who are evacuated from a site or who are temporarily without anything to do after the crisis is over. Many evacuation plans fail to consider what needs to be done with evacuated personnel. When the crisis is real and impact damage has happened, many organizations need to consider allowing non-essential staff to depart from the site. By providing a contact telephone number, for example, personnel can check what they are required to do as time passes.

Media

Media coverage of the Andover tornado response management provides a reasonable example of the points of view often used by media personnel when a crisis happens. The initial focus was on the extent of the damage and reporting on the casualties and personal experiences of the survivors. This was accompanied by describing the efforts of the response agencies and by outlining what concerned members of the community could do to help those directly affected by the tornado. Two local reporters focused on assigning blame, bringing attention to claims of lack of warning and to the apparently indifferent and unfeeling attitude of the response and recovery management in wanting to quickly clean away the debris.

The managers responded to criticisms about the lack of warning by showing the media a videotape inadvertently made by the officer in the police car that gave the tornado warning. One segment showed the car driving past a woman walking a dog and led to criticism that the driver did not stop to ensure she sought safety. However, had the police officer stopped to warn each nearby individual, the area in which the warning was broadcast would have been reduced.

The accusations about the lack of warning also distracted many of the EOC managers who had committed themselves fully to the response effort, gone without sleep and done the best they could. They felt they deserved appreciation and credit rather than criticism. They pointed out that community education programmes should have taught people that a police car with the siren on means a tornado is nearby and people should have reacted properly. However, the reaction of community members was different. After all, these members claimed, was not a police siren used to signal that the officer was chasing some lawbreaker?

Overall, media coverage was quite positive. Fischer and Harr (1994) report that 12 out of 132 reports on television and 10 out of 151 print media stories were negative. Local emergency managers became angry over what they saw as unfair criticism, particularly when those involved in running the town and in responding to the impact of the tornado saw themselves as altruistic volunteers doing their best in a difficult situation. They spent around 20 per cent of their time undertaking media damage control.

Because Andover had no crisis management plan, there were no selected or specialized personnel with specific roles for:

- collating information;
- dealing with outside inquiries for information; and
- dealing with media needs and requests.

The failure to adequately plan for, and perform, these duties separately and effectively was a cause of many of their problems. Executives and managers need to design or adopt flexible crisis management structures (such as CMSS – see Chapter 10) that include these roles within the management approach.

Response and recovery personnel can easily develop a siege mentality due to the distracting pressures of the media for interesting and attention-gaining stories. Personnel need more than training in redirecting media inquiries or in presenting interviews and conference briefings. They need to understand the motivations and objectives of media representatives so that the members understand the interaction process they face with media representatives.

Management perspective

Executives and managers need to accept that proactive planning (rather than reactive or emergent procedures) is more efficient and effective in handling crisis situations. Plans should not be made too inflexible with too few options and so many details that obstruction in or failure of one part of the plan effectively stops the whole effort. Plans are 'guides' to action.

Likewise senior managers need to ensure that personnel have the skills to deal with crisis situations, the impacts from those situations, and the associated demands that come with working in such situations. Three clear features are needed – good integrated incident (or response or recovery) management systems, the ability to properly use alarm warnings (or assess situations which have unusual or incomplete warnings), and the ability to quickly contact and assemble the necessary specialists and support personnel to deal with the likely impacts. This is demonstrated in the next Reality Bite covering a fire incident at the PNC Bank in Philadelphia, USA.

REALITY BITE

Reacting to non-normal signals –
PNC Bank, Philadelphia, USA, 1996

Background
PNC Bank is the tenth largest bank holding company in the USA, with headquarters in Pittsburgh (Pennsylvania) and operations that extend within the USA through eleven states and to branches overseas. The bank has an experienced emergency response team that includes groups focused on continuity, facilities, security, human resources, public relations and risk management. In Philadelphia, the PNC regional headquarters is situated in a 45-floor building.

Incident
At 8.30 am, 10 June 1996, a security person telephoned in a report of smoke in the front teller area. The duty crisis manager was placed in a quandary. While the security person reported a possible fire, none of the fire alarms had been activated. Attempts to contact the person reporting the smoke were unsuccessful as he had quickly left the site. The manager alerted the fire department and decided to place the bank's security and business continuity teams on alert.

Response
At 8.35 am the groups belonging to the emergency response team were alerted, along with the designated insurance adjuster. By 8.45 am, there was still no confirmation of any fire. A virtual command centre – one in which command team members are linked by electronic means rather than being physically in the one room – was activated. Security and continuity teams were dispatched to the site (some five minutes away).

Within a few more minutes the fire was visually confirmed. The firefighters had rapidly attacked the source of the flames, leaving visible water, smoke, fire and access damage. The on-site business incident manager assessed there was a need for specific continuity and recovery service providers to be called in. Before any suppliers and vendors and any of the bank's staff could and would be allowed on the premises, building safety and environment testing needed to be performed (contact engineers and safety and health specialists). There was likely to be damage to electronic equipment (contact electronic restoration vendor, using pre-arranged agreements), to records and currency (contact specialist restoration and salvage service providers), and to the interior structure (contact general clean-up contractor) and internal air-conditioning (contact HVAC vendor).

Due to the speed of the PNC response and the trust and confidence built up through the combined training with the local response agencies, PNC regained control over the site within two hours from response and recovery activation. The emergency response team had their personnel on site and had called in the insurance adjusters and vendor contacts. The team had established a secured perimeter and scheduled a press conference. Damage assessment established that the first floor (Banking Branch) was a total loss, that there was smoke damage to the floors above, and that there was smoke, water and heat damage to equipment, furniture, stationery, records and currency.

By the end of the day, the site command centre had been established on the 16th floor. Time lines for assessments and then recovery processes were established. Salvage and restoration had already begun. Customers were already being redirected to alternative branches and additional security had been deployed around the site. Air quality had been tested and found satisfactory and a decision had been reached to close the branch for restoration. Active accounts and recovered safe deposit boxes were relocated to a nearby branch, and a toll-free telephone number was advertised for customers to use for any inquiries. Electronic and computer equipment had been retrieved for restoration, water had been completely removed from the building, the insurance claim had been lodged and restoration authorized, the salvage vendor had more than 50 personnel working on site, and debris was already being removed.

By the end of the next day (11 June), all fire debris had been removed, the clean-up of smoke and water damage was nearly complete, and all damaged records were undergoing restoration by specialists. The business continuity process was terminated and all teams stood down when senior management decided to absorb the restoration process in a complete facility rebuilding project.

So what caused the fire and why did the alarms not work? The answers were quite simple. A small plastic fan had been accidentally left on over the weekend in one of the teller boxes. This fan had overheated leading to the fire. The alarms had not worked because a building manager new to the premises had turned the alarms off to allow repair work on one of the higher-level floors. He had simply forgotten to turn the alarms back on.

Statistics
The response-to-recovery process took less than 48 hours and was formally stopped with the decision to renovate the building.

Comment
The two keys to successful crisis management are clearly underscored in this incident. These are the quick and appropriate communication with those involved in the crisis (and the media and general public) and the rapid response that can reduce impact damage and downtime for recovery. By using the multi-group approach and using prearranged contact lists of specialists, lead starting times (when people can start their tasks) for response and recovery activities are reduced and the time taken to determine appropriate impact management and then recovery management is similarly reduced.

This incident falls somewhere between the local small crisis of a flooded critical-activity room and a full structure failure. Crisis planning and preparedness needs to be scalable and relevant to the task. There was an incident in the head office of a bank in which a pipe leak threatened some critical data-processing operations. Preparations were well in-hand for an evacuation to a distant site across the city (according to the business continuity plan) until someone pointed out the presence of nearly empty rooms elsewhere in the building that were well away from the threatened area. Crisis managers and planners thus need to determine what options and levels of management can quickly handle and resolve different sizes of crisis situation.

Management perspective

PNC has an interesting multi-group approach to physical crisis management and business continuity that reflects the general advice given by experts. By having specialist combat groups, a crisis manager can select appropriate groups according to the demands of a given incident. The different groups can assist in, or separately manage, each of the multiple aspects of a situation. These aspects include:

- employee and customer safety;
- site security;
- liaison with professional response agencies;
- supporting specialists on site;
- retrieval and recovery of off-site backed-up data and documents;
- monitoring any emergent issues (such as environmental damage);
- preparing to handle requests for information from customers, the general public and the media.

By adopting a multi-group approach, specialists can work in their area of expertise while the overall effort is linked and integrated by the incident crisis manager and the managers of the groups.

Note the usefulness of a virtual command centre approach. There is no substitute for having the crisis management team present in the one room. This enables quick exchanges of data, easy operational status check-up, and the ability to read the body language as well as the verbal message. The time taken to assemble such a team can be critical, however, as members may have to converge from different sites (and even from different countries). By using virtual centres until the team can physically interact in one place, two clear advantages emerge:

- more time is gained to respond to the situation;
- specialist managers can actively monitor and manage operations at separate sites.

For a virtual command centre approach to work, all communication connections need to be available for all members for all of the time. Once one member drops out of the communication loop then the effectiveness of the system is limited. Members need to be able to effectively use their communications links.

One of the clear lessons for managers from this example is the need to establish good relations with the likely response agencies involved in dealing with various crisis situations. By establishing trust and belief that the organization can safely and properly manage affairs on-site (or on the part of the site occupied by the organization), more access and freedom of action may result.

Three final points are worth considering. First, crisis situations can arise from simple mistakes, not just from large inevitable processes. In fact, many crisis situations emerge as the result of a number of events or actions (fan left on, alarms left off, weekend rather than workday).

Second, executives and managers need to establish a working policy that allows managers to declare a crisis situation with minimal negative effect should the situation prove to be a false alarm. Managers need to decide whether they should act from the available evidence and on what may result should a crisis situation declaration not be made, rather than basing a decision on the consequences to themselves should the alert prove unfounded. Waiting for confirmation of information before activating a crisis response can prove costly.

While a crisis alert that includes activating response and recovery actions may prove costly in terms of vendor and response agency penalties when the situation is a false alarm, the activation is a real test of the response and recovery capabilities of an organization. Draw out what positive learning aspects can be gained from a false-positive event (one that declared a crisis when a crisis did not exist).

Third, note the integrated approach used by the PNC emergency response team. There is an emphasis on speed of response using virtual centres and an equal emphasis on access to factual information that is regularly updated. Such access by customers, media and employees can help reduce misunderstandings and minimize conflicts and concerns.

References

Drabek, T. E. (1986) *Human System Responses to Disaster*. New York: Springer-Verlag.

Dynes, R. R. and Quarantelli, E. L. (1977) *Organizational Communications and Decision Making in Crises*. Newark: Research Center, University of Delaware.

Fischer, H. W. III and Harr, V. J. (1994) 'Emergency operating center response to media blame assignation: A case study of an emergent EOC', *Disaster Prevention Management*, 3(3), 7–17.

Foster, H. D. (1980) *Disaster Planning: The Preservation of Life and Property*. New York: Springer-Verlag.

Perry, R. W. (1985) *Comprehensive Emergency Management*. Greenwich, Conn.: JAI Press.

Perry, R. W., Lindell, M. and Greene, M. (1982) 'Crisis communications: ethnic differentials in interpreting and acting on disaster warnings', *Social Behaviour and Personality*, 10(1), 97–104.

chapter 5

EXERCISE

This exercise introduces participants to the simulation map and exercise format used in later chapters.

The key objective of this exercise is to enable users to try out the static and dynamic forms of warning and alert. Note that the exercise also provides a chance to practise information management approaches and skills (*see* Chapter 6), media or 'pressure group' management (*see* Chapter 7) and image-shaping of responses to questions from these groups (*see* Chapters 7 and 8). Do spend time discussing and working on these areas as well as on planning and making game-turn moves (described below).

When you have finished the exercise, critically consider the strategies and actions you made and the consequent outcomes. Should you be doing this exercise in a small group, discuss your impressions and criticisms. Remember to acknowledge the positive aspects as well as analyze any 'what went wrong' aspects. You may wish to consider the brief comments made on this exercise on pp. 447–8 in Appendix 2 to help generate your analysis and discussion.

Beginning the exercise
Find the simulation map in Appendix 1 and follow the preparation instructions.

Map descriptions
The map shows part of the Nation of Angst. There is a coast running east to west at the top of the map. There are three cities (Thumpe [T17, T18, U17, U18], Bashe [T1, T2, U1, U2], and Rage [F7, F8, G7, G8]), a VIP resort, a large gold mine, and an oil and gas production facility.

A mountain range (mountains numbered from 1 to 20) runs parallel to the coast with rivers running through it (entering the sea at F6, H10 and H15). South of the mountains and rivers is a large area of flat country with farming and livestock production (hatched squares).

Roll a dice to place the VIP resort, mine and oil well tokens on the map.

Resort   1 = L8, 2 = I9, 3 = M13, 4 = C2, 5 = C19, 6 = H16

Mine   1 = L1, 2 = M8, 3 = M13, 4 = L21, 5 = L24, 6 = H23

Oil well   1 = N1, 2 = S9, 3 = Q12, 4 = S16, 5 = G19, 6 = C24

Piece descriptions
All pieces may be moved up to four squares horizontally or vertically, or any combination of horizontal and vertical movement – but not diagonally. No more than four pieces can be placed on any square at the same time, and any piece can move through a square regardless of the number of pieces placed on that square.

HQ	Field Command: controls own square.
S	Heavy Support: controls own square; can fire into each vertical and horizontal square adjacent to its own square. This piece has a value equal to two combat pieces.
P1, P2	Paramedic Units (cannot attack or defend): reduce casualties and effect of any attacks within up to two squares in any vertical and horizontal direction from their own square. If attacked, Paramedic Units suffer casualties similar to civilian estimates.
TL, UL	Group Command Units for Group T and Group U: can elect to be team command and co-ordination piece in which case these pieces defend their squares but do not attack, and can direct their group precisely in any operations; or can elect to act as a fifth combat unit, in which case the other units may or may not follow instructions (*see* game instructions below).
T2, T3, T4, T5; U2, U3, U4, U5	Combat Units: these defend their own square and can attack any square adjacent to the square they occupy (but not diagonal squares) by moving onto that square.
X1, X2, X3	Units of the Kalmist Forces: these units will appear according to directions of the various Modules. They have a combat value equivalent to one T or U combat unit.

Scenario

The Angstian government has discovered that an unspecified number of armed Kalmist insurgents intend to strike one or more targets, probably in Northern Angst. As a result, two combat groups, paramedic units, and head quarter and support units have been moved into the region. These pieces start from any one of the three cities.

The Kalmists are fighting for the independence of the Island of Kalme (not on map but lies east of mainland Angst). Many units of the Angstian military are trying to maintain the peace and prevent violence on the Island of Kalme.

A crisis committee is formed. This is a crisis because there exists a threat to humans and resources, there is uncertain and missing information, and there are too few units to protect the whole region (or, indeed, to cover the three cities and the three important sites). Should the sites be closed down? Should mobile patrols be used? Or static defences placed on cities? Or a combination of these? How much should the public be told? Businesses be told? Business shareholders and staff be told?

The crisis committee consists of a general-in-command (the CM), a brigadier (field commander of one of the two combat groups – the FC), an unassigned colonel (the OO), the minister of police (representing the state government), and two business leaders who respectively own the oil well and the resort and represent the Angst business community. Add more members if you wish – mayors of the cities, the company owner of the gold mine.

The mission is to protect the interests and people of North Angst from attack.

Take some time to consider and discuss strategies. Ensure someone keeps track of these discussions, decisions, actions and outcomes so that the exercise can be evaluated and discussed afterwards.

General game instructions
There are 12 game turns in this activity. The turns can be tracked on the Timetrack line found at the bottom of the joined maps, using the piece with the 🎇 symbol.

To introduce a sense of time pressure found in crisis situations, set a time limit for each game turn. A suggested limit would be somewhere between 15 and 20 minutes per turn.

The CM (in consultation with the FC and OO) starts the 14 pieces from any of the starting points (the dark hatched squares covering F7, F8, G7, G8 and T1, T2, U1, U2 and T17, T18, U17, U18).

In each turn
1 Move one, some, or all pieces up to four squares up, down or sideways on the map in any combination of those moves. Pieces cannot be moved diagonally across the map.
   (a) Note that when pieces are not in contact with their command pieces (within 12 squares of the HQ piece, or four squares of the TL or UL pieces, then response to orders changes.
   (b) Roll a dice for each piece not in contact with its HQ (12 square radius from the HQ piece) or group leader (four square radius from the TL or UL piece) and which is moving or under orders that require movement: 1 = still in contact and follows existing or new orders; 2 = shift one square north; 3 = shift one square south; 4 = shift one square east; 5 = shift one square west; 6 = still in contact and follows existing or new orders. If units were under a prior movement order, then pieces continue toward the previous objective but along the verticals and horizontals (no mixture of these) from the new position. For static or stationary units (or those ordered to remain on one square) which are also out of contact with HQ or UL or TL, the roll of the dice means: 1, 6 = still in contact; 2, 3, 4, 5 = remain on the square but do not respond to new orders.

2 Roll a dice to determine whether you receive a report from the 'Situation' or the 'Incident' Module. The Situation Module contains reports on what is happening while the Incident Module contains reports about incidents or crisis-sourced changes in the environment. Situation = 1, 3, 5; Incident = 2, 4, 6.

3 Once you have found whether you are dealing with the Situation or Incident

Module, roll a dice to see which of the six Situation or Incident reports your crisis committee receives.

4   Respond to the information from the report from the Situation or Incident Module. You may only move those pieces that are directly indicated in the report you receive and only in terms of the instructions presented in that report.

5   Roll a dice to determine whether you receive a message from the 'Information' Module or a question from the 'Public Comment' Module. The Information Module contains messages that give soft or hard information about the situation while the Public Comment Module contains questions from the media, from pressure groups or from groups affected by the situation. Information = 1, 3, 5; Public Comment = 2, 4, 6.

6   Once you have found whether you are dealing with the Information or Public Comment Module, roll a dice to see which of the six messages or questions from the Information or Public Comment Modules your crisis committee receives.

7   Verbally respond to any questions from the Information or Public Comment Modules. You may decide to divide your committee into sub-groups to handle the game moves and information management. You may only move those pieces that are directly indicated in the report you receive and only in terms of the instructions presented in that report.

Begin the next turn

Situation Module (from a dice roll of 1, 3, 5): roll the dice

1   Unrest causes a request for one combat unit to be stationed in each of the three cities. Move the nearest unit toward each city that does not have a combat unit on one of the four city squares.

2   Communications failure in HQ facility. No new orders or new moves can be made next turn.

3   Transport failure is believed to have immobilized one of the field units. Roll a dice twice and add the scores to determine which unit cannot move for the rest of the exercise: 2 = report is disconfirmed; 3 = UL; 4 = U2; 5 = U3; 6 = U4; 7 = U5; 8 = TL; 9 = T2; 10 = T3; 11 = T4; 12 = T5.

4   Government advisers point out that the oil well and gold mines contribute substantially to the economy and must be protected. Base one unit at each of these locations as soon as they can move to those sites.

5   The Mayor of [roll a dice: Rage = 1, 2; Bashe = 3, 4; Thumpe = 5, 6] gets the Angst government to pressure the committee to place more protection in the city. If not already present, base two units in the city as soon as they can get there.

6   Heavy rains wash out bridges and most roads become temporarily unusable. All Angst units cannot move or be redeployed in the next two turns. They can only defend the squares they occupy.

Incident Module (from a dice roll of 2, 4, 6): roll the dice
Remember that any unit sustaining casualties has the casualty figures halved if within two vertical or horizontal squares of a P1 or P2 unit.

1 People report possible sightings of Kalmist forces. Roll a dice to see if this is confirmed by your personnel (6 = confirmation). If confirmed, roll the dice twice and combine the scores to identify the confirming unit: 2 = report is disconfirmed; 3 = UL; 4 = U2; 5 = U3; 6 = U4; 7 = U5; 8 = TL; 9 = T2; 10 = T3; 11 = T4; 12 = T5. Roll the dice yet again to determine an outcome: 1 = contact lost; 2 = contact made then broken off, explosives removed from vital structures; 3 = contact made with casualties to the Angst and Kalmist Units; 4 = contact maintained, no casualties at this point; 5 = Kalmist unit captured, casualties on both sides; 6 = Angst combat unit defeated, unknown casualties for Kalmist, casualties for Angst unit which is removed from the board (unless adjacent to or with a P1 or P2 unit, in which case casualties are halved and the unit remains on that square for the rest of the exercise. Roll a dice for casualties separately for Angst and Kalmist forces (similarly for number of personnel captured): dead = casualty dice number multiplied by 3; wounded = casualty dice number multiplied by 10; captured = dice number multiplied by 10. Unless specifically stated in the above report, future movement and operational capacity of all pieces involved is not affected.

2 One of the combat units appears to be infected by a highly contagious disease. Roll a dice twice and add the scores to determine which unit is removed for the rest of the exercise: 2 = report is disconfirmed; 3 = UL; 4 = U2; 5 = U3; 6 = U4; 7 = U5; 8 = TL; 9 = T2; 10 = T3; 11 = T4; 12 = T5.

3 Explosion strikes an Angst combat unit. Roll a dice: 1 = no casualties, probably faulty storage of high explosive; 2 = wounded casualties only, some suspicion of sabotage; 3 = error by private, dead and wounded; 4 = explosion due to vehicle accident, dead and wounded; 5 = no Angst casualties, at least three probable Kalmists are killed by the bomb they were setting; 6 = source unknown, unit and civilian casualties. Roll dice separately for combat unit and civilian casualties: dead = casualty dice number multiplied by 3; wounded = casualty dice number multiplied by 10. Unless specifically stated in the above report, future movement and operational capacity of all pieces involved is not affected.

4 Kalmist supply base captured with no casualties. The base is claimed to be five squares from Rage, at L7.

5 Kalmist units (roll dice: 1 unit = 1, 2; 2 units = 3, 4; 3 units = 5, 6) strike key target (roll dice: 1 = Rage; 2 = Thumpe; 3 = Bashe; 4 = gold mine; 5 = VIP resort; 6 = oil well). If target is defended by an equal number of Angst units then casualties will remain among the Angst and Kalmist units. If Kalmist forces outnumber Angst forces (or there are no Angst forces present) then civilian casualties = a dice roll multiplied by 9 for the dead and by 30 for wounded. Severe structural damage is suffered in the cities. If the resort, gold mine or oil well is overrun then these are destroyed. For unit-to-unit combat outcomes, roll the dice: 1 = Kalmist unit is defeated and is removed (for basic casualty figures for both sides: dead = casualty dice number multiplied by 3 and wounded = casualty dice

number multiplied by 9; the Kalmist casualty dice roll is trebled before being multiplied by the death and wounded factors); 2 = stand off, no casualties; 3 = heavy fighting, casualties both sides (for basic casualty figures for both sides: dead = casualty dice number multiplied by 3 and wounded = casualty dice number multiplied by 9), no ground is lost; 4 = Angst forces counter-attack and drive off the Kalmist forces, some casualties (for basic casualty figures for both sides: dead = casualty dice number multiplied by 1 and wounded = casualty dice number multiplied by 3); Kalmist forces retreat and merge into the terrain; 5 = Angst forces retreat toward the nearest untouched city, casualties are sustained and this retreat continues until that city is reached; 6 = Angst unit is defeated and is removed – Angst casualty dice roll is trebled then multiplied by the dead and wounded factors: dead = casualty dice number multiplied by 3 and wounded = casualty dice number multiplied by 9. Unless specifically stated in the above report, future movement and operational capacity of all pieces involved is not affected.

6 A formal complaint is lodged over the behaviour of one of the Angst units. Roll the dice twice and combine the scores to identify the unit: 2 = complaint is withdrawn; 3 = UL; 4 = U2; 5 = U3; 6 = U4; 7 = U5; 8 = TL; 9 = T2; 10 = T3; 11 = T4; 12 = T5. The complaint includes harassing civilians, being drunk and disorderly in public, and refusing to pay for food and drink consumed at various restaurants, cafes and bars.

Information Module (from a dice roll of 1, 3, 5): roll the dice

1 Several unconfirmed reports state that Kalmist forces may have left the Angst mainland for the neutral neighbouring nation of Kalamiti.

2 All units report no contacts and no problems.

3 The leader of the MAMS (Mothers Against Military Service), Maree Motha, claims to have video and victim evidence of torture being conducted by Angst forces on villagers in East Angst.

4 Rumours claim that the companies owning the gold mine and the oil well have paid a 'freedom tax' or ransom to Kalmist leaders in return for no attacks on their operations or key personnel.

5 A message allegedly from Kalmist leaders warns that the supply of power and water to the three cities in the region will be disrupted within the next 48 hours.

6 The Transport Workers Union calls for an unlimited strike in support of danger money claims for the risk they take in delivering goods in the region. This will restrict supplies and personnel movement for the Angst military units in the region.

Public Comment Module (from a dice roll of 2, 4, 6): roll the dice

1 Major foreign backers of the gold mine demand guarantees that their investment is secure, otherwise they intend to withdraw further development finance.

2 A media reporter asks the military commanders 'Should people evacuate the region?'

3 The leader of one of the main opposition parties wants to know why family and friends of the governing party are getting preferential protection and treatment by Angst military forces.

4 An international reporter files a story that claims that the Angst military forces suffered a severe defeat the previous day, with 78 dead and 215 injured, but has concealed this from the public.

5 Law enforcement union leaders demand that the military personnel cease interfering in the daily actions of the law officers when performing their duties.

6 The leading journalist of the largest television station, Kris Krosse, is preparing a detailed review of the situation for the weekly current affairs show, *In A State Of Angst*. Krosse has three requests: permission to film an Angstian combat unit at work in East Angst, for someone from the military command to answer questions on the current military conduct of the situation, and for interviews with some community and business leaders on the impact of the current situation on their business and whether they feel that the Angst military has performed appropriately in the region during this new situation.

Communications

Communication is the most important tool of crisis management. The existence of a crisis and the effects of that crisis cannot be measured and assessed without communication between those experiencing the crisis situation, those coming into contact with the crisis situation and those co-ordinating the management of that crisis situation. Crisis management depends upon exchanges of information and the ability of managers to use the gathered information to make effective action decisions. Such management also uses data drawn from sources outside the crisis environment, including scientific and expert knowledge, past experience and pre-crisis preparation. All this information needs to be made available as quickly and as clearly as possible.

Traditional communication theory and practice

At a basic level communication as a concept covers all types of exchanges of data between two or more devices or people. Communication mechanisms include visual and audible signals that inform of changes in the environment (fire and burglar alarms, for example), exchanges between electronic devices, electronic transmissions of human communications (television, radio, tele-phone calls) and face-to-face interactions. Traditional definitions of communication begin with a single exchange between a transmitter and a receiver. Transmitters (be these people or machines) send information to receivers (other people or machines) that collect and interpret that information. The clarity and accuracy of transmitted information can be ruined or impaired at the transmission source, during the passage of the transmission or while the information is being received and interpreted. This impairment or interference is called *noise*. Noise includes the distractions and competing sounds of other transmissions as well as the interference due to environmental conditions. Managers need to ensure that exchanges of information are accurate and thus seek ways to reduce any noise that may surround exchanges of messages.

Interference also comes from communication *barriers*. Barriers are obstructions to clear exchanges of information and can be human-based (different languages, different perceptions and meanings assigned to words, different beliefs and psychological orientations). Communication barriers can also come from within the physical environment – loss of telecommunications systems, for example, or obstruction by physical materials. Various natural geographical shapes (such as mountains) and man-made structures such as buildings can impede radiated transmissions and prevent line-of-sight communication systems (such as mobile telephones) from working.

Barriers and noise include *background noise* (machinery, voices, alarms and static) as well as intrusive thoughts and states of physical sensation (such as heat or cold, difficulty in breathing). Extraneous messages and messages that are non-crisis related are also likely to distract attention and block more relevant messages from being properly transmitted and received. Crisis managers consequently need to develop strategies to eliminate or reduce the effects of noise and barriers. When undertaking realistic exercises, organizers need to include communication barriers and noise to test and improve communication systems and to enable participants to learn how to operate in 'noisy' and distracting environments.

Developing noise- and barrier-resistant systems

An example of barrier and noise reduction may be seen in the cockpit of modern aircraft. Pilots use internal telecommunications systems to speak with other members of the crew and talk on radio systems with air traffic controllers and pilots in other aircraft. This helps reduce interruption from other sources. Given the large number of tasks a pilot needs to undertake, status signals for aircraft operation use several different forms and systems to attract attention (flashing lights, sounds, warning statements and even vibrations in control systems such as the steering mechanisms). When pre-set parameters of the systems are approached or breached, the warnings are communicated in ways that capture attention without overly distracting the crew from other tasks. The air crew and air traffic controllers also use a pre-established set of words to improve clarity of understanding when information is exchanged. Of course, these attempts at reducing barriers and noise are by no means foolproof. Radios and internal communication systems do fail and aircraft have crashed due to flight crew becoming too focused upon the meaning of warning signals they have received.

Communications and the crisis manager

Crisis managers need to consider the effects of outside influences on an emergent crisis event and environment. Dependence on telephones, for example, may lead to failures in communication because:

- the telephone system becomes disrupted;
- other users engage the available lines; or
- those people with whom the crisis manager or respondent wishes to communicate are talking to someone else on the phone.

Power failures disrupt electronic forms of communication, from facsimile machines to computers. People turn off mobile phones and computers. Even alarms that signal a need for response can be left sounding and consequently act as barriers to effective communication and as impediments to good decision making. Communication flows (the exchanges of communication between two or more transmitter-receivers whether people or machines) can be impaired because:

- people are calling for assistance, reassurance or information;
- people are continuing to use non-dedicated systems for normal and ongoing communication and business;
- people are making media inquiries;
- equipment is being repaired or updated; or
- people are absent from expected positions.

Crisis managers consequently need to determine ways of controlling, limiting or circumventing such aspects within a possible crisis environment before the crisis situation arises.

Formal and informal communications

Most analysis of communication in organizations suggests that two general forms of communication exist: formal and informal. Formal communication systems are deliberately constructed to enable an organization to achieve its goals. These systems include electronic transmission (telephone, facsimile, computer, radio), written material (memoranda, letters, reports, records of transactions) and oral interactions (from telephones to face-to-face encounters).

Formal communication

Formal communication tends to operate along lines of command. As a consequence, most formal communication channels can be deduced from any organizational chart that shows the structure and key positions in that organization. Communication flows are in two directions: *upward* from subordinate to superior and *downward* from superior to subordinate. Upward and downward flows are also called *vertical* communication.

Two major problems emerge in using vertical communication:

- The speed of the flow of information depends upon the number of levels and the number of interconnections within an organization. More connections and levels mean that messages take longer to be exchanged and the contents of the message are thus more likely to be soft (not reliable) and distorted (changed).

- Those receiving or transmitting messages may often filter the contents of upward and downward communication.

Information flow

Many formal communication flows are narrow (single-channel) and sequentially linked, with many receiver-transmitter positions between message originator and the ultimate target or original information request source. The time taken for a message to climb up or down a formal organizational communication channel depends on four factors:

- the length of the channel from point of initial transmission to point of final reception;
- the number of transmission-retransmission nodes or links within that channel;
- the degree of urgency involved in the need for information exchange; and
- the degree to which task activities match the communication demands of respondents.

As the communication channel lengthens, a message will take longer to move from original transmitting person to intended recipient. Likewise, as the number of links or handlers of a message within a communication channel increases, the likelihood that the message will take longer to arrive at its ultimate destination also increases. Messages may be delayed or blocked because of bottlenecks in a channel that arise when one particular link acts as a conduit or connector for a number of communication channels. Telephone services, for example, are constrained by:

- the number of lines (or aerial receptions for mobile telephones) available for transmitting telephone calls;
- the number of cross-connecting switches that allow lines to be connected between caller and recipient.

Should an organization have communications rigidly channelled through specific links in the organizational chain, then these links are likely to become bottlenecks between incoming and outgoing transmissions of messages. In times of crisis, such bottlenecks prevent the flow of information throughout the organization and cripple management of that crisis.

Message filtering

As the number of people receiving then retransmitting a message increases, the likelihood of message corruption and filtering also increases. People condense messages, select what they believe are the important elements of a message, insert their own interpretations or opinions, and even deliberately modify or remove 'bad news' or hold onto data from incoming messages for their own use. The information conveyed consequently changes.

Filtering of information arises for a number of reasons. Sometimes messages are filtered because the person undertaking the filtering retains information that gives that person knowledge power in that organization. Many superiors provide subordinates with information on a 'need to know' basis that restricts the accuracy and quality of consequent information transmission. Messages are filtered because those passing on messages do not like the consequences involved should they pass on bad news. This can lead to decision makers having an optimistic picture of what is happening. Failing to pass on all hard information (no matter how unpalatable or how negative) is unpardonable in crisis management.

People also filter the content of messages because the messages are poorly received. Conversations that are forgotten or the rapid reading of written material may contribute to misunderstandings of meaning. People use the same words to mean different things. Often people attempt to maintain calm and appear in control by using euphemisms or deliberately selected words. Pilots talk of 'small problems' when something has dramatically gone wrong. Managers of luxury hotels tend to have 'moments of interest' rather than problems with guests, and many of us talk about being caught in ticklish situations – when what we are really experiencing are feelings of stress, panic and loss of control.

For crisis managers existing formal communication channels may be too restrictive, subject to delays and inaccessible as those not involved in handling the crisis use the systems. Moreover, use of day-to-day systems can reduce the confidentiality of the crisis management activities. Executives and managers need to carefully consider shortening any formal communication networks and ultimately developing unique or dedicated crisis communication systems.

Informal communication

Informal communication systems are those that are not formal. These systems emerge through repeated contacts between people (from family and friendship groupings to colleagues inside or outside the organization). Not surprisingly, informal communications often use formal communication channels and systems.

Informal communication systems are random in appearance and structure. These systems range from lateral or horizontal communications (sideways to colleagues rather than up or down an organization) to friendship and associative clusters that provide hearsay (non-witnessed) information and rumours.

Lateral or horizontal approaches are often semi-formal in nature. Often these approaches are adopted within an organization to speed up information exchange. In a formal communication system, an inquiry may go from subordinate to superior, then on to that superior's superior and so on until an appropriate connecting management position is reached. The message then goes down an inquiry chain from superior to subordinate until the person holding the required information is reached. The response message then returns along the same path. In horizontal or lateral communication, a more direct path is followed. The person needing the information contacts the person holding that information – or their immediate superiors interact to get the information. This approach is useful because:

- the information exchange is accomplished more quickly;
- less work is generated for the intervening links in the organization;
- the imparted and received information is more likely to be accurate, and any perceived error can be more quickly investigated and corrected (given the smaller length of communication channel and the fewer connecting links involved).

Many managers worry that informal communication systems help generate rumours and unsubstantiated fact. Surprisingly, research shows that much of the information conveyed by informal systems is highly accurate, *provided that the information carries no significant impact on the transmitters*.

Rumour

When information directly impacts on recipients and transmitters *and their fears or uncertainties are not reduced* then rumours emerge. Managers can minimize the effect of rumours by:

- maintaining open communication systems (where the uncertainties and fears held by subordinates can be reduced by access to correct information);
- broadcasting specific information on the formal *and* informal channels; and
- listening to what is being said within the organization.

Crisis managers need to understand that a crisis situation can make people feel stressed, fearful and uncertain. Steps need to be undertaken to reduce such tensions and uncertainties in using formal communication and informal communication approaches.

Points for crisis management

From this review of organizational communications, nine basic points clearly stand out for executives and managers, particularly when developing response and recovery capabilities.

1 Consider the effects of the crisis environment on communications

Explore how the various crisis environments may affect communication systems and the users of those systems. The likelihood of too much sound in an environment, for example, may indicate a need for soundproofing (headphone sets or rooms).

2 Consider the effects of non-crisis communication users

Most communication systems likely to be used in crisis management are not dedicated systems. Non-dedicated systems are always at risk of being overloaded by non-crisis-related communications. For example, mobile telephones may not work in a crisis situation due to the relatively small number of channels available in any particular relay transponder. The media can gridlock mobile telephone transmissions in some crisis situations. Likewise, concerned citizens, worried family or friends or disquieted stakeholders and shareholders can impede the communications needed for managing a crisis response. The answer is to limit outside access to the systems or develop dedicated systems for sole use by crisis respondents.

3 Develop user-friendly communication systems

Communication systems can only be effective when all possible users are able to operate the systems. Managers and communication system designers ought to consider:

- the needs of the system;
- the likely impact of the crisis environment;
- the likely skill level and aptitude of users;
- the types of information exchanges likely to be made by transmitters and receivers, respondents and managers alike.

Some solutions are as simple as sticking a list of clearly written operating instructions on communications equipment (such as radios), or developing flexible templates for oral and computer-aided exchanges.

4 Develop information gathering and analysis skills

Perhaps the most important action managers can take is to develop their own skills and those of their subordinates in gathering, assessing and transmitting data. These skills are even more important for crisis management where speed and accuracy of message transmission and reception can make or break the response.

5 Validate information

Managers need to try to reduce information filtering and corruption. As crisis managers do not have the time to do so *during a crisis event*, proactive training and the development of appropriate techniques and skills needs to be undertaken. Pre-event practice (during an exercise, for example) can include checking the accuracy of message reception by asking transmitters to repeat their statements or by having recipients to restate what they heard the transmitters send. Crisis managers need to get themselves and their staff trained in remaining calm, in communicating in unambiguous statements and in cross-checking for understanding and accurate transmission of information.

6 Keep the length of communication channels as short as possible

Managers (and crisis managers) need to avoid the filtering that comes from having too many transmitters in the process. The best communication channels are those that are immediate (contain the fewest links or retransmitter persons) and are the most direct. Hence the most effective communication systems and channels are those with the shortest distance between message sender and message receiver.

7 Develop redundancy in communication systems

One fundamental cause of communication failure is the lack of physical and verbal redundancy in communication systems. System redundancy means having more channels and communication equipment (or access to these) than necessary.

Verbal redundancy means stating important information in at least two different ways so that receivers can check that they understood the message. Hence 'We will send our personnel to our regional office, so expect all our people to assemble at our office in Surbiton' conveys the same message twice. Effective redundancy includes repetition of main points, making summaries and getting receivers to repeat what they transmitted.

8 Identify and overcome bottlenecks

Three basic approaches used to overcome bottlenecks are:

- eliminate the bottleneck (by redesigning and expanding the system);
- evade the bottleneck by going around it (using, for example, dedicated systems or parallel systems);
- increase the volume of communication traffic processed at the link-point that is the source of the bottleneck.

9 Use informal communication systems

By using informal communication systems (and informal leaders), managers can establish channels of communication that bypass bottlenecks and reduce the amount of misinformation and rumour in circulation. The sense of openness, usefulness and trust consequently created among organizational members when informal systems are properly used may improve communication in most organizations.

Emotions and communication

Communication can also lose meaning when people directly communicate with each other. Different languages and dialects make communicating difficult. Even differences in vocabulary development and verbal experience of the meanings associated with words can lose precision. The word 'rain' may conceptually mean the same thing for all English-speaking people – condensed droplets of water that fall from the atmosphere. However, the mental picture of rain drawn from physical experience may differ: compare heavy tropical downpours with light misty showers.

Mental and emotional 'noise' also impedes communication. People become distracted by their own thoughts, by sounds from the environment and by other sensory stimuli. Their feelings and emotions may also hinder information exchange. Respondents, co-ordinators and managers need to train regularly in techniques that increase relaxation and concentration, and to practise common ways of exchanging information.

Communication between humans is very visual. Around 85 per cent of a message is actually conveyed by the non-verbal processes involved in conveying a message between humans: from body language to vocal volume and pace. Indeed, a majority of a message is 'read' by looking at the small and very rapid facial expressions (called microexpressions) displayed during interactions. This is a major reason why interpersonal communication decreases in accuracy and increases in levels of uncertainty and frustration when communicators use radios, telephones or computer-based transmissions. People need to see and sense each other when communicating.

When communications are important and personal for at least one of the parties engaged in information exchange, make the process face to face.

Flight or fight

Humans have inherited a survival instinct that readies them to run away (flight) or to deal aggressively with a situation (fight).

Both activities have similar tell-tale signs as the body prepares for action: increased heart rate, rapid breathing, tensed muscles and a mix of biochemicals that enhance oxygen supply to muscles and make body and mind more alert. One effect of these chemicals is a feeling of time warp. Because senses are heightened and concentration is increased and focused, time seems to slow down. Similarly, the fatigue produced by the chemical interactions within the body may make time seem to pass slowly.

Flight characteristics include:

- a paler face (especially among Caucasian races);
- reduced body shape (or small silhouette) as if the person in flight contracts to avoid drawing attention to themselves;

- fidgeting movements (as if seeking paths of retreat);
- reduced eye contact;
- rapid yet short breaths;
- small and shielding or placating arm gestures; and
- a softer than usual voice.

Many *fight characteristics* appear as the opposite of these flight characteristics, including:

- a red-flushed face for Caucasians;
- increased body shape (or large silhouette) as if seeking a confrontation;
- sharp and large movements of limbs;
- increased eye contact (or staring);
- deep rapid breaths;
- large and challenging arm gestures (including pointing and finger jabbing or arm spearing); and
- a louder than normal voice.

Both approaches lead to problems. In human-to-human interactions, fight or flight responses intensify conflict because these are the *predictable* options for most people involved. One expects another party either to fight or flee from a conflict situation. When respondents adopt either approach, they are likely to exhaust themselves more quickly as fatigue from increased muscle tension and the biochemical stimulus sets in, and the resulting heightened mental concentration drains energy. Decision making and rehearsed action can diminish. *Indeed, a huge advantage in a conflict situation can be gained by encouraging the other party or parties engaged in the conflict into excessive anger or fear, as their ability to think and act purposefully consequently diminishes.*

Empathic problem-solving mode

Executives and managers need to train their personnel in techniques that change fight or flight characteristics into a more controlled (even neutral) response style, such as demonstrated in the *empathic problem-solving mode* (EPSM). EPSM works by reducing the effects of the reactant stimuli. Many martial arts disciplines adopt a form of EPSM by emphasizing balance, stillness, readiness and economy of movement. Three components of any EPSM approach include:

- a *defuser* (often called a stopper in some psychological and behavioural counselling approaches);
- a goal-centred *focus*;
- behavioural *indoctrination*.

An example of a defuser is the PBR method, wherein users Pause, inhale slowly, then exhale slowly (Breathe) while saying silently to themselves, 'Relax'. Used properly and appropriately, PBR increases enjoyment and performance in most work activities and sports. PBR also works well in many conflict situations, as parties expecting either fight or flight reactions encounter neither, leading to a pause in their own aggressive behaviour. This is one reason why EPSM is a defusing technique in human interactions.

The goal-centred focus for crisis managers is one similar to the *CrisisThink* principles outlined in Chapter 13. This procedure works in normal business decision making as well, because attention is placed upon gaining information, managing time and reducing costs. Managers (and crisis managers) use a mantra-like set of three questions which need to be learned until almost automatic in nature to enable users to concentrate more fully on their actual missions and jobs. The three questions are:

- 'How can I get more and better information?'
- 'How can I gain more time to get this information and to manage the tasks I have to do?'
- 'How can I reduce the costs involved in this situation?'

Behavioural indoctrination involves learning to undertake tasks in a semi-automatic fashion. Soldiers, for example, do a lot of training in obeying orders and being able to perform tasks under almost any conditions. Such training is necessary because the actual shock of battle conditions can negatively impact on any capacity to undertake considered action and thinking. Most professional response agencies provide similar conditioning training for their personnel and use simulation training to reduce the impact of the crisis situation.

By training in EPSM approaches, managers can reduce stress and burnout. People who learn to change their fight-or-flight responses to the EPSM approach may find that they feel more in control of themselves, and more able to find solutions to the problems they encounter and the demands made upon themselves.

Using EPSM

In face-to-face use, EPSM involves making responses and gestures that are not characteristic of fight or flight. By employing the Pause–Breathe–Relax technique users calm themselves down and present an attitude that is neither confrontational (fight) nor evasive (flight):

- normal even open posture (minimal shielding gestures);
- normal eye contact;
- normal to slow even breaths;
- normal arm gestures;
- a medium volume firm voice.

The EPSM user needs to focus on three key features and rehearse regularly. Remember any behavioural change requires sufficient repetitions to overcome the thousands of previous performances of the behaviour being changed.

1 Practise a smile that is neither tight nor too wide (as both of these can be seen as challenging).
2 Practise speaking a little slower than usual, and with the voice pitched a little lower than normal. High sounding voices tend to suggest stress and nervousness to listeners. Most people speak too fast for clear and comfortable listening.
3 Practise presenting a relaxed and normal-looking body posture that suggests openness. Shielding gestures (crossed arms, crouching behind desks) and thrusting gestures (fast sweeping arm movements, large hand-pointing movements) tend to suggest flight or fight behaviours.

These three elements help a user to present an image of calmness, fairness and openness. With regular practice and use, users can find themselves becoming calmer and more able to solve problems.

When the interaction is remote (via telephone or radio, for example), attention focuses even more sharply upon the voice, the choice of words and on the way in which the interaction is processed. The person making the contact (the sender) may need to be calmed down. This can be accomplished by the recipient remaining aware of the feelings of the sender, keeping their own voice steady and 'calm', and by helping the sender to focus on the information he or she wishes to give (or the questions she or he wishes to ask).

Thus when taking an outside call:

- Use PBR.
- Keep voice even, moderate and slower than usual.
- Keep words as simple and concrete as possible.
- Ask a question or repeat a response using different words to ensure message information is exchanged.
- Use interactive statement checking (repeat in your own words as accurately as possible what the other person has told you).

One quick way of remembering these factors is called CALLER. Recipients can use this procedure to gain information from unknown sources. The sender may or may not be self-conscious or in flight or fight mode. As a result, the recipient may need to calm the sender down by using the above vocal procedures and by helping the sender to give their information as factually as possible. The five elements in CALLER are not used sequentially but as the need arises.

- *Clarity.* The prime objective of the interaction is a clear exchange of information, wherein the sender feels satisfied and calmed down by the process. Clear messages mean using concrete or hard communication (nouns and active verbs) as opposed to muddy or soft communication (emotive adjectives and adverbs and indirect or passive verbs). Recipients need to focus on simple language that helps senders focus on the content of the information exchange.

- *Active Listening.* Active listening is a key approach in taking messages as well as in cognitive debriefing and counselling. The process involves encouraging the person speaking to talk, using phrases such as 'Go on', 'Ah-ha' or 'Yes'. Because such phrases minimally interrupt the speaker they are called minimal encouragers. After a few minutes or when a significant set of 'facts' has been stated, the recipient states in his or her own words what the speaker has said to check the recipient's understanding and asks any questions that fill in missing information. From time to time, during a long interaction (and at the end of any interaction), the recipient checks the information by working through a summary of what has been said. The process is 'active' in that the recipient works with the speaker to gain a clear message rather than passively listens to what is being said.
- *Listing.* One means of acquiring hard information is to ask senders to list the data they wish to impart. Listing is improved when recipients use a sequential list of mixed directive and open questions. Directive questions are those that focus on names, ages, relationships, location, needs and reasons for calling, for example, while open questions elicit free information. Examples of open questions include 'Tell me more' and 'What happened next?'
- *Empathy.* Recipients need to seem interested in, concerned with and trying to understand the position of senders. This is not the same as sympathy (emotional agreement with the feelings of senders) and involves an ability to relate with the sender while remaining objective and helpful rather than being subjective and passively affirming the emotional state of the senders.
- *Repetition.* Along with listing, repeating key statements and facts helps senders relax, as their message appears to be getting through. This relaxation often enables them to recall further information and, very importantly, correct misunderstandings or misstatements being recorded by recipients. A recipient can use repetition in two ways – using the recipient's own words to check the understanding of the message and listing concrete phrases given by the sender to see if any further data can be gained.

Patterned reporting styles

Presenting information in standardized formats holds a number of advantages that enhance effective communication. These include:

- the use of pre-established template forms for recording verbal reports;
- the ability to quickly log and collate reports because of the standard formats being used;
- the ability to quickly note important information;
- the ability to calm both transmitter and recipient through the use of familiar patterns.

A simple PRS can be used by recipients receiving messages from untrained and outside callers and by trained crisis management staff who contact the crisis management centre. Where recipients use the template to prompt responses from outside callers, trained crisis staff can use agreed information 'templates' to report and record information in a speedy and efficient process.

The foundation for any PRS involves three important information data 'bytes':

1 an identifier
2 a subject
3 an action.

The identifier section has three parts that are reported and recorded:

- who is reporting;
- the location from where they are reporting;
- the time of the report (which may be done automatically by recipients).

These parts enable a quick record of who–where–when, and give recipient and receiver a little time to establish contact. The PRS then moves to the cental hub of information exchange, the subject phase. Here, three elements are dealt with in sequence:

- identify the location or site of the subject;
- state the facts (hard information only);
- give the interpretations or opinions (clearly identified by the sender).

The final section reports any action decisions from the sender or delivered by the recipient. Again, this can be divided into three parts:

- immediate action being undertaken;
- proposed next action;
- requests for assistance from recipients.

Note that crisis respondents need to state the three parts of the action section. Crisis management needs to know what the respondents are doing and are about to do. An example (see box) may help show how PRS works in terms of trained personnel reporting on a situation.

> A duty security manager has responded to a fire alarm at one of an organization's sites. The manager is now reporting back to head office. The nine elements of a PRS are indicated by square brackets.
>
> *This is the Duty Security Manager (name)* [who] *reporting from outside the Regional Head Office at (specified location)* [where] *at nine fifty hours* [when].
>
> *At the Regional Head Office* [location of subject] *I can see flame and smoke issuing from the front and right-hand side of the building* [concrete information]. *The fire brigade is in attendance* [concrete data]. *The streets around the building are closed off by the police* [concrete information]. *My current estimate* [signal for interpretative opinion] *is that all ten floors have suffered smoke and fire damage. The fire may be contained to the ground, first and second floor* [interpretative opinion]. *My understanding is that no one has been hurt or is missing* [interpretative opinion].
>
> *I intend* [immediate action] *to find out more from the officer in charge if I am permitted through the cordon. I will either stay at the fire brigade's incident command centre or move to the lobby of the Grand Hotel at (specified location) which is a block away from the site* [future action]. *We need our full response and recovery teams here and probably a team of security people* [action from recipients].

An effective respondent (and recipient) will ensure that the message components are repeated. In some cases, manager-to-manager interaction may look for more information or decision actions. Note that this type of message allows a recipient to quickly note key elements on an existing form or computer-driven template. Even without such prompts, the sequence in which the information is given reduces the length of the time of the exchange and increases the likelihood that all facts will be presented and that fact is separated from opinion or uncertain information. The action statements allow the respondent (and his or her team if a team is present) to be tracked and located at a subsequent time.

Dealing with outside callers

Outside callers need to be handled with care in order to gain information and reduce negative perceptions in those callers. They can be quickly yet attentively handled using the attributes in CALLER and PRS templates. The templates need to be modified so that the questions are open-ended and sequential, and not forced upon the sender. Figure 6.1 provides an example of a template covering threats to an organization from a sender.

Recipients usually log the times of the messages when they initiate contact with the senders. For people passing on information, the focus is on gaining

---

TELEPHONE THREAT DEBRIEFING FORM

Date:　　/　　/　　　　Time:　　　　　am/pm　　　_____

Call received by:　　　　　　　　Phone:　　　(Work)

　　　　　　　　　　　　　　　　　　　　　　(Home)

What threat is being made:　☐ Assassination　☐ Bomb　☐ Poisoning　☐ Other

Ask caller:

When will threat be carried out?　　_____

Where will threat be carried out?　　_____

How will threat be carried out?　　_____

What will cause threat to happen?　　_____

What will identify threat?　　_____

Why is threat being made?　　_____

　　　　　　　　　　　　　　　　_____

Where is call coming from?　　_____

　　　　　　　　　　　　☐ Local call　　☐ Long distance

Indicate your immediate impression about this call. Give your FIRST IMPRESSION.

Caller was:	Sex	☐ Male	☐ Female		
	Age	☐ Child	☐ Teenager	☐ 20–40	☐ 41 or more
Speech was:		☐ Local	☐ Foreign		
		☐ Slow	☐ Normal	☐ Fast	☐ Taped
		☐ Calm	☐ Excited	☐ Angry	
		☐ Soft	☐ Normal	☐ Loud	
		☐ Husky	☐ Lisping	☐ Accented	
		☐ High	☐ Normal	☐ Deep	
		☐ Clear	☐ Slurred	☐ Stutter	
		☐ Incoherent	☐ Disguised		
		☐ Familiar (sounds like who)			
Background noise:		☐ Static	☐ Clear		
		☐ TV	☐ Radio		
		☐ Office	☐ Street	☐ House	☐ Motors
		☐ City	☐ Country	☐ Animals _____	
				☐ Machinery _____	
		☐ Trains	☐ Aircraft	☐ Traffic	
		☐ Other sound _____			

Phrases/sentences used by caller:

Fig. 6.1 An example of a template for receiving telephone threats to an organization

information. While using CALLER and PRS templates, recipients need to focus on the needs of the sender. Most senders need to feel they have done 'the right thing' and that the information will be acted upon. To reinforce such feelings, recipients can employ a further four elements of interaction skills. These are to keep the interaction:

- *Simple.* Use short questions with simple word choices. Where appropriate, ensure questions are open and prompt more information ('So what did you see?' 'Anything else?' 'What happened then?').
- *Affirmative.* Reinforce the positive feelings of senders by affirming their contribution – 'You really are remembering a lot of useful material for us' 'That's really great information you've given us'. At the end of the exchange (after checking the identifier and subject information given by senders) do not forget to get action statements ('Where can we contact you if we need to get back to you shortly? In the future?') and to affirm the effort of senders by thanking them for making contact and passing on the information.
- *Favourable.* As with affirmative skills, recipients need to ensure that senders are gaining positive feedback as they present information. Judgemental comments – 'You should not have done that' 'Can't you remember more than that?' – tend to close down the interaction and the gathering of information. Recipients need to make favourable statements like 'Go on, you're being very helpful' 'Good, thanks a lot for your time.'
- *Encompassing.* Recipients need to ensure they gain as much information from senders as possible. This is done by asking open questions and by stating back to senders what they said, so that more information may be triggered.

People making specific inquiries need to be handled with similar care. In some crisis situations, many of these callers may be upset and even angry. As a contact point for senders, recipients may meet with hostility and verbal abuse. When such emotional messages are being made, recipients can forget that these senders are angry with the situation or with unidentified people. More training in dealing with difficult and abusive interactions may be needed. Recipients can use more specific 'HELP' skills to reduce the anger and gain a clear understanding of what is wanted by a sender. These skills are non-sequential and involve being:

- *Helpful.* This is a broad skill that needs to be active in use (and in the communication strategy of the organization). Recipients focus on helping senders gain answers to their questions.
- *Empathic.* In many cases, recipients need to show that they understand the feelings and the points of view of senders. By empathizing (not sympathizing) with a sender's feelings and points of view, recipients can move the interaction toward identifying the sender's needs and the necessary actions that may help the sender.
- *Listening.* Defusing emotion and gaining insight into the questions being

asked by senders often means recipients need to actively listen to what a sender is saying. Too often the volume of calls and monotony of call centre work can make recipients sound bored and uninterested (and thus unwilling to help). Recipients need to deal attentively with senders, mixing active listening with gentle impetus towards helping resolve the needs of the sender.

- *Polite.* Essentially, recipients need to remain polite and respectful of the feelings and needs of senders. Politeness and personal respect are two key negotiating skills and tactics that can reduce friction and influence positive outcomes.

Communicating with others (whether from outside or inside an organization) is not an easy task that can be done instinctively. Personnel need to be trained in these skills and to regularly practise them. When a crisis (or business continuity) exercise is being planned, add some time (in parallel and separate if necessary) for the people likely to be communicating with others to practise their skills.

Hard *v* soft information

Hard information is information assessed as being reliable and certain. For most of us, hard information is something we have witnessed for ourselves and has a physical and evidential aspect to it. Thus 'the building has collapsed' is hard information if (a) we saw the collapsed building and (b) the collapsed building can still be physically seen by others.

Soft information is information assessed as being unreliable and uncertain. Information may be deemed soft when (a) we cannot see the evidence for ourselves, (b) information comes from others and from some distance away, and (c) the physical evidence for the information is missing or lost. Hence unless we have access to video, film or aerial transport, we are less likely to be certain of what buildings were damaged when a report comes in that 'several buildings have collapsed'.

Whether information is assessed as hard or soft may depend on the attitude and training of the crisis management team and, specifically, of those on the team who collect and evaluate the information. Self-witnessed situations that are still visible are easily deemed hard information, although speculation about damage, casualties, loss of resources and associated problems may be very soft. Crisis managers will tend to face more soft than hard information. In fact, the 80–20 rule often appears to be applicable in many crisis situations. Of the information existing during a crisis response (and early recovery actions), around 80 per cent is likely to be soft.

Some managers trust crisis team-sourced information more than information from others within the organization or from those outside the organization. Trusted sources are often classed as giving 'hard' information. Most professional response organizations tend to trust their own members, discount information presented by other professional response organizations, and treat with vague cynicism information gained from anyone else. This does not mean that they will not respond. It does mean that initial decisions will tend to be 'check that information' orders to their own personnel.

A rule of thumb for defining hard information is when that information is:

- directly witnessed by the decision maker (or directly witnessed by a person highly trusted by the decision maker); or
- confirmed by two or more independent sources at much the same time.

Most information comes from a number of sources so emphasis needs to be placed on 'independent' and 'same time'.

If information sources are sequential in nature there exists some chance that one report will be 'hearsay' restatements of the earlier report. After CBS broadcast a specific story about the human cost of the Chernobyl nuclear reactor disaster (*see* The Reality Bite later in this chapter), others reported the figures as being true. As more media outlets expressed the same or similar information, these reports seemed to confirm each other and made the reported information appear to be 'hard' data.

The need for independence and immediacy of source material is another reason why victims and respondents need to be debriefed as soon as possible. The longer people are left to reconsider what they felt and witnessed, and to discuss what happened with others (or to listen to statements by others about what happened), the more likely such information will be rationalized and tend to be unreliable and soft in nature.

Soft information can be grouped into two broad categories:

- unconfirmed reports;
- speculative assertion.

The key to differentiating between these is the eyewitness nature of a report. Should the information be a first-hand 'I saw …' type, then this most often can be classed as unconfirmed. On the other hand, should the information be a second-hand 'They say …' type, then this is classed as speculative. Such classifications are made as information-value judgements for decision-making purposes and not as reflections on the characters of the informants.

Coding information

Once information has been assessed and classified, decision makers need to know the reliability level of the available information. Few organizations realize that simple colour coding by font colour on computers or ink colour on whiteboards can quickly convey such status. Another approach is to use coloured markers to indicate the current status of each bit of information, as information assessment is dynamic and reliability assessments may change over time.

One simple process is to use the three basic colours available for most media.

Black is used to signify hard information (or white on the dark background of a computer screen or blackboard). Blue can be used to indicate that the information is unconfirmed. Red is used to denote speculative information.

The selection of colours and grades of soft to hard information are choices each organization and crisis team may make themselves. In doing so, some precautions need to be taken. These include:

- Avoid colour combinations that confound colour-blind people (e.g. red and green).
- Do not use too many gradations as frequent colour changes detract from the information.
- Ensure that all users understand the coding system.
- Ensure that all organizations involved in integrated or combined operations share the same coding system.
- Keep the coding system easy to use and remember.
- Remember to keep checking the status of information.

Executives and managers need to ensure that an information-gathering, collation and evaluation process is in place and that the people doing these tasks are trained and experienced. Information management is the key to speed of response and recovery, and to the ability to make correct decisions. By being aware of the hard to soft nature of various 'facts', decision makers can develop flexible responses for the possible situational factors that may occur. In so doing, management of crisis situations can be improved.

Information systems – IT and computers

Information systems and computer-based processing generally fall under the title 'Information Technology' (or IT) and are useful tools in aiding response to crises. This utility is due to the speed of inter-computer transmission of information and the relative ease with which information can be quickly stored and collated. Use of laptops and microcomputers allows greater flexibility and mobility. Users can work in the field, in vehicles, or quickly move to alternate sites. Combinative use of mobile telephones, modems and laptop computers can allow interconnected decision making without the immediate need for all decision makers to be in the same room. The decision makers can exchange information and ideas in what is called 'virtual offices' (*see* the PNC Reality Bite in Chapter 5).

Computers may also generate or exacerbate crises. Consider an organization with which you are most familiar and ask yourself these two questions:

1 *Given a computer failure, what operations would cease and what operations could continue?*
2 *Given a computer failure, how soon would all services be restored and what would the direct and indirect cost of that recovery be?*

In most cases, many information and transaction activities would cease, which may mean difficulties in trading for many businesses. The consequent cost of recovery (and of loss of business) can be high. As a result, many organizations need to consider not only using computers and information systems to help manage crises, but also construction of crisis management plans for the IT or computer systems.

Benefits

Benefits include:

- the ability to make automated cascade contacts in a very quick time (as alert or warning systems, as well as providing detailed information);
- the ability to store and enable quick access to large amounts of data;
- the ability to record information rapidly for evaluation and transmission (including the use of templates to help sort and collect such information);
- the capacity to provide ready access to specialist response information (from methods of dealing with hazardous materials to crisis and recovery plans);
- the ability to use software for risk assessment, business impact analysis, business continuity planning and crisis management planning (over 400 software titles available);
- the ability to allow decision makers to operate as an interconnected team when they are not in the same physical environment (the virtual office).

The availability of IT-driven communication systems also provides three important crisis management aids. IT systems can enable and improve:

- distribution of information between different agencies, departments and groups involved in dealing with a crisis or with impacts from a crisis (leading to more accurate and faster access to the same information and thus better decisions);
- the capacity of organizations to monitor where people and assets are placed within the crisis situation (thus providing ongoing safety monitoring and – separately – better capacity to collect inquiries and provide information to those people needing to check on the status of potential victims);
- the capacity to quickly provide information (including graphics and images of the situation) for media organizations – with a greater accent on common information and less immediate variation due to human interaction factors (rumours, misinterpretation by those supplying the information, and reduced distortion of information through emotional and presentation accentuations).

Problems

Problems include the following:

- There is the possibility of penetration by computer users (often called

134

hackers) with innocent or malicious intent (who may cost lives, void assets and money, and even inadvertently trigger large-scale wars between countries).

- Access to information is likely to be either too open and free (with loss of confidentiality) or too restricted for adequate use in crisis situations.
- The reliance on electricity means increased risks under crisis situations where there is electric power involved.
- Systems are vulnerable to poor programming, viruses (hostile programs that can contaminate an IT system and corrupt stored information or prevent access to stored information), and system collapse through overload and insufficient processor capacity.

Computers and IT systems have been linked to a number of modern crisis situations. Some falls in share prices in the 1980s were linked to the speed with which computer-based share acquisition and disbursement decisions were conducted. Similarly a number of aircraft accidents have had associated computer-based program problems.

While IT systems provide a faster and generally more accurate capacity to monitor complex processes (such as nuclear-fuelled electricity power generators), such systems are only as good as the manufacture, programming and assembly of equipment allows. Over-reliance on inadequate processing and dissemination capacity can foster crisis situations. In the following Reality Bite on the meltdown of a nuclear reactor plant at Chernobyl (now in Ukraine), for example, the time taken to process status reports and the distance from operators of a printout containing such measures helped transform a critical problem into a crisis situation.

REALITY BITE

Chernobyl reactor meltdown, USSR, 1984

Background

Chernobyl is one of 16 identical nuclear power stations operating in the states of the former USSR. Construction of the power station started in 1961 with pressure to complete the project and produce electricity. The first reactor unit began work in September 1977 (two years behind schedule) and delivered around one thousand megawatts of power, a saving of over three million tons of coal each year. The fourth unit was brought into production in March 1984. A fifth and sixth set of units were then commenced.

Deficiencies in quality control were identified during the construction of the power station units. Under the early influence of the *glasnost* period, an article outlined some of the pressures and problems involved, including defective and lost prefabricated reinforced concrete (almost twenty per cent of the ordered quantity), defective sealant and disorganized workforce practices.

Operations were controlled by scanning many monitors and were assessed by a computer that measured the status of the reactor every five minutes. The printouts from this computer were produced 50 metres from where the operators worked.

In April 1986 Reactor Unit Number 4 was scheduled to be shut down for routine repairs and maintenance. Management took the opportunity to conduct a series of tests during the shutdown process. These tests included measurement of the effect of modifications on the turbogenerators and whether the generators held sufficient energy to pump the water coolant around for the 40 to 50 seconds needed for emergency generators to start feeding electricity into the system and thus to keep the coolant circulating properly.

Incident

On 24 April operators of Reactor 4 decreased the electricity output and shut down the reactor, including the emergency coolant system. A new shift took over at 8.00 am. The reactor was at half power by 1.00 pm. At 2.00 pm tests on one of the unit's generators were started. The emergency system was disconnected as the fall in water supply due to this test could trigger an emergency alert with associated emergency flooding of the core-cooling system which in turn would completely close down the reactor. At one point, an electricity supply manager in Kiev required the power generated by the Reactor 4 for another eight hours, so the complete shutdown was discontinued. At 11.10 pm permission was received to take the generator off the electricity distribution grid, and the delayed power-down testing commenced. Power output was reduced from 1700 megawatts to 700 megawatts.

To gain more control over the system, operators switched off the local automatic control of the rods (which helped maintain the constant 700 megawatt power level). An operator then noticed that power had sunk to around 30 megawatts and that the system had possibly developed an iodine well in which radioactive emissions were being blanketed by the surrounding xenon and iodine gases. Recovery from this point was hazardous and difficult, and the test should have been aborted.

Dylatov, the deputy chief engineer for Reactors 3 and 4, ordered the unit operators to withdraw control rods to increase the power. Seven rods were lifted, leaving 18 control rods in place. At 1.00 am a cooling pump was connected to the heat transport system. This action further reduced the power output and consequently required more rods to be withdrawn (leaving only 13 rods inserted in the core – two under the safety limit of 15). The steam that powered the generators to produce the electricity also fell to a point where automatic shutdown was triggered within the system. The operators bypassed this automatic shutdown.

At 1.22 am (25 April), a supervisor noted that the reactivity reserve margin was half the recommended level in operational guidelines and alerted a senior manager who tried to shut down the system by lowering all control rods into the core. The moment this was done a number of thuds were heard from deep inside the building. The senior manager saw that the rods had not completely descended and disconnected the rods from their electric servomotors to allow them to fall into place under their own weight (a built-in safety feature). The rods did not move and a loud explosion shook the building. The lighting to the rooms failed.

Dylatov ordered two operators to go to the water coolant tanks and open the valves by hand. Finding their way blocked, they went outside the building and found half of the structure had disappeared. Another two operators were instructed to manually lower the control rods. Even though these rods no longer existed, this pair sought to carry out their task – 'orders were orders'. The first two operators returned to Dylatov and told him that the reactor was destroyed. Dylatov calmly replied that this could not be true and decided to see for himself. He first looked through a window into the turbine hall then ran out of the building and found that the roof was on fire. On returning to the control room, Dylatov ordered the fire brigade be contacted. He then descended into another part of the building and found that around 250 square metres of the roof had collapsed, a pipe was pouring water onto electric cables causing sparks and fire, and the inside of the reactor was glowing.

Response

The Number 2 Chernobyl fire station despatched its units at 1.23 am. On the way, the officer in charge ordered a region-wide alert. The regional fire brigade commander arrived at 1.56 am and concentrated on preventing the fire from reaching the nearby Reactor 3. None of the firefighting personnel were equipped with radiation protection gear. After 30 minutes, the first firefighting teams at the scene began to feel giddy and sick. The chief manager of the Chernobyl nuclear facility was unofficially informed of the incident at 2.00 am. He arrived at the site and contacted his superiors and the chairman of the local Communist Party Committee of the nearby town of Pripyat (where many Chernobyl workers lived). The chief manager advised them to prepare the town for evacuation. The chairman protested that this would cause panic. The chief manager realized that he may be in trouble for allowing news about the accident to become public as all nuclear accidents were Soviet state secrets.

By 4.00 pm, firefighters from as far away as Kiev had arrived on site.

The civil defence response started badly. When the duty officer was alerted, he was not told the correct code word and dismissed the alert as a joke. However, the informal communication networks had functioned and most heads of civil organizations (fire brigades, schools, institutes and workshops) had assembled. The chief manager told them that an explosion had occurred but the reactor was intact and the dosimeters recorded a radiation of only 3.6 rems an hour. This data was contradicted by one administrator who was then told that his measuring device might be broken.

As Reactor 3 was losing water coolant in the effort to douse Reactor 4, it was shut down. By the morning of 26 April, Moscow administrators (believing the incident was under control) requested a schedule for the repair of Reactor 4 and a date for its return to the electricity grid. Many on-site managers still refused to believe the reactor had disintegrated. During the response, the rest of the Chernobyl power station workforce continued operating and took few precautions. The 268 personnel working on building the Reactors 5 and 6 continued work, farmers continued working their land around the site, and people in the region's towns and cities continued normal activities. The chief manager, Brukhanov, continued to state that the situation was not serious (after all everyone knew that Soviet reactors were perfectly safe). He operated on the principles that secrecy was most important and that superiors needed to be reassured until further information was available.

By 10.00 am on 26 April, 120 people had been admitted to hospital suffering suspected radiation poisoning. Helicopters and heavy equipment of the nuclear response brigade moved to the nearest airfield. An order commissioning a formal inquiry was signed. The commander of the chemical war division was sent to the power station. One of the response team finally reported back after overflying the site. He found that the reactor had disintegrated and that millions of curies of radionuclides were being released into the environment. By 8.00 pm a conference at Pripyat was told that significant radioactive fallout was being measured 50 kilometres away in the direction of the wind. Some 850 buses and 300 cars were made available to evacuate the 50 000 people living in Pripyat. The decision to evacuate was deferred until 7.00 am the next day and not then activated until 10.00 am. By midday, the town was evacuated. Most evacuees took only a change of clothes and expected to return soon.

Careful reconnaissance by lead-protected helicopters enabled the conclusion that even when the fission of nuclear material was over, the 2500 tons of burning graphite could continue to burn for upwards of two months emitting dangerous radioactive fallout. The core needed to be cooled to prevent actual meltdown of the uranium. This led to the decision to dump sand (mixed with boron, dolomite and lead) on the ruined reactor to absorb the heat. At first the helicopter pilots and crew used shovels to slowly load sand into bags from the river bank of the Pripyat River. Labourers and troops later supplied tools and work parties to increase the supply of the dumping material.

The helicopters could only accurately dump the material from a height of 200 metres while moving at 50 kilometres an hour. This meant that the crew would be quickly exposed to potentially lethal doses of radiation. On 27 April, around 44 helicopter missions to dump the sand mix were flown by two helicopters and their crews.

On the morning of 28 April, a radiation alarm was triggered at Fosmark Nuclear Power Station 100 kilometres north of Stockholm (Sweden). Fearing a nuclear leak, evacuation of non-essential personnel was ordered. Weather stations across Sweden also reported higher than usual levels of radioactive particles coming from across the Baltic Sea. While government officials first thought that the Soviets had tested a nuclear bomb, analysis of the particles established that the source was more likely to be from a nuclear power station. The Swedes requested information from Moscow. Calls were made to three Soviet government agencies. Each denied any accident had happened. At 9.00 pm, the Soviet government announced that something had happened but that there was little damage.

On 29 April, the Russian airforce sent special helicopters into the region to measure the radioactivity. The radioactivity was found to be 100 times the estimates of the physicists. The first regional maps of contamination would not be ready until 1 May. Helicopter sand-dropping missions had reached 180 deliveries a day and were using upturned parachutes to drop the sand thus increasing the load the helicopters could carry.

By 30 April, around 1000 tons of sand mix had been dropped and radioactive emissions were found to be smaller. An evacuation zone with a 10-kilometre radius was completed.

At 1.00 pm on 1 May, after the May Day Parade, the Moscow-formed inquiry met. It was soon clear that the regional and Ukrainian ministries could not cope. The army medical corps was ordered to assist, as were health ministries from neighbouring states. The first regional pollution map showed deposits of pluto-nium within a 30-kilometre zone and significant surface contamination that could be measured in Belorussia. As a consequence, all people within a 30-kilometre radius were evacuated.

Conflict over the use of the sand mix arose. One side argued that each drop of the sand mix caused radioactive material to vent out of the unit. They wanted the sand bombing stopped and the fire be allowed to sort itself out. The other side argued that they needed to be seen to be solving the problem and thus the sand-mix drops should continue. Doing so, however, meant some likelihood of allowing the fire to continue under the sand cover which would increase the heat. Conse-quently, a massive heat-exchange concrete structure was to be built beneath Reactor 4. Contaminated water had to be extracted from Reactor 4 to prevent steam-based explosions. Specialist fire service pumps and hosepipes were brought in on 6 May. By 7 May the water was drained from the structure. Measurements found the radioactive emissions were continuing to fall and the fire in the reactor was apparently extinguished by 9 May.

Recovery

An estimated 128 casualties were evacuated for specialist treatment in Moscow. These were distributed among three hospitals. Just under 400 were being treated in Kiev. Medical personnel dealing with (and in some cases being contaminated by) these victims were given a 25 per cent increase in their salaries. For many vic-tims, one hope for survival was bone marrow transplants. Armand Hammer, an American entrepreneurial businessman, donated modern equipment and the ser-vices of a Dr Robert Gale. Gale brought in an assistant and an expert from Israel. All three were confined to one hospital with 129 patients (including 111 acute radiation cases).

On 6 May, after first pictures of the accident were publicly released, residents in Kiev were finally warned to take precautions. The instructions included washing vegetables, keeping windows closed and staying indoors. Rumours that party chiefs were evacuating their families led many residents to try to withdraw money from their banks in order to leave Kiev. Within hours, Kiev banks ran out of cash. Hearing that iodine prevented contamination, people quickly bought all available iodine-based products. The contamination of 1500 square kilometres of land (stretching out 300 kilometres north of Chernobyl) was not made public, nor was the information that significant radioactive deposits were also found up to 500 kilometres west of Chernobyl (and less than 200 kilometres from Moscow).

Three of the firemen died of the effects of radiation on 10 May, followed by ten more firefighters and Reactor 4 personnel over the next five days.

On 14 May, the Soviet President finally spoke to the nation about the accident. He was economical with the truth, stating that only nine had died and that the people living near the site had been evacuated within hours. His main objective was to counterattack the exaggerations of the media from Western nations who reported thousands of dead and the poisoning of the entire state of the Ukraine. On 29 April, rumours of 80 dead on site and 2000 dead in the region spread throughout Europe and the United States and were given credibility on CBS news. The Soviet government refused to release any concrete information. Two officials from the International Atomic Energy Agency in Vienna were invited in to view the situation on 7 May. These officials were given a tailored set of facts and conveniently did not ask any difficult questions.

On 17 May, the Soviet government announced that a large concrete and metal structure (called the sarcophagus) was to seal the ruins of Reactor 4. Large lumps of radioactive fallout around the unit were picked up using remote excavation tools on the reconnaissance vehicles. Small robot-type vehicles were unsuccessfully used to clean up the roof areas. Individual soldiers were used to gather material on shovels or in tongs and quickly dump the material back into the hole where the roof had collapsed in Reactor 4. Because of the high radiation exposures, the individuals were shown what to do and where to go by television before they went on the site. They could only work for one to two minutes before receiving the maximum allowable 25 rem of radiation dosage. Over 260 000 personnel were used as human radioactive material collection tools. As personnel increasingly fell sick, maximum exposure was reduced in stages from 25 to 10 rems (and a total lifetime dose of 35 rems). Contaminated topsoil and trees were bulldozed and buried in concrete lined pits.

By July, response personnel were housed in five cruise ships moored 50 kilometres from Chernobyl on the shore of the Kiev Sea. A rotation system meant they worked for 15 days in Chernobyl then spent the next 15 days in Kiev with their families. A new town for the power station employees was built 40 kilometres east of the power station. Even with the policed exclusion zone, looting increased at Pripyat and property owners were allowed to venture into the closed zone to retrieve less contaminated items that had been under cover.

On 25 to 27 August, Soviet scientists presented a polished assembly of partial facts to an audience of diplomats and Western scientists in Vienna. They spoke about the poor testing procedures that led to the loss of control over the rods in the reactor and presented a number of apparently convincing yet dramatic facts including the supposed quick evacuation of 135 000 people. The scientists concluded that the long-term effects would thus be non-significant for the region, the Soviet Union and the world.

By 23 September the sarcophagus was completed. On 1 October, Reactor 1 went back into power production, followed by Reactor 2 on 5 November and Reactor 3 a year later.

Due to the prevailing view that the structure and facilities at Chernobyl must have been safe because these were Soviet-made products, the Soviet legal and political systems decided that the accident must have been due to human error by those working on site. This decision protected off-site party members and superiors in Kiev and Moscow, and avoided any investigation into the construction efforts at Chernobyl or the design and safety of the reactor. While 32 defects in the reactor were noted, focus was fixed on those charged with the crimes against the state. Consequently the senior management at the power station and those conducting the tests were found to be guilty of negligence and convicted on 27 July 1987.

A Chernobyl Law was passed in the Ukraine, Belorussia and the Russian Federation. This law entitled Pripyat residents to early retirement on full pensions. The law also offered those who worked in recovering the contaminated zone special passes that gave them free travel on government transport, the right to go to the front of queues, extra holidays and compensation for invalids. Despite public commitments, this offer was poorly funded by Moscow. The number of people who claimed to have worked in clearing up the zone increased dramatically. Non-recipients resented the favouritism the special passes implied, and people affected by previous nuclear accidents sought equal access to compensation.

Statistics
Even five years later, the Soviet government insisted that only 31 deaths were caused. Estimates of the death toll have ranged from 7000 to 300 000 (Barton, 1993), with an open-ended finding due to consequential illnesses likely to be caused over the next 50 to 100 years. At least 28 died directly from burns and exposure to lethal radiation doses in combating the meltdown.

Over 180 000 people were eventually evacuated. An estimated 600 000 personnel were used in response and recovery work within the contaminated zone.

At a conference in Kiev (May 1988) a larger picture emerged. At least 17 500 000 people (including 2 500 000 children under seven years of age who were thus more likely to absorb nucleides) were exposed to some level of fallout radiation. Contaminated land covered at least 25 000 square kilometres containing over 2000 towns and villages. An estimated 50 tons of radioactive material went into the atmosphere.

The cost of the accident was initially estimated to be in the order of 2 billion roubles (September 1986). This was revised in March 1990 to a conservative 180 billion roubles.

Comment
While few business organizations may confront a situation on this scale, some important issues need consideration. These issues include the effects of communication, the issue of long-term contamination by hazardous materials, and the pressure for a quick return to work-based normalcy.

Communication
The Chernobyl crisis illustrates a number of points discussed in this chapter. The length of communications channels giving rise to slow information transmission is illustrated by the computer printout – that reflected a state that existed five minutes previously – being produced 50 metres away from the operators who needed it. Likewise the slowness of formal systems can be seen in the slow exchanges of messages between relevant political and government departments. One filtering effect is particularly noted in the early response actions by Brukhanov who realized that he might get into trouble for publicly warning anyone and who 'operated on the principles that secrecy was most important and that superiors needed to be reassured until further information was available.'

Managers need to ensure that filtering effects are diminished by encouraging accurate information exchange (and by not allowing those presenting negative information to feel that they may be somehow punished). Likewise, managers need to insist on communication systems that are close to operational demands, short in length and contain the minimum necessary retransmission links to make information exchanges as fast and as error-free as possible.

The dependence upon formal approaches to management meant not only slow and filtered communication, but also an inability of those present to respond effectively to the situation. Many continued standing by their posts until struck down by radiation sickness, and others continued to perform what had become meaningless tasks because they were not instructed to cease operations or were instructed to continue working. This latter point is clearly illustrated by the decision of the pair told to lower the rods to continue to try to do so even though there was no way this could be done – 'orders were orders'.

The impulse to check with one's own eyes (confirmation of warnings, as discussed in Chapter 5) when non-normal signals and situations are reported is also clearly illustrated in this case. Dylatov sent people out to report on the situation, then 'calmly replied that this could not be true' when they returned and told him what they saw. Dylatov continued to check for himself (going to a window view of the turbine hall, going outside, going downstairs) which meant that his management presence was absent during the first minutes of the crisis and crisis response. This impulse to see for one's self not only reflects the difficulty in accepting signals of non-normal states, but also reflects the need for training in giving and receiving hard information, as outlined in this chapter. Managers need to be able to trust information supplied by their staff, and to be able to obtain detailed concrete information from those subordinates.

The lack of response to warnings is further illustrated by the reaction of the civil defence duty officer. Because the correct code word was not given, he decided the alert was a joke and went back to sleep. Managers need to reduce 'code word' encryption to a determined minimum, ascertain that all parties speak the same language (and thus the same code words), and train code-word recipients to check details of warnings.

Public communications were also delayed and filtered, with much of the presentation being shaped to counter the exaggerations made by Western media sources who reported vague comments and unsupported statements (due to the lack of sufficient official details). This effort somewhat misfired as further seemingly grudging revelations concerning the increased size and impact of the situation led most of the population to believe that they were being lied to by their own government and by the Communist Party. This case reflects the need for managers to ensure that credibility is not lost through misrepresentation and misdirection. Media and image management are covered in more detail respectively in Chapters 7 and 8.

Contamination

Obviously the Chernobyl case is the largest in terms of size and impact of contaminant exposure. The handling of mass situations by Western nations also provides concern. For example, the sluggish response by British government departments and politicians to the BSE (Bovine Spongiform Encephalopathy) problem in cattle led to increasing costs as well as product bans on British cattle. BSE was found to be probably associated with CJD (Creutzfeldt-Jakob Disease) which is a disease that attacks the human brain and has reportedly killed 28 people (27 in Britain – Geary, 1997). The sluggish and seemingly indifferent action and information delivery by British government and department officials generated a general mistrust over what was going on and being done among many members of the British public.

Much exposure to and contamination by hazardous material is invisible and migratory in nature, which (remembering the conditions for increased fear of risk

– *see* Chapter 2) engenders greater fears and stress among those potentially exposed to the contamination. Some reports (cited by Read, 1994) suggest that many of the illnesses now being uncovered since the event in 1984 may be due to dislocation stress and fears surrounding the long-term effects of exposure. Other experts tend to suggest that a large long-term health problem may still exist, when cancers and genetic malformations arise as the exposed population ages and produces children.

Return to work

This Reality Bite also reflects the pressures to return to normal (working) environments that can be made by those off-site and even by those on-site when recovery operations begin. In Chernobyl, managers were requested to report when the reactor would be fixed and how much the recovery would cost on the morning of the disaster. Such management concerns reflected the urgent need to fill the lost power supply (itself a critical ripple effect problem for the USSR) and the effect of filtered information on decision processes. In most natural disaster situations and major business or industrial crisis situations, much attention is directed toward a return to normal operations – if only through the demands of public (lifeline and lifestyle) and business (economics and cash flows) survival.

Management perspective

Managers need to work toward reducing the loss of information and time produced by many formal communication systems in organizations. Should the development of short dedicated communication channels with trained users be impossible for the day-to-day management of an organization, having these in place for use in crisis situations needs to be considered.

Ripple effects

Crisis situations rarely provide a single set of impacts. Crisis situations can generate other critical problems or crisis situations. These secondary crises are called ripple effects (*see* Chapter 1). The Chernobyl case illustrates some of these effects in the cash shortages induced in Kiev banks as customers tried to withdraw their money and the realization by government officials that the regional ability to cope with the response and health demands would be overwhelmed. Managers need to try to plan for consequential ripple effects as part of the response and recovery planning and training processes.

Image management

Managers like Dylatov and Brukhanov tried to do the correct thing and maintain the implicit (if not explicit) image required by their organization – secrecy, re-assurance, protection of senior management. Other senior people maintained the storyline that 'nothing can have happened in perfect USSR, and if it did it was minor and quickly controlled.' Some had different agendas that were somewhat concealed (protect senior agencies and the chiefs of these) or more transparent (attack Western media and governments as a means of distracting attention). The consequent effect of government bureaucracy, hidden agendas and mechanistic image management was that when these were seen to be wanting there was a loss of credibility which meant that:

143

- hard facts were lost (and would be regarded with suspicion when finally presented);
- image management became seen as concealment; and
- soft information from unassessed sources was accepted as more likely to be true.

Effective image management comes from being consistent with previous actions and statements, being seen to be open and calm and involving others in the resolution process. These points are discussed in more detail in Chapter 8.

Sterile zone
Impact effects can be diminished in many crisis situations by establishing a mental, system or physical 'sterile zone'. A sterile zone enables users to reduce the cost in terms of people and resources through the evacuation and containment of a crisis site. In the Chernobyl crisis, the sterile zone was the exclusion zone that was set – first around the site, then in a rough 10-kilometre radius around the site, and then the 30-kilometre exclusion zone. Managers need to consider how the concept of sterile zones can be usefully applied across the potential range of tangible and intangible crisis situations they may encounter.

Recovery planning and management
A significant aspect that managers need to assess and analyze is the effect of recovery programmes on people. The pressures of recovering the contaminated site at Chernobyl produced higher incidences of alcohol (vodka) addiction and stress disorders. Similarly, the reward and privilege programmes for those who helped in the response and recovery operations or who lived in the exposed regions were resented by those who were not so involved or who had no such support but had been affected by earlier (much smaller) nuclear crisis situations. Managers need to ensure that rewards and privileges:

- are supplied to all who should get the benefits;
- are distributed fairly according to need;
- do not become greater problems for recipients than the benefits they gain;
- do not discriminate against other deserving groups or individuals.

It could not happen in Western organizations
Western countries have produced similarly flawed crisis responses. A good comparison with Chernobyl is the Three Mile Island (TMI) incident in Harrisburg (USA) in 1979. TMI was a nuclear power plant operated by Metropolitan Edison. At 4.00 am on 29 March a potentially explosive gas bubble formed in Reactor Unit 2 when the main water coolant pumps failed and the emergency coolant system also failed to work.

The control room operators became confused as some indicators suggested that coolant pressure was dropping (leading to meltdown and blow-out) and other indicators suggested an increase in pressure. Contaminated steam leaked into the atmosphere by 4.07 am. Operators found that the emergency coolant system had been closed and not reconnected after a maintenance operation. Waste water tanks were vented at 5.40 am, exposing two technicians to more than 20 years of exposure and releasing more contamination into the atmosphere. At 6.50 am the emission alarm sounded and the Nuclear Regulatory Commission was notified of the incident.

At 9.00 am the mayor of Harrisburg was informed and the Pennsylvania Civil Defense organization was requested to develop evacuation plans for an area with a radius of 10 miles (16 kilometres) around the plant (some 160 000 people). As with Chernobyl, local authorities and citizens were not quickly alerted. The first public announcement was made at 11.00 am and schools were closed. Children and pregnant women were requested to leave the area. Within 24 hours, 10 000 people had voluntarily left the region. Some 14 days later the crisis was declared to be over.

As with Chernobyl, control of the reactor's operations was not helped by the number of flashing lights from indicators or by the delay in computer printouts on the state of the reactor (90 minutes in the TMI case – see Cohen, 1991). Smither (1994) suggests that some of the slow reaction may have been produced by the poor design of the control panels. When the alarm sounded, some 1600 indicators and instruments had to be examined, and around 200 of these may have been flashing. This 'noise' would have led to difficulties in concentration and information exchange among the operators. Fink (1986) finds that a senior engineer wrote a safety warning about a similar incident that had happened 13 months previously. This warning was lost in the formal communication system.

Residents around the TMI area reported being stressed and demoralized. Some time after the event, many residents were reporting symptoms as if an actual disaster had happened (Flynn and Chalmers, 1980). In 1996, the state court dismissed 2000 claims against the TMI operators on the grounds that the claimants failed to establish proof that their illnesses were linked to the leaked contaminated gas. In 1997, advertisements were placed in newspapers announcing the proposed sale of the TMI property with an estimated value of US$600 million (£375 million).

The parallels between Chernobyl and TMI are striking. Managers need to accept that the larger the organization, the slower and more constrained will be the response. Communications need to be shaped around strong internal report and information exchange systems and properly managed media and public communications.

References

Barton, L. (1993) *Crisis in Organizations: Managing and Communicating in the Heart of Chaos*. Cincinnati, Ohio: South-Western.

Cohen, D. (1991) *Aftershock: The Psychological and Political Consequences of Disaster*. London: Grafton Books.

Fink, S. (1986) *Crisis Management: Planning for the Inevitable*. New York: AMACON.

Flynn, C. and Chalmers, W. (1980) *The Social and Economic Effects of the Accident at Three Mile Island*. Washington, DC: Nuclear Regulatory Commission.

Geary, J. (1997) 'Hitting a nerve', *Time Magazine*, 15 December.

Read, P. P. (1994) *Ablaze: The Story of Chernobyl*. London: Mandarin Books.

Smither, R. D. (1994) *The Psychology of Work and Human Performance*. 2nd edn. New York: HarperCollins.

7

Media management

Media management is an essential element in successful crisis management. Successful management of the media may lead the general public and media commentators to be less negative and judgemental about mistakes and failings that arose in managing the crisis. This, in turn, may reduce agitation from pressure groups, decline in customer spending and depreciation of stock market price. The less negative impression may influence politicians not to set up parliamentary inquiries or may sway prospective jurors and even witnesses in their attitude toward the crisis managers and respondents (*see* Chapter 8 for more on image management).

Most managers have a cynical and even negative attitude about media reporters and their reporting. Part of this problem is that many managers do not learn skills that help them interact with the media, and when given such skills often fail to fully rehearse them in a meaningful and realistic way. Managers need to think beyond the media interaction toward the effect that interaction has upon the listeners, viewers and readers of the consequent edited media stories. By understanding what makes media representatives 'happy' and by developing skills that enable managers to present material that satisfies the general needs of media and organizational desires, managers can establish effective media management.

Why bother about media management?

Organizations inadequately equipped to manage media interest in any crisis and the impacts of that crisis are likely to feel threatened and isolated. Such organizations may develop a siege-mentality. These attitudes stem from the quick impact negative media stories have on an organization. Myers and Holusha (1986) note that 'even if all the details may not be right, ... once a company has been identified as the bad guy, the beating is out of all proportion as the media, in their competitive battle, fight for new angles and scoops.' While no media management strategy can guarantee complete success, effective management can reduce conflicts and misunderstandings and the consequent images of an organization as incompetently managed or with something to hide.

On the other hand, poor media management can destroy a company.

Media and Garibaldi

One strong element in the demise of an Australian small goods company, Garibaldi (based in Adelaide), was the lack of media interaction skills held by the directors of that company. In the period December 1994 to February 1995, 22 cases of food poisoning were hospitalized and a four-year-old girl died after eating salami with infected HUS – Haemolytic Uraemic Syndrome. The pathos of the victims shown in media reports aroused public sympathy.

On 25 January 1995, Garibaldi was identified as a likely suspect. The resulting non-management of the media included hiding behind locked doors, aggressively stated 'no comment' responses and the directing of fire-hoses on to media representatives. These actions created an image of uncaring managers who were avoiding responsibility. Management claimed that they had never had an incident of contaminated products affecting their customers. This claim was proved wrong within 24 hours when a current affairs television show broadcast a report of a wedding party a year earlier at which Garibaldi small goods products were the suspected source of food-poisoning among 80 guests. Management refused to respond to media questions and refused to recall their products.

By March, Garibaldi small goods was under formal liquidation. In filing for liquidation, the liquidator (Stephen Young of Arthur Andersen) claimed that Garibaldi had 'lost consumer support for its product and no longer has the available cash flow to meet either its existing or future commitments.' Three years later, victims of the Garibaldi-sourced food poisoning vowed to sue the directors after the directors walked free with fines of only AUS$10 000 each for creating a risk of harm by failing to issue a recall of contaminated salami.

Some obvious lessons for media interaction emerge from this example. By acting aggressively to media personnel, greater attention was focused upon the activities of the organization. Making 'no comments', hiding behind locked doors and refusing to appear interested in resolving a crisis allow a negative media image of concealment and wrong-doing to be drawn – whether this is correct or not. Managers need to interact with the media to sell the point of view (POV) of the organization, otherwise media reporters will seek interesting stories from whatever sources become available. Such sources can be ex-employees with a grudge or people who claim to have witnessed or experienced wrong-doing from the organization simply so that these people can achieve some notoriety and self-esteem from the reporting. Some sources may even reveal 'facts' that the organization's personnel have concealed over the years.

Media and Exxon

Where media may cause the collapse of a small to medium-sized organization, larger organizations may survive due to their size. Nonetheless, poor media management may impact significantly on the operations and public trust held by a large organization, as is shown by the problems faced by Exxon (USA) when one of the company's oil tankers ran aground in Prince William Sound in 1989. The oil tanker, *Exxon Valdez*, lost over 260 000 barrels of oil in an enclosed body of water, devastating fisheries and wildlife. Exxon's CEO, Lawrence Rawl, was uncontactable for the first six days.

When Exxon (and Rawl) did respond to media interest, two actions led to negative corporate images. The first was to release full-page advertisements ten days after the incident in which Exxon asserted that the company had acted 'swiftly and competently'. Media reports, on the other hand, showed a spreading tide of oil and a seemingly sluggish response. This reportage cast doubts upon the competence of at least two senior officers on board the *Exxon Valdez* and the apparent contradiction resulted in a public image of Exxon being aloof, remote, uncaring and seemingly out of touch or untruthful.

In the second action, Rawl was interviewed on *CBS This Morning*. During questioning about how the oil would be cleaned up, he responded that it was not his job to know details of the very technical plans for clean-up in the Sound. While this is a valid point, the presented public image was of an uncaring and dismissive senior manager who may be reflecting the attitude of the organization. The Exxon-Rawl approach may have worked better had they adopted any or all of three tactics. These were:

1 To provide a 10–30-second response that covered what Rawl *did know*.
2 To have available an expert or experts who *knew sufficient detail about the plans*.
3 To admit that such plans had complexities and difficulties beyond immediate comprehension – then to provide a simple statement *from the viewer's POV* of what would be attempted.

Given the approach used by Exxon and Rawl, negative media and public perceptions continued to grow. Exxon did make a concerted effort at cleaning up the area, drawing resources including boats and paid workers from all over America. There was some outfall from the negative media image. Numbers of Exxon customers shifted to competing organizations. Conflict also emerged between local Alaskans, the imported workers and Exxon managers. Exxon mounted a belated media management programme in which they showed what was being done.

Barton (1993) cited a subsequent costly media interaction by Rawl and Exxon. The judge adjudicating on penalties for Exxon for polluting areas of Prince William Sound outlined a settlement for civil damages of $900 million and four fines that totalled $100 million. Rawl commented that 'the settlement will have no noticeable effect on our financial results.' He intimated that these were non-significant in terms of profit, business turnover and business costs. Given that this decision was announced close to the annual general meeting of shareholders, Rawl was probably trying to ensure that there was little adverse movement in the share value of Exxon and to retain shareholder confidence. The comment, however, seemed to demonstrate a lack of remorse for the incident as far as the judge was concerned. As he had not written the penalties in a formal decision, the judge withdrew the decision and began to determine increased costs. He felt that penalties should not be regarded as the costs of doing business and saw that the original penalties appeared to send the wrong message – 'suggesting that spills are a cost of business that can be absorbed'. Exxon announced a profit of over $2 billion on the same day the judge made this statement.

The Garibaldi and Exxon examples show a slowness of response and a lack of understanding about media management and about how outside consumers of media reports may view a crisis. In some ways Exxon executives directed their attention toward dealing with the problem and not toward dealing with the perceptions of the problem that may be held by others. Garibaldi directors, on the other hand, appeared to try the appealing but rarely successful strategy of shutting their ears, eyes and mouths and hoping the issues will fade away.

Many crisis managers (especially among professional response agencies and from large organizations) tend to do the same. They feel surprised and even betrayed that the media (and the public) do not appear to appreciate the efforts of the managers in dealing with the situation. Physical resolution of a crisis is only half the work that crisis managers need to do. They also need to handle the internal and external communications with stakeholders and the media. This corresponds with the left-half of the crisis management sphere presented in Chapter 1.

Putting media management into our perspective

That crisis managers feel they are insufficiently appreciated for trying to resolve a crisis suggests a clue to the basic clash between managers (and their personnel) and the media. The other clue is that media reporters (and their editors) need to present interesting 'news' that holds and increases the viewing or listening or reading audience that buys the products of a given media outlet. In short, media reporting is less focused upon telling a 'truth' (which after all depends upon what selection of 'facts' is made) and more upon reporting the facts of a story in an interesting way that sells their product. Sherman (1989) points out emphatically that news organizations 'earn their keep by producing stories that attract audiences, and thus advertisers' (p. 57). Even non-commercial media operate to keep their sponsors happy. Such sponsors may be governments, religious or political organizations, or commercial enterprises. In this way media organizations make profits and media personnel retain their jobs.

When a crisis situation strikes, respondents are focused on dealing with the crisis and the impacts of that crisis. Communication and information management is rarely given sufficient importance in conventional planning and training for managing a crisis, as the planning and training tends to focus on resource and personnel management and on operational training. Managers and organizational personnel need more training in skills for interacting with others and for dealing with the media. Without planning and practice in internal communication, information is lost or distorted, orders become confused or take too long for useful application in the field, and effective management of that crisis can be diminished.

Regester (1989) reinforces the need for effective skills in dealing with the media. He finds that 'effective management of communications is as vital as effective management of the crisis itself. After all, external perceptions about the crisis, among key audiences, will depend entirely on what they hear, see and read about it' (p. 12). This echo of 'perceptions' leads back to the key differences between media and managers. Managers generally see themselves as the doers that are criticized by non-doers who get in the way. These non-doers are the media. This is echoed, for example, in the distraction shown by those managing the impacts of the Andover tornado (*see* Chapter 5). The media, on the other hand, see themselves as providing information to their customers about what is happening in the surrounding world. Both are doing their jobs, and both perceive each other as sometimes deliberately preventing them from accomplishing their work.

Point of view

'Point of view' (POV) is an important concept for executives and managers to understand. POV analysis helps people try to see the perspectives or positions adopted by another person or group of people. People who try to see the POVs of other parties or groups of people often find that they interact more successfully with those parties or groups. Consequently, any real attempt at POV analysis can improve the ways in which organizational and personal image is maintained, and may reduce conflict between parties with different perceptions about the world, how organizations should function and what work the given party has a right to do. Just as adopting a different frame for questions and for seeing how the surrounding environment interacts (or should interact), POVs involve adopting specific points from which the environment (and thus the crisis situation and the people and organizations involved in that situation) are viewed.

Managers need to try to determine what the POVs of a given party may be. This can be done by brainstorming, trying to place one's self in the situation of the given party, or even by asking (while listening non-defensively) the person or people for their POV.

POV analysis can suggest why media and managers clash. They hold different POVs. Once managers understand the specific media outlet POV (or the general media POV), interactions – and subsequent reporting – can become more positive.

Common media POV

A common POV for media organizations includes the following items, though the list is not exhaustive:

- Get an interesting storyline that appeals to current consumers and encourages others to become consumers.
- Interesting storylines usually reflect human interest perspectives or conflicts.
- Achieve the storyline as quickly (given deadlines for print media, radio and television news) and as painlessly as possible.
- Do not get caught reporting false information. Here, false information is that which cannot be attributed to a credible source (even if that source proves wrong or malicious in intent). Media organizations are susceptible to loss of consumers due to loss of credibility.

Obviously, managers who help media personnel obtain timely and interesting storylines are far more likely to influence the coverage and nature of the subsequent reporting.

The conflict between managerial and media POVs is accentuated by a trust that many media audiences unthinkingly place on media reports to 'tell the truth'. In many cases the 'truth' may never be fully seen or understood, so managers and media are often left with different versions of facts. Eyewitnesses rarely can really give a 'true' account of what happened. Mixed in with their experience of the facts of a situation are other distracting noises, emotional reactions and even rationalizations about their experiences or adjustments made while listening to other people's accounts of what happened. All of these 'truths' tend to paint a picture about what happened, which then can cause conflict between managers and media people.

With this understanding of POV in mind, the following comments upon media activities from the POV of a crisis manager or organizational manager can take on a different perspective. Harold Stuart, the Crisis Coordinator for the Newcastle City Council response to the 1989 Newcastle (Australia) earthquake, found that:

> *The local media responded well in the first few days while the 'outside' media tended to sensationalize the situation. Much of the misinformation may have been avoided if the Council's media response had been set up immediately.* (Stuart, 1993, p. 20)

Here, the need to more promptly manage and disseminate information is recognized.

Pijnenburg and Van Duin (1991) are more graphic. In discussing the *Herald of Free Enterprise* ferry disaster at Zeebrugge in 1987 the authors state that:

Shortly after the news of the disaster got round, a number of local 'freelance' photographers had arrived on the scene. Some of them succeeded in climbing aboard tug-boats that carried a rescue team and headed for the wreck. Soon other journalists invaded the working harbour's landing stage where the survivors of the disaster were put ashore. They seriously hindered the work of the emergency services and regularly the police had to intervene to clear the way. (p. 65)

Here, the charges are more worrying as media personnel hindered response operations. Had managers proactively sought media POVs, however, there may have been a clearer understanding of the likely actions media people would undertake. Crisis managers may then have had strategies and facilities in place to help media capture dramatic human interest storylines while being less of an invasive hindrance. Use of barriers, better policing, access to victims, witnesses and respondents who agree to be interviewed, and access to good (perhaps shared) audio-visuals of the site and of the response operations are just a few strategies that would moderate such pressures.

Incidents subsequently outlined by Pijnenburg and Van Duin illustrate what may ensue when control is loose or absent. The authors claim that:

Some journalists also behaved very badly when a funeral chapel was installed in Zeebrugge's sports centre ... it was impossible to prevent aggressive photographers from pursuing and harassing completely distressed relatives of victims on their way to and entering the chapel. (p. 66)

Part of the conflict emerges from the lack of attention by crisis managers and their planning teams to the major media interest that comes with a crisis situation that has a very visible human impact.

The simple common media POV may be more sharply focused by examining some research findings that indicate how storylines are selected and shaped. Galtung and Ruge (1981, p. 60) suggest that criteria used to select and shape a story include whether the story:

- fits the time frame of the presenting medium;
- is intense or dramatic (the more dramatic or intense, the more likely it is the story will be broadcast);
- is more meaningful to the audience (the closer to their home and experience, the more likely it is a story will be broadcast);
- is unpredictable or rare;
- balances other already reported events (adds to a bigger picture or fits a theme that has been or is being broadcast);
- has already been defined as newsworthy by previous broadcasts (or by other competing media organizations);
- will continue to be defined as newsworthy;
- involves elite nations or known important people (or celebrities);
- can be seen in personal terms;
- has increasingly more negative consequences.

These criteria may help managers identify likely newsworthy issues or situations and so enable some pre-crisis preparation to help manage consequent media interest.

One other point worth noting is that media reporting may compound a crisis situation through its presence at that situation. The on-site presence of media (particularly with video cameras) may trigger greater displays of action by those being filmed. Similarly, media reports may appear to worsen crisis situations. In discussing the effects of media presence in Los Angeles during the riots that followed the acquittal of four Caucasian police officers charged with assaulting an Afro-American (Rodney King), Alter (1992) concluded that:

> At least a dozen of the helicopters on the first night – a presence that helped create a wartime atmosphere – belonged not to police but to local media outlets. – As Los Angeles-based radio host Tom Snyder says, 'That's like saying "We've got the cameras on, you can start any time now." Several local TV reporters described both the exact locations of looting and the fact that police were doing little to stop it.'

This outcome invariably reinforces the conflict between crisis respondents and media personnel.

Positive contributions by media outlets

Managers need to balance the possible threats that media coverage of crisis situations may produce with the positive contributions that media outlets can bring. The media can:

- provide information to educate the public in what to do in various crisis situations;
- increase public awareness of hazards and threats;
- alert the public when a crisis threatens;
- alert organizations to the concerns and feelings held by their stakeholders;
- present information on what to do, where to go, who to contact, and on what is being done to manage and resolve a crisis;
- provide information for crisis managers – use of media helicopters and sophisticated video equipment can help managers comprehend and analyze a large crisis.

Organizational plans and actions can be quickly communicated so that interested people can act accordingly. Quick use of mass media outlets can reduce the communication pressures that arise when people try to contact someone in the organization for information about what is being done or what to do in specific circumstances.

General principles of media interaction

Having noted a number of factors that influence media reporting, some general principles about how to better interact with the media can be determined. Once these principles are understood, managers can better design facilities for media interaction and can more readily identify interaction skills that need to be acquired or enhanced.

1 Control where the media may go

Where possible, organizations need to determine ways in which media intrusion can be reduced. If the crisis situation is small, media response may be local and thus few in numbers. Large and visible crisis situations tend to attract local and regional (or even international) media interest. In these situations, reactive or unprepared media control measures will result in chaotic control with greater intrusion upon respondents and victims, more interference with response and recovery operations, and a greater probability of conflict and disparity between reports (which leads to suggestions of cover-ups or incompetence). In the latter situations the media will have:

- more lines of physical approach;
- greater need to differentiate their storylines from each other; and
- a reduced acceptance to remain part of a work-inhibiting crowd.

The general rule of thumb for managers is to *control the journalists on the site by determining and policing where the media can and cannot go*. This works well in tightly specified localities, or when the crisis situation can be secured. The Chernobyl incident (1986) and the Gulf War (1991) are good examples of these situations.

When the site is too large to control or the media cannot be told where they can or cannot go, then the alternative rule of thumb is to *screen the respondents and victims from the media attention*. This can be achieved by erecting screens, by using portable shelters and by providing transport to and from the crisis site(s). Screening of victims and respondents reduces the invasion of privacy and allows them to deal with their emotions and thoughts. At the same time such screening also places information access under greater crisis management control. Note that effective media management means that managers need to find appropriate victims and respondents prepared to be interviewed by the media.

Another means of exerting control is to allow limited access by representatives of the media selected by the media personnel attending the crisis site. The audio, visual and print reportage consequently gathered by these representatives is then shared among all media members. Ensure that the media personnel do the selecting of their representatives as this reduces any subsequent argument over preferential treatment and even takes some of their time that otherwise may be used to place pressure on those involved in the crisis situation. Another means of doing this is to establish an interview signal accepted by all parties – media, victims and respondents. In the response and recovery process after the Oklahoma City bombing of the Murrah building, personnel moving between the site and their command centres or their accommodation could signal willingness to be interviewed by walking on the side of the road nearest the media sites. Those walking on the far side of the road signalled no interest in talking to the media and were generally allowed their privacy.

2 Shape the answers to interviews toward those areas that suit the interviewee and/or the organization

Those being interviewed (the interviewees) need to know what they want to talk about and to be prepared to direct the interview to those points they wish to make. This can be done by rephrasing the question ('I think what you are trying to ask is ...') or by bridging from a weak response to a strong response ('While I need more information to fully respond to that, I can point out that what we are doing at this moment is ...').

3 When undertaking verbal interviews develop some short statements of between 10 and 30 seconds in length to convey important positional information

Unless presented live, interviews are usually edited into one to three short 'bites' of an interviewee's responses to a question. By fitting important points to a similar time frame, interviewees are more likely to have their 10 to 30 second statements broadcast in full. These succinct statements are also difficult to edit into a response that seems different to the response given by the interviewee.

4 Appear open and honest when interviewed, and deal with concrete 'facts' and not with assumptions

Interviewees need to focus on what is seen as correct, true and factual, no matter how negative these may appear for them or their organization. These 'facts' and 'truths', however, can be worded in terms that best suit the interviewees and the organizations they represent. Most media representatives and their audiences tend to believe the interviewee is doing this regardless of the interviewee's performance.

5 Remain calm and open to questions, and speak as a person not as a mouthpiece

Personalize any comments or statements, so long as this does not conflict with the aims and objectives of the organization and/or crisis management effort. In doing so, portray a calm and open position – avoid too much emotionality (which suggests loss of control) and avoid seeming distant or untouched by events (especially where people are hurt or killed). Interviewees need to appear interested and concerned about crisis situations and the impacts these situations have on people. Consequently, they need to express sufficient feelings that show they appropriately relate to the information being conveyed.

Most people believe they can identify when an interviewee is being genuine and open. These people may reject an apparently hostile approach by interviewers if an interviewee seems honest and open. An interviewee may express feelings of dismay and concern over the effects of a crisis. These expressions of dismay and concern can make further critical questioning appear insensitive and abusive.

6 Adopt a position in an interview situation that seems ready to help, fact-based and non-blaming, and avoid conflict with members of the media

Avoid saying 'no comment'. Such responses appear to conceal information. Try rephrasing the question or bridging across to safer areas of discussion. Interviewees can be honest and admit that they have insufficient information for factual comment. One further option is to claim that current legal obligations prevent the question from being answered.

Avoid misrepresentation. Report the facts that are currently known and which are cleared by the crisis manager for communicating to the public audience. Do not fall into the trap of trying to minimize (or exaggerate) situations and impact damage. Interviewees can be honest and admit that current information changes previously reported information – so long as the changes are due to improvements in the situation rather than due to attempts to minimize or maximize the details involved.

Avoid speculation. Any direct response to a question that is 'hypothetical' or 'assumes certain facts' is likely to rebound badly upon an interviewee. When asked to speculate on alternative scenarios or practices:

- refuse to be drawn into a speculative response;
- outline other speculative scenarios and then conclude that speculation is consequently not helpful; or
- acknowledge that the speculative question is interesting and worth considering given time, resources and a more predictable situation – none of which is currently available.

Avoid assigning blame to organizations or people. When questioned about possible guilt or mistakes by others, any answer that attributes guilt or error to some person, group or organization risks hostile reactions from these people. This can lead to distracting conflict, lack of unity in handling the crisis and even to litigation. Interviewees need to make one or more of the following statements:

- such judgements are not useful at this point in time;
- all the facts are being examined by the appropriate authorities; or
- such speculation distracts from the current effort of managing and resolving the crisis.

Avoid **clashes with the media.** Any accusations of reporting bias or personality clashes with specific members can unite the assembled media into defending their integrity and 'rights'. This may happen even when the target media person is not liked by many of his or her colleagues. The result of this unified defence is usually a negative perception of the conference, the accuser and consequently of the organizations involved in dealing with the crisis situation. Those interacting with media representatives need to continually remember that these people and their organizational staff ultimately control what information and perception of the situation will be broadcast to their audience.

Contact with the media during a crisis

Five types of contact with media personnel can arise during a crisis situation – on-site interaction, off-the-cuff or ambush interviews, appearance interviews, press releases and media conferences. These are considered in greater detail in the following sections.

On-site media interaction

As noted earlier, large and visible crisis situations usually attract large numbers of media personnel. These large numbers may become difficult to manage without appearing dictatorial and obstructive. The general approaches to controlling on-site interviews and reporting use a mix of:

- media self-regulation (media people selecting representatives who share the material they gather);
- provision of specific media sites (made more enticing by providing necessary facilities – power supply, telephones, refreshments and seats); and
- controlled but ready access to situation updates and witnesses, victims and respondents.

On-site interviewees may have some advance notice of the interview through early contact between media people and an organization. In these situations (which may seem similar to appearance interviews), the interviewer is seeking a 'live' background feel to what is an otherwise studio-type interview. Remember to wear appropriate clothing and to avoid being placed where wind whips hair across the face or lighting causes squinting and apparently shifty and nervous head movements. Interviewees who have time to prepare for an on-site interview need to establish clearly in their minds at least three key points with short yet concrete-sounding statements for each of these points.

Off-the-cuff or ambush interviews

Given the portability of electronic media equipment, media reporters are likely to appear very quickly at the site of a crisis and outside any location used to handle or manage that crisis. This means that organizational personnel are likely to be confronted or ambushed by media representatives as soon as they step off site or can be found in a non-controlled zone. Media people like to gain these off-the-cuff or street interviews for three reasons:

- They appear to be actively 'chasing down the story'.
- The interaction between reporter and an unready interviewee makes good actuality content for media stories.
- They may get a 'scoop' over other media organizations and representatives.

Interviewees undergoing street or off-the-cuff questioning are more likely to make unguarded responses and their comments are likely to be less rehearsed and less considered than those made in formal settings such as media conferences. Consequently personnel need to be trained in responding appropriately to such questions.

Should such training not be in place, then one rule of thumb is to refuse to get caught in informal or ambush interactions. If necessary, find alternative routes or seek a protective screen made up by other people or assistants. The primary rule of thumb when caught in a media ambush, however, is to have some simple short 'helpful' statements in mind.

When approached, the targeted interviewee can try to avoid the interview through a three-stage disengagement process. The first stage is to make a statement that indicates a readiness to communicate but a plausible inability to do so (not enough facts, legal impediments from outside authorities): *'I really would like to discuss with you what has happened today. At this point, however, we need to be more certain of our facts and we are conscious of the requirements placed upon us by [legal need or outside authority]'.* Properly done, this may prevent later reports that suggest that the interviewee and the organization were unwilling to speak to the media.

The second stage is undertaken after persistent questioning on technical issues and is made to reflect the person's (and the organization's) concern for people threatened or harmed by the crisis: *'Again, I would like to discuss the causes of what has happened. At this stage, however, I am more concerned about those affected by this crisis and in getting something done to help them.'* By showing concern for the victims of a crisis, the interviewee makes any further questioning on other more technical matters appear insensitive and even negative.

After further persistent questioning, the interviewee may seek a means by which he or she can exclude the interviewers (by driving off in a car or passing through an entry or exit point through which the interviewers cannot move), and make a third statement. This statement is a helpful redirection of the media interaction: *'This really is an issue which needs more attention than we can give here.'* This statement acknowledges the question and deflects an answer by saying that the question is too important for instant answers. The interviewee then concludes with a helpful direction to another time and place for the question(s) to be presented: *'Perhaps you can raise this matter at our next press conference [or interview situation] which will be held at [place] at [time].'*

The three stages of responding are more effective than the use of 'no comment' responses, or making awkward and often defensive sounding responses, or trying to ignore the questions and questioners. Many media organizations have experienced editors and interview teams who can make a silent or squirming target look guilty and 'on the run' and who can make a 'no comment' response appear to be a cover-up.

Should an interviewee elect to be interviewed in an ambush or field setting, a number of interaction skills can help. These include:

- Make silent use of the PBR technique for remaining calm.
- Make body language appropriate to the question and situation. Do not smile when questions cover impact costs and losses, for example, and try to present an EPSM non-flight and non-fight body language.
- Keep voice lower and slower than normal.
- Show that the question is being listened to (this gives some more time for composing a response).
- Share time between camera (the real audience) and the interviewer as much as possible, making transitions between interviewer and camera and camera to interviewer appear natural.
- Use thoughtful restructuring of questions as an apparent attempt to help the interviewer ask his or her questions – compliment the question and the questioner, rephrase the question, bridge to what the interviewee needs to emphasize, or redirect the question back to the interviewer and audience (as politely as possible).
- Where appropriate, take time to consider the question and the possible responses to the question. In some situations, this conveys thoughtful respect for the question.
- Learn to disengage after responding to sufficient questions. If necessary use a modification of the three-stage disengagement approach. The statements may take a form similar to: *'Thank you for giving me time to help you and your viewers/listeners/readers understand this situation. As you will realize, I now need ...' 'I think I have stated all I can tell you at this point ...' 'Why not contact [specify name or location] as they may help you with information about this ...'*

These skills may appear difficult or awkward to use. This is why learning and practising such skills is emphasized.

Appearance interviews

Appearance interviews are generally granted to people who host specific media shows (morning shows, chat shows or current affairs). The media organization (and host) will still try to obtain a natural (as opposed to prepared) response that creates interest if not 'scoops' the opposition. The interviewee, however, often has more warning about making an appearance and thus has more time to prepare. Used carefully, an appearance interview allows the interviewee to get his or her messages over to the listening audience, particularly in live shows where less editing can be applied by the host organization.

The major advice for appearance interviews (and, indeed, for any interview) is for interviewees to know what they want to talk about and to be prepared to direct the interview to those points they wish to make. This can be done by rephrasing the question ('I think what you are trying to ask is ...'). Alternatively, one can bridge from a weak response to a strong response ('While I need more information to fully respond to that, I can point out that what we are doing at this moment is ...').

In general, people being interviewed on appearance shows need to prepare for likely questions. They need to have some strong concrete points to make. One important tip is to dress according to the situation being discussed as well as in accordance with the expected interview setting. Try to remember that the interviewee has granted the interviewer an audience, and so should appear relaxed and confident.

Press releases

Press releases are less interesting for media representatives than organizational managers and most of their advisers seem to believe. From an organizational POV, press releases can be edited and groomed to inform (sometimes without much substance), or conceal deficiencies in the organization presenting the release. Managers and their advisers seem to act as if a press release will satisfy everyone while limiting and controlling any outflow of information. Therein is the problem. From a media POV, press releases are of reduced value because everyone gets the same information and the information supplied is often limited and uninteresting (in presentation, if not in content). At best, press releases can be viewed by crisis managers as a starting point from which information flows will expand.

Effective media releases contain four elements. These include:

- a concise and clear outline of why the statement is being made and what has happened;
- a comment that shows human interest in (be it concern or happiness) and an understanding of the impact the event may have on people;
- a succinct yet clear statement on what has been done, what is *currently* being done and what is intended to be done in the future; and
- a clear statement on how and where to gain more specific information, and where and when any media conference will be held.

By making the information content of a statement or press release more concrete and precise, users establish credibility and reportage impact. Misunderstandings and misrepresentations are likely to be reduced.

Press releases have added value when a lot of background material is also supplied. In crisis management, such material may outline:

- factual details about the organization (management structure, safety records and operational features);
- the crisis management (or recovery) programme used to handle the given crisis (or get the situation back to normal); and
- locations where further information can be gained.

Such material may include diagrams and photographs. Producing and collating this material needs to be done *before* any crisis is encountered as this generates less distraction and displacement of effort during a crisis. Pre-crisis information-gathering and presentation-packaging needs to be part of a crisis or business recovery plan.

Media conferences

While media conferences are the most important means of meeting the basic needs of media representatives and the crisis managers, media emphasis on live reporting of crisis situations means that ambush, field and on-site interviews are more likely to be undertaken before any conference has begun. As a result, managers need to ensure that personnel are prepared for ambush, field and on-site interviews. Many of the skills gained in these settings can be effectively used in more formal activities like media conferences.

Conducted properly, media conferences provide information, access to expert and senior management personnel, and a source of initial and ongoing information that gives no particular media outlet an advantage. Media organizations are likely to select what they need from this material. They will differentiate their product through their own mix of replays, expert opinion and eyewitness, victim or bystander 'fillers', and any interesting field interview.

From the POV of organizations and crisis managers, media conferences enable organizations and crisis response teams to establish a number of positive factors on their own behalf. These factors include the opportunity to:

- succinctly outline what has happened (their story about the crisis);
- develop how the situation has been, is being and will be managed;
- establish and maintain the lead in defining and interpreting the crisis situation (and the consequent perceptions of successful resolution);
- be seen as people with emotions and feelings who feel concerned for those affected by the crisis situation.

These opportunities increase the chances of having the media and thus those outside the situation see the situation from the crisis management and organizational POV. This will only happen, however, if the conference carries sufficient impact, information and credibility with those media personnel in attendance.

Through careful preparation, crisis managers can control the main sources of information available to the media and thus regulate when and how much key information will be released. Crisis managers cannot control informal information that comes from former employees, pressure groups, bystanders and victims who have moved off-site. Consequently, media conferences need to generate a volume of information and reportage that reduces the impact of any non-mainstream coverage. Media conferences achieve this by becoming the main source of information from those handling and managing the crisis situation or recovery process.

One example of a conference-driven supply of main source material was that of the Allied media presentations covering the Gulf War of 1991. A senior officer (a brigadier-general) hosted the conferences and linked presentations from various experts and commanders. This allowed senior commanders like General Schwarzkopf (the Commander of the Allied Forces) and experts to be introduced, make their presentation, answer a limited number of questions and depart 'to return to operational command duties'. By having a co-ordinator (or master of ceremonies) information supply was co-ordinated and the amount of information released and timing of that release could be controlled. At the same time, presenters had some protection against awkward or hostile questions. Through this control and restrictions on how many reporters could go into restricted areas, the media conferences became the single important source of information about the Allied management of the war. In this case, of course, the crisis managers had two advantages denied most other crisis managers – secure military control over the crisis site and the plausible case of not responding to questions because of the risk to the success of operations and the lives of allied combat personnel. Even in this circumstance, however, a number of reporters were able to penetrate closed areas without the military command knowing the reporters were there.

The central features to note from this are as follows:

- Design the conference(s) to be the main supplier of information.
- Use a co-ordinator or master of ceremonies who is not the commander or CEO or managing director or chairperson.
- Ensure some control over media intrusion.
- Have appropriate experts, eyewitnesses and respondents available who can provide media-friendly information and human-interest storylines.

From this point, managers can begin developing effective conference strategies by looking at the needs of the media (another use of media POV analysis). Facilities, presentations and presenter skills can then be enhanced to meet those needs.

Effective media conferences

The effectiveness of a media conference depends upon the preparation, training and practice undertaken by those presenting information in the conference. The success of a media conference can be increased or diminished by the effort placed into four major elements: the facilities, the process strategy, the presentation strategy, and the level of skill of those presenting information at the conference.

Facilities

Basic requirements include:

- sufficient room to accommodate the number of media representatives likely to attend and for the assembled presenters to feel comfortable and be easily seen;
- ready access to power points (and communication outlets);
- separate entrances for media and presenting personnel;
- adequate lighting and ventilation;
- appropriate facilities to support the presentations.

Unhappily, few crisis and recovery planning efforts pay adequate attention to media interactions as a whole and to the intricacies involved in presenting effective media conferences. As a consequence, most media conferences become more tense and stressful than necessary. At one police media conference, seven officers from four response organizations sat on uncomfortable chairs behind a bench-type table, hard up against a wall. There was only one way in and out of the room and this was behind the assembled media personnel. The seven members looked stiff and uneasy, and appeared on the run as questions were still being asked while they scrambled through members of the media and their equipment at the close of the conference. The senior police officer involved in the conference tripped on a cord and fell onto a number of people while still being filmed.

Other facilities that can aid in holding media personnel at a conference location include:

- general power and phone access;
- places in which the media can hold their own strategy and work meetings;
- shelter and chairs;
- food and drink
- toilets and washing facilities;
- a media help and information centre that is fully operational 24 hours a day.

Process strategy

With the venue and facilities for a media conference in place, the host organization needs to define a process strategy that enables the presenters to promote the information, attitudes and beliefs the management of the

163

organization desires to be communicated. Process strategies cover *how* the media conference will be presented.

Aspects considered include:

- the order of presentation;
- how the key points will be made during the conference;
- the length of question time;
- any background or support material.

To be effective, a conference needs smooth transitions and the repetition of key points. Organizers also need to balance a number of conflicting needs. These include:

- the media's need for specific information and issue clarification which is satisfied by presentations by experts and ample question time;
- the limits placed on the conference (when to conduct it and how long it should run);
- the need to regulate the flow and detail of information (avoiding inadvertent or premature release of information and fitting in with crisis management cycles such as changes of shifts or moments of significant change in the situation); and
- the need to protect presenters from over-exposure or hostile questioning.

The first step in a process strategy is to determine what impact and feeling the presenting organization wishes to achieve from the whole conference. Senior managers from all organizations involved should meet with the chief crisis manager to decide the key facts for release, the timing of this release and who will present these facts. At this meeting, the managers need to determine the mood and attitude to be conveyed throughout the conference.

Having decided on the main content, the process of delivering that content, and the mood and attitude desired for the conference, a co-ordinator or master of ceremonies needs to be carefully selected. This person hosts the conference, links the presentations together, monitors the question time given each presenter and acts as an on-stage support and protection person for each presenter. The co-ordinator usually welcomes the attending media personnel, outlines the main points and agenda and may state a set of rules for the conference. These rules may range from the length of time available for questioning presenters to house-rules for using any facilities made available to the media. She or he may also recapitulate the situation and the management of that situation up to the moment of the current media conference.

The conference host needs to have a good overall picture of the crisis situation, *as far as he or she is informed*. He or she will have specific knowledge about the management of the situation in terms of:

- what the media already know;
- what will be presented at the current conference;
- what the meeting of the senior managers and chief crisis manager deem appropriate for the host to know.

In this way, the co-ordinator cannot reveal information prematurely. Moreover, she or he cannot lie to the assembled media by concealing information.

Some attributes needed by the co-ordinator or master of ceremonies are worth noting:

- The co-ordinator needs to hold adequate status and level of authority in order to appear credible.
- He or she should not be a public relations or media relations person, as the media and public usually believe that people in these positions are professionally putting the best picture on the situation. Most public relations people and ex-journalists also have close relationships with some of the media personnel and this can lead to suspicions that these people will be favoured.
- He or she needs to have tact, firmness, clarity of expression, an ability to be unruffled by stress and tension, an ability to be seen as having a pleasant even temperament and an apparent readiness to be open and honest with the members of the media.
- He or she needs to be experienced through ongoing and realistic simulated practice, if not from hosting actual media conferences.
- The same person needs to be the co-ordinator for most if not all conferences.

This list is not exhaustive and reaffirms the need for proactive selection and training. No one is likely to prove an effective co-ordinator without practice and corrective feedback in simulated pressure situations.

After selecting a co-ordinator, the senior managers need to look again at the content to be presented in the conference. Here, managers agree on an order of presentation of the material and thus determine the number and nature of the presenters needed to convey the message and the information. The order of presentation may depend on whether the conference is the first or one in a chain of conferences subsequent to the initial conference.

The chief crisis manager and/or the most senior management person need to attend the first conference and are introduced early in the conference programme. Their attendance creates an impression that those involved in managing the crisis take the crisis and the conference seriously and are not hiding from public scrutiny. This image of serious and open management is strengthened by having these people demonstrate a broad grasp of the management currently undertaken, and *by having them express compassion for those affected and warm appreciation for those assisting in handling the impact of the crisis*. These speakers can plausibly leave soon after their presentation, as they 'need to be back attending to the management of the crisis'. In an initial conference, the senior managers customarily are followed by experts on the various issues involved, and finally by eyewitnesses.

Eyewitnesses need to be carefully selected as these people can influence how the media evaluates the usefulness of the conference. The eyewitnesses can also reveal information prematurely and can adversely comment on the organizations involved with the crisis situation. From a media POV, eyewitnesses need to be:

- interesting;
- able to express themselves clearly;
- drawn from those close to the key crisis events.

The presence of the senior managers is less essential in subsequent conferences, unless an important event has happened. Likewise, the sequence of presentation can be varied, with interest segments interspersed with drier and more verbal expert material. At any conference, however, key organizations managing the crisis need to have senior representatives available as organizational experts to present supporting material if needed. The impact and authority of a sequence of media conferences is enhanced by retaining the same experts (or set of experts), by ensuring that any needed expert opinion or commentary is available, and also by ensuring that interesting eyewitnesses (including on-site response or recovery managers) are present.

Presentation strategy

Once the process strategy of the conference is determined, the senior managers and the chief crisis manager need to define a set of operating limits for the conference. These limits are developed from the process strategy decisions and are communicated to each presenter (and potential presenter). This process helps unify and integrate the conference. In most cases the conference is then likely to have fewer hesitations, less conflict in information and reduced chances of premature release of information.

The objectives and operating limits which have been outlined become a blueprint for the interaction of each presenter with the media. The four elements of effective media release may prove useful for these presenters. The elements cover what has happened up to the time of the conference, the human interest or concerns involved, what is being done currently and what will happen in the future.

Presenters from senior management need to find a balance between appearing too remote and detached (thus uninterested) and appearing to be too involved and accessible (thus not managing properly). Avoid looking too well groomed (*Don't they get their fingers dirty? Do they really care?*) or too weathered and untidy (*Don't they trust anyone else? Who's actually running this thing?*). In many situations, senior managers need to show concern and care for those affected by the crisis and for those helping to resolve the effects of the crisis. They also need to demonstrate a grasp of the strategies involved and be positive in interest and leadership. The senior managers need to balance these attributes with brevity in the statements they make and in the time they spend 'on stage' making their presentation.

If this appears difficult to successfully manage, it is. Again, such skills need training and regular practice.

Most media conferences are well lit. Media personnel often add their own lighting as well. The combination of these can create a hot, humid and eye-dazzling operating zone for presenters. As a result, presenters need to avoid wearing too much white clothing. This is true when the clothing is close to the face (shirts, blouses and scarves). Modern cameras can deal quite naturally with bright to dull contrasts between a face and the surrounding environment, but less easily with large contrasts between the face and close objects such as clothing. Presenters wearing white clothing often look bright-faced or like pale ghosts. In these cases, facial features and even arm movements tend to blur uncomfortably for a viewer, distracting attention from the message and diminishing any image of calmness and control a presenter may wish to convey. Pastel colours soften the difference in contrast. Presenters who wear blue and some red convey psychological connotations of calmness and energy (at least in Western countries).

In delivering the content of their presentation, speakers need to work from what is believed to be factual. Any attempt at misinformation in a media conference will be uncovered at some point, and once that attempt is uncovered, *all* the information and presentations will become suspect. Presenters need to focus on what is seen as correct, true and factual.

All presentations need to be cleared by the chief crisis manager. Likewise, presenters need to have their organization-specific information cleared by the appropriate manager for their organization. This limits conflict between presentations, avoids premature release of information and enables greater management of information flows. Incidentally, these actions provide some protection for presenters should the material released become controversial or damaging to management and the organizations involved.

Presenters need to carefully consider how they make their statements effective. Some field-proven recommendations include the following:

- State the material clearly, logically and in a recognizable sequence.
- Speak slower than normal, and try to lower the pitch of the voice. Doing so creates a better reproduction of sound on most electronic recording equipment.
- Avoid jargon and too many technical terms. Carefully explain the meaning of any technical terms.
- Do not speak in a monotone. This is visually and audibly boring and increasingly hard to absorb. Personalize the presentation, so long as the personality shown does not conflict with the material being presented or the objectives of the conference.
- Where appropriate, use pictures and graphics to illustrate what is being said.
- Dress to match the image to be conveyed to the media's audiences.
- Remember there are two audiences in media conferences. The obvious audience is the physically assembled media personnel. The real target audiences, however, are the people reached by the assembled media.

How well presenters manage their effort depends upon the macro-skills outlined above and their ability to manage their own self-presentation.

Skill level of presenters

The degree to which process and presentation strategies are successful depends on the skills held by each presenter. The pressure of dealing with modern media in stressful situations is a major reason why conference co-ordinators and presenters need ongoing practice under realistic conditions. Many need careful instruction in the techniques and skills used to appear calm and open, to get key points across to the audience, and in handling questions.

One fundamental skill is to appear relaxed in conditions where many bright lights, microphones and cameras are directed towards the speaker. Regardless of the degree of control placed on the media, the presence of many people seeking sellable storylines has an unsettling effect on presenters who may feel hunted and besieged before they begin to speak. Presenters can use techniques like PBR to regain some calmness.

The most difficult skills needed by presenters are those that help them handle questions. Even with a conference co-ordinator assisting and a set period for questioning, presenters can face a period of tense interaction. Reporters see question time as a chance to clarify what has been presented, to get more information and to elicit any information being held back. They need to add interest to their reports and the interest may be a sense of cover-up, heroic deeds, personal tragedy or triumph. Questions tend to be searching and specific (*What exactly is this methyl isocynate and how toxic is it?*) or seek some form of comment (*Is it true that the safety procedures were not properly followed in this case?*). For presenters, question-time means making unrehearsed responses. To be effective, they need to balance the desire to appear open and helpful with not having sufficient information and prohibitions on releasing particular information. Slip-ups do occur. Presenters may wish to review the general principles outlined earlier, particularly the last principle on avoiding responses which provide no comment, misrepresentation or speculation or which assign blame.

Presenters need to practise the non-verbal skills of active listening, of summarizing and reflecting questions, and of monitoring and managing their body language. Some key non-verbal skills include the following:

- Slowly scan audiences when presenting information.
- Look at a questioner when responding.
- Share time with the media audience by looking directly into the cameras.
- Convey an appearance of relaxed openness.
- Make normal gestures.
- Avoid too many body shielding signals.
- Avoid signalling flight or fight responses.

To improve these skills presenters can rehearse in front of mirrors, within small groups of potential presenters who take turns in evaluating the performance of each member, or by using audio-visual equipment to replay their practice or live performances.

Tips for effective presentations and media conferences

The following are a list of further points that can help make presentations and conferences more effective.

- Be a source before becoming a subject.
- Do not take media questioning personally.
- Keep statements in an active voice.
- Increase credibility by using independent authorities as presenters.
- Avoid displaying the organizational logo or brand, as this reduces the association of the crisis situation with the organization.
- Monitor press reports.
- If conducting more than one conference or multiple interviews then keep the story current yet consistent, retell the story as often as needed, and focus on presenting an image of caring control.
- Face the facts.
- Consider the public interest in every operating decision.
- Avoid making the CEO directly responsible for communicating with the media. Changes in outlook and corporate or company policy become less easy to make once a CEO has spoken on these in public.
- Go public with mistakes or misdemeanours as soon as (1) the facts are clear and certain, and (2) positive plans for rectifying these are made.
- Spell out repeatedly the positive steps the organization is taking that can contribute to answering the problem or crisis.
- If wrongly accused, prove that the accusation false – remember mud sticks.
- Try to get everyone (at least within the organization) saying much the same story.
- Make certain at the end of any interaction that details of future information releases are presented.
- Ensure that any agreements to supply future information are met.

References

Alter, J. (1992) 'TV and the "Firebell"', *Newsweek*, 11 May, p. 43.

Barton, L. (1993) *Crisis in Organizations: Managing and Communicating in the Heat of Chaos*. Cincinnati, Ohio: South-Western.

Galtung, J. and Ruge, M. (1981) 'Structuring and selecting news', in Cohen, S. and Young, J. (eds), *The Manufacture of News: Deviance, Social Problems and the Mass Media*. London: Constable, pp. 50–63.

Meyers, G. C. and Holusha, J. (1986) *When It Hits the Fan: Managing the Nine Crises of Business*. London: Unwin Hyman.

Pijnenburg, B. and Van Duin, M. J. (1991), 'The Zeebrugge ferry disaster: elements of a communicating and information processes scenario', in Rosenthal, U. and Pijnenburg, B. (eds), *Crisis and Decision Making: Simulation Oriented Scenarios*. Dordrecht: Kluwer Academic.

Regester, M. (1989) *Crisis Management: What To Do When The Unthinkable Happens*. London: Business Books.

Sherman, S. P. (1989) 'Smart ways to handle the press', *Fortune*, 19 June, 57–62.

Stuart, H. (1993) 'The Newcastle earthquake: local government response', *Macedon Digest*, 7(4), 17–21.

chapter 7

EXERCISE

This exercise enables users to try out a number of the skills and techniques outlined in this chapter – handling questions, disengagement and presentation micro-skills.

Review the short brief on doing this type of case-based exercise in Appendix 1.

When you have finished the exercise, critically consider the strategies and actions you made and the consequent outcomes. Should you be doing this exercise in a small group, discuss your impressions and criticisms. Remember to acknowledge the positive aspects as well as analyze any 'what went wrong' aspects. You may wish to consider the brief comments made on this exercise on pp. 449–50 in Appendix 2 to help generate your analysis and discussion.

Begin the exercise.

Diamonds'

Diamonds' is a large and successful retail chain that sells produce including fresh food, grocery items, clothing, footwear, furniture, gifts, electrical goods, house linen, and sports and leisure goods.

You are a senior member of the store's crisis management team. On your way to work you overhear an excerpt on the early morning news.

> '... The number of people admitted overnight to the city hospitals with what may well be E Coli food poisoning stands at ten. Medical spokespeople admit that they expect this number to increase over the next three days. Unconfirmed reports suggest that a common factor may be products bought from Diamonds' city stores.'

What are you going to do?

Take around 20 minutes to outline the initial steps you think should be taken. Remember to note the beliefs and assumptions on which you base your choices and decisions. If working in a group, you may find it easier to get one of the members to note these down as the discussion proceeds.

Take the next 20 minutes to quickly review the assumptions and beliefs in the decisions you made.

Would the action choices be different if the assumptions were:

(a) not made?
(b) less than estimated?
(c) greater than estimated?
(d) different to those expected?

How could the beliefs and assumptions be better assessed before these were made the basis upon which action decisions were made?

Proceed with the next part of the exercise

Given the nature of the news item, your organization is likely to become a media target. Sure enough, as you arrive at work you find yourself surrounded by journalists and cameras.

Try to quickly jot down how you would respond and what you would say to each of the four questions below. If repeating this exercise or working in small groups you may wish to use some of the alternative questions supplied below. If working in small groups, try doing the exercise 'live' with someone asking the questions. The rest of the group needs to note what impressions they got and critique each answer after the four questions are made and responses presented. Once the question and answer routine feels good, participants may wish to practise the disengagement process mentioned in the chapter.

- *'Is it true that your company is already being investigated for other health and safety issues?'*
- *'How many deaths and injuries may result from this?'*
- *'Are the companies supplying you with security most likely to be at fault?'*
- *'When are you going to come clean and really tell us what is going on?'*

Alternative or supplementary questions

Public safety/corporate negligence:
- *'What about that accident that happened last year?'*
- *'Why wasn't the public told about ... ?'*
- *'What actual protection did the public/user/customer actually have?'*

Negligence/blaming:
- *'Who caused the accident?'*
- *'How could you let this happen?'*
- *'Why wasn't this found out before now?'*

Blaming/uncaring:
- *'So your management has no idea about what is going on in your company?'*
- *'Why haven't you paid out compensation for your last disaster three years ago?'*
- *'Care to comment on claims that you use unskilled and untrained workers on those technically complex tasks?'*

Uncaring/concealment:
- *'Isn't it a fact that the safety practices you mention are a public relations sham?'*
- *'Why can we not visit and film the site?'*
- *'Why can't we interview the managers involved?'*

chapter 8

Image management

What is image management?

Image management is the set of activities used to establish a 'right' image for an organization. Green (1992) sees image management as 'a formal structuring of those skills and techniques used to protect a company's reputation' (p. 1). The reputation may be that of the organization itself or may be of the brands held by an organization. Green sees crisis management as a strand of reputation risk management and this is correct from a narrow consideration that places a crisis as the end result of a lack of reputation management. In reality, crisis management covers much more than this.

For crisis managers, image management is how an organization, group or individual shapes the perception of the crisis and the crisis response for those in the crisis environment and, perhaps more significantly, for those outside the crisis environment. Image management is concerned with shaping perceptions held by people about organizational management and operations (and group or personal behaviour and performance). This shaping competes with attempts to influence these perceptions from sources that include media outlets and pressure groups. In everyday operations, image management is commonly expressed in terms of internal corporate cultural indoctrination and external public relations. External public relations cover any activity that influences the organizational image – advertising campaigns, community relations and dealing with product or service issues and complaints.

When a crisis arises, managers need to intensify the attention given to image management. In many crisis situations, image management becomes part of a media interaction domain. Consequently the interviews and audio-visual footage used by media outlets shape the way in which the general public perceives the crisis, the crisis impact(s) and the organizational response. Those caught in dealing with a crisis need to get the image 'right' or suffer from negative public perception.

'Right' image management succeeds when four criteria are appropriately met. These are:

- being consistent with pre-crisis attitudes and actions;
- reflecting the real attitudes and actions of the organization;
- being seen to have an outward focus; and
- maintaining the presented image after the crisis is over.

By matching actual effort with being seen to make that effort, those involved with a crisis situation can consolidate a positive 'right' image. Sometimes the image even expands positively within public perception. When Tylenol responded quickly to the 1982 poisoning scare, the company management also moved to protect their image with the public. This was done by increasing the resistance of the product to tampering – first with tamper-proof packaging then by introducing the solid capsule (called a caplet). So successful was their effort that the public perception of the organization changed from a fairly normal American corporate 'indifferent to people' image to that of a 'consumer champion for safety' within a year.

Being consistent with pre-crisis attitudes and actions

If an organization has a tarnished image before a crisis, then many outsiders may regard a sudden shift to a good and caring image with suspicion. They will suspect that the pre-crisis image is closer to the true organizational picture, and this suspicion is likely to haunt and taint any image management and crisis management efforts by that organization. Most law enforcement agencies suffer from histories of apparent heavy-handedness and overreaction when a public order crisis arises. As a consequence, members of the public readily accept suggestions that the same behaviours will happen in a given situation.

Managers need to look at existing public and stakeholder perceptions of the organization and begin work toward improving the nature of these images where the currently held images appear negative. By encouraging a pre-crisis positive image executives and managers are more able to shape a positive crisis image.

Reflecting the real attitudes and actions of the organization

Any organization found to be presenting inconsistent images during a crisis is likely to be suspected of being a villain. Inconsistencies between pre-crisis and crisis attitudes and statements lead to negative images. Thus an organization with a pre-crisis public image of indifference and remoteness has to work very hard in a crisis situation to achieve a public perception of a caring and close organization. Similarly an organization that has a positive image may lose that image should its members act defensively and dismissively under the pressure of a crisis situation.

Inconsistencies between statement (often called espoused behaviour) and action (often termed actual behaviour) also lead to negative images. For example, people who say they will return a telephone call and do not do so establish a negative image. Negative images quickly develop when crisis managers state something is being done or will be done and the actually perceived action is less than the statement suggested. Thus when Lawrence Rawl of Exxon stated that the situation in Prince William Sound was under control and people saw expanding oil tides creating more pollution, a negative image formed about Exxon. Likewise when the chairman of Occidental, Armand Hammer, flew to Britain in response to the Piper Alpha oil platform fire he stated that all affected Occidental workers would receive £100000 compensation. This statement was assumed by the public to mean that all workers on the rig would be compensated. Only 31 of those killed on the rig were Occidental employees – the rest were contractors and did not gain compensation. The result was a negative public image about Hammer and Occidental.

Being seen to have an outward focus

Negative images quickly develop when representatives of organizations involved in a crisis situation focus on concerns within their organization. Being seen to be concerned about protecting the organizational image or ensuring one's position is safe creates a poor image with the public. Similarly, emphasis on blame-assignment or recovering physical assets can promote a negative image of not caring about people who are affected by the crisis.

People often react defensively when publicly perceived crises occur. By avoiding normal interactions and relying only on formal statements, executives and managers can appear uncaring and unconcerned. Effective image management places attention upon positive actions done to help those affected by a crisis. Such attention means that executives and managers need to determine who has been affected (and even what has been affected) and act positively to reduce the hurt. Thus a primary focus of crisis management is outward to the stakeholders and people in the surrounding community who are affected by the crisis situation.

Maintaining the presented image after the crisis is over

Because of other distractions many stated intentions and activities commenced during a crisis situation seem to cease when the crisis situation no longer exists. This lack of follow-through into recovery and post-crisis (or new normal) operations can generate negative images among stakeholders and the public. Ensure that any action commitments and publicized attitudes made during a crisis are continued after the crisis is over.

Some useful image management terms

In the last few chapters the term 'shaping' has been used. *Shaping* is what people do when they determine the shape or nature of the image they wish to present to other people. By selecting how information is released and how those releasing the information will look and behave when that information is released, users 'shape' the consequent image received by other people.

Other useful terms include seeding, painting and glossing:

- *Seeding* involves planting ideas or concepts early in an interaction process so that these ideas and concepts can be used positively in subsequent interactions. Many companies who have had to recall contaminated products (Tylenol, Perrier, Arnott's, for example), try to reduce the loss of market share by planting the seed 'we will be back.' When the Garibaldi small goods company in Adelaide, Australia, was publicly suspected of being the source of contaminated salamis, the directors tried to plant some seed defences by pointing out that other companies could be culpable as could the transport company used to deliver the meat products to Garibaldi.
- *Painting* covers the activities involved in setting out the desired image. Users try to paint in the background (previous good record, adherence to regulations) then add the foreground focus – the crisis and the response and recovery management. Painters need to select carefully the appropriate style of presentation and words used to convey the atmosphere and image they are trying to create.
- *Glossing* is the process of highlighting a painted image. Gloss is used to add the right amount of shine and sparkle that helps the image look positive and appealing. As with painting, gloss can be used to cover over unwanted details or less positive facts. Used too obviously or too often, people begin to see the gloss and not the substance. At this point, whether the resulting image becomes negative depends upon the appeal of other image presenters from media outlets, pressure groups, dissatisfied stakeholders, competing companies or ex-employees.

How to conduct image management in a crisis

Ideally, proactive managers will already have in place some positive images, people looking to see what negative images may arise given certain situations, and trained staff, consultants and information packages. By looking for possible crisis events (and issues likely to prompt scrutiny by media or pressure groups), positive positional strategies for an organization's image may be identified or even already established.

Five general activities help define how to implement a given strategy:

- Make the appropriate personnel available.
- Shape interactions toward making concrete statements.
- Be seen to be open and honest.
- Be consistent.
- Involve those who are upset.

These activities are similar to the recommendations made about managing the media in Chapter 7. This should be of little surprise given the nature of media attention and the consequent negative or positive public perception of a situation, organization or person.

Make the appropriate personnel available

As with media conferences and interviews, having the appropriate experts, witnesses and respondents available improves the chances of the organizational POV being heard. Avoidance of involvement is seen as having something to hide. Avoidance of explanation is seen as being distant and dismissive. From an image management perspective, when pressure groups or media personnel do not get access to the appropriate personnel they begin to see the organization as trivializing or rudely dismissing the interaction.

Shape interactions toward making concrete statements

Most scrutiny situations (whether from investigation, media interactions or pressure group actions) involve increasing amounts of emotionality. By remaining polite, non-confrontational and apparently open and honest, people can focus attention on factual or concrete statements about issues and examples, and thus upon resolving those issues. This is not easy to do. The three hardest aspects involved in dealing with scrutiny are:

- the stress of the interaction;
- the uncertainty over what will ensue;
- the feeling that the survival of the organization (and of one's job) may depend on statements one makes in moments of intense pressure.

One way to cope is to learn to listen to what people say and then present a considered response. This is difficult to do without a lot of training. Most people would prefer to tell others to 'shut up while I am thinking what I will now say to you'. Even when they do actually listen, people react to emotional cues. Scrutiny (particularly by media) can lead to emotional statements. Consequently, people need to learn and practise skills that defuse emotional outbursts and move dialogue toward concrete statements. Concrete statements have reduced emotional content (accusative generalities) and increased factual content (non-accusative specifics, phrased in simple language with a high level of nouns and simple active verbs). The key skill is to get people to change from inflammatory 'You' statements (*You don't care about the pollution you cause so long as you make lots of money*) to 'I' statements (*I am concerned about the pollution caused by these operations*). Any effort to gain concrete statements and use empathic listening enables users to appear calm and willing to set things right while others are out of control and unreasonable.

Be seen to be open and honest

Note the emphasis on being seen to be open and honest. While this may suggest that people can simulate these attributes, the strategy really works when the appearance is actual, genuine and real. The emphasis on 'being seen' is made with a different purpose. Many people perform appropriate and positive actions in crisis situations. They tend to do these unseen, however, and are often surprised or bewildered when others doubt that the actions were done or doubt that the actions were done in good faith. The scrutineers and the public need to see the openness and honesty being displayed.

Be consistent

As emphasized in the general principles for 'right' image management, a key condition for successful image management in crisis conditions is to be seen to be consistent in attitude, behaviour and action. Consistency has multiple levels. Be consistent in what is said across time, unless the inconsistency is due to a change of information that is acceptable to the scrutineers. Maintain consistency between what is said and what is done. Remain consistent between espoused values and action values. This consistency or congruency between statements and actions (and between pre-crisis, crisis and post-crisis situations) becomes the foundation for effective image management.

Involve those who are upset

By involving all those who are upset in the process of resolving the problems – particularly stakeholders and pressure groups – managers improve their chances of gaining positive public images about themselves and their organization(s). Positive images can emerge from any, some or all of:

- an earnest search for a workable solution;
- a calm and rational honesty and openness;
- an actual all-party solution; or
- being assailed by people who have no wish to look for solutions and thus only wish to make trouble.

Involving scrutineers in resolving the issues they raise can also place pressure back onto the scrutineers. Failure by the scrutineers to suggest reasonable and workable solutions can make the scrutineers appear simply to be agitators.

One well known case involving this process was the boycott of Nestlé products (1977–84). In 1977, Nestlé successfully sued a Swiss pressure group over a pamphlet claiming that Nestlé helped kill children in third-world countries through the way the company marketed its infant formula products. The long court case led to an image of profit-making righteousness. Nestlé responded to media interest by claiming that the problem was one of nutrition and health-care and thus not the concern of a product supplier like Nestlé. This led to an American-led international boycott of Nestlé products.

Nestlé management tried to discuss the complaints with leaders of major groups of critics but tended to regard the positions adopted by these critics as being politically motivated. The resulting mistrust by Nestlé managers then led to their assuming that there existed no legitimate case to which they had to respond. This led to an attack by the managers on the motives of the groups involved and the tactics they employed.

By 1980, Nestlé executives decided that the conventional approaches of litigation and public relations campaigns were costing a lot of money while producing little positive effect. This led to the formation of the Nestlé Co-ordination Centre for Nutrition in 1981. The Centre employed independent consultants and involved the groups campaigning against Nestlé in the decision making and operations aimed at co-ordinating research into nutrition and the nutrition problems experienced in third-world countries. At the same time Nestlé managers refrained from making confrontational statements about the politics or ideologies of their critics. By March 1982, Nestlé management had given detailed instructions to its overseas marketing managers to comply with the recently produced Code of Marketing Breast Milk Substitutes by the World Health Organization of the United Nations.

To ensure public perception of this compliance, Nestlé created an independent organization called the Nestlé Infant Formula Audit Commission that was staffed by church leaders, scientists and educators who were publicly perceived to be independent (even critical) of Nestlé. This led two of the key leaders of the boycott – the American Federation of Teachers and the *Washington Post* – to call for the cessation of the boycott. In 1984, the International Nestlé Boycott Committee formally ended their actions.

Note that the situation lasted a long time. The initial negative perception was so reinforced that some people still will not buy Nestlé products. The positive image only started with the involvement of the scrutineers or pressure groups in overseeing positive contributions of research into nutrition and of compliance to an independent code of practice.

What to do in image management in a crisis situation

The *what to manage* component has five basic steps:

- Identify the problem.
- Solve the problem.
- Reshape the outcome.
- Emphasize the positive elements of the situation and the solution.
- Inform stakeholders.

By implementing these steps managers will strengthen the image they are trying to establish by directing attention to strengths rather than weaknesses.

Identify the problem

Sometimes this step is not as easy as it may seem. Too often the issues or problems are poorly or vaguely identified. The result can be serious for the organization involved. If, for example, a product is under scrutiny, managers tend inadvertently to transfer the focus from the product to the organization. Careful analysis is needed to identify the what is wrong, and the approaches used in risk evaluation (Chapter 2) and in situation and management evaluation (Chapter 17) can be adapted for this purpose.

Solve the problem

Once the issue or problem has been identified, a solution or treatment is often simultaneously suggested. Most solutions tend to be:

- get rid of the problem;
- redesign the situation to design out the problem;
- contain the problem;
- solve the problem.

Again these solutions are very similar to those outlined for risk reduction.

When faced with suppliers that use unethical practices, businesses can get rid of the problem by ending the contracts with those suppliers. On finding that a poisoner had tampered with their capsules, Tylenol personnel redesigned the capsules as a tabletlike capsule and redesigned the packaging of their products to be tamper-proof, thus designing out the problem. Containment may be achieved by contacting media outlets, suppliers and buyers with information that counters the perceived problem or that shows the problem is being resolved. Finally, problems can be solved by repairing the failure and compensating the affected people. Note that all four approaches may be used singly or in any combination. The key for these to help foster a positive image, however, is that the public and the scrutineers see the effort, not just the result.

Reshape the outcome

Most executives and managers fail to grasp the possibilities of positively building upon a crisis. By using the marketing and strategic management SWOT (Strengths Weaknesses Opportunities Threats) tool, managers can identify likely issues of scrutiny as obvious threats and determine what weaknesses could be exposed to such scrutiny. These weaknesses and threats may be turned into opportunities and even into strengths. The Johnson & Johnson management of the Tylenol capsule contamination, for example, took advantage of their product solutions (the caplet and the tamper-proof packaging) to shift the situation from a weakness into a strength. They converted an image of a potentially poisoned medication into an image of the safest product that can be produced by a community and safety conscious corporation.

Emphasize the positive elements of the situation and the solution

Managers need to emphasize the positive elements of the situation and their response. As with the reshaping of outcomes, managers and executives need to direct attention to the positive aspects – what was not damaged or lost, what is being done, what has been learned, and what can be done to eliminate or reduce the crisis or crisis impacts in the future.

Inform the stakeholders

Clear and timely information can offset rumours, speculation and fears held by the groups of people needed for an organization to survive and recover – the members of the organization and those people who deal with the organization in some fashion. For business and industrial organizations, important stakeholder groups include staff, investors, shareholders, creditors, debtors, suppliers, statutory authorities and customers.

The information needs to be clear, as honest as possible and expressed in simple direct statements. Where possible individual or personal communication should be used as this makes those receiving the communication feel important to the organization. Senior personnel need to be appointed to maintain contact with the most significant people within these groups.

Of these groups organizational members or staff are often poorly informed, yet they often need to cope with rumours, fears and the fallout from the scrutiny. Poorly informed staff are likely to become disgruntled and resign, or even wittingly or unwittingly provide contradictory and inconsistent statements and points of view to scrutineers and the public. Managers thus need to ensure that sufficient facilities, strategies and staff are deployed to quickly and calmly inform organization personnel about what is happening and how the situation and response affects each of them. Organizations need to consider the use of information contact telephone and/or Internet addresses through which staff can acquire relevant information and which may be used to instruct members or staff in what to do next.

Who to manage in image management in a crisis situation

Those who need to be managed in a crisis situation include the stakeholders, any scrutineers (media and pressure groups) and the general public. Each of these groups may need a different image of the organization and crisis management, depending on the main concerns entailed in each group's POV.

When organizational image is brought under pressure

The need to manage images arises in all crisis situations. People undertake image management in many less crisis-driven situations. For example, describing a car accident to family members, law officers, insurance agents and owners involves selecting information and highlighting (glossing) some points for some people and different points for other people. For crisis managers, image management is needed in situations that are very visible – natural disasters, major accidents or the destruction of large structures. Lack of appropriate image management worsened the perception of the Chernobyl nuclear reactor meltdown. Image management becomes increasingly important when the crisis is less physical in nature or when a situation is used subsequently to question the operational integrity of an organization.

In Hong Kong in 1996, a company called Vitasoy faced an image crisis over the way in which product contamination was handled. Vitasoy produced a range of soya bean-based drinks and traded in Hong Kong (95 per cent market share) and internationally. In January 1996 complaints of sour-tasting drinks led to a quick recall of 30 000 000 cartons. When a second contamination arose, however, the company became too internally focused on trying to solve the problem. Public reassurance seemed a piecemeal action (Tracey and Moir, 1996).

What seemed at first a quick response by Vitasoy became seen as a set of faltering reactions. The first complaints and product recall (50 000 cartons) had been made on 24 October 1995. A second contamination incident happened on 4 January 1996 requiring a recall of more than 8 000 000 cartons. Blame was placed on the packaging process and share value fell by 8.5 per cent (Tracey and Moir, 1996). Complaints continued until the manufacture of paper-based packaged soya drink completely ceased on 9 January 1996, with a recall of 30 000 000 cartons. Share trading was suspended and market share lost. More important, however, was the image of a distracted and piecemeal response to the situation. The resulting negative image for consumers and investors meant that Vitasoy was confronted with a very hard task to regain market share.

Many multinational companies face pressures because of the size of their operation. Size is often publicly seen as a predictor of acceptability – large organizations are quickly painted as being remote, uncaring, profit-oriented and destructive while small organizations can be seen as close, caring, people-oriented and constructive. These images need not be accurate.

Oil companies like BP have often encountered criticism as they seek to maintain or increase their access to reserves of oil. These additional reserves tend to be in less developed regions that seem less resilient to the impact such large-scale drilling and collecting operations entail. In 1996 BP came under scrutiny over its operations in the Department of Casanare in Colombia, where reserves of two billion barrels of oil are estimated to exist. A European Member of Parliament claimed that local BP officials have confessed to weekly oil spills, chemical overflows, water contamination, illegal sites and invasion of protected jungle. He also alleged the company (along with others) paid blood money to the government over and above the 7 per cent war tax (Fidler, 1996).

In response, BP claimed to be the victim of a campaign of disinformation and exaggeration that left them having to disprove a negative. The company managers claimed that the European Member of Parliament never visited the region and had based his accusations on a report that the Colombian government claimed was based on uninvestigated assertions. To help dispel the negative images of remoteness produced by these accusations, some executives were moved from the distant capital of Bogota to the town of Yopal in the region so they could hear local concerns.

Incidents and crises can be subsequently used to paint a picture of negligence and incompetence. In 1991, Coors (USA) accidentally allowed 150000 gallons of beer to leak into Bear Creek, Colorado, killing 17000 fish. Coors faced penalties of US$50000 plus US$10 per fish. Should Coors have a similar accident they could find they have a negative corporate image that is at best one of being accident-prone and inefficiently managed or at worst one that appears negligent and indifferent to both the environment and the public.

Image management covers physical and less tangible situations. Negative images may arise from media investigations, media reports on a crisis situation or from pressure groups that want targeted organizations to change their operations.

Assaults on an organization's image

Assaults on an organization's image tend to come from three sources: action or cause-driven groups, warring parties in hostile takeover situations and journalists investigating a specific organization or industry group. Many different types of product or operational assault exist.

When a Danish investigation revealed that a chemical preservative, formaldehyde, was used within the products Carrot Moisture Cream and

Elderflower Eye Gel, executives and managers of the Body Shop had little time to react before a serious image problem emerged. Formaldehyde is suspected to cause cancer at 1000 parts per million according to Danish government authorities. While the cream and the gel were well below this level (220 and 160 parts per million respectively), two sources of image management problem remained. One problem was the possibility that the existing levels could trigger allergies among users with sensitive skin. The other problem was the damage this could cause Body Shop in terms of its carefully crafted image of an ecofriendly company which uses only natural products.

In England, the retail chain Marks and Spencer encountered an image problem when scrutinized by an ITV programme, *World in Action*, in early 1996. The two issues raised were the selling of goods allegedly produced under unfair employment practices in foreign countries and allegedly copying fashion items designed by other people or organizations and which were not licensed to Marks and Spencer. While the first problem could be resolved quickly through changing the contractors for the supplies, the second problem was not so simple. Given the size of the Marks and Spencer operation and the relatively small size of those organizations claiming infringement, direct legal action may have been unlikely, but for Marks and Spencer, the concern raised by this issue was likely to be the damage to its retail image.

Pressure groups and image management

Single-issue groups place pressure on how an organization (and any crisis management effort) is perceived by stakeholders and the general public. As a consequence, managers and executives need to manage their interactions with pressure groups effectively. Image management needs to be proactive rather than reactive as the first image statement or position is often the best remembered and accepted by the audiences of the media outlets. The key is to determine clearly the focal interests of the pressure group.

One approach to determining likely focal interest is to analyze the scrutiny or pressure being applied or likely to be applied. Six questions help reveal the substance and scope of interest of a scrutiny by pressure groups:

- Who is undertaking the scrutiny?
- Why are these people or groups of people making this scrutiny?
- What is their position or goal?
- Where are they currently making this scrutiny?
- When are they doing this scrutiny?
- What are the outcomes for (a) the scrutineers: and (b) those being scrutinized?

The answers to these questions help managers assess the likely points that may be touched on by special-interest pressure groups.

Pressure groups are usually single-issue organizations. They may focus on environmental protection, transportation safety, noise abatement, anti-arms trade, anti-racism, anti-smoking, anti- or pro-abortion, use of animals for experimentation and testing, anti-pollution or even getting a specific industry or perceived threat removed from a local community. Over 1000 pressure groups have memberships that span national borders, the largest being Greenpeace with over four million members.

Pressure groups undertake a wide range of tactics and strategies to influence public opinion against their target. These activities may include:

- delivering damaging information to likely litigants;
- challenging actions in legal courts;
- attention-gaining demonstrations and public picketing of premises and access points;
- devising deliberate incidents that range from obstruction through to violent protests and acts of terrorism;
- consumer boycotts.

Pressure groups also enlist support from celebrities, demonstrate at annual general meetings, and sometimes threaten the health and safety of the stakeholders of targeted organizations. These groups also use direct marketing of their vision and criticisms, opinion poll shaping and photo opportunities. These tactics support a strategy that is a combination of nuisance-making, public visibility, increasing the costs of the targeted organizations and isolating support for their targeted opposition by reinforcing public perceptions that the targeted organization is confrontational and reactionary.

Members of protest groups generally share four attributes that make them difficult to handle:

- They are emotionally committed to the group's cause. This means they will publicly display 'missionary' zeal and appear as bright, attractive and earnest individuals.
- They sell simple solutions that appear attractive because of the apparent ease with which simple solutions can be applied.
- They focus on the single issue they hold. Members of the organizations they target, on the other hand, need to focus not only on the issue(s) raised by the pressure group but on other goals and activities – such as public good, profit for shareholders and ensuring safe operations for members of staff and the surrounding community.
- They present themselves as being a small group of earnest individuals who are opposed by impersonal technocratic giants with faceless managers and implacably inflexible organizational mouthpieces. Many pressure groups work hard at appearing individualistic, small and weak in apparent resources, as they realize that the resulting public impression of being a public champion and an underdog gains the support of a largely unquestioning public.

These four attributes mean an ease of focus and high-energy behaviours

among pressure group members, many of whom quite genuinely see themselves as 'good people' or 'modern-day knights in shining armour' serving
good causes. One problem with this zeal is the possibility that any behaviour
or action will become acceptable so long as the 'good cause' prevails. As with
any other cause-driven groups or individuals (including terrorists and serial
criminals), the appeal of 'being someone' through gaining public attention
and of holding power over others can lead to aggressive and arrogant behaviours and actions. The attraction of these behaviours and actions may increasingly have less to do with the original 'good cause' for which the group
formed.

Before encountering action by pressure groups, managers and executives
need to improve communications with all stakeholders – from those likely to
bear the brunt of a protest campaign to those who make up an initially disin-
terested general public. Such communication needs to be open and truthful
but can be positively skewed in terms of organizational image. The key is to
get the organization's story across to the people likely to support the organization when a pressure group campaign begins.

Executives and managers have a number of options to consider once a pressure group begins their campaign. As with any negotiating situation the fundamental choices consist of an attempt to remove the pressure by finding a
solution acceptable to all parties (what is often called a win–win approach) or
of a confrontation with the pressure groups (a win–lose approach). The advantage of the co-operative win–win approach is that the solution can last a long
time. The main disadvantage of this approach is that it takes time, patience
and a willingness to share information and solutions. A competitive win–lose
situation seems much quicker and more easily adopted. Unless the losing parties disappear completely, however, the chances are quite strong that conflict
will occur in the future with people who resent the costs imposed by their
earlier loss.

The Nestlé example contrasts the potential image outcomes of both these
approaches. At first, Nestlé executives tried a competitive win–lose approach
by mounting a successful libel case against the Swiss pressure group. These
people did not disappear, however, and were joined by a much larger pressure
group in the form of the International Nestlé Boycott Committee. When
Nestlé executives deliberately stopped the competitive approach – avoiding
the name-calling, litigation and deliberate public relations campaigns – and
sought a win–win approach through co-operation, they quickly secured the
end to the campaign. Note this later strategy meant using an independent
third party that included people acceptable to all sides and adherence to an
acceptable third-party determination (the WHO Code of Marketing Breast
Milk Substitutes).

Skilled managers and executives may use the win–win approach while holding some competitive tactics in hand should the approach fail. Since the Gulf
War of 1991, the United States of America and the United Nations have tried
win–win tactics of negotiation with Iraq, while applying trade embargoes and

threatening to use force. Over time, the win–win position has moved toward a win–lose situation. The Iraqi government uses the embargo to maintain internal control over the country and as a means of blaming any deficiency on those outside the country. As a consequence, the Iraqi government is able to secure a positive image of national resistance that is supported by repressive internal force.

If managers choose a win–win approach then they need to be seen to be reducing any confrontational image. Instead of confronting protesters from pressure groups, organizational representatives may offer the groups chairs, umbrellas, food and drink, and may even help them demonstrate. This creates a public image of tolerance and calmness and can mute the effect of the protest. This is because many pressure group members tend towards confrontation and cannot readily cope with non-confrontational behaviours. They tend either to go elsewhere (letting the protest fade) or become publicly seen as increasingly confrontational and obstructive. In this way they lose public support. Managers need to make their interactions with members of pressure groups appear tolerant of multiple opinion, ready and willing to listen to *constructive* opinion, willing to learn, and always polite and sensitive to the issues involved.

Should executives choose to be confrontational then a number of tactics may lead to a truce. Organization members may undertake a counter-protest (not necessarily at the same place or time) that challenges the lost jobs or lifestyles which may ensue if the changes pushed by the pressure groups are accepted. Where a protest group excludes all news media (or favours a specific few outlet organizations), crisis managers can appear willing to assist the media. When a protest group asserts specific points, managers may avoid challenging such assumptions directly by encouraging other *independent* parties to make those contradictions. Managers can try to check the authenticity of data used in a protest group's media campaign. Two choices arise in this effort. The *soft approach* contrasts points made by a pressure group media effort with counter-points that pre-empt debate. The *hard approach*, on the other hand, does not deal with the data or information presented by the other party, but undermines the credibility assigned that party by the surrounding audience.

Co-operative win–win and competitive win–lose approaches need to adopt similar publicly seen postures of being rational, fair and flexible. 'Behind closed doors' arrangements need to be avoided, as these appear secretive and deceptive and are often later denied or retracted in public. Managers and executives need to be publicly seen to be ready and willing to talk *constructively*. This approach includes very visibly and publicly involving the protest groups in the process of finding solutions.

Should the pressure groups join in the search for solutions, their members need to be seen to be providing more than 'don't want' statements or they risk appearing incompetent and unhelpful. Should they reject involvement, the pressure groups publicly appear obstructive, confrontational and non-constructive. The search for solutions needs to be done through a mediating independent third party otherwise the process is likely to collapse, with charges and counter-charges being made over control, distortion and unwillingness to co-operate.

Where the win–lose and win–win approaches differ is in the use of these public forums. Competitive win–lose strategies are used to make the other party look bad to the media and the general public. By adopting a posture of open and constructive participation, users can shape the responses of others into appearing competitive, obstructive and aggressive. The single-issue simple solutions can be made to appear naive, unworkable and even dangerous.

Win–win approaches take the openness and honest-dealing as a means of uncovering a workable solution accepted by all parties involved. The display of openness and honesty and willingness to talk, listen and adjust behaviours if needed is genuine. This approach takes time and may require patience due to the willingness of other parties to assume more competitive responses and actions. Ultimately, however, win–win based solutions are likely to last longer and generate fewer interruptions as time passes.

REALITY BITE

Shell, Greenpeace and the Brent Spar oil rig, 1995

Background
Oil companies are often seen as aggressive organizations that seek profit before safety and abet pollution. This stereotype makes such companies easy targets for pressure groups. Given the oil exploration 'boom' of the 1970s in the North Sea (off Britain and Norway) and in the Gulf of Mexico, the rigs and oil storage platforms from this period are becoming increasingly obsolete and unused. One of the first of the oil storage platforms was Brent Spar.

Incident
In 1995, senior executives from Shell (UK) decided to dump the Brent Spar in 2000 metres of deep water in the Atlantic ocean. Their scientists and specialist managers advised that this was the most efficient and safest means of disposal. As soon as the decision became publicly known, Greenpeace mobilized world-wide, European and local protests. Such organization was accelerated by the use of computer networks on the Internet. Protests were visible and threats were made to Shell operations and employees. In Germany, for example, some Shell service stations were petrol-bombed.

Response
At first the Shell senior executives maintained their stance and decision. They had government backing, particularly from the Conservative government of the United Kingdom. This support seemed insufficient given the threat of openly hostile action in Europe (particularly Germany) and the massive media management directly presented by Greenpeace.

At one stage Greenpeace boarded the Brent Spar and occupied the platform for a number of days. The group reported that their scientific personnel had examined the rig and estimated that around 5000 tonnes of contaminant oil remained on board. Shell denied this was so. Later, Greenpeace conceded that their personnel had miscalculated badly, losing a deal of credibility among members of the public. Nonetheless, as Greenpeace had publicized their estimate first, the image of likely pollution stuck.

By June 1995, executives from Shell (UK) reversed the decision to dump the Brent Spar and called for public consultation. The Shell executives requested an 'honest dialogue' with all interested parties. This move stranded external supporters (especially the government of the United Kingdom) and lost Shell some backing from these sources.

After the Brent Spar was diverted to a Norwegian fiord until a further decision over disposal could be made, members of the oil industry were determined not to be caught out again. Suggestions to gain public support have included advertising campaigns, more direct contact between the oil industry and the various environmental pressure groups involved, more contact with representative governments and regional political bodies, and better communication with the industry's stakeholders.

By October, Shell again appeared to raise the possibility of dumping the Brent Spar in deep sea, but stated that the company would wait until all options were explored. Suggested options were requested from all interested parties, including pressure groups and members of the general public. The options were to be assessed in terms of the best practicable option – viewed from environmental, public opinion and economic perspectives. In 1996, Shell enlisted participation from a third and independent party in brokering this solution process, involving a European Union organization – the Environment Council. Some 250 submissions were received and assessment reduced these to six 'finalists' by 1997.

Statistics
Brent Spar is 450 feet (138.5 metres) tall and weighs 14 500 tonnes. The cost of the aborted dumping has been estimated at over £10 million, none of which qualified for tax relief. An estimated 15 rigs and associated platforms were due for decommissioning and removal in 1996. The number of offshore oil rigs and associated structures in waters around the United Kingdom exceeds 210.

Comment
The use of computer networks (the 'superhighway') enables the rapid transmission of data and information around the world virtually immediately. One of the surprises for Shell executives was the rapid escalation of the protest from a local English dispute to a regional European affair and then to world interest and action. Multinational organizations can expect similar escalation when confronted by major pressure groups.

One concern emerging from this and other recent situations is the readiness with which some members of support groups resort to violence to further their protest. Setting aside the implications of a desire for power over others and an attempt to be someone as psychological drivers for such violence, managers and executives now have to consider the safety of staff and other stakeholders in making action decisions that may trigger a pressure-group protest. What has to be recognized is the ease with which highly emotionally held beliefs can move from committed lawful support to acts of unlawful behaviour that include violence.

Commitment to a cause can become obsessive to the point where the end justifies any means of obtaining that end.

Protest groups are as capable of managing (or manipulating) the media as any other organization. The news media were somewhat trusting and naive to accept single-source audio-visual material from Greenpeace that was not validated by any other independent party. As noted in Chapter 6, such single-source unvalidated information has to be treated as soft and unreliable in nature. Use of the available material needed to be qualified by the broadcasting media so that their audiences could assess the facts for themselves. In the Brent Spar case, Greenpeace used their own media equipment and deliberately excluded other news media personnel. This latter action should have warned media reporters and editors who would have rejected such material had it come from sources that media people traditionally regard as suspect – like business organizations. Some footage was used to create public outrage over the treatment Greenpeace representatives received while boarding and remaining on the platform. This was later found to be biased and incorrect.

Managerial perspective

This Reality Bite illustrates why organizations need to establish strategies for managing pressure group campaigns. As the credibility and support for both the protest groups and the target organization depend upon public trust and acceptance, managers and executives need to determine proactively strategies for gaining and holding that support. Such strategies may mean a change in the day-by-day organizational image. By being involved with community issues and publicizing any beneficial or positive actions undertaken, organizations can establish a public image of a beneficial organization that a community desires to retain. To do so, managers use approaches that help the organization appear honest, open, positive and empathic. By then showing a public willingness to listen and seek mutual solutions, managers can establish a reputation for fairness and willingness to resolve issues that reduces the virulence of an image assault.

Executives and managers need to note that workable solutions may mean organizations change their practices and ways of operating. Instead of resisting such change, organizations could make the change very public and positive for their image. Visible steps to implement change 'for the good of all' is one way in which pressure-group campaigns are brought to an end and an organizational image is enhanced. Both Nestlé and Shell demonstrated that adopting a deliberately public positional change does end the pressure-group campaign.

Dealing with specific pressure groups: NIMBYs

What Nestlé and Shell experienced were global forms of a specific type of pressure-group campaign where groups of people desire that an action should happen 'Not In My Back Yard' (NIMBY). NIMBY groups protest over actions or structures near where they live ('back yards') which the protesters believe will detrimentally affect their quality of life and the value of their properties.

NIMBY groups have protested over religious groups building in their neighbourhoods and churches ringing church bells. They have objected to dump sites being placed within their region (especially for nuclear and industrial chemical waste) and hospitals or housing development projects being built (because of the noise and loss of property values). Likewise, protests have been made about road and rail developments and airport locations due to the pollution, loss of environment and increase in noise. NIMBY activities have taken on regional and global perspectives due to growing fears that organizational practices in one region may affect other parts of the world. Pollution, the effects of unregulated industrialization and unethical work practices have become some of the issues leading to regional and global action campaigns from NIMBY-styled pressure groups.

A number of steps can be taken to reduce the impact of NIMBY groups upon an organization's operations and image. These steps include:

- Appoint a community affairs manager to meet with, get to know and monitor community people and their attitudes to the organization. Get employees to join local community organizations.
- Meet with leaders of community groups *before* any public meetings.
- Undertake careful and independent impact studies, and make the complete data freely available to all community members.
- Keep community groups and members informed about what is happening and what is being done through newsletters, articles in community newspapers and reports on local radio and television stations.
- Involve community leaders and any NIMBY group leaders in the decision-making and action-determining process.
- Monitor attitudes in the target community through environmental monitoring processes, including use of clipping services to extract any reports or items from local media that mention:
  - the organization;
  - the activity or trade undertaken by the organization; and
  - any local grievances or expressions of community unquiet.
- Where possible, employ local labour and contract with local companies for services and supplies.
- Involve the organization in community affairs, so that the company is seen as part of the community fabric as time goes by.

Managers and executives need to avoid name-calling, lecturing or making statements that infer blame. Eight particular statements to *avoid using* with NIMBY groups include:

- *'No comment.'*
- *'I don't need to put up with this.'*
- *'You do not understand.'*
- *'We need more time to ...'*
- *'Wrong.'*
- *'The media have blown this out of all proportion.'*

- *'The media lied about ...'*
- *'This is the only time this will happen ...'*

These statements show negative reactions that close out dialogue, suggest avoidance of responsibility and increase confrontational tensions. Managers and executives need to make statements that infer a willingness to listen and work together over the issues. Some examples include:

- *'I understand your point of view.'*
- *'May I restate your position?'*
- *'We are here to listen to what you wish to tell us.'*
- *'We care about the community in which we work.'*
- *'Join us in resolving these issues.'*

REALITY BITE

McDonald's and Greenpeace, London –
The McLibel case (UK)

Background
Large organizations always run the risk of being seen as too large to care about the community or communities within which they operate. Such organizations are also visible targets that bring public attention to the pressure groups or individuals needing to advertise their POV issue. McDonald's, as one of the largest worldwide fast-food organizations, is one such target. McDonald's executives were harassed by pressure groups over a number of alleged failings including the treatment of staff, the health and safety of their product and their association with questionable activities in third-world countries. At the time of the trial, the company had 21 000 stores in 101 countries. Sales for McDonald's were around US$32 billion (£15 billion) in 1996.

Incident
In January 1985, London Greenpeace launched a campaign to expose their perceived reality of McDonald's operations. In 1986, the group published a pamphlet, *What's Wrong With McDonald's?* London Greenpeace activists distributed this pamphlet outside London outlets of McDonald's and the London head office for the United Kingdom. In September 1990 McDonald's sued five alleged writers and distributors of the pamphlet for libel. The activists set up a McLibel Support Campaign Fund. Three of the five formally apologized in January 1991, leaving David Morris and Helen Steel to face prosecution. Neither Steel nor Morris were full-time workers or had any personal wealth. Any damages that McDonald's received were thus unlikely to be financial.

Response
The court case (with adjournments) lasted from 1994 to 1997.

McDonald's hired one of Britain's leading libel lawyers, Richard Rampton, to lead their case. Rampton successfully argued to the court that the trial should be conducted without a jury given the complicated evidence over diet and disease.

Morris and Steel unsuccessfully applied to the Court of Appeal and then to the House of Lords to reinstate the jury. Rampton also successfully had parts of the defence case struck out from the proceedings. This was reversed by the Court of Appeal, which found that the defendants could base their defence on witness statements, on future disclosure from McDonald's documents and on what they may reasonably expect to discover through cross-examination.

In March 1994 McDonald's released 300 000 copies of a leaflet, *Why McDonald's is going to court*. This leaflet claimed that the court action was not about freedom of speech but about the right to stop people telling lies. Morris and Steel counter-sued for libel in April. In the initial libel case Morris and Steel had to prove their pamphlet expressed true or fair comment and this comment had to be supported by direct or primary evidence and not by media reportage or common public beliefs. With the counter-suit in place, McDonald's had to establish that the facts in the Greenpeace London pamphlet were lies and that Steel and Morris knew that such facts were lies.

By June 1994 the parties had engaged in 24 pre-trial hearings. The trial began on 28 June 1994 and was presided over by Mr Justice Bell. During July evidence was proffered over McDonald's operations – the environmental effects of the food packaging, the nutritional value of the products, animal welfare issues and food poisoning complaints. On 12 September 1994 one of McDonald's expert witnesses unwittingly found that the claims made in the pamphlet over connections between diet and disease were 'very reasonable'.

The pressure group also pursued a public strategy. During October, 30 bags of McDonald's packaging litter were picked up from London streets. World-wide protest action took place. In Australia, for example, seven benefit concerts raised support money. In court, evidence on McDonald's advertising techniques was presented.

The trial resumed in March 1995, and by April had moved on to look at McDonald's employment record. Anti-McDonald's demonstrations were held in at least 20 countries on 15 April (McDonald's 'birthday'). An advertisement production for McDonald's being made in London's Ruskin Park was abandoned at a cost of £100 000 as demonstrators kept on appearing in front of cameras with McGreedy posters.

On 28 June Morris and Steel confirmed reports that McDonald's had offered them a settlement deal. The two claimed that the offer came from American directors with money being settled on a third party so long as they legally bound themselves not to criticize McDonald's. They declined the offer. In July McDonald's ended an agreement to supply the defendants with copies of official court transcripts, claiming that much of the material supplied then seemed to find a way to national and international media storylines. On 16 October the 11th Annual Worldwide Day of Action Against McDonald's took place. Protest leaflets were distributed outside half of the 300 McDonald's stores in Britain. Protests took place in 20 other countries. During October, the defendants began examining 30 ex-employees in their case against McDonald's employment practices.

In February 1996, the defendants launched the McSpotlight Website. Over 12 000 000 visits to this site were made in the next 18 months. At one time the site had 1300 files in 12 languages available for viewing. During February, the defendants examined witnesses on the effect McDonald's may have had on rainforest depletion. Last evidence was presented in July, and closing addresses were to be made on 7 October 1996. Morris and Steel lost appeals on being made to present their case first. Morris and Steel began their closing address on 21 October and finished on 28 November. Rampton submitted his closing address in writing on 28 November, and was questioned on aspects of this in early December. On 11 and 13 December, the defendants responded with their final legal arguments, propounding that big corporations should no longer be able to sue their critics to silence them and that the English libel laws were oppressive and unfair.

In his judgment, Mr Justice Bell ruled that the leaflet was libellous (and thus found for McDonald's). He also found some substantiation for the claim that McDonald's targeted young children. McDonald's had claimed around £200 000 (US$320 000) in damages and perhaps around £10 million (US$16.6 million) from Morris and Steel. This money was unlikely to be gained as Morris was unemployed and Steel worked part-time for £64 (US$105) a week. The defendants proposed to take the judgment on appeal to the European Court of Human Rights, as well as seeking damages from three private investigators hired by McDonald's to infiltrate the London Greenpeace organization.

Statistics
The court case began in 1994 and lasted 313 days until late 1997 when a judgment was declared. Around 44 000 pages of documentary evidence were presented and 18 000 pages of transcript testimony were recorded.

Comment
Perhaps the most interesting outcome from this case is that no one really won. McDonald's gained a qualified legal judgment in their favour, but had little expectation of material gain from the defendants. In exchange for this victory, the company presented pressure-group activists with 313 days in which to argue their case publicly. In pressing the litigation, McDonald's helped expand the protests against their operation into an internationally orchestrated campaign. The establishment of the McSpotlight website undoubtedly helped this orchestration and growth of protest. Perhaps the most ironic twist was the fact that the move by McDonald's to sue the five Greenpeace London activists was made around the same time that this group decided to end their leaflet campaign against McDonald's.

On the other hand, the defendants gained little from the effort. They still claim in 1997–8 to be taking appeals onward. Morris and Steel certainly had their moment of fame and recognition in the public spotlight, and gained some impact on McDonald's with the judge's adverse comments on the strategies employed by McDonald's in aiming their advertising at children. On the other hand, targeting specific types of people and interest groups is a common practice by most commercial organizations – and even pressure groups are not innocent of such practice. Advertising aimed at children is not unique to McDonald's. Meanwhile, McDonald's continues to expand and produce profit, and millions of people still eat their products. Like Exxon, this multinational or transnational organization has a size that prevails over such events. In this sense, the defendants had no impact on McDonald's.

Management perspective
The real question remains: why did McDonald's choose to lash out with a win–lose

coercive tactic like litigation? Surely the very public outcomes of the Nestlé predicament should have cautioned them against this approach. One possibility is the use of SLAPP (Strategic Lawsuits Against Public Participation) litigation in the United States. This approach has been used not only to silence pressure groups but even to pressure individuals who write letters of complaint to newspapers. Advice given to McDonald's may have been that all five people would back away (indeed three did formally apologize). If this were the case, however, surely the managers, executives and directors of McDonald's would have explored the impacts of 'what if the activists go to court?' One possible determination was that pressing this case through would make other pressure groups avoid confronting McDonald's. Perhaps McDonald's executives and managers, like those of Exxon, know that they are selling a consumer product that will continue beyond adverse image effects. If this latter belief were part of the corporate thinking then the response surely would be to act as if the protests did not exist and hence not seek legal redress.

From an image management POV, this case illustrates the strategies used by pressure and NIMBY-type groups. Litigation approaches play directly into the stereotypic image contrasts between the 'Goliath' of the large organization and the little 'David' of the activist being sued.

Beneath the surface the actualities may be different. Managers and executives cannot focus on the litigation issue only – they have to continue their work within the organization. Pressure-group activists, on the other hand, often have little other than the litigation to preoccupy them. While large organizations will hire the correct representatives to handle the case, many activists make a grandstand play to handle the case themselves – pleading they do not have the money to afford lawyers. By tackling the court appearance themselves defendants can build a picture of oppressed innocents trapped in the chicanery and unfairness of due legal process. This helps seed and paint the David and Goliath images and excuses mistakes, delays and incompetence. For many pressure-group defendants there exists a concealed support that can exceed the investment placed in the case by a large organization. Pressure groups enlist dedicated widespread support and advice from many equally antagonistic scientists and legal advisers virtually free of charge. They can set up websites that will be regarded as truthful because the defendants are earnest people expressing concern and bewilderment in an increasingly indifferent and hostile world. Any equivalent effort by a large organization will be too readily dismissed as an obvious and cynical public relations job, and thus probably a set of lies.

Managers need to consider carefully any hardline approaches (aggressive counter-tactics, litigation). They really should only choose to litigate when the likely costs of the pressure campaign on consumers buying their product or service can be expressed in financial amounts that exceed the costs of going to court and the costs of being made to appear less favourably in the public spotlight.

References

Fidler, S. (1996) 'Oil giant in troubled waters', *Financial Times*, 8 November, p. 17.

Green, P. S. (1992) *Reputation Risk Management*. London: Pitman/Financial Times.

Tracey, E. and Moir, J. (1996) 'Bitter blow for Vitasoy', *Sunday Morning Post*, 14 January, p. 9.

chapter 8

EXERCISE

This exercise focuses readers and users on the delicate skills required to deal with image-shaping issues. Try to identify what choices are open to Diamonds' representatives, how these choices may affect the image of that organization and how the strategies may be tactically conducted.

When you have finished the exercise, critically consider the strategies and actions you made and the consequent outcomes. Should you be doing this exercise in a small group, discuss your impressions and criticisms. Remember to acknowledge the positive aspects as well as analyze any 'what went wrong' aspects. You may wish to consider the brief comments made on this exercise on pp. 450–1 in Appendix 2 to help generate your analysis and discussion.

Begin the exercise.

Diamonds' and the pressure group PAPPAW

Diamonds' is a large and successful retail chain that sells produce including fresh food, grocery items, clothing, footwear, furniture, gifts, electrical goods, house linen and sports and leisure goods.

On your way to work you overhear an excerpt on the early morning news.

> '... On Midnight Views last night, Pat Goodworks, president of PAPPAW (People Against Poverty, Pollution And War), angrily called for protest action against Diamonds', the large general goods retailer. This call for action followed confirmation that Diamonds' was directly linked to the company running the slum factory that burned down in Copha City in Nirvana last week, killing 58 people and injuring hundreds more. Goodworks claimed that 'Companies like Diamonds' need to be stopped from using virtual slave labour in order to increase their obscene profits.'

As a senior member of Diamonds' crisis management team, what are you going to do?

Take 20 minutes to outline the initial steps you think should be taken. Remember to note the beliefs and assumptions on which you base your choices and decisions. If working in a group, you may find it easier to get a group member to note these assumptions down as the discussion proceeds.

Take the next 20 minutes to quickly review the assumptions and beliefs in the decisions you made.

Would the action choices be different if the assumptions were:

(a) not made?
(b) less than estimated?

(c) greater than estimated?
(d) different to those expected?

How could the beliefs and assumptions be better assessed before these were made the basis upon which action decisions were made?

After discussing these issues, continue with the material below.
Given the nature of the news item, your organization will soon need to interact with a number of pressure groups.

Take 20 minutes to determine how you will interact with these groups, again noting the assumptions and beliefs associated with these action decisions. You should explore the profiles outlined below to help guide your choices for action.

Take the next 20 minutes to quickly review the assumptions and beliefs in the decisions you made.

Would the action choices be different if the assumptions were:

(a) not made?
(b) less than estimated?
(c) greater than estimated?
(d) different to those expected?

How could the beliefs and assumptions be better assessed before these were made the basis upon which action decisions were made?

Explore the strategies you or your group chose. Were these win–win or win–lose? What were the potential outcomes for the worst-case result for your organization?

Profiles

Diamonds'
Diamonds' is a large national retailing operation that includes home products, electronics, gifts, clothing and foodstuffs. The operations are aimed at a broad market base, offering an upmarket ambience and quality at value-for-money prices. In many cases, products similar in style and quality to market-leading brand names are offered at prices much lower than those brands.

The capital base of Diamonds' is approximately $4 billion, with a turnover of around $16 billion and a profit of nearly $500 million. Diamonds' employs 60 000 staff nationwide.

The issue
Diamonds' has contracts for their very popular Sparklers (children's leisurewear) and Scorers (sports/leisure trainer) shoes with Ah Fat Enterprises, which subcontracts the actual production orders. Currently a successful advertising campaign has boosted sales figures for Scorers, with a slogan 'How can you score without your Scorers?' and the participation of sports stars.

Without the cheaper overseas manufacturing of most of the value-for-money products that parallel the dearer brand names, prices would be increased by nearly 100 per cent, Diamonds' would possibly have to cut its staff by 8 per cent and the overseas workers would have no employment. Diamonds' attitude has been to indicate that it is up to its suppliers to enforce ethical standards, that one cannot tinker with different standards of living around the world, and that Diamonds' would be very willing to reconsider its strategy should its competitors be likewise constrained by evenly applied regulations.

PAPPAW

The People Against Poverty, Pollution And War is a multi-focus protest group aimed at the impact developed countries and their commercial organizations have on lesser-developed environments. Past actions by PAPPAW have included picketing, boycotts, public destruction of the product(s) in question and legal actions.

While Diamonds' had not directly clashed with PAPPAW in the past, the new leadership of PAPPAW is said to have a target hit-list of 20 national and multinational companies against which PAPPAW will mount long-term campaigns.

Media interest

Media interest seems based on the human interest storylines of poor slave-like foreign workers and on the likely confrontation of Diamonds' with PAPPAW.

Community interest

The general public seem sympathetic to the plight of the lowly-paid workers overseas (and the fire tragedy at Copha City). Union groups are considering their position on the fairness of the situation, with especial attention given to loss of local employment and the plight of the workers overseas. Possible work bans and boycotts may be proposed and accepted.

c h a p t e r **9**

Management and crisis management

Along with Chapter 10 and Chapter 13, this chapter looks at factors associated with the third 'R' of the RRRR model – Responding to a crisis situation. While Chapter 10 looks at crisis management structures and Chapter 13 provides advice on managing in crisis situations, this chapter explores four key factors in crisis management:

- the structure and culture of organizations;
- strategic and tactical management;
- strategic crisis management;
- approaches to decision making.

Once these quick perspectives are established the techniques and approaches to crisis management can be more easily understood.

Managing and organizational structure

Organizations hold elements that can facilitate and obstruct a response to a crisis situation. While most crisis managers are likely to be senior managers or executives within an organization, other senior managers and executives can restrict the freedom to act when a crisis arises. Crisis managers consequently need to understand how organizational structure and culture can influence how a crisis may be handled.

Without this understanding, crisis managers may be impeded by the actions of other managers and staff. Many impediments may be avoided by informing all members of an organization of the crisis management actions to be undertaken and by determining ways around possible impediments when planning and preparing for managing crisis situations.

How organizations react to a crisis situation differs according to size, culture, experience and preparation. Many professional response agencies – such

199

as law enforcement, firefighting and paramedic – cope well with small and local critical problems. These critical problems are those that contain elements of crisis but do not place demands on resources greater than the resources available for use. With large and catastrophic crises – those that do demand more resources than are available – response agencies do not often adapt particularly well. Poor adaptability comes from the organizational red tape and legal requirements that surround them, as well as from an over-learned response behaviour that means their personnel will tend to react as if dealing with the smaller critical problems.

Stallings (1978) introduced a basic set of established, expanding, extending and emergent organizational structures that seem to be present when crisis situations arise. *Established organizations* are those crisis response organizations available on a day-to-day basis, such as law enforcers, firefighters and paramedics. *Expanding organizations* are organizations filled by volunteers who act as 'reserves' for assisting with or managing particular elements of a crisis. These organizations include the Red Cross (or Red Crescent), any civil defence or emergency services, and religious or community bodies such as the Salvation Army. These units 'expand' as the emergency situation demands and the volunteer members assemble for crisis response duties.

Extending organizations are those that are brought in to help in specific situations. These may be civil organizations that provide construction or clean-up crews or may include community groups (Rotary, Lions) or boy scouts and girl guides brought in to help clean up litter or convey messages. Extending units are organizations that normally have no crisis mission but meet specialist or support roles when requested. *Emergent organizations* are temporary or situational 'organizations' that arise from the circumstances of the crisis situation. These organizations or groups emerge during the crisis to manage the response.

From these four types of organization, Stallings (1978) makes some interesting points. First, the likely number of response organizations involved depends on the severity of a crisis situation. As the severity (or size) of the crisis increases, the likelihood increases that different types of organizations will be involved. For example, a car accident or building fire is readily managed by the three professional response agencies that take over from amateur bystanders. A large passenger aircraft accident, on the other hand, is likely to require a response from more organizations – from government investigation agencies to voluntary organizations providing refreshment and support for bystanders, victims, respondents and meeters-and-greeters. An earthquake or flood, however, will stretch the organized professional and volunteer organizational response, leading to local community and commercial organizations emerging to meet the response need.

While established organizations may find their personnel less flexible in dealing with large crisis situations, expanding organizations often face a problem due to their reserve role and volunteer membership. The role of many expanding organizations is usually loosely defined, their operational boundaries are vague, and the regular or full-time members may be less effective when they move from normal to crisis environments. Authority becomes stretched and inhibited in expanding organizations because there is little time for the expanded organization to consolidate their new authority structures and pre-crisis and unexpanded ways of operating remain.

Extending organizations have problems getting their members to assemble and tend to be hard for other organizations to control. These organizations generally have a local focus.

According to Stallings (1978) emergent groups are more likely to arise from the interaction of responding organizations than from the type of crisis or disaster. Emergent groups or organizations appear where lack of information, co-ordination and control seem to be lacking, or whenever people are isolated from professional response organizations. Emergent groups can be quite visible when rescue work is prominent. These groups can appear where lines of communication intersect, when there is a common perception of a need for co-ordinated action, and when information appears to be uncertain or problematic.

Crisis managers need to identify the likely types of organization involved in responding to particular crisis situations. By doing so, crisis managers can assess the key problems resident in each type of structure and can operationalize ways of coping with them when a crisis situation arises.

Structure and cultural aspects

National culture can add complexity to crisis management. Where some cultures favour individualistic responses, others need the shared decision making of a group. Three key interaction measures are outlined in Figure 9.1 below. These are:

- *Individualist/collectivist.* Does the culture generally focus on individual decision making, actions and satisfaction or is the culture more likely to encourage group (family and organizational) consensus decision making, action taking and satisfaction?
- *Uncertainty/certainty.* Is the culture more likely to function on being uniform and certain about how things are done or on being diverse and uncertain and accepting of different ways of how things may be done?
- *Power distance.* Does the culture emphasize formal authority and thus distance staff from managers and junior managers from senior managers, or does the culture place more emphasis on personal power and thus reduce these distances between members of an organization?

Crisis managers may find such referential tools helpful in dealing with actual crisis situations, when analyzing specific crisis responses and in dealing with transnational or global responses to a crisis. Many transnational and multinational organizations have crisis management teams that are geographically remote from the site of a crisis situation and staffed by members of a different culture. In these cases, executives and managers need to be

Country	Individualist/ collectivist	Uncertainty avoidance	Power distance
Australia	Individual	Moderate	Small
Austria	Individual	Strong	Small
Canada	Individual	Weak	Moderate
France	Individual	Strong	Large
Great Britain	Individual	Moderate	Small
Germany (West)	Individual	Strong	Small
India	Collectivist	Weak	Large
Israel	Individual	Strong	Small
Iran	Collectivist	Strong	Large
Italy	Individual	Strong	Moderate
Japan	Collectivist	Strong	Large
Netherlands	Individualist	Weak	Small
Singapore	Collectivist	Weak	Large
Switzerland	Individual	Strong	Small
United States	Individual	Weak	Small

Fig. 9.1 Three dimensions of cultural differences

(drawn from Hofestede, G. (1980) 'Motivation, leadership, and organization: do American theories apply abroad?', *Organizational Dynamics* (Summer), pp. 42–63).

sensitive to the likely ways in which personnel interact and approach problems. Where an American, Canadian or Australian may take an individualist look at a crisis response, other cultures (Japanese and Indian, for example) may use group-driven consensus approaches.

The inertia of structures and organizations

As organizations increase in size, the organizations seem to become more inert in their ability to receive and transmit information and to make decisions. This inertia can be a problem when a crisis is encountered. Inertia also appears to increase with:

● the greater the degree of rigidity and formality within the culture of the organization; and

• the greater the fear of post-crisis evaluation of actions and behaviours.

Inertia also may arise because of the unexpectedness and unpredictabilty of warnings and communications in the early stages of the onset of the crisis.

Drabek (1986) and Perry (1985) find that a sudden and unexpected message (especially of a threat to resources or people) may generate disbelief. Given such disbelief, decision makers and communication 'gatekeepers' (those who receive and pass on messages) may avoid any action choices other than to ignore the communication, to wait or to seek confirmation of the warning or threat. Many crisis situations show this characteristic. The refusal of the Civil Defence Duty Officer to believe the alarm about the explosion at Reactor 4 of the Chernobyl power station (*see* Chapter 6) illustrates this attitude.

Early information can be confusing and even contradictory in nature, and so reinforces response inertia. Any loss of communication facilities due to (or as a subsequent impact from) the crisis event can reduce the chances of confirmation or clarification of the original warnings or alerts. At least one site continued pumping oil through to the burning Piper Alpha platform because the duty engineer would not make an early shutdown command while trying to find out what was happening. His attempts to contact Piper Alpha were fruitless as the communications centre on Piper Alpha was destroyed early in the disaster.

As time passes, lack of ability to communicate may increase as communication systems fail due to overload (too many messages) and gridlock (incoming and outgoing messages block communication channels so that no new message can be transmitted). The equipment in these systems may also fail, and further reinforce inertia. Allinson (1993), for example, finds that 'crisis or disaster will strike at the weakest links of an organization, and the weakest links of an organization are those links where there is a stoppage of the flow of information' (p. 43).

In integrated responses that span several organizations or semi-autonomous divisions within an organization, stoppages generally arise between these organizations or divisions because of the use of different equipment, terminology and goals. Communications also fail when strangers are involved or when people who rarely interact with each other try to communicate vital information.

Crisis managers need to assess how inertia may affect the management and response to a crisis. By increasing the familiarity (*see* the FPC model in Chapter 12) with non-normal signals, managers can help the relevant organizational personnel become more willing to act when a crisis alert is signalled. Similarly, by trying to standardize equipment and terminology and by making communication systems redundant in capacity and as direct as possible, inertia due to failure to exchange information can be reduced.

Strategic preparedness

The effects of organizational inertia, time lags and the size of the crisis can be reduced through placing more attention on planning and preparedness at a strategic level. Strategic management helps reduce these effects by developing appropriate pre-event preparedness.

Strategic crisis management may be seen as a process involving environmental scanning, risk assessment, contingency planning, resource deployment and appropriate personnel development. These are interactive and dynamic elements that exert changes on each other. Deal with one element and the nature of the other elements will change. Over time, environments and risks change and resources deteriorate or become redundant. These changes affect an organization's state of readiness and ability to respond.

Robbins (1994) finds that executives and managers are 'putting less time into highly detailed, quantitative plans and instead are developing multiple scenarios of the future' (p. 193). Events that become dynamically complex become less predictable and thus need to be considered in terms of probable and worst-case scenarios. Crisis situations often arise from prevailing conditions within an environment. As a consequence, the amount of crisis resistance (or resilience) held by an organization may determine whether a crisis (as opposed to a critical problem) emerges and the severity of a situation if a crisis does arise. Environments may influence organizations and organizations may influence environments (Richardson, 1994).

On one level, for example, the structure of the organization and strategic deployment of resources to physical locations influences the subsequent speed and effectiveness of response. When resources and crisis respondents are placed close to where a crisis situation happens there is a greater probability of a fast and effective response to that crisis – provided that the resource base is relatively unaffected. Proximity and capability (enough resources and trained people) reduce the effects of a crisis.

Strategic crisis management

Strategic crisis management involves two key activities:

- establishing an acceptable fit of crisis management within the 'big picture' of the organization and the surrounding physical, social and political environment;
- developing the capacity to respond to potential crisis situations as these may arise.

These two activities roughly match the Reduction and Readiness and the Response and Recovery components of the RRRR model. Likewise the two activities respectively cover pre-crisis preparation and the capability and capacity to respond and recover when a crisis arises.

Effective pre-crisis preparation involves:

- determining the risks and needs involved;
- establishing the policies to reflect an effective way of dealing with these risks and needs;
- devising and erecting the structure of the crisis management response;
- appropriately deploying the crisis management response resources within a given environment.

The pre-crisis activities of strategic crisis management thus seek an optimal match between the available capability to respond to a crisis, the day-to-day organizational environment in which the crisis response structure exists, the structural needs of the crisis response effort and the high resource demands of dealing with a crisis.

Effective capability and capacity to respond and recover from a crisis involves:

- acquiring needed resources and skills to deal with crisis situations;
- developing plans that help resolve crisis situations;
- ensuring a quick and efficient translation of response and recovery strategies into tactical actions within the crisis situation; and
- providing the training to enable effective use of the resources and appropriate response actions in crisis situations.

Thus the capability and capacity activities need policies and procedures through which crisis situations can be effectively managed. Where pre-crisis activities reflect the setting up and maintenance of crisis management functions within an organization, the capacity and capability activities focus on responding to, and recovering from, crisis situations.

The ultimate goal of both activities is to free on-site response and recovery managers from structural and supply activities so that they are able to deal with the crisis situation.

This approach to strategic management can be seen in a letter written by General Grant, Commander of Union Forces, to General Sherman in the American Civil War. The letter outlines the policies for dealing with the crisis situation (war with the Southern States) and the crisis situations likely to arise in the campaign by the Union armies of the Northern States in 1864. Grant had already undertaken the pre-crisis strategic activity of determining the risks, establishing the response policies, developing the army structures, gaining the resources and deploying the Union Armies. He thus freed the army commanders from much of the supply and support distraction so that they could plan for, and implement, their parts of Grant's overall strategy. He then communicated the policies and requirements for the individual response armies. Grant wrote to Sherman:

It is my design, if the enemy keep quiet and allow me to take the initiative in the spring campaign, to work all parts of the army together and somewhat toward a common center. For your information I now write you my programme as at present determined upon.

I have sent orders to Banks by private messenger to finish up his present expedition against Shreveport with all despatch... With [his] force he is to commence operations against Mobile as soon as he can. It will be impossible for him to commence too early.

Gilmore joins Butler with 10,000 men, and the two operate against Richmond from the South side of the James River... I will stay with the Army of the Potomac, increased by Burnside's corps of not less than 25,000 effective men, and operate directly against Lee's army wherever it may be found.

Sigel collects all his available force in two columns ... to move against the Virginia and Tennessee...

You I propose to move against Johnstone's army, to break it up and to get into the interior of the enemy's country as far as you can, inflicting all the damage you can against their war resources.

I do not propose to lay down for you a plan of campaign, but simply to lay down the work it is desirable to have done, and leave you free to execute in your own way.
(Murray, 1992)

Three qualities of a good strategic manager are found in this letter. First, the directions and explanations are clear and simple. Grant communicates his vision ('my design', 'work all parts of the army together') and the overall direction ('toward a common center'). Second, there is a succinct and clear definition of the elements of the strategy (*'I have sent orders to Banks... to commence operations against Mobile...'; 'Gilmore joins Butler ... the two operate against Richmond on the South side of the James River...'; 'I will ... Sigel collects all his available force...'*). Grant then offers Sherman clear instructions on what he desires Sherman to accomplish (*'You I propose to move against Johnstone's army, to break it up and to get into the interior of the enemy's country as far as you can, inflicting all the damage you can against their war resources.'*) In so doing, Grant illustrates the third quality. Having defined Sherman's objectives, Sherman is freed to manage – *'I do not propose to lay down for you a plan of campaign, but simply to lay down the work it is desirable to have done, and leave you free to execute in your own way.'*

Good strategic crisis managers need to express their vision of the grand strategy for overall crisis management quickly, succinctly and in simple terms. The message needs to convey the precise goals and convey permission to then manage the situation as best can be done from the subordinate's understanding of the nature of their assigned task and the environment within which that task is to be undertaken.

So what are the elements involved in strategic crisis management?

Strategic management has two levels of concern. The higher level, often called *meta-strategy*, involves the determination of an overall strategy within which more situation-specific strategies may then be devised. Hence meta-strategic thinking involves two elements:

- determining an overall strategic goal;
- determining the operational content needed to achieve that goal.

The second level of strategic thinking involves devising the *process* (or how) these meta-strategies may be achieved. This means converting meta-strategies into operational strategies that conform to, and work to produce, the meta-strategic principles.

Once the operational strategies are communicated, crisis managers convert the strategies into *tactical* actions. Strategic management positions the resources and co-ordinates logistics and supplies, while tactical management undertakes the appropriate local actions likely to achieve the communicated strategic goal.

Suppose, for example, a community faces a major flood. The community meta-strategy is to preserve life and property. As a result, teams of response personnel deploy to enact three operational strategies – diversion or prevention of flooding by building walls of sandbags or levees of soil, evacuation of people and threatened resources, and acquisition of more accurate and relevant information. Tactical activities can be placing sandbags and barriers, using small boats to rescue people, or establishing better communication links with people measuring flood heights upstream.

Note that this approach reflects the *CrisisThink* principles of gaining time (slowing the impact of the flood down by building barriers), reducing costs (evacuating people and other resources) and getting more information. Strategic crisis management can follow the principles of *CrisisThink: how can I gain more time? how can I gain more information? how can I reduce the cost in resources?*

War as crisis management

Not surprisingly many of the approaches to managing crisis situations and for determining strategies come from professional response agencies and from military command. This is not so surprising on three fundamental levels. First, warfare is a critical problem that can produce a number of crisis situations. Second, warfare provides many examples of crisis management where success or defeat emerges from the ability of each combatant to respond to critical situations and demands upon their resources. Third, military and professional response agencies are involved in community and national crisis situations.

War provides useful hints on how to successfully regain control and resolve a crisis situation. Sun Tzu (a very successful Chinese general who wrote a doctrine on warfare, *The Art of War*, at the time of Confucius – around 400 BC) repeatedly emphasizes the need to prepare for any oncoming battle by knowing the ground on which to fight and having near-perfect information.

Napoleon and Wellington succeeded because they surveyed their environment very carefully, often exploring the topographical features of the region in person. Admiral Nelson and General Grant showed the effectiveness of having specific yet flexible plans. Their plans were specific in terms of intent and objectives and flexible in terms of how the intent and objectives were to be accomplished.

War management is crisis management

Management of war is a specialized version of crisis management. Even when a war is conducted over a long period of time (from months to decades) there are battles and events that become crisis situations. During the Second World War, for example, when the Allied forces were forced to retreat into the Dunkirk enclave in 1940 a crisis grew from the urgent need to evacuate as many of the troops as possible. This evacuation was one of many crisis incidents in that war.

As with crisis managers, military commanders often face demands that exceed the resources they have to meet those demands. Consequently they need to determine priorities of attention and establish how the overall process can be flexibly managed. Military commanders often need to communicate with those outside their command, and thus become information managers dealing with politicians, community leaders and representatives of media companies. Consequently military forces undertake crisis-like response and recovery activities.

Fog of war equals smog of crisis

Many commanders and commentators discuss the experience of war as being like shrouded in a fog. Many battlefields over the last few centuries have been covered in a fog of smoke, originally from the musket-fire from infantry formations packed tightly together. More recently, high explosives and chemical smoke add to the sense of a fog of smoke descending upon a battlefield or naval engagement.

The real meaning of the term 'fog of war' is found in the limited ability of army commanders to see what is happening once a battle started. In earlier centuries commanders literally lost sight of a battle due to weather or the smoke of guns. Commanders would select a central feature from which they and their general staff (the crisis management team) would manage the battle. In the course of the fighting much of the battlefield became increasingly invisible. As battlefields increased in size, any ability to see the course of a battle decreased. Commanders increasingly used maps and written orders as references and listened to reports on what was happening.

Contemporary wars and battles may range over thousands of kilometres. Commanders are increasingly dependent upon communications. Advances in satellite technology and in miniaturization of video and film technology allow commanders to see live footage of what is happening when those commanders may be hundreds or thousands of kilometres away from the scene.

Crisis management also involves a loss of information certainty and lack of situation visibility akin to war. This is not so surprising as war is a special form of crisis management. The fog of war becomes *the smog of crisis*.

The smog of crisis

Crisis 'smog' comes from three features that are present in every crisis situation. The smog, in fact, is a key reason for the sense of lost control that permeates crisis management, especially in the initial stages of a crisis response. Crisis managers lose 'sight' of the event and the impacts of that event. Crisis managers even contribute to the resulting smog through their interaction with the crisis event and the impact(s) of that event. The three features are:

- the *chaos in the environment* surrounding the crisis;
- the *distortions that arise from communication* systems operating under conditions of stress;
- the *cloud of cognitive uncertainty* that covers any manager's insight into what is happening and what best can be done.

The chaotic environment

A fundamental feature of a crisis is that the crisis situation overwhelms the surrounding environment and the human senses. Because people expect systems to behave in predictable ways to produce specified outcomes, systems that lack certainty of outcome and are unpredictable in process are deemed to be out of control (and thus threatening). *Loss of control* can be seen as the onset of uncertainty about what is happening and what predictable outcomes may emerge. Consequently crisis management may be described as the art of *regaining control* of a situation.

Smog can literally arise from the crisis. Smoke and noise from a crisis situation can form smog that promotes greater chaos. The ability of respondents and managers to think and communicate can diminish as their senses become overwhelmed by the sound and stimulation of a crisis. Similarly, a major crisis requiring different tactical responses can create a confusing picture to an onlooker. This distorted and confusing picture is often augmented by distorted communications.

Distorted communications

The features that help distort communications in a crisis situation include:

- people often mean different things in choosing particular words;
- the noise and bustle of a crisis can impede clear communication exchanges;
- communication systems often fail.

Smog from distorted communications is not physically obvious, although signals of the onset of smog can be present. Some possible signals of increasing crisis smog include:

- increasingly expressed frustration;
- raised voices;
- repeated requests for information;
- hesitant decision making.

The end result of communication smog is an increase in cognitive uncertainty and consequent poor and delayed decision making. Communication smog can be reduced by using common terminology, having sufficient working communication systems, and by designing crisis management structures that remove confusion of tasks and enhance certainty of information.

Cognitive uncertainty

Cognitive uncertainty emerges from the combination of being unable to see clearly all the elements of a crisis situation and from the lack of hard or certain information available to executives and managers. Managers and executives may handle cognitive uncertainty by refusing to make decisions, focusing only on one aspect of a decision task or by taking a quick stab at solving the situation. In any of these cases a crisis manager dramatically increases the risk of worsening the crisis.

So what can be done about the smog of crisis?

The smog of crisis will always be present in a crisis. A situation is unlikely to be a crisis if the situation does not produce uncertainty, uncertain or missing information and unexpected or unwanted outcomes and impacts. Crisis smog is a cognitive product that comes from distortions of our senses. In simple terms, the smog of crisis is ultimately inside our heads. This is one reason why members of post-crisis inquiries find it difficult to place themselves in the situation of victims and respondents.

A number of actions can help reduce the effects of the smog of crisis. First, managers and respondents can try to reduce the stimuli that distort our senses. By eliminating or reducing those distracting stimuli some of the sensory load that contributes to a feeling of enclosing smog can be removed.

Second, respondents and managers can prepare themselves for the stimuli that help create the smog of crisis. This is done by learning to cope better with crisis situations through planning and training for their likely onset and resolution. Planning and training increases the familiarity with the possible stimuli and effects involved in the crisis situation. Consequently managers and respondents feel able to predict some or all of the effects and the nature of the crisis situation and thus learn to allow for (or shut out) the distracting smog of crisis.

The smog of crisis can also be reduced by:

- using dedicated communication systems that secure the system from interference and other users;
- developing additional or alternative communication systems – including use of messengers;
- using weatherproofed communication and command centres that are large enough to reduce the noise of crowds;
- the development and training of specialist information 'scouts' (*see* Chapter 10).

Realistic training can also reduce the distractions of background noise and other stimuli produced by a crisis by acclimatizing respondents to likely crisis environments. This is why the military undertake 'live ammunition' training in geographical terrain similar to a likely operational territory, firefighters use 'smoke rooms' and other controlled environments to provide experience of smoke and heat while undertaking assigned tasks, and airline and airforce pilots train in flight simulators.

From a strategic perspective, two complementary approaches help reduce the effects of a crisis on response and response management. These approaches are redundancy and specialization. *Redundancy* approaches involve having more systems or elements in place than may be needed. Aircraft and ships, for example, often have extra struts and bulkheads added to provide more strength and impact resistance. Redundancy in communication systems may mean sending messages by more than one system, having back-up systems and appliances, or even having alternative ways of communicating.

Specialization approaches involve assigning resources or people to specific tasks, such as information gathering, transmission and collation, or maintaining breathing apparatus. Specialization enables specific people to give greater attention to a small number of tasks that, in turn, enable a more robust and smog-controlled management and response.

Both strategies and the previously outlined skills and actions improve the capacity of executives, managers and respondents to focus more clearly upon dealing with the crisis situation.

Crisis management

In Chapter 1 four broad areas of crisis management were described in the RRRR model. These areas were:

- Reduction
- Readiness
- Response
- Recovery.

The RRRR model provides a 'what to do' foundation for crisis management. Managers and executives need a structure (whether physical and/or conceptual) within which crisis management can be organized. Simply relying on existing organizational structures and processes is unlikely to be adequate. As noted earlier, existing structures tend to impede response and recovery action decisions. Disasters or crisis situations need to be seen as more than just big accidents. These situations may produce a different social order and cannot be managed by the same organizational structures used to deal with day-to-day operations and accidents (Quarantelli, 1995). Taking Quarantelli's observation to a logical conclusion crisis management needs a fluid and adaptable structure that meets the needs and demands of each crisis situation.

Whether practitioners use PPRR, MPRR or RRRR models (*see* Chapter 1), there is a strong probability that response and recovery activity clusters are overemphasized at the expense of the mitigation and prevention activities. Such emphases illustrate a reactive approach to crisis management that is non-optimal. Allinson (1993) sees such emphasis on response and recovery action planning as essentially *band-aid* in nature. He argues that greater attention to communication and prevention measures would reduce many business-type crises. In some cases this is quite true. However, natural disasters and human error are likely to require band-aid management on a regular basis.

Towards crisis management

Nearly everyone involved in crisis management has some concept of how to construct and staff a crisis management group. Most of these concepts have common crucial elements which can include:

- a preference for the crisis manager to be as senior as possible;
- a preference for the crisis manager to be capable of managing the crisis;
- the need for fixed membership so that everyone knows who does what;
- the need for flexibility or adaptability because of the demands of crisis situations;
- a strong focus on command and control structures;
- the need to co-ordinate the efforts of diverse groups in large-scale crisis situations.

Not surprisingly these crucial elements tend to form pairs of conflicting requirements. Seniority does not necessarily mean capability to manage crises nor does fixed membership lead to flexibility of approach (or vice versa). Most managers with command and control backgrounds – military, law enforcement, firefighting, paramedic – find co-ordination difficult. They tend to command and control the total effort. Within their own organization the organizational culture may accept command and control. Once combined service operations arise, however, high levels of facilitation and communication skills are needed. Orders are not sufficient. In community and business or industry settings, management by command and control alone will probably fail as too many independent and loosely structured groups are likely to be involved. On the other hand, crisis management needs quick and decisive action that does not occur when consensus and co-operative management approaches are used. Therein exists a central problem of crisis management.

Fast decision making is most likely to come from single decision makers who exert authority in centralized structures. In other words, *crisis situations require a central commander to whom (and through whom) all information and decision making is placed*. This requirement suggests that a senior manager running a specific group of people in a command and control setting would provide the best crisis management.

Most crisis situations, however, are beyond the management of a single person or a small unit. Moreover, many crisis situations require specialist responses from different groups of people. Diverse groups of people are likely to resist and resent command and control from a person outside their group, and are likely to be more motivated when they have input into the decisions about what they do. Groups with important specializations are likely to use the importance of the specialization to operate as they see fit rather than as an outside manager may require. From this POV, *responses to crisis situations require consultation and decentralized decision making to make full and effective use of all respondents*. This requirement suggests that a crisis manager who uses decentralized and consultative decision making and co-ordination rather than command and control will generate a more motivated and goal-directed effort from respondents, and thus offer the best crisis management.

The reality of crisis management is that it needs highly motivated respondents operating in a flexible yet robust decision environment that uses both authoritarian and democratic decision processes. The skill is to find the balance between speed of decision and involvement in the decision by all those connected with it, and between enabling field managers to manage parts of the crisis situation and working toward the same central goal or set of goals. One fundamental way of combining these apparently opposite requirements is to use participative management in reduction and readiness stages – the pre-crisis components of crisis management. By effective participation in the planning stages, the response and recovery components can become co-ordinated actions of already self-selected and agreed task management that accepts the direction and support of command and control teams.

This brief discussion highlights one of the central issues involved in crisis management – making timely and appropriate decisions in an environment full of distractions, noise and disruption. Before an appropriate crisis management approach can be established executives and managers need to identify the decision-making styles they need to use.

A quick guide to models of decision making

Crisis management involves two forms of decision making – pre-crisis and crisis decision making. Pre-crisis decision making needs to be participative and optimal. Crisis decision making needs to be as optimal as possible, is likely to be restricted in terms of including all personnel involved, and may need to incorporate decision aids. Where as in non-crisis settings time can be taken to assess and evaluate all options carefully, time is very limited in crisis situations. Crisis decision-making processes need to:

- reduce time loss to allow more time for enacting the decisions;
- help evaluate the options; and
- lead to an acceptable decision.

Efforts that help find more time are discussed further in Chapter 13. Decision tools like OMT and RPP (*see* Chapter 13) help managers by substituting pre-planned actions and pre-learned decision option tools for complex and time-consuming activities. These substitutes need to be carefully designed and robustly constructed for use in the field.

Pre-crisis decision making

Where time is available and information is fairly concrete and complete, decision making needs to be made optimal through associative and combinative decision assessment. This form of decision making takes eight steps or stages:

1 Identify the problem or need for a decision.
2 Identify the criteria or 'facts' of the decision.
3 Determine the means of assessing the criteria or facts, including assignment of 'weights'.
4 Determine and define alternatives (or choices or answers).
5 Analyse the alternatives or choices.
6 Select an alternative or choice.
7 Implement the alternative or choice.
8 Evaluate decision process and outcome impact of decision.

This process represents a typical attempt to systematically make a decision.

Identify the problem or need for decision making

Most decisions start with a perceived problem that is often an apparent gap between a desired situation and an actual situation. Decision makers can:

- make a decision or choice;
- choose not to make a decision or choice; or
- ignore the need to make a decision.

Any identification of a need for a decision is consequently most likely to be subjective in nature, relying on decision makers being aware a problem exists.

Identify criteria or 'facts'

Decision makers need to define the decision. As noted in Chapters 2 and 3, care needs to be taken in asking the question that covers the problem. Changes in words, emphasis or data can lead to different options and choices.

Decision makers often rush toward deducing alternatives or choices before fully understanding and exploring the terms and assumptions in the decision-prompting question. Thus decision makers need to look at the meanings they assign terms used to define the decision they need to make. For example, decision makers looking at the decision 'Where do we place a firefighting station?' need to analyze a number of assumptions including 'we need to place a fire station somewhere' and 'a firefighting station needs a place of its own'. A list of questions may lead to a better defined decision. Some of these questions would be:

- *Who are those people included in the 'we'? Are these the appropriate people to make the decision? Are there other people who can provide appropriate information for this decision?*
- *What is a firefighting station? How big is it? What does such a station need to be effective? Is such a station necessary?*
- *What is the meaning of 'where' in the context of this decision? Is this an initial firefighting station, or a replacement firefighting station, or an additional firefighting station? What is the area expected to be covered by this station? What are the likely types of fires to which this station needs to respond?*

Good analysis of the decision question or proposition often clarifies and determines the content, and thus the criteria, for making a decision choice.

Decision makers often complicate a decision by seeking an infinite set of criteria. Useful criteria are those elements that are clearly seen as contributing to the desired outcome. While a search for all likely criteria is necessary, the criteria then need to be evaluated for contribution toward outcome. In selecting a site for a firefighting service, less useful criteria may be siting the station as close as possible to where the firefighters live. Over time, people and addresses will change thus making this a poor criterion and not worth including on the list.

Assessment of the criteria

In being systematic and consistent, the same measures and meanings for each criterion should be applied across the perceived alternatives or choices. In most cases, however, decision makers use assessments made on one or a few criteria or make evaluations across criteria and add them up into a single integrated value. The optimal choice is then usually the option with the greatest single integrated value.

Sometimes multiple criteria can distort the decision. As an example, take a decision to acquire protective gear for firefighters. Core criteria may be seen as the degree of protection offered, ease of putting on, comfort, ease of supply, cost, reputation of supplier, style, and compatibility with tools and accessories carried and worn by firefighters. Half the criteria are user-defined (protection, comfort, compatibility, ease in putting on), while the other half are acquisition-defined (cost, reputation, supply, style). Values for the acquisition criteria may bias a decision toward a less protective and useful outfit. To reduce this bias, decision makers intuitively or deliberately make some criteria more important than others. This is called *weighting* the decision variables or criteria.

Weighting can involve any numeric system so long as the selected system is applied consistently. In selecting the firefighter gear, the eight criteria may be weighted more strongly towards protectiveness and comfort, and less strongly in terms of style. Thus assigned weights may appear as:

40	*Protection*
15	*Comfort*
10	*Compatibility*
10	*Ease of putting on*
10	*Cost*
5	*Supply*
5	*Reputation*
5	*Style*

In this case, the decision is shaped toward the degree of protection offered the user (40 out of 100) and the usefulness to the user (75 out of 100). This set of weights reflects less concern for style, cost and source of supply, and far greater concern for the safety of those wearing the gear.

Determining and developing alternatives or choices

The next step for systematic decision making is to generate as wide a set of alternatives or choices as possible. To some extent this set is uncovered by the analysis of the prompting decision statement and by the selection of evaluation criteria. Some choices or alternatives readily appear, while others need to be actively uncovered and considered.

Three questions help shape a fuller set of alternatives and choices. These questions are:

- Do we need to make this decision?
- Do we need to make this decision now?
- Can we decide not to make a decision?

These three questions rebalance most decision makers from a tendency to make decisions simply because action choices are available. The questions offer a choice of negating, deferring and deciding not to decide.

Overall, the object of this stage is to generate all the possible alternatives, options and choices. This can be accomplished by brainstorming, asking informal groups for advice and more formal processes.

Analysis of alternatives or choices

Once the most complete set of alternatives or choices has been generated, decision makers need to evaluate these for their contribution toward effectively resolving the problem.

In many situations, decision makers use simple weights to reflect the importance or relevance of criteria by multiplying the raw score by the respective weight, then summing the modified scores for each alternative or choice across the criteria. In the example of choosing protective gear for firefighters such simple models may generate the outcomes presented in Table 9.1 where four choices are assessed.

Table 9.1 A weighted decision model for protective gear for firefighters

Criteria*	ABC Firewear	Protect Ltd	People Protection Wear	CoolGuard Systems
Protection	7 × 40 = 280	5 × 40 = 200	8 × 40 = 320	7 × 40 = 280
Comfort	7 × 15 = 105	8 × 15 = 120	5 × 15 = 75	8 × 15 = 120
Compatibility	8 × 10 = 80	7 × 10 = 70	5 × 10 = 50	8 × 10 = 80
Ease to put on	6 × 10 = 60	7 × 10 = 70	4 × 10 = 40	5 × 10 = 50
Cost (cheap)	8 × 10 = 80	7 × 10 = 70	3 × 10 = 30	8 × 10 = 80
Ease of supply	10 × 5 = 50	7 × 5 = 35	2 × 5 = 10	4 × 5 = 20
Reputation	5 × 5 = 25	6 × 5 = 30	10 × 5 = 50	8 × 5 = 40
Style	6 × 5 = 30	7 × 5 = 35	6 × 5 = 30	5 × 5 = 25
Total	710	630	605	695

*All criteria scored on a 1 = very bad to 10 = excellent scale.

In Table 9.1, a local supplier, ABC Firewear, appears to be the best overall choice. While the protectiveness was not as good as the product supplied by People Protection Wear, the degree of comfort, compatibility with equipment and ease of putting on the protective gear was superior. Note that Coolguard Systems provided the best user-defined choice, but was less able to meet acquisition-defined criteria.

Selection of best alternative or choice

As illustrated in Table 9.1, aggregate decision models generate a highest score for the best choice. When scores are close, re-evaluate the alternatives or choices to check the accuracy of the final selection. Check that the criteria and weights being used are appropriate.

If time is available, a review of criteria and weights may prove beneficial at this point. When aggregate or integrative models are employed users can find that some of the choices and alternatives turned out to be inappropriate, or other criteria appeared relevant, or that criteria or weights of criteria were not appropriate. Be careful, however, about changing the decision model, as decision makers can feel weights or criteria were wrong simply because intuitively favoured choices or selections scored poorly.

Implementing selection

Sometimes decision makers believe that their task is finished once the decision has been taken. Implementation means that decision makers convey the decision outcome to those affected and those undertaking the activities surrounding the decision. Implementation also means checking to see that the enactment processes of that decision are undertaken.

Evaluate decision process and outcome impact of decision

Many decision makers forget to spend time reviewing the two products of the systematic decision-making process. First, decision makers need to review the process(es) used to generate the decision outcome. Each of the stages outlined above needs critical consideration so that decision makers can improve their decision making. Likewise, the impact of the decision needs to be reviewed. Key questions here include:

- *What happened?*
- *Did the selection prove successful?*
- *How did the decision affect those involved?*
- *If the decision selection proved less than expected, why?*

The goal is to establish objectively the consequent impact and effect of the decision.

Decision making in crisis conditions

Many decision-making models are based on an assumption that decision makers are rational. *Rational decision making* in this context assumes that:

- the decision or problem statement is clear and unambiguous;
- a well-defined goal is sought;
- all facts and consequences are known and certain;
- preferences are clear and consistent across time;
- time and cost constraints over the decision-making process do not exist;
- the final choice will maximize economic payoffs.

Under these conditions, decision making approaches an ideal state that is not likely to be found in many management settings. In crisis situations, time is limited, information is missing or uncertain, costs are likely to be rising and unpredictable, and demand for resources will appear to be exceeding the available resources. Rational decision-making models are unlikely to be naturally used and would appear to be too complex and time-consuming to be properly applied.

Rationality is quite limited in real decision environments. Solutions and problem or decision statements tend to be mixed together. This is why decision makers need to analyze the frames of reference and terms used in the decision-prompting question. The culture of an organization may distort decision-maker perceptions that lead to blindspots in which managers and executives sometimes will not see what they believe cannot be there. Decision makers may even increase their commitment to a poor decision rather than seek new alternatives or choices.

In reality, decision making is more likely to resemble some form of *bounded rationality*. Decision makers are likely construct simplified models rather than complex ones. In many cases, decision makers may make *satisficing* decisions in which the first alternative or choice that meets acceptable levels of criteria evaluation is adopted. This saves time and effort, although optimality of choice selection and outcome is sacrificed.

Recently several natural approaches to real-world decision making have been suggested. Klein et al. (1993) find traditional normative models (as outlined above) unsatisfactory in that these focus on option generation and simultaneous evaluation which is not reflected in what the authors termed *naturalistic decision-making environments* (NDM). The NDM environments are characterized by:

- dynamic and continually changing conditions;
- real-time reactions to the changes;
- ill-defined goals and ill-structured tasks;
- people with knowledge.

Decision making in NDM environments involves the above four characteristics plus:

- uncertain, ambiguous and missing data;
- shifting and conflicting goals;
- time pressure;
- high stakes;
- multiple players;
- organizational culture and norms.

This perception reflects much of our daily decision making. Even more strongly, the ten NDM characteristics mirror conditions found in crisis decision making. Consequently some theorists and researchers (e.g. Frederico, 1995; Klein et al., 1993) suggest a concept called *recognition primed decision making (RPD)*.

RPD models focus on how experienced decision makers determine appropriate courses of action. The focus thus falls on:

- situation assessment;
- satisficing rather than optimizing;

- serial generation and evaluation of options;
- mental simulation of option choice for workability;
- elaboration and improvement of option;
- being primed to act.

Proponents of RDP claim this focus reflects real-world decision making. The result has been a number of training courses in professional response agencies based on RPD.

Interestingly, these arguments re-invent the 'decision-making research' wheel. For more than 30 years researchers and decision makers have argued for and against static versus dynamic environments and optimality models versus subjective determination models. Neither approach fully encompasses an effective result for real-world decision making. This failure is due to the constraints built into each approach by the assumptions made by the users. Optimality models, for example, detach the decision maker from an inter-active environment. These approaches consume much time (which is in lim-ited supply in crisis situations) and require near perfect information (which is unlikely in crisis situations).

Subjective determination models, such as NDM and RPD appear to support, assume that consensual expert knowledge equals a good satisficing outcome. There can be a deal of difference (and subsequent inquiry proceedings and lit-igation) between the best possible choice of action and one which just satis-fices because the choice more or less works. Moreover, many satisficing decision choices are 'first cab' actions – ones which appear first as the most workable. Users of RPD approaches may also tend toward delivering inflexible 'book decisions' that can be wrong in a given set of circumstances. RPD would be acceptable when applied by earnest, experienced and flexible practitioners. Unhappily, the reality of training in RPD alone is that average people with limited experience and flexibility will apply half-understood principles in a crisis situation. Seat-of-the-pants actions are likely to emerge. These actions may or may not work, or may reflect a specific training example that is less appropriate to the crisis.

What is really needed is a compromise between the two positions. Where time and information is plentiful, any approach that seeks an optimal out-come is more likely to generate near-optimal outcomes. Hence the reduction and readiness stages of crisis management can usefully apply optimality approaches. When time and information is uncertain or in short supply, then we need to accept that the human decision maker is more likely to reflect an NDM environment and probably an RPD approach. To counterbalance group-think, mindsets and personal cognitive decision-making flaws, three useful training and practice elements could be added:

1 Ensure decision makers gain experience in the option generation and evaluation processes suggested by approaches like RPD – where experience mediates with mental practice in quickly generating and evaluating options.

2 Establish skill-techniques that seek to increase time and information made available so that decision makers can search beyond the first workable action.

3 Develop decision tools that aid rational and optimal judgements while being quick to use and reflecting RPD approaches and NDM environments.

These practical emphases move action-choices in crisis situations toward better and more defensible decision making that can lead to effective crisis management.

Decision making in the real world is often based upon heuristic (rule-based) short cuts that may omit important information. Decision makers also can encounter psychological reactions (*see* Chapter 14) that lead to decision distraction or freezing. The stress involved in the situation and in making decisions in a crisis environment may affect the decisions being made. Brehmer (1996), for example, outlines three pathologies of decision making that may occur when decision makers are under stress. These three pathologies are described as:

- vagabonding (flitting from goal to goal, also known as butterflying);
- encystment (focusing on one goal at the expense of others); and
- refusal (not making any decisions).

These decision pathologies can also precipitate crisis situations.

Vagabonding

This pathology may be hidden in what appears to be either encystment (focusing on one decision, the last apparently touched upon) or refusal (no apparent decision made). Decision makers suffering this pathology seem to flutter erratically from issue to issue and from 'fact' to 'fact'.

Encystment

This pathology can cause crisis situations to develop. As an example, some aircraft accidents may have happened due to crew focusing on a specific issue or concern to the exclusion of other issues and concerns. The Eastern Airlines Lockheed Tristar crash at Miami (Flight 401) in December 1972 and the United Airlines DC8 crash at Portland in December 1978 (both in the USA) were mostly due to an increasing preoccupation on whether the undercarriages of the aircraft were lowered and locked for landing. The Tristar simply drifted into the ground as the crew failed to note that the autopilot was locked into a gentle descent mode. The DC8 ran out of fuel.

In response management, many instances of encystment are likely to become buried by the resulting impact damage. The Hillsborough crowd crush disaster, for example, may be seen as having elements of encystment and refusal. Certainly the mindset of the law enforcement agency that was focused on preventing a pitch invasion led to slow recognition of the crowd crush situation. Lord Justice Peter Taylor, who chaired the inquiry into the Hillsborough disaster, found that the overall commander 'froze' (1989, p. 50).

221

This perception that group mindsets can lead to disasters brought Janis (1983) to propose a concept called *groupthink*. Characteristics of groupthink include:

- a lack of search for all data and all answers;
- a reluctance by any group member to oppose a course of action;
- aggressive support of a choice by one or more senior members of a group;
- stereotypic views of situations and people;
- an illusion of unanimity;
- an illusion of being right and invulnerable.

Managers and executives need to develop strategies to counter groupthink decisions. Such strategies may include:

- searching for the underlying assumptions and POVs;
- encouraging dissent that is more than rejection of an option;
- deliberately considering the worst-case outcomes for each option;
- using sub-groups rather than one key group to generate solutions and to analyze the possible good and bad outcomes of these solutions.

These are by no means an exhaustive set of strategies to counter groupthink. Three particular groupthink-related mindsets to avoid are:

- conventional wisdom;
- book answers; and
- 'last time' experience.

The main problem with using any of these mindsets is that decision makers shift from looking at the detail of the actual problem to looking at only those details that fit the approach. All major wars tend to be fought on concepts based on the previous major war because the commanders are hampered by 'last time' experience and war college 'book answers'. Community and business decision makers may often look for conventional wisdom (how most 'experts' and experienced personnel see situations should be managed) and overlook the idiosyncrasies and unique elements resident in their particular organizations, the surrounding environment and the likely crisis situations. Crisis management entails using past experience, contemporary planning and training, and a readiness to see the situation as it is.

REALITY BITE

Piper Alpha, 1988

Background

Much oil production comes from the dry areas of the Middle East or from offshore areas off southern USA, Scotland and Norway. Offshore production faces crises from the weather (and consequently the sea) and from the volatile potential of oil and gas, as well as complications from people-caused problems.

Piper Alpha was a 34 000-ton oil rig platform over 190 kilometres (120 miles) northeast of Aberdeen, Scotland. The platform commenced operations in 1975, run by Occidental Petroleum. A crew of over 200 worked 12 hour shifts to produce an estimated 167 000 barrels of crude oil and 23 million cubic feet of natural gas a day. The accommodation module – made of wood and fibreglass – was housed directly over the main production area, unlike Norwegian platforms where the accommodation is placed on a separate platform or as far away from the production area as possible (and shielded by blast walls). The British government had permitted the wood and fibreglass accommodation modules as a temporary measure that would be replaced by the appropriate steel modules and fire protection walls. One module had been replaced.

Incident

On 3 July, production routine on Piper Alpha changed. Excess gas was being burned off. On 6 July, maintenance work commenced around the gas condensate pumps. A technician removed the pressure safety valve on Pump A, closing the open pipes with special flanges. The valve was serviced but could not be returned immediately because the crane needed to shift the valve was being used elsewhere. A change of shift occurred at 18.00 (6.00 pm) and work proceeded as if the valve had been restored. Automatic fire suppression equipment had been switched to manual controls because divers were working in the surrounding waters.

By 21.45 (9.45 pm) on 6 July 1988, the gas processing system began to display non-normal system behaviour. At 21.58 (9.58 pm) a large amount of gas led to a large explosion in Module C. The pressure safety valve that could shut down production was lost in this explosion, as were the manual controls to close down the production. Moments later a further explosion set the platform on fire. All the platform's communication systems were destroyed.

At 22.22 (10.22 pm), the largest explosion occurred as gas pipes leading into Piper Alpha exploded. Flames from the fire were estimated to reach 120 metres (135 yards) in height. A support barge, *Tharos*, had to move away to avoid catching fire. Many platform personnel died, others jumped into the sea. Those in the sea without survival suits had less than five minutes to be rescued before the intense cold sapped their lives.

Response

As the *Tharos* moved away, smaller boats (Z ships) were dispatched from two trawlers (converted into work boats) to rescue survivors. At least one of these boats, half filled with survivors, was incinerated in a gas fireball.

The response from those on land seemed slow. The first helicopter arrived an hour after the explosion. Survivors came ashore intermittently. Several survivors wished to make personal calls home to their families but were not allowed to do so.

As the home port for Piper Alpha was Aberdeen (Scotland), the Grampian Police and the Procurator Fiscal (the Scottish equivalent of a coroner) began collecting and identifying bodies and commenced investigations into the event.

Red Adair (the premier oil troubleshooter in the world) was brought in to cap the flow of oil and gas. Over 80 per cent of the rig was destroyed, leaving a cluttered and dangerous structure on which the Adair team had to quell individual fires before sealing off leaking wells. The operation started on 9 July. Within two weeks they had quelled the fires and capped the wells.

Statistics
Only 62 survived out of 228 on board the rig when the accident occurred.

Comment
Some interesting data exists on safety in North Sea (Scotland–Norway) oil and gas production. Smallman (1994) reports that only 2 per cent of accidents occur in the actual work of extracting oil and gas. Around 12 per cent of accidents happen while people are transported to and from a platform, and 86 per cent of accidents happen in or close to living quarters. These figures are influenced by three major events that killed many workers – the crash of a Chinook helicopter in 1986 (45 dead), the Alexander L. Kielland structural failure off Norway in 1980 (123 dead) and the Piper Alpha fire.

The Piper Alpha fire had the first specifically designed offshore oil multipurpose barge, the *Tharos*, nearby. The barge was a twin-hulled self-propelled barge that had accommodation for 300 people, an 88-bed hospital, decompression chambers for divers and four computer-controlled thrust propellers that stabilized the vessel according to sea conditions. The barge had fire monitors (virtually water canon) that could pump 40 000 gallons of water (over 70 000 litres) per minute a distance of 80 yards (73 metres). In responding to the fire, a response crew primed these monitors too quickly and lost much of this water volume. The gantry structure that could have helped to rescue some personnel took far too long to extend to be of use. In the end, the *Tharos* could only assist in retrieving survivors from the surrounding water.

Management perspective
This example shows a clear division between crisis event (gas explosion) and the immediate crisis impacts (fire and immersion in freezing seas). Likewise, the example illustrates the escalating nature of crisis. Only 13 minutes spanned the time from irregularities in performance and the first response-crippling explosion. Note that the first explosion wrecked manual controls and communication equipment while automatic fire-suppression mechanisms had been turned off because divers had been in the water. These factors surely should have been considered in a worst-case scenario.

The Piper Alpha case shows signs of a response lag when non-normal signals were received. People tend to seek confirmatory information before acting. In the Piper Alpha example, confusion over the level of seriousness of the event caused some delays. Some reports (e.g. Cook, 1989) suggest that gas from other wells was allowed to flow through to Piper Alpha for an hour after the first explosion.

Site and structure design also plays a part in physical disaster crisis situations. Management needs to remember the benefits of safe design as a means of reducing impact damage. As with the Coode Island chemical storage fire (*see* Chapter 10) where the water suppression system was destroyed within the first few explosions, the explosion on Piper Alpha quickly eliminated both control and command and fire-suppression centres which were almost directly above the probable initial explosion site. With these systems out, and thus no command and control communication working on Piper Alpha, individuals and small groups had to make local decisions based on limited knowledge. Most of those who survived did so by breaking a 'rule' about jumping 100 feet (32 metres) into a very cold ocean.

Response management is almost always criticized about the slowness of response. This is particularly likely when response locations are distant from the situation. Part of the reason for such criticism resides in the psychological impact crisis situations tend to have on those caught in the situation – minutes can feel like hours. Another part of the reason may be the time lags between exchanges of information along the warning and then the response information channels (see Chapter 5). A third reason for slow response may arise through the need to change or add specific equipment on general purpose vehicles (such as helicopters). Given the delays for confirming the alert, checking aircraft systems and modifying internal cabin configuration, such time lags can be expected. No matter where a crisis arises, the vital first few moments have to be handled by those on site – many of whom are likely to be suffering some shock and some distress.

Executives and managers also need to be careful about how their response appears to those around them and to the outside world via the media. When Armand Hammer, the chairman of Occidental, arrived from America he promised that all affected Occidental workers would receive £100 000 compensation. This statement was taken to mean all workers on the rig would get this compensation – which was not to be the case. Only 31 of those killed on the rig were Occidental employees – the rest were contractors and thus not eligible. The media and victim hostility to Hammer and Occidental management consequently increased.

Other actions by Occidental led to accusations of insensitivity. On the anniversary of the accident, only the families of the unrecovered 31 victims were invited to pay their respects at the Piper Alpha site. Those not invited felt angered by the apparent rejection. When Aberdeen Council decided to establish a rose garden within which a memorial to the dead of Piper Alpha could be placed, Occidental management declined to contribute, claiming that there should not be a proliferation of memorials. Such actions tend to leave a negative impression.

The Piper Alpha crisis was a key factor in Occidental's decision to leave the offshore oil and gas production industry. Crisis situations can change an organization and its mission.

References

Allinson, R. E. (1993) *Global Disasters: Inquiries into Management Ethics*. New York: Prentice-Hall.

Brehmer, B. (1996) 'Dynamic and distributed decision making', *Journal of the Fire Service College*, 1(2), 211–41.

Cook, J. (1989) *An Accident Waiting to Happen*. London: Unwin Books.

Drabek, T. E. (1986) *Human System Responses to Disaster*. New York: Springer-Verlag.

Frederico, P. (1995) 'Expert and novice recognition of similar situations', *Human Factors*, 37(1), 105–22.

Janis, I. L. (1983) *Groupthink*. Boston: Houghton Mifflin.

Klein, G., Orasanu, J., Calderwood, R. and Zsambok, C. (eds) (1993) *Decision Making in Action*. New York: Abbex.

Murray, W. (1992) 'What took the North so long?' in Cowley, R. (ed.), *Experience of War*. New York: Norton, pp. 177–86.

Perry, R. W. (1985) *Comprehensive Emergency Management*. Greenwich, Conn.: JAI Press.

Quarantelli, E. L. (1995) 'Disasters are different, therefore planning for and managing them requires innovative as well as traditional behaviours', in *Proceedings of the Third Emergency Planning and Disaster Management Conference*. Lancaster: Lancaster University.

Richardson, B. (1994) 'Crisis management and management strategy – Time to "loop the loop"?' *Disaster Prevention and Management*, 3(3), 59–80.

Robbins, S. P. (1994) *Management*, 4th edn. Englewood Cliffs, NJ: Prentice Hall.

Smallman, C. (1994) 'Offshore safety management systems: current practice and a prescription for change', *Disaster Prevention and Management*, 3, 33–48.

Stallings, R. A. (1978) 'The structural patterns of four types of organisations in disaster', in Quarantelli, E. L. (ed.), *Disasters: Theory and Research*. London: Sage, pp. 87–103.

Taylor, P. (1989) *The Hillsborough Stadium Disaster: Interim Report*. London: HMSO (Home Office).

chapter 9
EXERCISE

Now that you have covered aspects of communication (Chapter 6), media (Chapter 7) and image management (Chapter 8), and have been introduced to some of the basic concepts of crisis management, return to the Exercise outlined at the end of Chapter 5. Try this exercise using the concepts and knowledge you have gained.

When you have finished the exercise, critically consider the strategies and actions you made and the consequent outcomes. Should you be doing this exercise in a small group, discuss your impressions and criticisms. Remember to acknowledge the positive aspects as well as analyze any 'what went wrong' aspects. If you have already performed the exercise in Chapter 5 and have kept records of what you did and your post-exercise analysis of what was effectively and ineffectively accomplished, compare the outcomes and feelings held then with the outcomes and feelings after doing this exercise. What was done better or worse? Were the outcomes better? Where? How? What led to this difference? Once again you may wish to consider the brief comments made on this exercise on pp. 447–8 in Appendix 2 to help generate your analysis and discussion.

Ways of undertaking crisis management

This chapter explores some existing perceptions on how crisis management operations may be designed before outlining an approach that encompasses more of the full crisis management task activities.

Some suggestions about crisis management structures

Theorists and practitioners generally agree that crisis management needs to be conducted through a central focal point (usually a crisis manager or incident commander). Where crisis situations are complex and/or large, most practitioners and theorists accept the need for a crisis management team that co-ordinates and/or controls the approaches adopted in dealing with the crisis and the impacts produced by that crisis. Just how the organizational structure for the response and the management team composition are integrated into a strong yet flexible unit depends on how the theorist or user views the mission of the crisis management response.

Meyers and Holusha (1986), for example, prefer *ad hoc teams* that are called together by a CEO or very senior manager. This preference is because of the flexibility this approach can encourage. However, there are some problems. Members of *ad hoc* groups suddenly called together may not have all the skills and training for their group member roles. The time taken to select members of an *ad hoc* team could be better used in obtaining more information on the crisis.

Where crisis response teams are more permanent in business or industrial settings because the organization confronts crisis situations regularly or is exposed to major crisis situations, Meyers and Holusha believe that team members should:

- have frequent contact;
- work in close proximity;
- be able to effectively interact together.

These crisis team members need to be able to set aside their work and their personal lives for the duration of a crisis and should be well compensated for their efforts. For Meyers and Holusha team membership needs to include:

- the most creative senior executive in the company who can take the pressures involved;
- a person with a broad and substantial knowledge of the organization and how the organization functions;
- the most senior (power-wielding) executive available;
- a person from outside the organization that is knowledgable about the type of work undertaken by the organization.

In essence the authors propose that a team needs to have sufficient conventional authority to enforce the crisis management instructions, sufficient understanding of the intricacies of the particular organization, innovative skills, and a member that may hold a different POV than those within the organization. This latter feature can help reduce the effects of mindsets and groupthink.

Barton (1993) finds that several managerial level positions from within an organization are needed to make a crisis management team. This team includes:

- a lawyer;
- a public relations co-ordinator;
- technical experts;
- a financial officer;
- a telecommunications manager;
- a public affairs expert; and
- the CEO or delegate.

One problem arising from this type of team is the potential for over-caution and administrative slow-downs. Lawyers tend to argue for limited and non-committed responses while financial people try to curb and control expenses. While such actions are beneficial when time is plentiful, the same actions can be inhibitory and even costly when dealing with a quickly changing crisis situation. On the other hand, an understanding of legal points of a situation is important and properly maintained financial records will be needed for the survival of an organization once the crisis ends. Consequently the real question is not should such personnel be included but rather should such personnel be included in a crisis response or recovery management group as opposed to advisory or support management sub-groups?

Existing structures

Two widely supported site management structures exist: the *incident command system (ICS)* and the *standardized emergency management system (SEMS)*. The strengths of both systems are that they have been tested in a wide range of physical crisis situations, most of which have been natural disaster and major accident types. Military and paramilitary (law enforcement, firefighter, paramedic, civil defence) organizations generally use variants of ICS. The weaknesses in these structures are that the systems are:

- designed and operated by organizations with strong command and control POVs;
- designed for a strong physical mission orientation and are less user-friendly when dealing with the larger strategic picture or non-physical situations;
- designed for tactical rather than strategic and meta-strategic use.

Within these limits, ICS and SEMS approaches cope well with physically defined situations.

The incident command system

The incident command system (ICS) is an American approach for direct management of an incident or crisis situation. The approach links actions and activities required to resolve a crisis or disaster at a specific point or site. ICS is an accepted and recommended management approach for physical crisis situations that are local and specific.

The principles underlying ICS are as follows:

- The system is relatively simple and flexible. ICS can be conducted by single users, a key user with others in support, or multi-users in a unified command.
- The organizational structure meets the requirements of any likely crisis or disaster and is readily adaptable to new technology.
- The system can expand in a rapid and logical manner and involves common terminology, modular organization, unified command structure, integrated action plans, workable spans of control, resources appropriate to likely responses and integrated communications.
- The ICS structure is shaped according to the size and type of incident, and expands (where necessary) upward and downward from an incident commander who has overall authority at the site of an incident.
- Sections involving planning, operations, command, logistics and finance-administration are capable of expansion into separate divisions when necessary.

The basic ICS operational procedure is to:

- establish a location for primary command activities (the *incident command post*);

- establish an area for temporarily storing and holding resources (the *staging area*);
- establish a place where the primary logistic functions for an incident may be co-ordinated and administered (the *base*);
- establish a location for provision of sleeping, food, water and sanitary services (the *camp*);
- establish a site or sites for use by helicopters for parking, refuelling and maintenance (the *helibase*) and for safe landing and take-off operations within the crisis environment (the *helispot*).

These locations are activated and determined when needed.

Primary functions of the ICS approach

As ICS is designed for field management of a crisis event, the approach has an *incident commander (IC)* who manages the response to the crisis. Note the military-based terminology. The organizational structure devolves from the IC and the IC's immediate staff into four section commands that resemble closely a military headquarters structure – operations, planning and intelligence, logistics, and finance and administration (*see* Figure 10.1). Each section can be further split into divisions, branches or specialist units when necessary.

The operations section is responsible for the co-ordinated tactical response to the crisis event. The IC may assume an operations management role in small crisis situations, and this allows flexibility in scale. The planning and intelligence function involves collecting, evaluating and documenting all the information about the crisis, crisis response and status of available resources. In small crisis situations, an IC may also manage this section. The logistics section is a broad support service that provides facilities, services, personnel,

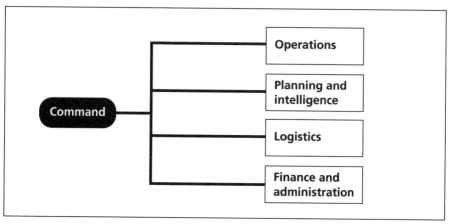

Fig. 10.1 A typical ICS structure

equipment and materials to support the crisis response effort. Given the size and nature of the crisis situation, logistics units may include communications, medical, food, supply, facilities, ground support and transport. The finance and administration section monitors financial and cost analysis during the crisis response, and acts as an umbrella section to handle any other functions not covered by the other three sections.

One immediate strength of the ICS is the flat structure (a simple command to section, or two-level structure). This flatness contributes toward quick interactive communication. Another strength lies in the simple division of labour into four sections. Additionally, the four sections can function simultaneously and semi-independently.

A major weakness of the ICS is that intelligence (or information gathering and assessment) is given secondary importance as an attached subsection. Information collation and evaluation is a central requirement for effective crisis management, so this needs increasing in importance. Such a status perhaps reflects a more significant weakness in that little attention is given to communications – particularly with those outside the crisis response group and the crisis environment. The poor emphasis on communication may be one reason why ICS users tend to appear off-balance and even secretive when dealing with media representatives and special interest groups (including any victims of the crisis).

ICS can be used for multiple response agencies through a *unified command structure*. Unified command enables responding agencies to establish a common set of objectives and a single incident action plan. Effective unified command structures increase efficiency and minimize the inter-agency friction. Primary features of a unified command system include:

- establishing an integrated incident management structure;
- sharing facilities (particularly at the on-site incident command post);
- using a single-strategy planning process;
- establishing a single and common incident action plan;
- sharing of planning, logistical and financial/administration activities;
- sharing or co-ordinating a process for ordering resources.

Benefits of adopting unified command structures include:

- a common mission for the whole crisis situation;
- improvements in information flows between the responding agencies;
- greater understanding of the priorities and limitations for each responding agency,
- reduction of duplicated activities.

In reality, unified command can be implemented physically but may be less successful given differences in response–action priorities, clashes between different organizational cultures and use of unique within-organization terminologies.

Incident action plans

Incident action plans are developed by field managers to outline the strategy or strategies, tactics, resources and logistics required to resolve the crisis over a period of time called the *operational period*. Incident action plans cover:

1 a statement of measurable objectives;
2 how management will be organized;
3 assignments and tactics;
4 required logistical support;
5 referential material (site plans, weather data, safety precautions, important messages).

While the incident action plan may be verbal for small single-agency situations, the details really need to be written down. Written outlines of plans help managers reconstruct events and actions for post-event reports and any investigations or inquiries.

Wenger, Quarantelli and Dynes (1990) find that the handover of command as the response force expands is the weakest element of the model. The lack of strong and purpose-built information management and communication planning could reduce response effectiveness over time. They find that 'in several of our studies, the position of incident commander changed a number of times and such action resulted in loss of information about the earlier situation.' (p. 9). This deficiency arises from the flaws resident in the ICS model. The ICS design primarily suits local situations in which the effort has a short-term and concentrated management.

The standardized emergency management system (California)

The standardized emergency management system (SEMS) was developed as a direct result of the East Bay Hills fire of 1991. Because of the different response management structures and equipment used by the different response agencies called in to deal with this urban wildfire, errors allowed greater loss of resources than necessary. The California state government enacted legislation (effective on 1 January 1993) empowering the Office of Emergency Services of the State Governor to establish a standardized emergency management approach to disasters and community crises. Future funding of response-related costs of any response agencies in the state was conditional upon meeting and implementing SEMS requirements.

SEMS operates on five levels, each being activated when appropriate. These levels are:

1 *field response* (tactical decisions and activities conducted in direct response to an incident);

233

2 *local government* (management and co-ordination of overall response and recovery activities within their jurisdiction);

3 *operational area* (manage and/or co-ordinate information, resources and priorities among impacted local governments; serves as a communication link to the regional level);

4 *regional* (manages and co-ordinates information and resources among impacted operational areas; assists state level in co-ordinating state agency support);

5 *state* (manages state agency resources).

All five levels undertake their own planning functions, management activities, operations activities, intelligence gathering and dissemination, logistical support and administration.

A SEMS approach may help facilitate information flows, co-ordinate all responding agencies and improve supply and logistics management. While SEMS can be described as an expanded ICS structure, the approach is seen as a means of providing better flows of information among and between responding agencies (that is, *within* the crisis environment). By trying to standardize the operational structures, equipment and terminologies, a SEMS approach works to provide an integrated response management of a crisis situation.

The base level structure (field response) uses an ICS approach. The SEMS structure really begins when the scale of the crisis escalates management. As the scale of response increases, SEMS activates the appropriate emergency operations centre (EOC). This EOC activation begins initially at the local government level, then moves up through regional to state levels as the response demand increases.

Recommended standards include span of control, personnel accountability, common terminology, the way in which resources are managed and integrated communications. An optimum span of control is set at one manager or supervisor to five resource units or five people. The SEMS approach also requires proper use of personnel accounting with check-in forms, position logs and status monitoring systems being used to account for every respondent. One of the strengths of SEMS is the use of common terminology that streamlines multi-agency efforts. Likewise, insistence upon effective resource management and integrated communications hopefully increases efficiencies and commonality of response effort.

Identifying appropriate levels of command or management

ICS and SEMS approaches are structure oriented. As many crisis situations involve at least three levels of response – operational, tactical and base-strategic – organizations often need a means of differentiating field respondent from base respondent, and between tactical, operational and strategic management.

One approach is to assign each of the three tiers a colour or metal label. The tiers enable management to interact so that task, situation and event are appropriately managed. Operational management (undertaking task or task cluster management, usually at the site of the crisis) is Bronze. Tactical management (allocation of resources and co-ordinating effort, often on site at an incident command post) is Silver. The strategic level (policy formulation and situation co-ordination, usually at an off-site central headquarters) is Gold. Front-line work is the province of Bronze managers, site management is the function of Silver managers, and off-site event co-ordination the place for Gold managers. Liaison and media management is left to Gold-level managers.

At first this seems an effective link system, and this probably is so within the confines of response agency missions and perspectives. Three real concerns emerge on closer examination.

The first of these is the effect of tier labels, particularly of Gold, Silver and Bronze, upon those assigned the colours and on those interacting with the various colour holders. Many sports awards (such as the Olympic Games) use a similar ranking of achievement – gold for first, silver for second and bronze for third. Consequently tier labels may lead to psychological perceptions of relative worth and contribution among users and outsiders that has little to do with the level of response management. A Bronze-level manager may be regarded as being less important than a Silver or Gold manager. Tier labelling is likely to encounter problems when situation management expands and from potential job demarcation conflicts ('That is not my job – so it is not my concern').

The second concern is the reduced emphasis on liaison and integration of multi-agency response at the base level. Integration needs to occur all the way down to local site actions for effective, safe and efficient crisis management. Yet there are few recorded cases (even in big accident scenarios) where interaction and co-ordination does not reportedly fail between different agencies and between different organizations.

The third concern is that of keeping liaison and media management at the Gold level. While some Gold operatives may be on site for liaison and media duties, the resulting external or outside impression gained from headquarter-based liaison and media management is of ponderous and remote management that is likely to be behind the times with what is happening. Groups of threatened or concerned people see this stiff and remote activity as being dismissive of their local and urgent concerns. The public and organizational stakeholders need to see localized concern and media management, and need to feel they can access the right people where the crisis situation is based.

The Herald of Free Enterprise ferry capsizes outside
Zeebrugge, Belgium, 1987

Background

At 7.30 pm on Friday, 6 March 1987, a roll-on roll-off sea-going ferry, *Herald of Free Enterprise* (HoFE), capsized and sank just outside the harbour of Zeebrugge. The HoFE was owned by Townsend-Thorenson, a recent subsidiary of the Peninsular and Oriental Navigation Company, at the time of the capsize. Zeebrugge is a port on the northwest coast of Belgium that services passenger ferries, freight carriers, fishing vessels and the Belgian navy. Ferry services carry 1 700 000 people and 970 000 vehicles through this port.

Incident

The HoFE sailed for Dover (England) at around 6.24 pm with approximately 500 people on board, 81 cars and 50 transport vehicles. Four minutes after passing the harbour entrance, the HoFE swung to starboard and filled with water. The ferry capsized two kilometres outside the harbour.

Response

Upon the report of a watchkeeper, a captain of a dredge moored outside Zeebrugge harbour raised the alarm. The captain contacted the port admiralty and ordered the dredge to move toward the site of the capsized ferry.

The duty officer of the port admiralty contacted the pilot and sea rescue service. One sea rescue boat and two tugs arrived at the site at 7.40 pm. The port admiralty alerted the coastal emergency services and fire brigade. The alert message was ambiguous, only mentioning that a ferry was adrift. The contacted response services consequently waited for clarification and confirmation messages.

The chief of the pilot and rescue services requested medical services. A tug, a freight ferry, two fishing boats and a crane barge were also moving from the harbour to the site. Search and rescue helicopters from the airforce had been alerted.

By 7.50 pm, boats and tugs on site had rescued around 250 people. A full alert and response was in place by 7.52 pm.

The policy centre had most core representatives turn up for duty by 8.15 pm. Centre managers turned down assistance from amateur divers and requisitioned a large holiday complex (*Duinse Polders*) as a holding area for survivors along with the Novotel and Olympia Hotels.

At 8.45 pm the first of the rescued people were disembarked onto the largely unoccupied working dock.

By 9.30 pm, law enforcement agencies had sealed off all roads leading into Zeebrugge. This created a major traffic jam of vehicles carrying media people and sightseers.

Over 300 survivors were rescued by 10.30 pm. Medical units were still arriving, some having travelled over 120 kilometres. The landing stage for victims was also changed (due to tidal effects) to the quays nearest the pilot and sea rescue base.

At 1.30 am the first press conference was convened.

The last survivors were recovered at 3.00 am. Medical respondents from distant bases were released.

The Sheen Inquiry (England) was set up on 9 March. The inquiry tabled a report seven weeks later.

Statistics
Seven provincial hospitals accepted 165 casualties. An official total of 193 lives were lost. The HoFE sank in around five minutes.

Comment
The Zeebrugge response illustrates the number of organizations that may share a piece of the plan. Key organizations included the port admiralty, the company managing the port, the pilot and sea rescue service, the coastal emergency services, the fire brigade, the municipal police force, the mayor, the district gendarmerie, the provincial hospitals, the governor of the province and the civil defence unit(s). Each organization needed to be co-ordinated and integrated into the action-decision strategies to manage the situation.

Delays in responding to the HoFE situation may have been increased through a number of factors. The lack of a call for help from the ferry, the lack of visibility due to the onset of night, and the location of the situation outside the harbour may have contributed to sluggish response efforts (Pijnenburg and Van Duin, 1991).

Management perspective
Executives and managers need to include managing outside interest in their policies. Four particular outside groups can create problems on and around the site and distract those who need to focus carefully upon the situation and the response to that situation:

- the media;
- concerned groups (including pressure groups);
- volunteers;
- very important visitors.

Handling the media and pressure groups is discussed in Chapters 7 and 8. Volunteer assistance often emerges when the crisis is very large (natural disasters) or very visible. Problems with volunteer assistance include injury and psychological impact litigation (post-crisis), uncertainty over skills held and a lack of logistical support (food and accommodation, for example) that can make further demands on stretched resources.

Few plans and fewer incident command centres or EOCs have facilities and personnel available for handling important visitors. Where possible, plans and management centres need to include the means of handling important visitors so that these people may see and hear what is happening *without impeding or intruding on operations*.

Media management in this crisis was poor. The first media conference at 1.30 am on Saturday was delayed by 30 minutes. Most statements in Flemish were either poorly translated or unaccompanied by a translation – yet many of the assembled media came from outside Belgium. Many questions by foreign media representatives were never answered. Given the media conference delay and the lack of detail and information then made available, media personnel resorted to on-site reporting and filming – much of which bordered on invasion of privacy and coercion. Managers and executives need to place more attention on providing skills training for people likely to be interviewed on site, and to place far greater priority on information management during a crisis.

The HoFE case provides some insight into the need for separating on-site operational co-ordination (ICS) from policy and support management (EOC). The Zeebrugge crisis plan separated strategic (policy centre) and tactical (operational centre) management. Each centre was supposed to be located in a different place, with the policy centre usually at a fixed address and the operational centre near the crisis site. Members of the policy centre included the provincial governor (chairperson of the policy centre), the provincial head of the civil defence, the chief of the fire brigade, the commander of the district gendarmerie, the mayor and the port admiral.

Operational command is divided into four 'disciplines' – rescue (commanded by a fire brigade officer), medical (commanded by an officer from the provincial health inspectorate), public order and traffic (joint command by the gendarmerie and the municipal police) and support (headed by an officer from civil defence). This appears similar to many orthodox structures in community disaster management planning.

At Zeebrugge, the policy centre appeared to absorb many of the operational centre duties (Pijnenburg and Van Duin, 1991). One possible reason may have been that planning and exercises had concentrated on shoreline and on-shore multi-agency operations, with the fire brigade in charge. However, the fire brigade was inexperienced in dealing with rescue-at-sea settings, and by their taking a more direct 'field commanding' role, many policy issues were ignored or mismanaged by policy centre personnel. Information management was also poorly managed. Not only were the media poorly handled, but so too were efforts to exchange information about victims and survivors with their relatives and friends.

Introducing the crisis management shell structure

Structures like ICS and SEMS are heavily focused upon on-site co-ordination and management. This is not surprising as the designers of these structures come from professional response agencies that primarily attend localized physical crisis situations. These structures are weak when the crisis is less physically present, large-scale and where information management becomes critical over a distributed (rather than local) environment. Many business, commercial and community crisis situations have some or all of these factors. Assaults on business reputation, stock market failures, industrial relations failures, product failures and greenmail activities are less physical in situational appearance. Large-scale disasters such as floods, wildfires, volcanic activity, earthquakes or cyclonic windstorms create region-wide demands on resources and priorities. SEMS and ICS-type approaches will tend to operate less capably under such environments.

Executives and managers need to develop structures for crisis management that aid information management, remove distractions from ICS-style operational management at crisis sites, and which allow better transfers and rotation of command. These structures need to function in terms of crisis-related tasks and activities rather than through traditional departments, position titles and procedures. As suggested over the preceding chapters of this book, crisis management differs from managing in day-to-day situations.

One structure capable of supporting the broader demands of large-scale community and less tangible business and industrial crisis situations is the *crisis management shell structure (CMSS)*. This structure is purpose-designed to meet the strategic and policy demands of a crisis situation, while retaining clear connection with operational (ICS-type) field command and response processes. The CMSS is a flexible structure that can fit any size organization, from a single-person business to a national government. Management and personnel fill roles and positions according to their skills and abilities, rather than seniority of office or years served within the organization.

CMSS provides a number of features that meet the requirements for effective crisis management established over the preceding chapters. These requirements include:

- a simple and easily understood structure;
- short and simple communication and command paths;
- flat management that reduces loss of time in giving information and commands;
- centralized decision making;
- delegatory task management and associated decision making at the task level;
- a focus on co-ordination more than tactical command;
- collection, evaluation and distribution of information;
- ability to communicate effectively among groups *inside* the crisis environment;
- ability to communicate effectively to groups *outside* the crisis environment.

As shown in Figure 10.2 the CMSS has an information element (the right-hand half of the figure) and a decision-action element (the left-hand side of the figure). These elements respectively separate into advisory and information components and decision and operational components. The information component has an information collation office (INCO), a public and media office (PUMO) and an advisory image management office (IMMO). The advisory component involves an advisory image management office (IMMO) and a principal advisory group (PAG). The decision component holds a management interface between the crisis manager (CM) and higher authority (including, where there are a number of crisis situations, a chief crisis manager (CCM)). The operations component has a co-ordination and command office (CACO) and the field-based or speciality-based tactical response units (TRU) that may be organized along ICS approaches where the field or speciality operations require management of more than two teams of personnel. The crisis

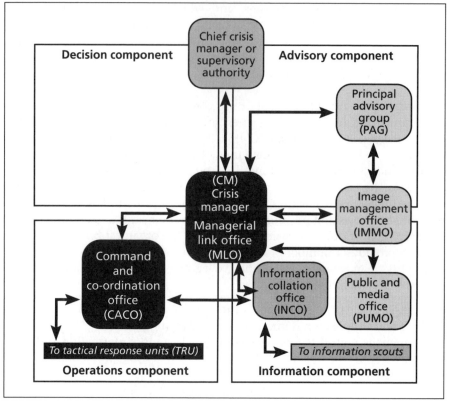

Fig. 10.2 The crisis management shell structure

manager (CM) and her or his immediate support staff in the managerial link office (MLO) span the boundaries of each of the four components.

Starting with the CM position, the following brief tour of the CMS structure provides a fundamental understanding of the rationale and contribution of each unit. This is achieved through a standardized description of each unit that conveys its essential functions and its links to other units in the CMSS. The description covers:

- what the unit is;
- why the unit is there;
- who works in the unit;
- when the unit is activated;
- where the unit is placed.

Crisis manager (CM)

What The CM is the central manager of a crisis situation. A chief crisis manager may run a separate co-ordinating CMSS allowing each CM to operate a tighter CMSS team if there were a number of physically separate and different crisis situations happening at the same time. The CM makes all the strategic decisions although she or he may delegate operational authority to a deputy in situations that require more than eight hours to manage.

Why By placing co-ordination and control through the one position of CM, the resulting central authority can lead to faster decision making and a comprehensive perception of the crisis situation or the resulting recovery operation. The CM may use advisory groups and information analysts to assist in determining information validity and options and thus retain some consensus and co-operative inputs. These extra opinions can reduce the influence of mindset and groupthink on action choices.

Who A CM needs sufficient authority to make decisions and to take control of the crisis environment. While some further discussion on crisis managerial traits is presented in Chapter 14, a CM needs to be able to manage in confusing situations. By crisis definitions, such situations involve missing and uncertain information, have almost no time in which to decide and respond, entail a demand for resources that exceeds the available resources and have high levels of stress and performance expectations. The CM needs to have the skills and training necessary to manage the crisis. If the CM is a middle or junior manager (as can arise in the field) executives and higher management need to accept the authority vested in the CM for the duration of the crisis.

When Once a crisis response has been activated, the CM takes control. Only the CM can formally close a crisis response operation.

Where A CM usually operates in a command centre or headquarters. This centre or headquarters may be on-site or off-site depending upon the size and nature of the crisis situation and the size and structure of the crisis response component of an organization.

The managerial link office (MLO)

What The MLO is run by a small number of people who act as links between the needs and requirements of the CM and the needs and requirements of the other units within the CMSS. The mission of the MLO is to ensure continuity of information exchange between the CM and the rest of the units in the CMSS, and between the CM and the rest of the organization.

Why By having a permanent link unit, the continuity of information exchange enables faster interactions and ensures ongoing exchange when the CM may not be present. This frees the CM and senior subordinates from acting as their own secretaries, reduces potential gridlock in communications by having more than one receiver for transmissions, and enables simultaneous reception of multiple messages.

Who MLO operatives are generally junior staff who are trained and skilled in accurately receiving and recording information. Medium to large crisis situations would need a minimum of three MLO staff. For crisis situations that require more than eight hours to manage, MLO staffing needs to be multiplied by the number of shifts (multiples of six to eight hours) required until a complete 24-hour rotation is completed.

When The MLO assembles when a crisis response is activated.

Where MLO staff work where the CM is generally based.

Information collation office (INCO)

What INCO personnel are the core information collators and assessors in the CMSS. They:

- provide information exchange facilities within the crisis response team (except for PUMO operatives); and
- sort, collate, evaluate and record information about the crisis situation.

Why The INCO unit relieves the CM and MLO of the burden entailed in continuously obtaining, updating and assessing information from inside and outside the crisis situation. The unit provides a centralized processing operation that frees CM, CACO and field personnel to undertake their response or recovery tasks.

Who INCO personnel need to be trained in collecting and evaluating information. Other skills include recording the information in ways that help operational CMSS units (the CM, MLO, PAG, CACO and IMMO) define the crisis and crisis response issues. Medium to large crisis situations probably require three sub-units to be formed – inquiry–reception, collation–validation and recording. Personnel need training in dealing with people upset by the crisis, in obtaining concrete information and in using patterned information-gathering techniques. INCO operations may use trained personnel who move around a crisis situation gathering information – information scouts (see below).

When The INCO team assembles when a crisis response is activated.

Where The team is placed within the crisis command centre or headquarters. The INCO site is physically separated from the PUMO site with no permitted direct access between the two units.

Information scout

What Information scouts provide information-gathering capabilities for the INCO team. The information scouts are used as specialized source gatherers (radio, television, newspapers) or as on-site observers and information seekers. These personnel function as the eyes and ears of the CMSS operation.

Why Information scouts provide a dedicated information-gathering service.

This service is faster and more accurate because the personnel concentrate on gathering information rather than on responding to the crisis situation. Scouts use communication systems that are independent of those used by response units (such as the TRUs). If response communication systems fail, the information scout communication network may be used as a last-resort option for a brief time. Scouts help speed up the information-gathering process, and through their training and discipline can add concreteness to information supplied to INCO and thus on to the CM. This helps meet one of the key elements of *CrisisThink*.

Who Information scouts are staff trained in gathering and reporting objective information (often using a set pattern). Scouts need to be appropriately and independently equipped and accepted by the various operations units as equals doing a support task (and not as spies).

When Information scouts assemble when a crisis response is activated.

Where Information scouts used for gathering field data either assemble at the designated INCO site or move to predetermined locations according to a given crisis response plan. Scouts may be assigned to sift radio, television, newspapers and the Internet.

Public and media office (PUMO)

What Personnel working in the PUMO unit deal with media agencies, interest groups and people outside the crisis situation. They:

- receive and respond to inquiries from outside the crisis situation for help and information;
- transfer any information contacts from the outside world to the appropriate INCO personnel;
- provide routine information briefings for media personnel.

PUMO personnel may relay information to INCO personnel but cannot request or gain information from them. All information made available by PUMO must be cleared by the crisis manager.

Why The PUMO unit provides information to those outside the crisis situation and who are not members of the crisis response. This frees the CM and other specalized CMSS units from handling these contacts, makes for faster response to inquiries from those outside, and allows the INCO personnel to concentrate on gathering and evaluating information that can help with managing the crisis. Isolating PUMO from internal information flows and requiring PUMO information to be pre-approved by the CM enables three specific improvements in crisis management:

- separation of internal and external flows of information to reduce rumours, inconsistent information and leakage of information;
- development of a centralized source for information to the outside world;
- faster supply of information to media personnel and other interested people.

PUMO personnel relieve the rest of the CMSS personnel of the need to deal with distracting public information issues.

Who People who work in PUMO need to be trained in dealing with those who are stressed or disturbed by the crisis situation. PUMO staff need to be able to effectively deal with media requests for information and to organize media interviews (including media conferences).

When The PUMO team assembles when a crisis response is activated.

Where The team is placed within the crisis command centre or headquarters. The PUMO site is physically separated from the INCO.

Image management office (IMMO)

What Staff employed in the IMMO unit analyze and advise on the effects the crisis and crisis management may have on the perception of the organization by the general public and any special-interest group. IMMO deals with organizational image management and may offer advice to PUMO and the CM on how information can be effectively released to those outside the crisis situation. IMMO personnel also advise on possible issues that may be raised by those outside the crisis situation.

Why IMMO is a specalized 'public relations' unit to help executives and managers make more balanced and appropriate statements. This assistance frees respondents from these distractions. IMMO also advises on how to counter rumours and speculation (or active attacks) upon an organization and its staff.

Who IMMO personnel need to be skilled and experienced in anticipating issues raised in the outside community over the crisis episode. They need to be skilled in:

- analyzing comments and criticisms;
- presenting positive yet truthful information;
- getting co-operation from groups with hostile points of view (POV);
- dealing with speculative or malicious opinion and publicly aired POVs.

In small organizations the CM may also manage the IMMO role. This is not optimal as the CM has many other activities to undertake or supervise and is thus likely to leave such thinking until far too late for effective image management to be enacted.

When IMMO needs to be activated once a crisis incident is tangible and obvious to outside groups. Less tangible situations may also prompt an IMMO presence – attacks on an organization's image, cash flow problems, takeovers and acquisitions, and major changes to an organization's operational mission or management process may need assistance from IMMO.

Where IMMO needs to be quite close to the CM and PUMO personnel. Given modern technology, the IMMO personnel may operate off-site. Remote or off-site operations, however, mean that IMMO personnel are removed from directly assessing the mood and attitude of crisis respondents.

Principal advisory group (PAG)

What The PAG provides a close source of expert advice for the CM. This allows more time and more POVs to be focused upon problems or issues confronting the crisis response. Gaining extra time fits *CrisisThink* criteria and the range of POVs available from this group can reduce mindset and groupthink. A PAG enables:

- the CM to concentrate on crisis response tasks and co-ordination;
- more than one person to know the general big picture; and
- quick access to expert advice (and even the ability to send well-briefed experts into the field to handle special issues or procedures).

Why Members of PAG relieve the CM of the need to be expert in all features of the crisis situation. These members have more time to consider the information and options available.

Who Membership of the PAG may change over the course of the crisis. These changes may be due to changes in the crisis situation or because specific experts move into the field to supervise particular response activities. An expert in handling hazardous chemicals, for example, may move from a PAG role to a more direct and tactical role in handling those substances. The PAG needs to include senior representatives of all groups responding to the crisis, especially those groups from outside the organization. Other useful members would be senior personnel likely to be co-ordinating post-crisis recovery activities, as these persons would then know what is damaged and what was done during the response activities.

When The PAG assembles when a crisis response is activated. Specific members are invited to join the PAG depending on the nature of the crisis situation.

Where The PAG team meets where the CM is based, usually at the field or base command centre.

Chief crisis manager (CCM)/supervisory authority

What A more senior authority may need to co-ordinate or at least monitor the crisis management. This may arise because:

- there is more than one crisis situation or more than one crisis site; or
- only a part of an organization (or community) is involved in the crisis.

In most crisis situations a CM reports to a higher authority that operates as a supervisory authority. This contact is one of accountability and information supply, and should not be used for micro-management by these higher authorities.

Why CCMs provide support and strategic co-ordination over multiple sites or situations. Supervisory authorities enable a process of accountability for CMs and their teams and can co-ordinate between affected and non-affected groups within an organization or community.

Who CCM personnel tend to be very senior executives or managers with requisite training and experience. Supervising authorities are those to whom a CM will eventually report and may include heads of organizations or government. Often both forms of higher authority are those to whom the CM reports on non-crisis day-to-day terms.

When According to the process used and the size and nature of the crisis situation, these supervisory authorities are informed of the activation of a crisis response. CCMs are activated when a crisis (due to complexity or size) is beyond single CM management, and when more resources and personnel are required for the crisis response (either in terms of shift-work or in terms of ongoing supply and resupply).

Where CCMs usually operate separate command centres or headquarters and have their own CMSS teams. Supervisory authorities are also usually located elsewhere.

Normal operations liaison office (NOLO) – outside CMSS structure

What In some crisis situations and crisis recovery operations a NOLO team helps liaise between affected and unaffected groups. NOLO personnel act as a link and buffer between normal operations and the crisis-affected areas.

Why NOLO personnel link respondents, recovery personnel and affected groups with the rest of the organization when communication systems are not operating properly or when the response or recovery activities require most effort and concentration. NOLO teams help:

- co-ordinate and supply support resources;
- look after the needs of unaffected groups; and
- maintain the balance between the intense focus of crisis management and the surrounding non-crisis environment.

NOLO thus eases any frustration and resource discrimination between internal and external elements. This group increases in importance should senior executives and managers of the overall organization have active CM and CMSS involvement.

Who NOLO staff are usually managerial in status and are not part of the

CMSS team. NOLO may also include subordinate staff to process requests and co-ordinate support to affected and non-affected parts of an organization or community.

When NOLO personnel are assembled when required.

Where NOLO personnel are often based at the offices of the supervisory authority or CCM.

Command and co-ordination office (CACO)

What CACO personnel provide the active translation of strategic plans from the CM into local response strategies for on-site management co-ordination. CACO has two missions:

1 converting strategic decisions into on-site tasks and assigning those tasks to tactical response units (TRUs);
2 monitoring the status and deployment of resources allocated to the crisis.

Why CACO provides direct co-ordination and command over the response effort. In large CMSS designs, CACO relieves the CM of direct and continuous tactical control of the situation. This helps the CM to give more attention to the broad issues of the crisis response, problem resolution and future strategy formulation.

Who CACO personnel are trained in transmitting strategic directions into tactical and unit level instructions and in other co-ordination and situation monitoring tasks. The person in charge of CACO is often the deputy crisis manager (DCM) who may temporarily assume the role of crisis manager when the CM is absent.

When CACO staff assemble once a crisis response activation is made.
  In extended crises, changeovers of CM and DCM need to be staggered to aid continuity of management. Ideally, CMs and DCMs who are about to take over management need to be present at least an hour before so that they can be properly briefed about the status of the crisis response.

Where CACO assembles at the designated command centre or headquarters.

Tactical response units (TRU)

The field crisis-response effort is divided into the number of general and specalized units that have the personnel and equipment to deal with the crisis incident and the impacts of that incident. These TRUs are linked to the CACO team for information exchange and transmission of instructions. Note that ICS-type structures easily fit into this area.

The benefits of using a CMSS-type approach

The CMSS process is a simple and flexible approach to putting structure into the crisis response. Task clusters are grouped into specific and general 'offices'. Regardless of the type, size or nature of the crisis, CMSS clearly defines the role and object of each team or 'office'.

Importantly, CMSS *separates* (and *keeps separate*) flows of communication within the crisis response and information made available to those outside the crisis response team. This separation reduces conflict, misunderstandings and poor image perception, through presenting a co-ordinated 'single' source of information. Given the emphasis on information collation, use of CMSS enables better recording of what happened during the crisis.

The CMSS approach enables rescaling according to the needs of a given crisis situation, and allows a flexible adaptation of the appropriate 'offices' and 'units' for that crisis. Note that the approach can be used by one to one million people, because the emphasis is on the skills appropriate to managing the crisis and not on non-crisis job titles, processes or ways of undertaking work.

REALITY BITE

Coode Island storage fire, Australia, 1991

Background

Coode Island was a storage facility and tank farm, 6 kilometres west of the downtown area of Melbourne (Australia). Within a 5-kilometre radius of this area live 150 000 people. The island is really a peninsula on which five companies operated chemical storage and cargo handling facilities. One of these companies, Terminals Pty Ltd, had 39 vertical storage tanks (the largest storing 5 500 000 litres) and seven horizontal tanks. Stored chemicals included benzene, acetone, phenol, acrylonitrile, methyl ethyl hexane, toluene and cyclohexane. The site of Terminals Pty Ltd operations covered one and a half hectares and was divided internally by earth bunds. The perimeter of the site consisted of an earth and concrete bund 3 metres in height.

Incident

At 2.20 pm on Wednesday, 21 August 1991, an explosion and fire on the site of Terminals Pty Ltd was reported from several sources, including an off-duty fire officer crossing Westgate Bridge.

Response

The section officer of the initial two fire units responding to the alert reassessed the situation as a Level 5 alarm. The units witnessed Tank 80 (278 000 litres of acrylonitrile) rip from its base, rise 15 metres in the air and land in flames over 50 metres from its base – damaging a truck and wrecking the above-ground fire suppression ring mains. As further units arrived the alarm was increased to a Level 8. Each increase of a level had associated increases in personnel, resources brought to the site and level of on-site management or command.

The intensity of the fire started exploding 200-litre drums of chemicals and forced firefighting operations to remain outside the external bund. Metal pieces up to 4 metres in length were thrown up to 120 metres from the site by the explosions.

The Metropolitan Fire Brigades Incident Control Unit was on site within 10 minutes. The Incident Control Centre was sited some 600 metres north of the site, with the staging area a further 200 metres north along Mackenzie Street. While this allowed some safety for Incident Centre personnel, the distance from the site and the narrow access roads in the area slowed communications and resource redeployments.

Concern over the toxicity of the smoke plume – heading towards the downtown and city business areas – was raised. The smoke plume caused main arterial roads to be closed and the evacuation of a major railway switch box resulting in trains coming to a halt in the path of the plume.

Police broadcast advice via television and radio, and announced a special public advice telephone number. Residents were advised to stay indoors, closing all windows and doors. The phone system, with a capacity of 500 calls per hour, was found to be limited to 50 calls in the first few hours, the capacity having been eroded by other government agency use. On-site, the police employed an expanding cordon. Westgate Bridge, the Footscray Markets and Dynon Road were closed, local power was shut down and four ships in Melbourne Port were evacuated. Closure of a main arterial road led to traffic jams which increasingly impeded the movement of emergency vehicles.

Within an hour, police communications personnel were receiving international telephone calls requesting information on how much of Melbourne had been destroyed. Images of the fire broadcast overseas had created the impression of a firestorm. School staff and parents wanted to know about evacuating school children. No concrete information was available for around two hours. There were media reports about school evacuations that did not happen (Munday, 1993).

Given the spread of the fire, a defensive containment strategy was adopted. Offensive strategic plans involve interior operations to provide search and rescue and to control and extinguish a fire. Defensive strategic plans involve exterior operations directed towards protection from exposure and avoiding unnecessary risk to firefighters (Hume, 1991, p. 8). As the hand lines and monitors seemed unable to cope, a request was made for high-pressure tenders from CAA and RAAF services. These tenders dramatically helped bring the fire under control by 4.30 pm with only Tank 49 still ablaze. Inspection showed that eight tanks were destroyed and five severely damaged.

Foam supplies became a major problem – reserves were called from nearby airports (downgrading the capacity of the airports to safely service large jets) and from Sydney and Brisbane. Reserves were also being requisitioned as far away as Singapore and Hong Kong.

On the second day, concerned groups raised political pressure over the presence of high volumes of stored chemicals so close to the city centre. Firefighters (in shifts of around 70) patrolled the site and tried to douse a fire in the base piping of Tank 49 with dry chemicals.

At 11.53 am the storage farm fire re-ignited resulting in a fire bigger than the fire of the previous day. The high-pressure airport foam pumpers provided a wall attack to damp successive fronts of the fire. The fire threatened other large storage tanks until brought under control by 4.00 pm on 22 August. A further 20 tanks were damaged or destroyed.

Statistics

At the peak of the fire, 180 firefighters (10 per cent of the MFB) and 120 support personnel were on site, as were 350 law enforcement personnel. Some 200 000 litres of foam were used on the fire out of a total throughput of 220 000 litres (around AUS$1 200 000). Total estimated cost (including clean up which took a further nine days) was AUS$9 500 000. Firefighters, for example, remained on site and provided 50 to 60 personnel to assist in the clean up.

Around 3000 tonnes of chemicals burned in the fire. Estimated insurance loss was AUS$50 000 000 – excluding any operational loss to surrounding businesses and any litigation.

Comment

Coode Island illustrates a multi-agency response to a major incident. The MFB were the lead agency, supported by the police. Terminals Pty Ltd had a constricted partial management role and appeared ineffectual – their fire-suppression system was eliminated early in the crisis, the fire prevented access to offices containing information about what was stored on site and the supply of useful information for response management appeared to be slow.

While the firefighting management was generally good, a number of observations could be made:

- Access to the incident command site became clogged due to narrow roads.
- Staging areas were far apart and thus difficult to supervise and maintain complete records of activities.
- Lack of information about what was on site and about what formed the plume of smoke placed response personnel in danger.
- An arrangement for the supply of interactive information to political and municipal leaders from a credible (senior) source was needed to remove distractions from the EOC manager.

Speculation over the cause of the explosion included sabotage, freak electrostatic discharge or lightning. A coronial investigation determined that lightning was the cause.

The incident reflects the concerns over evacuate-or-stay-put options in circumstances of chemical air pollution. Either way between 5 and 20 per cent of a target population will do the opposite to the action recommended by response managers.

Management perspective

Executives and managers need to examine existing plans for evacuation from threat. As outlined in Chapter 4, effective policies that require shutdown and closure to be sensibly conducted (such as ACCCE) help reduce over-reaction and asset losses. Plans need to cover the small percentage of people who may not follow the advised actions.

Reassurance over the safety of the smoke plume caused a deal of perturbation in the Coode Island situation. Few of those trying to reassure people in the path of the plume that the smoke was safe (and not toxic) did so from within the plume area. Advice from people visibly not at risk and in safe areas (and particularly from within air-conditioned offices) rarely reassures those exposed to risk.

The incident triggered a number of ripple effect impacts. These included commuters trapped in stationary trains and the need to provide cover for areas depleted of resources required to combat fires. Fire protection cover for areas reduced in MFB resources were provided by the Country Fire Authority. International flights were diverted to other airports due to the downgraded safety capabilities at airports close to Melbourne.

Managers and executives need to be aware of any changes in the environment due to any political reaction to a crisis situation. One outcome after the Coode Island fire was the downsizing of the Coode Island facilities. Chemical storage and manufacturing facilities were placed on the outskirts of Melbourne. This move traded the risk of a Coode Island-type situation for smaller yet probably more numerous transport-sourced chemical spills and accidents.

References

Barton, L. (1993) *Crisis in Organizations: Managing and Communicating in the Heat of Chaos*. Cincinnati, Ohio: South-Western.

Hume, B. (1991). *Coode Island Fire*. Melbourne: MFB Internal Report.

Meyers, G. C. and Holusha, J. (1986) *When It Hits the Fan: Managing the Nine Crises of Business*. London: Unwin Hyman.

Munday, J. (1993) 'Coode Island chemical spill', *Macedon Digest*, 8(2), 6–11.

Pijnenburg, B. and Van Duin, M. J. (1991) 'The Zeebrugge ferry disaster: elements of a communicating and information processes scenario', in Rosenthal, U. and Pijnenburg, B. (eds), *Crisis and Decision Making: Simulation Oriented Scenarios*. Dordrecht: Kluwer Academic.

Quarantelli, E. L. (1995) 'Disasters are different, therefore planning and managing them requires innovative as well as traditional behaviors', in *Proceedings of the Third Emergency Planning and Disaster Management Conference*. Lancaster: Lancaster University.

Wenger, D., Quarantelli, E. and Dynes, R. (1990) 'Is the incident command system a plan for all seasons and emergency situations'? *Hazard Monthly*, 10(3), 8–12.

chapter 11

Response and recovery plans

A cautionary tale

At the end of a meeting with the company's three regional managers, the chief executive officer (CEO) announced each region would get a one-off grant of money to help accelerate the crisis management planning being done in each region.

'Thank you,' said the first regional manager. 'This will help us centralize our resources so that our plan will truly be an integrated one.'

'Thank you,' said the second regional manager. 'The money will be divided among our sites so that each will improve their readiness for any incident.'

'Thank you,' said the third regional manager. 'This will buy some useful things.'

The first regional manager added: 'With this money we will print all the necessary copies of our integrated plan. Everyone will know what to do.' The first regional manager lifted up a 500-page hard-covered version of the integrated plan.

The second regional manager added: 'The money will allow each of our site managers to print their own plans. In this way, we harness everyone's expertise in the right way.' The second regional manager thought that the first manager was too inflexible: let the site managers and each of their departments make their own plans.

The third regional manager looked through some pages in a ring-binder and said, 'We will discuss what to do according to these guidelines our personnel determined last year.'

A year later a major earthquake struck the three areas. The CEO met the three regional managers at a briefing session.

'The response to the earthquake was slow in the initial stages,' admitted the first regional manager. 'Our central crisis office was destroyed. At first we were sorting things out in the car park, then we shifted to my deputy's house. No one knew where we were operating from because we lost our communications systems and contact lists in the crisis office. A lot of the staff waited at their homes to know what to do but we had no way of contacting them. Others turned up at their sites but did nothing because they could not find what to do in the plan, so they waited for instructions. That was not helped by the fact that our crisis manager was overseas on holidays.'

'You think that was bad,' said the second regional manager. 'No one told anyone else what they were doing till too late. On one site each of the departments tried to evacuate by the same stairs and these collapsed under the weight of the congestion. We will be sued for sure! Our transport departments were either damaged or could not deal with the demand – each department and site wanted so many vehicles! The police cordoned off the city centre and would not let our central office staff in. The same recovery specialists were on the books for each site – so they had to wait for recovery assistance. We spent two days sorting out what we were doing and how we could help each other.'

'I noticed that your people responded quite well,' the CEO said to the third regional manager. 'Indeed, I must congratulate you on your region's effort. What did you do that the other two regions did not?'

The third regional manager shrugged and said, 'I do not know. Our plans really told us what we wanted to achieve when things went wrong. We drew these plans up as guidelines, then met often and discussed what we could do if things went wrong. We invited the police and fire brigade and paramedics to help us establish what we could do and what they would do. This helped because on some sites when we turned up with engineers to check the damage they let us through the cordons. We had worked out that if all the crisis centres were down we would ring through on a mobile phone number and find out where the crisis centre would be placed. Each site had the same provision in their plans. Mostly we had an idea about timeframes, what we could try to achieve, and what we could do to help our staff and keep our products selling. That worked well. I guess we spent a lot of time discussing what to do when the plan would not work.'

Crisis plans are guidelines for co-ordinated action in a crisis. Plans are not inflexible regulations for action or procedures designed in isolation. A crisis plan is only as good as the planning that takes place.

About crisis planning

As indicated in the above anecdote, plans are really flexible guides to action outcomes and provide:

- a common picture;
- help in focusing decisions;
- descriptions of the roles and sources of the respondents.

Plans help provide a common and agreed POV from which managers can work when meeting unique crisis-driven situations.

Too often plans are treated as the only way tasks can be done and seen as 'being set in concrete'. Another problem with many plans is that they are so superficially written or out of date that the plans may constitute a risk of adding to the impacts of the crisis. Plans are often treated as venerated relics that are put away safely until the annual touching of the plan takes place. This ritual takes place because of lack of crisis response enthusiasm from superiors and because most planning efforts rarely involved those who have to carry out the tasks covered by the plan. Without enthusiastic support from above and ownership due to input to the plan by those who are designated to undertake tasks in the plan, the plan becomes unworkable.

Planning – from theory to practice

Robbins (1994) finds that planning is concerned with *ends* (what is to be done) and with *means* (how the ends will be achieved). He states that plans reduce uncertainty, give direction to managers and non-managers, reduce overlapping and wasteful activities and establish standards that aid control. Planning allows managers and executives to identify what needs to be done, how this can be done, and how such activities can be measured and controlled.

Robbins debunks three common myths of planning. The first myth is that *planning that proves to be inaccurate is a waste of management time*. Any planning undertaken in an organization is likely to make those in the organization identify what is being done and what should be done. This process of clarifying an organization's mission and goals can be beneficial. The second myth is that *planning eliminates change*. Planning does not eliminate change, as change happens regardless of plans. Plans can be used to predict and help assimilate change. The third myth is that *planning reduces flexibility*. Planning does involve commitment. This commitment becomes inflexible only if the planning activity ends after the first effort. Planning is an ongoing and dynamic activity.

For crisis managers, planning involves two sets of activities. The first set of activities includes those linked with the organization that supports the crisis management response. The second set of activities covers the response activities. Hence, firefighting organizations develop organizational plans to develop and maintain the resources needed for firefighting and also generate plans to handle the missions involved in firefighting. The two sets of activities may conflict with each other. Efficient management of resources as far as an organization is concerned may be achieved at the expense of efficient response capabilities. Likewise, developing effective response resources and personnel for response and recovery efforts may stress the overall budget and organizational structure.

According to Robbins (1994), plans may be specific or directional. Specific plans have clearly defined objectives, hold no ambiguity and are often stepwise and sequential in nature. An example of a specific plan may be that of how to put out a fire using a particular appliance and equipment. A directional plan, on the other hand, is looser. The plan may simply state 'Put out the fire'.

According to McCaskey (1974), directional plans are preferable when uncertainty is high and thus where flexibility is needed to be able to respond to unexpected changes. High uncertainty and unexpected changes are characteristic elements in crisis situations. Executives and managers need to ensure that their crisis plans are directional in nature rather than loaded with specific 'how-to and what-to' instructions. The exceptions to the use of directional plans are when the risk of worsening the crisis is increased should steps or actions not be undertaken or when actions are not undertaken in a specific and ordered approach.

Executives and managers need to remember that the complexity and length of any crisis response master plan removes readers from the physical presence of the real event. Sizeable plans cannot be read while trying to manage a crisis.

Ultimately crisis plans or guides need to be produced in three ways:

- a master plan or master guide;
- simple strategic or specific situation plans;
- short unit-level action plans.

The master plan or guide can be seen as an integrated blueprint that shows how different groups of people interact to resolve a crisis. The strategic or specific situation plans outline outcomes or specific action steps required by designated managers and their teams or units. The action plans outline the goals or tasks required by personnel at a unit level.

The blueprint for a universal crisis response plan

There are a number of books and journal articles that outline in some detail the form a crisis response plan or a crisis recovery plan should have. To an extent this reflects the organizational need for bureaucratic correctness. The layout, size of print and formal design appear at times to become more important than the strategies and tactics involved in handling crisis situations. Many practitioners join with these authors in stating that a crisis plan should be as short and to-the-point as possible then produce a many hundred page document that buries the plan under formalities and is stiff with organizational niceties. There are planners and would-be crisis managers in some of the biggest companies in the world who are more preoccupied in getting the company logo aesthetically correct on the cover than they are with having an up-to-date set of plans that may guide an effective crisis response.

Any question about how big plans ought to be is also pedantic and misleading. For large organizations or those organizations undertaking work that entails complex risks, plans need to be specific and extensive. The best approach is to use all of the three types of plans – overall, strategic and unit oriented. Fine detail can be presented at length in the large overall planning document. Co-ordinated response activities can be described in the strategy document. Actions taken by specified individuals and groups can be outlined in the short action-plan unit-level document. These documents can be placed in semi-permanent form so that the documents can withstand rough handling yet can be quickly updated. Many organizations use ring binder documents.

The problem with loose-form documents is that crisis planners and managers depend upon unit managers or their delegates to update their copies immediately the changed pages are delivered to the units. There is a risk that non-uniform changes due to people forgetting to do so or not being available to do so leads to confusion, as respondents then work from different versions of action plans and strategic plans. One way to get systematic and uniform changes made is to assemble all responsible for the unit level plans for an updating walkthrough of the changed plan. This means that everyone present inserts the changes and the old pages can be collected and destroyed.

Some organizations prefer a more permanent crisis management set of documents that are either updated by manual correction or reprinted in updated form. Problems remain as to whether the updates are actually made and whether the old version is properly replaced. Again, changes may best be made by assembling those responsible for unit-level plans and having the changes inserted or by having a specific crisis management-tasked person systematically replace old versions with new versions.

Components of a plan

The following is a basic blueprint showing the shape and contents of a plan.

Cover page

This carries details such as issue number/date/key telephone alert number.

Authorization page

This may take the form of a letter from the chief executive officer.

Who reads the plan

This outlines either the people who need to read the plan (overall) or the people needed to read the plan (strategy) or the specific person or group that uses the plan (action).

Confirmation form

Usually this is a form signed by the holder of the plan. Some organizations insist all who read the plan need to sign and date the form.

Policy section

This section outlines organizational policies. Contents include:

- policy on confidentiality of plans and of information held by the organization;

- aims and priorities of the organization in terms of crisis management (or recovery management);
- the overall mission or goal of the plan;
- who has what authority and responsibility;
- who changes policies and how policies are changed;
- any links between types of plan (overall to strategy, strategy to unit action);
- conditions for invoking plan.

Plan administration section

Sometimes this section appears at the end of the document. Some formats place checklists at the end of the document (as below) which means that the section needs to be placed before the response or recovery plans are outlined. This section states:

- who designs the plans;
- who maintains the plans;
- how changes are made to the plan (including time limits for any review or evaluation of incidents);
- plan review and audit procedures;
- exercise and training activities.

Risk assessment

This section indicates how and when risk assessments are conducted and outlines key or probable risks that may be encountered.

Pre-crisis section

This section deals with organizational policy on crisis management. Information includes:

- responsibilities of the organization;
- individual or group or department responsibilities for health, safety and crisis reduction;
- risk reduction and control;
- management procedures for dealing with non-organizational people on site when a crisis occurs;
- general instructions on information management.

Communication policy section

This section states the organization's policy on information management in more detail. Contents include:

- who is informed (internal and external groupings);
- how information will be exchanged;
- instructions on how the media is managed;
- instructions on dealing with inquiries from outside the organization;

- instructions on dealing with stakeholders (including staff, customers, shareholders, users, suppliers, creditors and insurers).

Finance, legal and administration section

This section outlines how these specialist activities will be used within the crisis management response (or recovery management) to monitor and co-ordinate activities.

Warning and alert section

This section outlines the alert and warning systems used in the organization. The information includes:

- what alert/warning systems are in place;
- who reviews these systems;
- who maintains these systems;
- what the alert and warning messages contain (descriptions of sounds, statements of any oral messages);
- obligations when alerted;
- evacuation and security procedures;
- safety or evacuation sites;
- contact telephone numbers or e-mail addresses and internal information procedures during and after a crisis.

Crisis command and co-ordination section

This section defines:

- lines of command and communication in terms of the crisis structure;
- the site and location of the crisis command centre (and alternatives);
- contact list of non-internal response agencies (contacts and authority);
- crisis manager contact and crisis team contact numbers (and alternatives).

Crisis resolution section

This is a large and often subsectioned set of outlines covering crisis response actions and activities. These include procedures for handling elements of the crisis event and procedures for handling elements of crisis impact. With each indicated group, team, department or unit will be an accompanying team leader and alternative contact list and a list of team member contacts.

Recovery management section

This section outlines steps to take to:

- implement security procedures;
- activate restoration or continuity plans;
- debrief personnel involved in the crisis situation;
- provide visitor and staff advice;
- gain assistance and counselling.

Note this section may become a full set of plans on its own (*see* below).

Aftermath management section

This section describes procedures for:

- dealing with outside agencies (insurers, professional response agencies);
- review and evaluation of the crisis situation;
- how formal closure of a crisis response may be made.

This section concludes with a master copy or multiple copies of a crisis response evaluation form that gains feedback on how those filling in the form perceived the warnings, impacts, management and outcomes of the crisis situation.

Checklist section

This section holds checklists for use in preparing for, and conducting, crisis management (or recovery management activities). Four critical groups of checklists form the PACE checklist set covering:

- *P*reparation (including equipment lists, skill lists, procedural lists);
- *A*ction (strategy and unit-action sequential checklists);
- *C*ontact (alert or warning contact lists, specialist assistants, teams and leaders);
- *E*quipment (supply and use during response lists, loss list, logistics and supply lists).

Organizations using decision and action assistance tools (such as OMT) may wish to insert a copy of each tool in this section.

Recovery planning

Recovery planning is often separated from response planning. This helps:

- separate the immediate (response management) and longer-term (recovery management) issues;
- establish a point at which organization efforts move from trying to resolve a crisis situation to cleaning up and managing the after-effects of the crisis.

Response activation should prompt activation of the recovery management process.

Some strategic response structures can provide a basis for recovery management structures. The CMS structure allows parallel efforts wherein specialist personnel can assist both operations. INCO, IMMO and PUMO staff and members of PAG and NOLO, for example, can provide the same services.

Recovery planning is particularly emphasized in business, commercial and industrial organizations. These use a number of terms to mean the same fundamental objective of recovery, but with accents on how quickly executives and managers of an organization believe recovery needs to be accomplished. Hence a general term used for recovery planning is *business recovery planning (BRP)*. Other similar terms include *business continuity planning* (with an accent on not losing business activities or services) and *business resumption planning* (where the accent falls upon the need to resume operations after some period of discontinuity). Business recovery planners and managers tend to use these terms interchangeably.

While BRPs have a similar profile to CRPs, there are some adaptations that reflect the need to interact with specialist outside agencies (engineers, insurers, recovery specialists, hot site managers) and outside agents for repairing or replacing damaged or destroyed equipment.

A typical BRP can look much like the above CRP, with many similar sections. A BRP is likely to include the following:

- cover page
- authorization page
- who reads the plan
- confirmation form
- policy section
- plan administration section
- risk assessment.
- pre-recovery section
- communication policy section
- finance, legal and administrative section
- activation section
- recovery command and co-ordination section
- team leader contact list
- team contact lists (including consultants and vendors)
- recovery strategies and action steps
- other contact lists (staff, major customers)
- recovery sites – including hot and warm sites for computer and call centre operations
- PACE checklists.

The planning process

Having provided the core components of response and recovery plans, some consideration of the process towards producing these plans may help planners. Revision of the chapters on risk assessment (Chapter 2), impact analysis (Chapter 3), crisis reduction (Chapter 4), warnings (Chapter 5) and media management (Chapter 7) will help develop guidelines for plans. The concluding section in Chapter 3 also provides some advice on steering analysis and plans through organizational requirements and procedures.

Organizational and community guides to action

Organizations responsible for community safety or with operations that may severely affect the community should crisis situations arise often provide documentary advice for that community. These guides for action need to include specific information that includes contact persons and telephone numbers, types of threat or risk, how and when warnings will be made, actions to take once warnings are broadcast, and simple basic first aid (CPR, breath resuscitation, dealing with shock, treating wounds and burns).

Such guides are generally laid out as follows:

- an initial page that provides contact numbers and the main action message;
- a simple outline of the threats under consideration, each with simple action steps for the reader to follow;
- a description of how and what warnings will be made should a crisis situation arise;
- a simple outline of the response processes that will be enacted for each of the threats;
- a section on being prepared for emergencies;
- a section on emergency supplies and equipment to have available (if appropriate);
- a section on checking for hazards in the surrounding environment;
- a section on first aid.

By making this material available managers may improve the response by bystanders and victims. The material also provides tangible evidence of 'due care' being taken by the executives and management of an organization. The improvement can be enhanced when executives and managers seriously and enthusiastically include hands-on practice and training in undertaking the actions outlined in the guide.

Some hints on planning

- *Define a crisis by the effect on response resources rather than by type of incident.* Too many planners try to plan for the situation or scenario rather than for the effective use of available resources. Planners need to work on the basis that a crisis situation is a situation in which there is a threat to resources and people that has little time to be resolved and which has demands that overwhelm the existing personnel, facilities, equipment and capabilities of an organization.
- *Plans are guides to action.* Do not overplan as this adds inflexibility. Rather maintain a focus on detailing objectives and missions, providing guidelines where the tasks require sensitive management or where severe risk is involved.

261

- *No plan will ever fully meet a specific crisis event in detail.* Probably the best level of planned readiness is to be able to discard reference to the plan because the response tasks and objectives are familiar to the users. The PACE checklists are then used to ensure that the operations are monitored and all tasks are undertaken.
- *One feature often forgotten in planning is to incorporate clear guidelines for regular updates.* Plans need to be regularly maintained (updated) and such activities need to be made part of the formal plan and need to have set deadlines for those reviews to be accomplished, reviewed, approved and implemented.

  Executives and managers need to remember that plans are a means to the objective of effective crisis management and not an end in themselves. Plans and users need to focus on:
  - dealing with information as well as the problem;
  - dealing with external as well as internal perceptions and realities of a crisis; and
  - maintaining links to ongoing operations of those sites or units not affected by the crisis.
- *Plans need to consider operational priorities in the event of more than one crisis situation occurring at the same time.* Simultaneous events do occur. For example, in 1982 an Air Florida aircraft crashed in the Potomac River within seconds of take-off from Washington City Airport. Thirty minutes later, a crowded commuter train was derailed less than a mile (1.37 kilometres) from the aircrash. Both of these situations had to be managed during a snowstorm.
- *Plans need to include provision for shift-work.* Should operations continue past eight hours, executives and managers need to develop shift-work routines for crisis response personnel. Shift-work procedures are particularly likely when undertaking recovery activities after a major physical crisis situation. Resources and staff need to be left in reserve to act as relief and rotation for on-site personnel. Without the crisis manager's intervention, there is likely to be an overcommitment of personnel in the early stages of a situation at the expense of fully fit and alert personnel hours later.
- *Have basic user instructions and job tasks listed for positions.* Planners and their plans often forget that full response teams will rarely be available. Some responders will be on training courses, sick, on leave, unable to respond due to crisis impact or no longer with the organization. Some may even refuse to respond. Accidents and task requirements may also remove normal users away from their equipment. Hence major job specifications and basic instructions for the use of equipment need to be clearly attached to workstations and equipment.
- *Design and implement standardized reporting procedures.* One of the attachments to a crisis plan and to equipment used in information reporting should be a standard reporting process. By using a standardized reporting procedure, respondents are helped to focus and calm down. Recipients are

able to quickly use standard received message forms. More aspects of a crisis are likely to be recorded and processed, and omissions of major details are less likely.

● *Ensure a clearly defined process through which the crisis response and management may be upgraded.* One feature often missing from crisis plans is how an upward shift of management is processed or 'triggered'. Some professional response agencies (such as firefighting agencies) operate on a size-by-alarm signal. In many cases, however, upward or even lateral changes of who takes overall charge of the situation depends on subjective judgement, with all the consequent biases of ego and organizational position blurring accurate assessment. One simple rule of thumb planners may use is that when 80 per cent of the resources available to a unit or department are committed; the next upward level of management needs to be brought into play.

● *Develop priorities and core plan objectives using the 80–20 cubed rule.* By using the simple 80–20 cubed rule, plans are based on use of 50 to 55 per cent of the total possible available resources. Identify key priorities that make best use of 50 per cent of the resources and regard any more resource availability as positive additions that can be used or deployed on secondary or tertiary priorities.

The 80–20 cubed rule works as follows: 80 per cent of equipment and personnel is likely to be available at any one time; 20 per cent is likely to be unavailable due to servicing and being absent or non-operational. Of the original 80 per cent, 80 per cent (that is, 64 per cent of complement) will actually respond to instructions from the crisis command and control centre; 20 per cent will be unable to respond or refuse to do so. Of the 80 per cent who actually respond, 80 per cent (that is, 51.2 per cent of complement) are likely to arrive where the crisis manager wishes; 20 per cent will get lost, held up, distracted by another facet of the crisis or simply break down. Hence smart planning uses just over half the available resources, and regards any increase in resources beyond that figure as a bonus. Note the positive psychological effects on a crisis manager should 20 or 30 per cent more resources be available beyond this minimum 50 to 55 per cent – decisions become positive rather than negative in nature.

● *Use forward planning as crisis situations can provide an opportunity for change.* Crisis plans (particularly for communities or organizations covering large areas such as industrial estates, airports, dockside regions) can include a restoration plan that redesigns the area or structures within the area. Through consultation processes and feedback from managers and users of the potentially stricken area, restoration plans allow resources to be more effectively placed within the community, estate or given area. Out of a crisis impact may emerge a better planned, more desirable site.

● *Ensure that alternative facilities and recovery agreements are valid in BRPs.* When developing business recovery/resumption plans, the contract and service level agreements need to be regularly updated. In particular, evaluation and identification of alternative facilities need to be:

- undertaken before a crisis happens
- comprehensive
- validated, and
- the capacity and equipment made available clearly noted and checked for compatibility of use.

REALITY BITE

Penton Publishing, Cleveland, Ohio, USA, 1995

This case study illustrates the benefits of planning for crisis management (recovery operations). The crisis was a burst water main that was a non-major (loss of structure) situation yet proved a complex operation. This example thus also illustrates a smaller crisis.

Background

Penton Publishing Inc. produces over 30 business-to-business magazines. The writing and publishing of all but four magazines and all the support services for the organization are undertaken in Penton's headquarters in Cleveland, Ohio, USA. The business occupies the second to the sixth floors of the 26-storey Diamond Building in Cleveland.

Incident

At 4.20 am on Saturday, 28 January 1995, a large 36-inch water main fractured outside the Diamond Building. The ensuing jet of water sprayed four floors (around 60 feet or 18 metres) into the air for 90 minutes, sending dirt and debris through 19 windows on the second, third and fourth floors along with thousands of gallons of water. Both the exterior and interior of the building were extensively damaged.

The force of the water moved furniture and computers. Everything in the offices was totally saturated. As the crisis happened in winter ice coated the furniture and hung from the ceiling. Electricity was out for over three days. Asbestos was exposed creating additional health hazards. When heat returned, pipes burst and led to more water damage. Most modern office equipment was lost. This included at least 100 desktop computers as well as printers, copiers, fax machines, modems, phones and furniture.

Response

The building managers notified the police and fire department and made sure that all employees were safe. Only three Penton employees were in the building at the time. These employees powered down the mainframe and followed other procedures in the response and recovery plan.

As the building was inaccessible, a command centre was needed. Penton's plans included the use of a printing press in a suburb about 15 miles (24 kilometres) away. The crisis management decided that somewhere closer was needed. The owners of the Diamond had a building across the street and they gave Penton space for a command centre and some conference rooms.

The technical team met on the day of the disaster. Production schedules for magazine material and mailing labels were due at the printer so priorities of recovery had to be determined. Team managers and the insurance carrier were also notified, as were appropriate vendors, mainframe services and computer resellers. The corporate communications director could not be contacted.

On the next day some entry into the building was allowed. Damage was assessed, the technical team unplugged all computers and all movable equipment was removed as quickly as possible. Assessment of clean-up, restoration and the dehumidifying needs was made. Vendors for services appeared on site. Consequently, work began on the second day on the repair and replacement of equipment. Back-ups of data and software were retrieved, and supplies and forms that were needed were ordered.

Estimates of temporary office space needed were made and arrangements were made for that space to be hired. Employees were contacted at home, and media coverage (including radio and TV) commenced. As there was little furniture at first, people sat on a floor with phones, pencils and paper and a script of what to say. The impact was played down. Customers were told that Penton was in business as usual. Arrangements were made to meet twice a day to check recovery status and progress, to identify and deliberate on any problems and to assign any re-evaluation of priorities. All expenditures were tracked separately from the ongoing costs.

Statistics
The cost to Penton was over $4 000 000.

Comment
The Penton case provides a number of issues that support points made earlier on planning. For example, Penton crisis managers could not get in touch with their designated crisis spokesperson who was their corporate communications director. This director was in the process of shifting to a new residential address. According to the plan, there was supposed to be one spokesperson to communicate with the media, so with no apparent spokesperson available, media representatives talked to employees who came to look at the building on the Saturday when the situation happened. Television cameras also recorded meetings that could be seen through the glass.

The plan proposed a cold site for recovery that was not used due to distance. The management effectively made flexible decisions on the spot and found a command and co-ordination centre and meeting rooms in a building across the street from the site.

Some planned details were well supported in practice. Recovery, technical and facilities teams did exactly what they were supposed to, enabling Penton's mainframe to be running within three days.

Other aspects in the plan that the managers found useful included the following:

● *Defining disaster as an interruption to the normal process*, as there were no mindsets as to what could go wrong. Mindsets arise when action decisions are bared on pre-situation beliefs rather than the realities of a situation. As pointed out in this chapter, crisis definitions need to be based on the concepts of threat, limited time and the sense that the demand for resources to resolve a crisis exceeds the available resources.

- *Having an inventory of all computers, peripherals and software and of all furniture and forms needed for quick recovery operations.* This is particularly valid for recovery planning. Ensure that these details are regularly updated and that improvement wishlists (*see* Chapter 15) are also developed.
- *Having available the phone numbers of vendors, police, team members, customers and other useful contacts.* These lists can be placed in the PACE section and near relevant action plans for specific scenarios or impact damage management. Do ensure that these are updated at least on a monthly basis as contacts (especially those within an organization) can regularly change.
- *Having off-site tape back-ups.* Do use geophysical separation for this principle. When the Docklands bomb exploded in London (1995), many organizations had their back-ups on site, on another floor of the same building, or only a few buildings away. Between the area of damage and the sterile zone secured by the police, many organizations could not access their own sites nor retrieve back-up storage of data.

Penton managers also used equipment and communication approaches that were not part of the planned response. These included:

- *Flashlights, walkie-talkies, pagers and cellular phones.* Note the emphasis on mobile communications equipment. Remember to have access to (or buy or rent) large numbers of spare batteries and battery chargers. Appoint a staff member to oversee the use of this equipment.
- *A daily employee newsletter.* Far too many plans provide little or no attention to communicating with stakeholders. Organizational members are important stakeholders and need to have ready access to reliable sources of information.
- *Agreement to be able to use temporary space was not in place.* Perhaps the most significant activity within a BRP is the access to hot (immediately ready to take over a full operation), warm (can be brought up to full operation within a few hours) or cold (space in which to bring in equipment and personnel) sites. These arrangements are either internal or external. In either case check the amount of spare room for storage and cleaning of retrieved documents and equipment, particularly with outside or third-party recovery vendors.
- As the event happened on a payday and at the end of January (a taxation day), employee pay cheques and their W2 tax forms became a major priority to be accomplished by the following Tuesday (31 January).

One benefit noted from the aftermath of the situation was that work spaces were rearranged more effectively. This is a key benefit that can be gained in recovery management, as outlined in Chapter 15. This improvement can be enhanced by undertaking regular wishlist activities that produce a list of preferred facilities, equipment, work procedures and policies that may be activated when a crisis situation damages an organization. Should the desired improvements be potentially financed by insurance, remember to check the fine detail of existing policies and discuss with the insurers what can be done.

One effective feature was the readiness with which the three employees on site at the time of the situation responded. By powering down the mainframe and following other procedures in the plans they were able to limit some of the potential damage that may have worsened the situation. Managers and executives need to evolve evacuation and impact reducing activities (such as ACCCE – *see* Chapter 4) that are clear, simple, logical and do not impose increased risk to people or resources.

Management perspective

This crisis situation did not include loss of structure yet threatened to overwhelm the Penton response and recovery plan. Part of the threat of being overwhelmed came from the insurance arrangements that required magazine deadlines to be met. At the same time, Penton crisis management generally adapted and worked effectively around the problems involved.

Once in the temporary crisis co-ordination centre and conference rooms, Penton personnel began some damage limitation and stakeholder communication. Note that an organization needs to do what their spokespeople say will be done. Once Penton employees, for example, reassured customers that the operation was in 'business as usual' mode, the organization needed to meet that commitment. Espoused actions (those stated to be so) need to be matched by enacted actions (those physically seen to be so).

In the Penton evaluation of the crisis and their recovery management, they identified a number of interesting points for future improvement to their plans and crisis response and recovery management. Among these points were the following:

- The length of time to recover had been underestimated. The plan gave an estimate of three months. The temporary space across the street was used for 18 months.
- Clean-up and restoration vendors just showed up and followed employees around looking for work.
- Representatives of the insurance carrier were out of town and did not turn up until late Monday. This insurer changed the vendors for clean-up and restoration from one company to three companies and this caused confusion, disruption and ill-will.
- Security was either too lax or too strict and thus caused conflicts.
- Besides being a potential hazard, the asbestos problem caused employee discomfort and concern.
- People on floors not directly affected still experienced odour problems and complained of feeling ill.
- Co-ordinators should have stayed at the command centre. When they were needed for decisions they often could not be found.

Notice needs to be taken of the points about the asbestos and smell. After a crisis situation, many people are highly sensitized to cues that suggest the crisis may not be over. Should these sensitivities not be addressed with understanding, tact and even action, then morale will drop and workplace absenteeism and employee turnover may increase.

Executives and managers need especially to note the last point. Managers are there to manage, not to do, though there are some circumstances when a manager needs to lead by example. Every time they do so, however, they let go of their grasp of the bigger picture of what is going on around them, of what next needs to be considered, and even of threats to the health and safety of those they are managing. Ensure that link personnel within the decision and operational chain not only remain linked to the information communication system but do so where they can respond with factual information on matters relating to the activities they are managing.

References

McCaskey, M. B. (1974) 'A contingency approach to planning: planning with goals and planning without goals', *Academy of Management*, 17, 281–91.

Robbins, S. P. (1994) *Management*, 4th edn. Englewood Cliffs, NJ: Prentice Hall.

Readiness

Having worked through risk and impact analysis, looked at ways of reducing exposure to sources of risk and consequent crisis situations, and prepared warning systems and plans, executives and managers need to ready themselves and other organization members to deal with crisis situations when these occur. Readiness is as much a state of mind within people and an organization as it is a planned and tangible process of resource acquisition and resource deployment.

This chapter introduces users to the broad concepts of readiness management. Beginning with the FPC concept, users are then directed to ways in which readiness can be continued and increased through assessing and maintaining plans and through training and simulated crisis response activities.

The FPC model

The FPC model consists of three dimensions – Familiarity, Predictability and Capability – which form a composite measure of effectiveness of response (*see* Figure 12.1).

Consider any human interaction and three of the core variables that lead to good or poor performance are:

- How familiar are participants with the situation?
- How predictable is the process?
- What levels of appropriate skills do participants hold?

Should the answers for all three be high then the interaction performance is also likely to be high. On the other hand should one or more answers be low then the corresponding level of effective performance will be somewhere between the best and worst estimates for the three measures.

Poor interaction performance occurs when measures for any to all of these three variables are low. For example, person-to-person interaction can move from co-operation to conflict simply because one of those interacting does

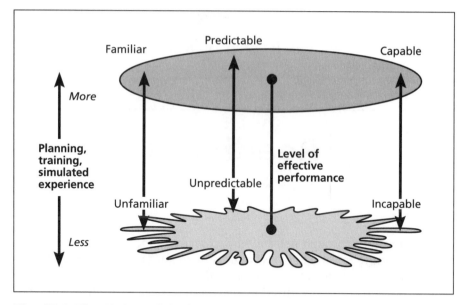

Fig. 12.1 The FPC model – high level of effective performance

something that appears unpredictable in terms of the behavioural model of that person held by any other person in the interaction. An argument develops because the behaviour of one person appears inconsistent and thus unpredictable from another person's POV.

Performance may also be low when one enters a new environment or begins a task that has not been done before or has been rarely attempted. Playing sport on a new site, driving in areas never before encountered or joining a new organization are activities where performance is lowered while the newcomer learns about the way the environment appears to interact and influence his or her activities. Those encountering a crisis situation without plans or previous experience tend to perform poorly because of unfamiliarity with the situation. As familiarity increases, performance can increase.

Performance is likely to be poor or low when trying out a sport for the first time, learning to drive a car or taking on a completely new job. This lack of skills or capability to do the new task lowers performance. Performance increases as the skills involved are practised and as the person becomes more familiar with the surrounding environment. A crisis situation is likely to be poorly handled if those involved have not regularly rehearsed or experimented with the needed behaviours and skills.

Executives and managers need to increase the knowledge, familiarity and skills involved in dealing with crisis situations. These elements mirror the variables of predictability (from pre-crisis knowledge and information gathered during a crisis), familiarity (through knowledge of the plan and any experience – including simulated crisis response and recovery activities) and capability (levels of appropriate skills held by those dealing with a crisis situation). While all three variables form necessary parts of a readiness pro-gramme, managers and executives can identify the variable with the lowest assessment and make the activity that improves that assessment a priority.

Each of these variables is interactively linked. Familiarity breeds assump-tions about the predictability of the nature and effects of a crisis. Perceived capability to respond to a crisis situation is often influenced by the familiarity with the situation held by those involved and how predictable a particular crisis situation appears to those involved. Predictability of the effects and nature of a crisis is based partly on the perceived familiarity with the crisis held by those involved and their belief in their capability to respond effec-tively to that crisis.

Figure 12.1 (illustrating the FPC model) shows a probable high performance given the high measures for the three variables. Conceptually, consider the three variables (labelled, with arrows at each end) as supporting a flat oval sur-face, the centre of which is the point from which the measure of effective per-formance is made. It may help to view the flat oval as a transparent grey glass surface on top of three supporting legs. Performance is roughly a measure of the interaction of the three variables, so the height of the table from the floor (or the crisis, which is represented by the splash in Figure 12.1) reflects this measure.

Each variable is a sliding continuum that runs from high on a variable (familiar, predictable or capable) down to low (unfamiliar, unpredictable or incapable). Planning, training and experience help increase these measures and thus improve response and recovery performance. This improvement is a prime reason why planning, skill training and undertaking regular exercises and crisis situation simulations are so strongly urged upon executives, man-agers and members of organizations. Response and recovery management is likely to be slow, costly, inefficient and potentially unsafe for those involved if planning is not adequate and up to date, if training is rarely done and erratic, or when crisis situations are not somehow made familiar to those people.

The Kobe earthquake (1995) illustrates this point. Part of the sluggish response was possibly due to lack of regular planning and practice. Van Biema (1995) found that:

> Longtime emphasis on the threat in Central Pacific Japan created an atrophy of vigilance in the western part of the country: in Tokyo 27% of homes kept emer-gency supplies; in Osaka the number had shrunk to 2.6%. While Tokyo's army and civilian officials conducted yearly drills to test their coordination, military officials reluctantly admit that in the Kobe area they did not. (pp. 20–1).

This reduction in preparation and planning may be due to the enervation of readiness and training that takes place over time when no crisis or disaster happens. Such lack of planning, training and experiential activity suggests that those involved were likely to perform more poorly than could have been possible.

FPC and experience

Familiarity, predictability and capability are dependent upon the experience held by those involved as well as the planning and information exchange capabilities of response and recovery structures. Experience comes from many sources. The best form of *experience* is a physical and mental encounter with crisis situations, and with a crisis situation similar or nearly identical to the one subsequently encountered. In terms of knowing of what 'happens', no experience can be better than 'having been there before'.

There is a negative side to actually experiencing a particular crisis. Too much reference to past experience can lead people to ignore the unique aspects of the crisis situation they are trying to handle. Preparing for crises purely on the basis of past experiences can lead to disaster. No crisis situation has exactly the same form, the same time limitations, the same demand for resources that exceeds the available resources, or the same temporal, social and economic threats. Past experience is, however, useful in defining common feelings, in planning possible actions needed and in suggesting some of the likely effects and outcomes of a crisis event.

Experience may be gained by watching others operating in a crisis situation. This indirect experience is called *vicarious learning* and is a more common and more available learning approach. Watching live crisis response and recovery actions or the management of situations recorded on video or film can help viewers see and hear the environment of a specific crisis and mentally register what their own experience of such a situation may be. This vicarious learning increases familiarity. Analysis of the environment and response or recovery actions performed can increase the predictability of the type of crisis situation being watched. News reports and documentaries similarly allow viewers to safely experience natural disasters and major accidents.

The problem with vicarious learning is that it is detached from actuality: seeing violent hurricanes or tornadoes is different from feeling them and having senses and thoughts numbed by the smog of crisis. The consequences and impacts of nearly all major passenger aircraft accidents in the Western world are quickly covered by media reports. Nothing, however, prepares one for the actual sight, smell, taste and sound of a major passenger aircraft accident.

Experience helps people learn about the nature of crisis situations and to identify possible crisis impacts on the organization and on the environment. In terms of the FPC model experiential learning increases:

- familiarity with the appearance, effects and processes involved in the crisis;
- ability to predict the cause and consequences of the crisis; and
- skill capability to operate in the crisis-impacted environment.

The effect of low measures of the variables in the FPC model

Many performances in crisis response and recovery will reflect values that fall between the extremes of optimal (very high) and worst (very low) performances. Performance can be estimated by examining the likely performance measure when one or two of the three measures are low. Given the dynamic and time-consuming nature of response and recovery activity, explanations for performance being better than the worst measured variable or even generally improving are likely to be based on experiential learning acquired during the crisis situation.

One low variable

When one variable is low and the other two are high, the result is a downward slope of the performance oval. The measure of effective performance will be moderate (between the low and the two high measures).

When familiarity is low, higher levels of skills and more certainty of information and the nature of the situation will contribute to higher overall performance than the lack of familiarity would suggest. The result would be a hesitant response with response and recovery performance increasing as those involved become more familiar with the situation and probably more confident in their capacity to operate due to increased perceived certainty of information and increased knowledge of the situation.

When predictability is low, the result would be a hesitant response or recovery operation once the initial effort to activate was finished. The apparent improved performance (against level of predictability) may lead to some dangerous overconfidence due to possible perceptions of local situation predictability ('familiarity breeding contempt').

When capability is low (*see* Figure 12.2), the higher levels of familiarity and predictability may provide an environment in which appropriate skills may be quickly, if roughly, learned as time passes ('learning by the seat of the pants'). In some situations this learning may increase overall response or recovery performance. In other situations, however, overconfidence due to apparent predictability, confidence in information and familiarity may result in poor decisions that lead to losses of resources and people.

Two low variables

When two variables are low, the result is likely to be an overall performance that is lower than the performance in a one low variable case.

When familiarity is the only high measure, the result probably will be a performance closer to the two low variable measures. That this performance may generally be better than measures for predictability and capability may lead to overconfident and poor decisions in early response or recovery activities. Performance may then further decrease. In some situations, increased local situation predictability and roughly learned field skills may increase performance,

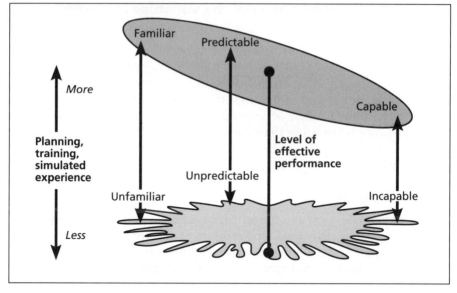

Fig. 12.2 The FPC model illustrating the effect of inadequate skill capabilities

given the benign effects of familiarity.

When predictability is high, performance may be slightly higher than the lack of familiarity or skills would suggest. This will be due to confidence in cause-and-effect predictions, learning undertaken during the crisis situation and information exchange revealing aspects of the environment and task procedures that appear to enhance familiarity and offer coarse skill acquisition. Lack of skills and familiarity may lead to sluggish and hesitant response and recovery actions for much of the early and middle periods of the crisis situation.

When capability is high (*see* Figure 12.3), the overall performance is likely to be slow at first, then quicken as possession of skills leads to successful decision making, then decrease as overconfidence in the predictability and familiarity of the situation leads to errors of action choices.

The FPC model, and the resulting visual figures, helps those responsible for crisis management illustrate the need for planning, skill and resource acquisition, and experiential training. By increasing the familiarity, the predictability and the capability to effectively respond, the smog of crisis and the possible effects of a crisis may be reduced. Regular training and refresher sessions in all types of preparation activities not only improve familiarity, predictability and capability (and thus levels of effective performance), but also maintain interest and readiness through the diversity of approaches that can be used. Experiential training eventually becomes one of the most important components of readiness preparation – increasing the potential performance

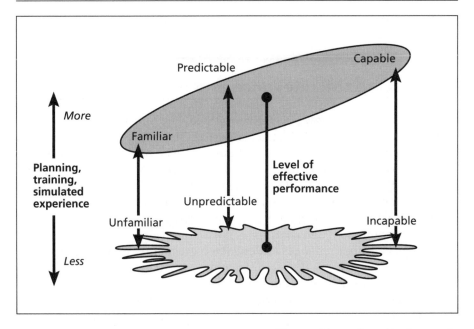

Fig. 12.3 The FPC model showing the effect of low familiarity and predictability measures

of organizational members and of the crisis team, testing crisis plans for defects, and helping executives and managers gain a hands-on feel for the tasks they need to undertake in crisis situations. The other important component is to evaluate and maintain up-to-date crisis response and recovery plans.

Maintaining plans

As suggested in the previous chapter, response and recovery plans need to outline clear guidelines on how the plans will be maintained, including specific details on:

- who keeps the plans up to date with organizational and environmental changes;
- who oversees such activities;
- who reviews and approves the changes;
- the procedures and timing for checking the details, changing plans and exercising the tasks outlined by the plans;
- how exercises and crisis situations will be evaluated;
- how recommendations from those evaluations will be implemented within the plans;
- how and when detailed assessment of the plans is undertaken.

275

These steps provide the framework for active maintenance of crisis response and recovery plans.

Checking the relevance and accuracy of plans

Two easy approaches allow plans to be checked. The first of these can be done at the lowest unit level for which a plan exists. This approach may be used as part of a familiarization programme should there be new unit members. The approach is simply to take the plan and 'walk through' the details with the members of the unit. This helps all members identify key response or recovery personnel and their deputies or alternates, while checking that those people are still undertaking the tasks and activities outlined in the plan. Changes to equipment and environment (structural alterations, unit transfers to different locations, changes to designated evacuation points) may also be identified.

On a larger scale, executives and managers can require an operational walk-through of the strategic and action plans by having a 'walk-through and walk-around' assessment undertaken by the planners and crisis managers and supervisors. Where the simple walk-through may consist of a few hours in a conference room reading through the plans and checking for changes, the walk-around assessment checks the environment while the plan is checked point by point. This mobility enables planners, section leaders, managers and executives to see the environment and check that the required actions and tasks can still be performed. Should such practices not be regularly undertaken, then post-planning changes may block and stop the plan from working. In many cases, existing crisis response and recovery plans have not been changed to cover:

- significant alterations to interior designs (including blocked off or removed emergency exit paths);
- new equipment;
- changes in storage of hazardous goods;
- changes in work practices (shift schedules, core resources and skills);
- changes in organizational structures.

Four specific issues need to be actively monitored by executives and managers:

- *Changes in organizational personnel structures can affect plans.* Organizations that have undertaken expansion, contraction, resizing, upsizing, or downsizing are likely to have removed, replaced or made redundant those persons and positions that contributed to response and recovery action.
- *Anticipated response and recovery processes outlined in plans may be untenable in reality.* Many organizations have a fallback position that states that response and recovery tasks can at least be done manually. These state-

ments tend to be untested. Many organizations do not have the resources to handle the manual management of records and organizational tasks nor sufficient staff numbers to do such time-consuming activities.

- *Changes in resources and equipment may mean that planned responses and recovery operations will not work.* In many cases, changes in software, hardware, work tools and organizational records are not automatically made to the designated hot or warm site resources and equipment.
- *Provision for lost organization members is not adequately implemented.* Plans usually assume that all personnel will be available for response and recovery redeployment and for continuing the mission-oriented activities of the organization. In some cases organizational personnel are incapacitated, injured or even killed. Strategic plans need to identify how these people may be quickly replaced. At an action level, resources and equipment may need to be clearly labelled and have accompanying basic instructions on their operation and co-ordinating task activities.

Crisis audits

Executives and managers need to undertake a detailed evaluation of the readiness and capacity of the organization to handle crisis situations. This process is similar to undertaking a financial audit and is, not surprisingly, termed a *crisis audit*.

Done comprehensively, a systematic crisis audit can be used to augment initial surveys of risk and impacts undertaken in BIA activities. As an ongoing process (used at least annually) the crisis audit helps maintain currency and identify weaknesses in a crisis management programme.

A non-exhaustive set of cued prompts is outlined below. These offer a skeleton around which users can add their own specific questions.

What early warning systems are present?

- How do these work? What are the strengths? What are the weaknesses?
- Who maintains the alarms? Are they properly qualified?
- How can the alarms be improved?

Is there a crisis management policy? Why? Why not?

- Who creates the policy? Why? How realistic and specific is the policy?
- Is the policy updated? Why? Why not? How? When?
- How can this policy be formed or enhanced?

Is there a crisis management strategy? Why? Why not?

- Who creates the strategy? Why?
- How realistic and specific is the strategy?
- Is the strategy updated? Why? Why not? How? When?
- How can the strategy be formed or enhanced?

Is a crisis response team available?

- Are roles and responsibilities clearly defined?
- Who is involved? Why? How? When? Where?
- How can this team be formed or enhanced?
- How experienced are the personnel? How well trained are they?
- Are the response managers experienced? How well trained are they?
- Who gives these managers orders or information?
- To whom are these managers accountable? Why?
- Who do these managers manage? Why?
- How can these people be helped to become better?

Is a crisis recovery team available?

- Are roles and responsibilities clearly defined?
- Who is involved? Why? How? When? Where?
- How can this team be formed or enhanced?
- How experienced are the personnel? How well trained are they?
- Are the recovery managers experienced? How well trained are they?
- Who gives these managers orders or information?
- To whom are these managers accountable? Why?
- Who do these managers manage? Why?
- How can these people be helped to become better?

Does an independent and separate budget for crisis management exist? Why? Why not?

- Who manages the budget? Why?
- Who is ultimately accountable for the budget? Why?
- How much is the budget? What are the outlays?
- How can the budget be formed or enhanced?

How good are response and recovery information management processes?

- What are the strengths? What are the weaknesses?
- Do the users hold sufficient skills? Why or why not?
- How can these processes be improved?

Is the organization and response or recovery management interface effective?

- What are the strengths? What are the weaknesses?
- How can the interface be improved?
- Does a mindset exist? Is groupthink present?
- Is management open to criticism and bad news?

Are sufficient resources available for crisis response and crisis recovery?

- What resources can be improved?
- Who maintains the resources? Are these the appropriate people to do so? Why?

Are organizational members introduced to their role in any crisis event?

- Why? Why not? How? When? Where?
- What resources are used/handed out?
- What training is undertaken? Why? When?
- Is this reinforced regularly? When?
- How can this introduction to their role in a crisis be accomplished or enhanced?

Are appropriate organizational members given training in the tasks they perform in a crisis situation?

- Why? Why not? How? When? Where?
- What resources are used/handed out?
- What training is undertaken? Why? When?
- Is this reinforced regularly? When?
- How can this training be accomplished or enhanced?

Are appropriate organizational members given training in the skills they need to perform in a crisis?

- Why? Why not? How? When? Where?
- What resources are used/handed out?
- What training is undertaken? Why? When?
- Is this reinforced regularly? When?
- How can this skill training be accomplished or enhanced?

Are response or recovery workshops conducted?

- Why? Why not? How? When? Where?
- What resources are used/handed out?
- What training is undertaken? Why? When?
- Is this reinforced regularly? When?
- Who participates? Who organizes the workshops? Who runs the workshops? Why?
- How can these workshops be initiated or enhanced?

Are experiential crisis exercises conducted?

- Why? Why not? How? When? Where?
- What resources are used/handed out?
- What training is undertaken? Why? When?
- Is this reinforced regularly? When?
- Who participates? Who organizes the exercises? Who runs the exercises? Why?
- How can the exercises be initiated or enhanced?

Do plans exist?

- What type are these plans (master/strategic/tactical or action)
- Are these up to date? Who updates the plans? How are these updated? When are the plans updated?
- Who manages the plans? Are these the appropriate people to do so? Why?

How is crisis response or crisis recovery activated?

- What are the strengths of this activation? What are the weaknesses?

- How can the activation process(es) be improved?

What crisis situations are included in plans and preparations? Why?

- How detailed are these plans and preparations? Why?
- Are the plans too detailed? Too inflexible? Too general? Why?

What control does the organization have over the crisis or crisis impacts?

- Full? Partial?

What crisis situations may be overlooked? Why?

- On what basis are crisis situations covered or not covered by plans? Why?
- Do the situations covered create a mindset? Why? Why not?

How are the plans presented? In what form (bound/loose-leaf/computer-based)? Why?

- Can the presentation be improved? How?
- Are the contents of the plan clear? Are the instructions clear?

Are crisis audits conducted on crisis response and recovery issues? Why? Why not?

- How? When? Where?
- Who participates? Who organizes the audits? Who runs the audits? Why?
- How can the audits be accomplished or enhanced?

Crisis response or recovery operations

What are the time-lines for any crisis situation?

- How soon may these situations be resolved? Why?

What are the response tasks needed for each phase?

- Are these the complete response tasks? Why? Why not?
- Can these be done differently? Why? Why not?
- Who makes these responses?

If response handling comes from outside the organization –

- Who are the respondents?
- Who lets them in?
- Who liaises with them?
- Who is in charge?
- What do those within the organization do?

Is there a crisis management centre for response and recovery operations? Why? Why not?

- Who works in the centre? Why?
- How realistic and specific is the centre?
- Are the resources updated? Why? Why not? How? When?
- How can the crisis management centre be created or enhanced?

Is there an inventory of resources for use by crisis response and recovery managers? Why? Why not?

- Who handles the inventory? Why?
- How realistic and specific is the inventory?
- Is the inventory updated? Why? Why not? How? When?
- How can the inventory of resources be accomplished or enhanced?

Is there an inventory of personnel and skills for use by crisis response and recovery managers? Why? Why not?

- Who handles the inventory? Why?
- How realistic and specific is the inventory?
- Is the inventory updated? Why? Why not? How? When?
- How can the inventory of personnel and their skills be created or enhanced?

What in-house sources can cause crisis situations? Why?

- What can be done to eliminate or reduce these sources?
- What factors or elements within these sources contribute to the risks? Why?
- What can be done to eliminate or reduce these factors or elements?
- What can be done to transfer or cover these factors or elements?
- What can be done to control or contain the possible crisis situations? Why?
- What can be done to improve the management of these sources of risk? Why? How?

What sources adjacent to the organization can cause crisis situations? Why?

- What can be done to eliminate or reduce these sources?
- What factors or elements within these sources contribute to the risks? Why?
- What can be done to eliminate or reduce these factors or elements?
- What can be done to transfer or cover these factors or elements?
- What can be done to control or contain the possible crisis situations? Why?
- What can be done to improve the management of these sources of risk? Why? How?

What regional sources can cause crisis situations? Why?

- What can be done to eliminate or reduce these sources?
- What factors or elements within these sources contribute to the risks? Why?
- What can be done to eliminate or reduce these factors or elements?
- What can be done to transfer or cover these factors or elements?
- What can be done to control or contain the possible crisis situations? Why?
- What can be done to improve the management of these sources of risk? Why? How?

What global or remote sources can cause crisis situations? Why?

- What can be done to eliminate or reduce these sources?
- What factors or elements within these sources contribute to the risks? Why?
- What can be done to eliminate or reduce these factors or elements?
- What can be done to transfer or cover these factors or elements?
- What can be done to control or contain the possible crisis situations? Why?

- What can be done to improve the management of these sources of risk? Why? How?

What will be affected by a crisis situation? Why?

What specific sources lead to what specific impacts? Why?

- What can be done to eliminate or reduce these impacts? Why?
- Are all sources and impacts able to be identified? Why? Why not?
- What resources can be used to assist in handling the crisis impacts?
- What resources can be used to assist in recovering from the crisis impacts?

Who are the likely victims? Why?

- What needs to be done for the victims?
- Who does this? Why?
- What are the organization's responsibilities? Why?
- Who manages this? Why?
- What can be done to help manage the victims? Why? How?

Who are the likely respondents? Why?

- What needs to be done for response personnel?
- Who does this? Why?
- What are the organization's responsibilities? Why?
- Who manages this? Why?
- What can be done to help manage the respondents? Why? How?

Who are the likely bystanders? Why?

- What needs to be done for the bystanders?
- Who does this? Why?
- What are the organization's responsibilities? Why?
- Who manages this? Why?
- What can be done to help manage the bystanders? Why? How?

Who are the stakeholders? Why?

- What needs to be done for the stakeholders?
- Who does this? Why?
- What are the organization's responsibilities? Why?
- Who manages this? Why?
- What can be done to help manage the stakeholders? Why? How?

Who are the likely special interest parties or pressure groups? Why?

- What needs to be done for these parties and groups?
- Who does this? Why?
- What are the organization's responsibilities? Why?
- Who manages this? Why?
- What can be done to help manage special-interest parties and pressure groups? Why? How?

Does the organization's philosophy support crisis management? Why? Why not?

- How can this be accomplished or enhanced?
- Is crisis management incorporated in organizational mission statements? Why? Why not?
- How can this be accomplished or enhanced?
- Is crisis management in the organization's strategic plans? Why? Why not?
- How can this be accomplished or enhanced?

Are expert consultants and advisers part of the crisis management team? Why? Why not?

- How can this be accomplished or enhanced?

Is there an emphasis on safety of product and workplace? Why? Why not?

- Who emphasizes safety issues? Why?
- How realistic and specific is this emphasis?
- Is the emphasis updated? Why? Why not? How? When?
- How can the safety emphasis be initiated or enhanced?

Are there redundancies built into the operations of the organization? Why? Why not?

- What are these redundancies? Why?
- Who maintains and/or manages these redundancies? Why? How? Where?
- How realistic and specific are these requirements?
- Are the redundancy requirements updated? Why? Why not? How? When?
- What do the redundant resources do? Who uses them?
- How can redundancy management be initiated or enhanced?

Are there financial audit and control systems in the organization?

- What do these audits and controls cover? Why?
- How realistic and specific are the audit and control systems?
- Are the systems updated? Why? Why not? How? When?
- Who manages the audits or controls? Who uses the audits? Who applies the audits or controls?
- Are these people appropriately skilled and trained?
- How can the audit and control systems be initiated or enhanced?
- How can the audit and control personnel gain or enhance their skills?

Are there legal audit and control systems in the organization?

- What do these audits and controls cover? Why?
- How realistic and specific are these audit and control systems?
- Are the systems updated? Why? Why not? How? When?
- Who manages the audits or controls? Who uses the audits? Who applies the audits or controls?
- Are these people appropriately skilled and trained?
- How can the legal audits or controls be initiated or enhanced?
- How can the audit and control personnel gain or enhance their skills?

Do financial and legal audits of potential crisis situations exist?

- What do these audits cover? Why?
- How realistic and specific are these audits?
- Are the audits updated? Why? Why not? How? When?
- Who manages the audits? Who uses the audits? Who applies the audits?
- Are these people appropriately skilled and trained?
- How can the financial and legal audits of potential crisis situations be initiated or enhanced?

Do human-impact audits of operational or potential crisis events exist? Why? Why not?

- What do these audits cover? Why?
- How realistic and specific are these audits?
- Are the audits updated? Why? Why not? How? When?
- Who manages the audits? Who uses the audits? Who applies the audits?
- Are these people appropriately skilled and trained?
- How can the human-impact audits be initiated or enhanced?

Do employee-impact audits of operational or potential crisis events exist? Why? Why not?

- What do these audits cover? Why?
- How realistic and specific are these audits?
- Are these employee-impact audits updated? Why? Why not? How? When?
- Who manages the audits? Who uses the audits? Who applies the audits?
- Are these people appropriately skilled and trained?
- How can the employee-impact audits be initiated or enhanced?

Do organizational-impact audits of operational or potential crisis events exist? Why? Why not?

- What do these audits cover? Why?
- How realistic and specific are these audits?
- Are these organizational-impact audits updated? Why? Why not? How? When?
- Who manages the audits? Who uses the audits? Who applies the audits?
- Are these people appropriately skilled and trained?
- How can the organizational-impact audits be accomplished or enhanced?

Further cued questions that reflect other organization-specific concerns, RRRR model variables and soft areas such as image and reputation management may be added as appropriate. Cued questions on type and level of insurance, workplace attitudes and the socio-political climate (changes in legal requirements, pollution measures, safety and duty of care regulations) may also be needed.

When undertaking a crisis audit try to have the group remain as objective as possible. Use brainstorming sessions to generate options and listen to stakeholders (especially the workforce and customers). These people can often indicate where things may go wrong and suggest simple response and recovery actions that may help.

Try to frame each cued question so that reasons for doing something and not doing something are explored (Why? Why not?) and look for strengths, weaknesses and ways of improving performance and readiness.

Training and experiential exercises

Once plans are in place executives and managers need to ensure that members of the organization learn the necessary skills and practise their response or recovery tasks. Training can use a diverse number of learning and rehearsal approaches, including:

- background reading
- lectures
- video
- case studies
- syndicate exercises
- computer-based exercises
- computer simulations
- table-top exercises
- field exercises
- full-scale field exercises (scenario-based exercises).

Reasons for training

A fundamental reason for training is that it increases familiarity and capability among those being trained. Effective training can reduce human response errors that can worsen the impacts of the crisis and can similarly reduce the time taken to begin responding to the demands of the situation.

Crisis management training programmes help crisis management in three ways:

- Walk-through practices acquaint participants with a crisis plan and their part within it.
- Rehearsals allow respondents to interact with each other and to determine task requirements and operational needs more readily.
- By practising mobilization, assembly and deployment of respondents, more time is created for dealing with a crisis when one happens.

Some benefits of training

Undertaking any exercise has positive effects for an organization or community. Two core advantages from working through a programme of increasingly realistic exercises are:

- an increased awareness of potential crisis situations; and
- an increased experience of managing a crisis.

Most people really only become aware of the nature and proximity of threat by encountering that threat. Training people in the basic skills and response tasks, and then increasing the complexity and realism of the exercises leads to familiarity with the threat and the behavioural responses required to deal with that threat.

Exercises can lead to crisis reduction solutions. In an oil refinery crisis exercise, for example, participants may conclude that more water and foam booster points are needed, or that wider and flatter access roads would decrease response time, or that the bunds (walls encircling storage tanks) need to be higher. Each of these solutions may reduce the impact or consequence of a real crisis. Likewise, a financial organization may run an exercise on the effects of a sudden plunge in stock market prices. Impact reduction solutions drawn from this exercise may include the need to have standby funding arrangements, or the need to ensure the organization holds a large stable mix of shares, or the need to develop early warning systems that use process models and close scrutiny of local and world trends. Even more importantly, evaluation of scenarios and exercises may lead to suggestions about how crisis situations may be eliminated altogether.

Other benefits of undertaking training and exercise programmes include the following:

- Exercises act as breaks from routine and can be motivational for members of organizations.
- Exercises can demonstrate an image of organizational resilience and readiness that can be used in public relations and community programmes to 'sell' the organization.
- Exercises help improve security and safety.

Exercise programmes without good management and balanced debriefing can give rise to some problems, including the following:

- The scenarios used for training become seen as the only crisis situations and the only way those crisis situations will occur. Without variety and proper debriefing, participants can develop mindsets about what crisis will happen and how it will happen. Such mindsets lead to paralysis of response when a different crisis occurs, or when a crisis situation does not match what has been rehearsed.
- Managers (and thus staff) regard the exercises as an interruption to their real work, so they just 'go through the motions'. The learning is minimal and the ability to respond is equally low. Executives and managers need to ensure that the exercises are treated seriously and are conducted with energy (particularly as the exercises become more complex and realistic).
- An exercise is only as good as the clarity of its design and the appropriateness of its outcomes. This means that those who design and conduct the exercise need to be competent in these tasks. They need to match the type

of exercise to the level of skill and response capability of the members and sub-units of the organization, create a positive learning environment either through the exercise or in the debriefing of that exercise, and be able to show the fit of the exercise to the crisis response or crisis recovery plans.

- Overconfidence can develop as participants translate a controlled exercise into a representation of their ability to handle a real crisis situation. Acting out roles in an exercise does not equate with the real thing. The pressures of costly decisions cannot be fully developed in exercises, nor can the chaos and clamour of distractions that arise in many crisis situations.

The benefits of undertaking regular exercises far outweigh most problems involved. Executives and managers need to develop these training activities according to the level of ability of the participants.

Early in crisis management development, training activities are best kept small and simple. Learning about what to do, becoming familiar with the planned response activities and gaining skills in doing the required tasks equate with training activities that include walk-throughs of the plans and simple, small-unit practice of specific response tasks.

As familiarity and knowledge increase, exercises reflecting some interaction with other participants or sequences of tasks may be undertaken. This stage may move onto simple field exercises that focus on deployment and communications interaction before reverting to on-site run-throughs of task activities. Executives and managers are likely to undertake simple table-top exercises to acquaint themselves with the bigger strategic picture and to aid interaction and decision-making practice.

As these exercises become effective, crisis management can move toward practising co-ordinated activities across the organization. These activities tend to be hands-on or 'field' activities in the sense that a crisis situation or storyline is used to stimulate the response and recovery operations. As the storyline and resulting details increase and become complex, organizations shift into undertaking experiential exercises often called *scenario exercises*.

Once crisis management has become a regular part of an organization's existence, an annual exercise or training programme can be designed. The detail and frequency of this exercise and training activity depend on the degree to which an organization is exposed to risks. As a base guideline, there needs to be at least three such activities performed within a calendar year, as follows:

- A walk-through of the plan that may take two to four hours in a conference room. Here the accent is on familiarization with the plan, with a useful secondary benefit of checking its accuracy and workability.
- A unit-level activity that enables participants to perform the steps of each required response or recovery activity. This is still most likely to remain focused on checking that people can perform the required tasks, with the useful secondary benefit of checking that the equipment and resources are present and in working condition. This activity can take between a half and a full day.

- A full-scale scenario crisis exercise in which many (if not all) elements and roles in the crisis response or recovery plans are undertaken over a period of time (usually one to three days). The object of this exercise is to test the response planning and training, with less emphasis on allowing people to slow down and learn what they should be doing. When things go wrong, the exercise organizers will either let the errors run their course or reconfigure the storyline so that the next tasks in the crisis plan can be tested.

By conducting such a series of training activities, executives and managers can focus on particular aspects of crisis management – strategic decision making and co-ordination (table-top exercises) integration of response or recovery plans (integration exercises) and situation management (scenario training exercises).

Scenario exercises

Scenario exercises can be performed by computer simulations or through on-site multi-hour real-time exercises. Computer-based simulators enable decisions and reactions to be input. These simulators are used extensively to train pilots, space personnel, weaponry personnel and even car drivers. While the construction and use of such simulators is expensive, such costs are relatively inexpensive when compared with the value of the aircraft, spaceship or military vehicle users would put at risk in learning and refining their skills.

Computer simulation of disasters and disaster response situations is likely to develop within the three-dimensional world of special effects known as virtual reality. When graphics become more lifelike and computer-chip power becomes even greater, more individual and team training and rehearsal is likely to arise. Firefighting training, for example, may include virtual reality graphics with physical effects such as the smell of smoke and the feelings of heat.

Field-based simulation exercises usually attempt to mirror aspects of a crisis situation. These exercises often add background elements such as fire or water and deploy the actual equipment. Participants are required to physically dress and behave as if the event were real.

Scenario training involves three general approaches:

- a case study for conference room analysis;
- a table-top exercise of the management team; or
- a field-based exercise storyline.

In the latter case, the scenario approaches may link together a number of field simulations and exercises.

In any exercise or training activity, planners need to keep in mind that the learning benefits are likely to be greater when the activity has fewer outcome objectives. A test of the level of integration by multiple response agencies in a response is weakened if planners also attempt to explore strategic decision making or response crew task training.

The first action of any exercise is to select the basic goal or purpose of the exercise. The situation, the required response, and the players and victims are then defined. Organizers can then decide whether observers (passive umpires) or facilitators (active umpires) will be used, and if they are used, how and when these officials may observe and intervene in the exercise. What needs to emerge is a clear definition of the involvement and expected actions of umpires and players.

In most exercises, two types of information are used. The first type is called *primary information* because this information is made available in the pre-exercise briefing and at the start of the exercise. Primary information defines the problem, sets the scene and activates the response or recovery effort. The second type of information is called *secondary information*, and is the data and information produced during the response or recovery effort and may include scenario information that is released on a time schedule.

As crisis management on one level is really about information management and consequent response decision making, exercises need to involve the use of information gathering and information assessment. One means of doing so is to produce a detailed pre-exercise briefing on the scenario, give minimal information when activating the situation, and then to add information from outside sources (bystanders, eyewitnesses, victims, response personnel, umpires and organizers). Similarly field exercises need to include media interaction and dealing with the general public and pressure groups.

Where a real response to a crisis situation may last days from activation to aftermath management, organizers rarely are allowed that much time for an exercise. Organizers may need to plan a series of exercises based around a central scenario activity. Some of these exercises may be run at the same time while others may be sequential but separated by several hours. For example, an organization may wish to exercise response and recovery operations. While both management teams can be activated together and can perform assembly, deployment and information-gathering tasks, recovery operations usually take over after the crisis is resolved. Thus a simulated crisis exercise may consist of four three-hour segments – activation of the teams, continuing response effort with some issues or problems added, transfer to recovery operational control, and an ongoing sample test of recovery operations with problems and issues added.

Many organizers need to add monitoring and accounting systems to exercises and real crisis management. Accounting systems include the traditional bookkeeping cash-flow assessments, but also need to encompass resource, personnel and goal achievement factors in their assessments and records. In high-risk or mass-threat events, for example, costs in terms of money and resources may be offset (even discounted) by savings made in terms of preventing casualties or reducing infrastructure damage.

Organizers and their supervising executives and managers often fail to give adequate time and attention to evaluating an exercise. This is unfortunate as the real value of an exercise resides in the time used to give useful feedback, to encourage creative *solutions* to the problems and impediments that arose during the exercise, and thus to encourage enthusiasm, commitment and cohesion from the participants. Evaluation needs to be critical and hard-nosed, but without assigning any blame or raising any personality issues. The focus needs to be placed on how to improve performance. By looking at what went wrong and what went right, and then seeking solutions rather than blame, crisis plans (or guides) can be improved, co-ordination and trust can be increased and the response time to enact appropriate tactical levels can be reduced. The best exercises are often the ones that do not run too well, provided that participants look toward fixing and improving the plans and the performances in response or recovery tasks.

Mansfield and Hoffman (1979) provide an example of a scenario exercise. They discuss what may be learned from a 2.5 day exercise conducted by Canadian provincial and national governments and their appropriate agencies. The exercise involved up to 80 participants and was centred in the Territorial Government Offices in Whitehorse in the Yukon. The scenario presented an oil-spill crisis, and used a control group to respond to the decisions made by participants and to present new problems as the exercise progressed. The main lessons outlined by Mansfield and Hoffman included the need for:

- a better defined command structure;
- better co-ordination;
- better logistic support and administration.

Many exercises today are likely to reach the same conclusions.

Perhaps the major disadvantage of scenario training (and of desk-top exercises) is the readiness of decision makers and respondents to overlook likely problems, to discount the effects of surrounding events and to grossly underestimate the time taken to resolve the crisis. In a large decision-making exercise using an earthquake scenario in a major city in Australia, for example, fire and rescue activities were announced to be completed within hours. The 'quake' was estimated at above 6 on the Richter scale, with an epicentre about 15 kilometres away from the city. The city, moreover, made heavy use of domestic gas and several areas had been built on reclaimed and alluvial ground. While completion claims help move an exercise along, debriefings need to remind participants that the real event is likely to be dirtier, longer and more demanding.

Specific issues in conducting exercises

Pre-exercise briefings

Formal briefings need to be made orally and in writing. The oral briefings include:

- the key objectives or goals of the exercise;
- the need to undertake the activity seriously;
- the key features and expected course of the exercise;
- reminders about safety.

Written briefings can make use of a standard format which includes:

- identification of the exercise – type, location, times (start and conclusion), location and time for pre-exercise briefing, and place and time for debriefing;
- list of participating organizations (or organizational units);
- rules of operation (including use of controllers and moderators);
- incident description (detailed enough to set a realistic atmosphere);
- activities/tasks/functions being tested in the exercise;
- requirements of participants (particularly for volunteer 'injured' or crowds) in terms of clothing, expectations, permitted behaviour to add to realism, transport and refreshment;
- requirements for any permitted non-participants (observers, media, community invitees, special guests – assembly areas, clothing and personal needs, refreshment facilities and clearly defined areas they may enter);
- people to contact for clarification and assistance (names, telephone numbers, locations on site of exercise);
- authorizing manager (name and contact telephone number).

Have more copies than participants, as many will leave these behind or lose the pre-crisis briefing notes in the initial stages of an exercise.

Post-exercise analysis

Three important outcomes may emerge after an exercise is conducted, as follows:

1 Participants can become more motivated and more able to undertake their tasks as they become more familiar with their roles and interrelationships, and understand the bigger picture of the crisis response or recovery processes. Crisis impacts appear more predictable and more familiar.
2 Crisis plans, management, interactions and communications can be tested and improved.
3 Participants help assess the exercise and consider how the exercise and their performance can be improved. This helps them to feel that they are part of the operation and thus establishes feelings of ownership of their tasks and jobs.

Too often debriefing sessions are allowed to become either a quick 'we all did well' superficial assessment or a series of exchanges blaming one group or another for some mistake or poor performance. Neither of these efforts produce any insight for future use, and can lead to diminished integration and co-operation among units or response agencies should participants feel frustrated by what happened or come to believe that their opinion is unwanted and unheard. Crisis and disaster exercise managers and organizers need to plan for debriefings as thoroughly as they plan and organize the exercise.

Those conducting a debriefing session need training and practice in learning to ask open questions, dampening any blaming or defensive reactions, and in refocusing attention on solving problems that arose and on improving plans and practice. When used appropriately, debriefing sessions can become the prime source of learning how to effectively manage crisis situations, and provide a foundation for forming relationships, respect and understanding between participants that enables greater co-operation and trust within an integrated crisis response.

Any evaluation needs to start with concrete thinking on cause and effect, starting with an appraisal of the exercise briefings, moving through the stages of the exercise, and even including (post-evaluation) the evaluation process used to debrief participants. Three simple questions to prompt responses would be:

- What actually happened?
- What were the consequences?
- How can these happenings and consequences be better handled?

Hard data is sought in responding to 'What actually happened?' Given the usual complexity of events being managed in many crises, an EOT record (*see* Figure 12.4, p. 300) may prove a quick recording tool. The event observation timeline record helps users to sequentially record events and interactions, as well as graphically recording meeting arrangements or crisis sites for future reference.

People conducting debriefing sessions need to keep the activity focused on:

- identifying and resolving problems and poor performance;
- identifying and resolving any problems or weaknesses in the plans;
- what happened and how it happened rather than why it happened.

Debriefing

Debriefing helps managers and response or recovery personnel to:

- gather an experiential picture of event, impact and response;
- record what was done for any subsequent inquiries or improvements to the response and recovery management;
- release some of the stressed perceptions held by participants;
- promote an increased feeling of belonging to a team.

Debriefings are not critical and hostile attacks on individuals or organizations, nor are debriefings a chorus of 'we done okay'. Skilled debriefing seeks:

- concrete facts;

- analysis of strengths (what went well) and weaknesses (what went wrong);
- an assessment of what would happen in a larger crisis;
- constructive discussion about how to improve performance.

Debriefers need skill training in:

- asking open questions;
- active listening;
- seeking feedback about feelings and beliefs;
- integrating loose, often brief statements into an accepted 'picture'.

Open questions

Open questions encourage multiple word responses rather than the 'yes' or 'no' responses that come from closed questions. Open questions thus take the form of the following examples:

- *'Tell us about ...'*
- *'Give us more details ...'*
- *'What happened next?'*
- *'How do you feel?'*

Closed questions prompt short non-informative answers and promote feelings of being interrogated or prosecuted. Some examples of closed questions include:

- *'So you are telling us that ...'*
- *'Nothing more to say?'*
- *'Then [this fact] happened next?'*
- *'So you felt bad about that?'*

In the context of a cognitive debriefing session (such as conducted during crisis situations as personnel finish their shifts or report back to a command or co-ordination centre, or in post-exercise or post-crisis evaluation sessions) 'factual' information is sought rather than emotional beliefs and responses. This means asking questions that use *what* and *how* rather than *why*.

Basic debriefing involves all participants (including facilitators and bystanders). Executives and managers may determine that there are too many people involved to provide a complete debriefing session at one time. In this case, a series of debriefs are undertaken, starting at the lowest group or unit level of response or recovery participants. All participants need to be encouraged to contribute. These groups then have some of their members represent the groups at a multi-group debriefing session. Once the highest level of debriefing has taken place, a detailed report of the overall findings is circulated so that all members of an organization find out what was concluded and what changes need to be made. Executives and managers may wish to consider the value of a public report on the exercise as a means of reassuring stakeholders and cultivating a resilient and positive corporate image.

Example of a group-based post-exercise debriefing report

Airline cabin crew presented this report after a major exercise at an international airport. Note the look at big-picture incidents as well as issues of immediate concern to the cabin crew involved.

1 On entry from the rear of aircraft, a firefighter began removing bodies – this is not supposed to be done until permitted by accident investigation officials.
2 The fireman removing bodies was told by flight attendants that nine injured were on board to which the fireman replied: 'The fire is contained and medical help coming. Stay put. You are safe.' This was on a damaged aircraft that had a burning engine and wing.
3 Medical help arrived 19 minutes later and was preceded by media intrusion.
4 No one asked if the crew were injured.
5 The safety of the exercise situation was questionable. There were no safety straps or fall protection for 'volunteer' passengers.
6 No directions were given or clear markers erected to guide crew and passengers away from the aircraft.
7 In the pre-exercise written instructions and the verbal briefing we were told that passengers were to be guided to a yellow 'field command' vehicle that had flashing lights and flags, and to listen for instructions from portable PA systems. The vehicle came late, was not yellow, had flags but no flashing lights and there were no PA instructions given.
8 After 20 minutes at the holding area near the supposed command vehicle, one ambulance officer began assessing passengers for injuries, including the walking wounded.
9 We cannot understand why the field command centre was placed *upwind* and triage *downwind*, with the crashed aircraft in between the two sites.

The comments show a mix of fact and opinion that is stated fairly non-accusingly.

Exercise blueprint

Having outlined some of the features and issues involved in conducting exercises, a basic blueprint for their design and conduct can be developed. Any extra details that meet the requirements of particular organizations and situations can be added as appropriate.

- Establish the organizational and situation POVs in the test scenario – the state of the organization and the nature of the crisis situation.
- Define the crisis situation in detail.
- Decide:
  - who needs to participate;
  - what resources need to be used or tested;
  - when the tests will be conducted;
  - where the test will be conducted;
  - why the test will be conducted.
- Define the type, nature and duration of the test.
- Define the impact(s) of the crisis situation being tested.
- Define precisely what is being tested.
- Define any additional tests or objectives and state why these are being tested.
- Determine when participants enter and depart the test environment.
- Determine the levels of realism to be incorporated in the test.
- Define the stages involved in the test – chronology, timing and duration.
- Establish how the test will be monitored – observers, adjudicators, controllers, facilitators.
- Establish how the test will be evaluated.
- Determine how test inputs and outputs will be recorded and analyzed.
- Establish debriefing and reporting procedures that lead to specific improvements in the plan.
- Inform participants, staff and important stakeholders of the learning outcomes from the test.
- Determine the implications of the exercise and have these accepted by senior executives and managers. Implications may include:
  - gaining acceptance of the costs in time and business;
  - getting sufficient resources allocated to the exercise;
  - gaining access to and participation of those who need to be involved (particularly senior management);
  - establishing acceptance of the test as 'proper work' that needs full attention.

Tips on training and exercises

Reality mirroring

Five brief points can be made about mirroring some of the likely aspects of a crisis. Reality mirroring is done to make participants more familiar with aspects of the crisis situation and crisis impact and with difficulties they may face in undertaking their tasks. Likewise, reality mirroring can test how elements of a crisis plan fit together under stress. The five points are:

1 Incorporate equipment failure when undertaking a simulation exercise.

2 Incorporate communication failures in simulation and integration exercises.
3 Use sensory elements such as sight, sound and smell where appropriate and safe.
4 Include within the exercise provision for media activity (and even undertake a media conference).
5 Test the integration of the response or recovery process.

Do keep in mind when developing and running reality (or proximal) exercises that:

- ongoing business is not lost;
- costs do not exceed gains;
- participants (and bystanders) do not think the test is a real event;
- damage to persons or equipment is not sustained.

If any of these elements arise the negative publicity and impact on the organization may limit interest in future exercises.

Try to ensure the exercise is taken seriously

Crisis conditions can be far worse than those in an exercise. At one full field exercise for a major airliner crash at an airport medical teams operated in everyday dress 'because the safety uniforms were too hot'. Without wearing these uniforms, no proper insight was gained into the amount of time these people should be on duty nor the amount of support (fluids, food, rest periods, air-cooling equipment) they may need. The teams did not experience the distractions such discomfort may provoke in a crisis situation. Crisis situations can have distracting elements (alarms, flashing lights, raised voices) and physical irritants (smoke, water, dust, heat) that sap respondents and their capacity to work and make decisions. Experiencing these in safer exercise conditions can help participants feel more familiar and capable when they find themselves in a crisis situation.

Where possible, film the training exercise

With modern camera and video technology, exercises can be filmed by observers. Audio-visual feedback of events prompts recall of problems or incidents and is useful when analyzing unit or group performance. Particular moments can be freeze-framed and discussed by all watching the replay. Given sufficient resources and personnel, consider attaching a film team to a crisis response team. Quick replay of a filmed crisis helps later management decisions, and any weakness in response or management can be seen and addressed (on site if the crisis is extended, or before the next crisis).

Expect equipment to fail in large-scale exercises

Equipment can fail when dealing with a crisis, so use such failures in an exercise as training activities. Two prime causes for equipment failure during a demonstration or exercise are:

- lack of clear instruction to personnel (who then attempt an activity at the wrong spot); and
- not providing adequate time for proper demonstration.

Consider adding equipment loss or breakdown in a complex exercise to test flexibility and ability to deal with unexpected issues, but do not add this until organizational competencies in task performance seem acceptable.

Establish clearance teams

When conducting an exercise that is constrained by time, use groups of non-participants to collect and store equipment that is no longer to be used by the respondents. The focus of participants on tasks and time constraints can lead to accidental loss or damage of resources as they shift from one task activity to the next. Clearance teams can reduce these costs and losses.

Rehearse removing victims from the crisis environment

Victims have a habit of going back to retrieve valuables or to find and save lost family or friends, so simulate such actions when attempting realistic exercises. Similarly the distraction and resource drain in dealing with victims, bystanders and media is rarely adequately added to exercises.

Scenario-based management exercises

If executives and managers are going to role-play various situations, have participants in the role-play take a role not currently held by them in the organization. This variation helps to:

- promote greater creativity;
- increase awareness of the POV of those positions among participants;
- provide valuable cross-training; and
- develop POVs of those outside the organization (other response or recovery organizations, stakeholders, pressure groups and media).

Run several scenes of a role-play in relatively realistic sequence. Each scene can take around 15 to 20 minutes and may include:

- a crisis manager talking to a reporter;
- a major stakeholder talking to the chief executive officer;
- union representatives interacting with a relevant senior executive of the organization;

- a leader of a protest group meeting with the public affairs director;
- a victim meeting with a senior executive; or
- a customer checking on the organization's ability to meet the customer's order.

Run the series of activities for no more than two hours, take a break, then evaluate each scene in terms of reactions, statements, skills used and consistency with organizational mission, culture and crisis planning.

Try to create some distracting crisis smog during role plays – extraneous telephone calls, memoranda, rumours, false information leads, other protestors, audio-visual footage and even suitable atmospheric settings.

Communication during an exercise

Remember to use exercise cues when activating an exercise, transmitting storyline elements or exchanging information over unsecured communication systems. In a British airport exercise, over-eager participants (acting out media reporting roles) contacted the regional hospital with requests for information about the number and treatment of crash victims, triggering a belief that an aircraft had crashed. Train participants to use the 'exercise parenthesis' technique – 'This is Exercise Fireball. I repeat, Exercise Fireball. An explosive fire has started in Tank 49. I repeat, a fire in Tank four-nine. This message is for Exercise Fireball. Over.' The warning that the message is for an exercise and not an actual crisis situation is placed like parenthetic punctuation brackets at the beginning and end of the statement. Note the repetition of both the warning and the activation message ('fire in Tank 49'). This is good communication redundancy that helps receivers tune in to the vital elements of the communication.

References

Mansfield, B. and Hoffman, J. (1979) 'Contingency plans for the Beaufort Sea', *Emergency Planning Digest*, 6, 15–19.

Van Biema, D. (1995) 'When Kobe died', *Time*, 30 January, 14–23.

Event observation timeline record (EOT)

Observers and participants need to keep an ongoing record of events and thoughts. While cassette recorders and video cameras provide real-time audio and visual records of situations, these tools are less able to record the human perspective in terms of thoughts, feelings and beliefs. Moreover, the real-time nature of replaying audio-visual records can slow down quick recall of what happened.

Pen-and-paper approaches still serve a purpose in recording an observer's objective and subjective impressions. A recommended approach is to use an EOT (event observation timeline) record – see Figure 12.4. Each page of an EOT has a page or sequence number, date, location, event and reviewer (top left-hand box). An area for making a quick outline sketch of a site or situation (such as a meeting room, as in the example) is provided at the top right-hand box. This allows users to quickly note physical aspects or interactions for future recall. Underneath these two boxes is an event record area, with a time track, event track and a column for queries and comments. By running the three elements in parallel, an observer records a sequential order for post-exercise feedback and for any subsequent report. Event observation is also separated from comments and queries, reducing contamination of data by observer opinion.

The example in Figure 12.4 represents a meeting of the main response agencies in a strategic command centre during an earthquake exercise. The records may be quite similar to an actual crisis situation. The record shows the beginning of the first full emergency management committee meeting since the 'earthquake' happened. At this stage, information is just beginning to come in and the meeting proceeds as a briefing service.

EOT records enable detailed debriefs and help ensure that important observations are not overlooked.

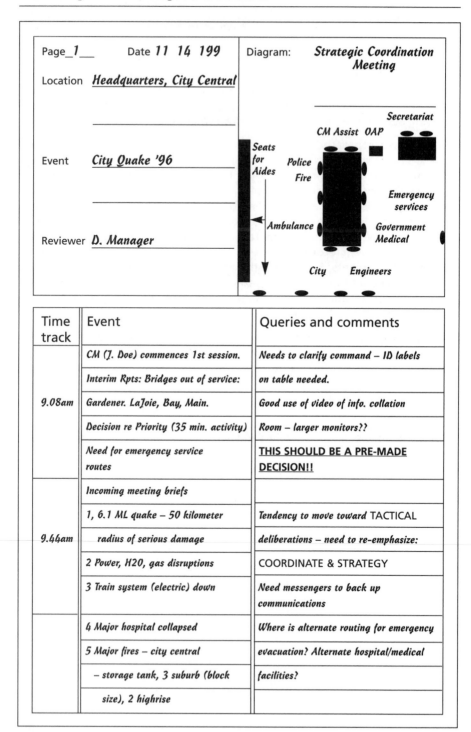

Page _1___   Date _11 14 199_

Location _Headquarters, City Central_

Event _City Quake '96_

Reviewer _D. Manager_

Diagram: *Strategic Coordination Meeting*

Time track	Event	Queries and comments
	CM (J. Doe) commences 1st session.	*Needs to clarify command – ID labels*
	Interim Rpts: Bridges out of service:	*on table needed.*
9.08am	*Gardener. LaJoie, Bay, Main.*	*Good use of video of info. collation*
	Decision re Priority (35 min. activity)	*Room – larger monitors??*
	Need for emergency service routes	**THIS SHOULD BE A PRE-MADE DECISION!!**
	Incoming meeting briefs	
	1, 6.1 ML quake – 50 kilometer	*Tendency to move toward* TACTICAL
9.44am	*radius of serious damage*	*deliberations – need to re-emphasize:*
	2 Power, H20, gas disruptions	COORDINATE & STRATEGY
	3 Train system (electric) down	*Need messengers to back up communications*
	4 Major hospital collapsed	*Where is alternate routing for emergency*
	5 Major fires – city central	*evacuation? Alternate hospital/medical*
	– storage tank, 3 suburb (block	*facilities?*
	size), 2 highrise	

Fig. 12.4 Example of an EOT record

Response management

This chapter shifts the focus from reduction and readiness to response. Previous chapters have dealt with aspects of response and recovery management – communication, media and image management, strategic management and decision making. This chapter explores *CrisisThink* in greater detail, then outlines applications of crisis response management in business-specific situations before looking at managerial issues in crisis situations.

CrisisThink

A major problem that confronts crisis managers is the choice of appropriate response strategies when (a) working under constraints of limited time and uncertain information, and (b) being well aware that resources and people may be at risk from the crisis or any impact(s) from that crisis. *CrisisThink* is one approach that helps managers focus on elements within the crisis situation that suggest optimal management approaches.

What is *CrisisThink*?

CrisisThink uses three essential mental questions that need to be semi-automatically cycled and recycled in a manager's mind during a crisis. These are:

- *How can I (or we) gain more time?*
- *How can I (or we) gain more information?*
- *How can I (or we) reduce the loss or cost of resources?*

This analytical assessment helps calm users while maintaining attention on issues central to their managerial responsibilities. In this sense, *CrisisThink* is a behavioural stopper that uses the three action-directed questions to promote a calmer and more reflective response to the situational stimuli.

Without trained response reactions, managers are likely to lose control of the crisis situation. Training means becoming familiar with what has to be done, increasing skills and capabilities to be able to perform those tasks, and seeking the appropriate information that helps make the situation appear more predictable. Consequently, training and exercises can help managers gain more time for actually finding and meeting the demands of a crisis when that crisis happens.

This is one reason why members of armed services spend so much time learning explicitly and promptly to obey orders. Most commercial civil aviation and military fighter pilots similarly spend much time rehearsing behavioural responses to such situations as the aircraft suddenly losing power in all engines. Should that event arise pilots are likely to adopt the optimal response actions enabling them to emerge safely from the crisis.

Crisis managers need to practise approaches like *CrisisThink* to help them concentrate during stressful times in crisis situations, and to help them determine acceptable response strategies and actions.

Implementing *CrisisThink*

CrisisThink is a simple process that helps users improve decision making and action choices. If desired, a number of strategies can support the focus on gaining time and information, and on reducing the costs of using or losing resources.

The search for more time may involve use of *time reduction* and *event delay* strategies. The search for more information can include *siphon* and *fact-talk* strategies. Reduction of costs in resources may be aided by *sterile ground* and *positive gain* strategies.

Gaining more time

Time is the most critical element in crisis management. Crisis situations are actually just difficult problems if there is sufficient time available for analysis and response. As a consequence, managers and executives need to seek more time between a crisis warning signal and the impact(s) of that crisis situation. Many of these gains can be achieved in pre-crisis planning and preparedness and response deployment. Time can be gained by becoming familiar with roles, actions and tasks outlined in plans and rehearsed in readiness exercises. Rehearsing deployment and initial action tasks helps reduce time wastage and thus increases time for examining the situation and making decisions.

Time reduction strategies

By reducing the time used in warning and deployment, crisis managers increase the available (if still finite) amount of time in which to act and react to the crisis situation. Two strategies that reduce loss of time are:

- better deployment to meet the situation;
- getting to the impact site as fast as possible.

Better deployment

Deployment is too often treated as a static decision with two components:

- placing resources at bases or agency sites; and
- deploying resources when a crisis situation occurs.

Community and organizational structures change over time, as do the assets held within these structures. As a consequence, these changes alter exposure to risks and vulnerability to damage. Crisis management plans and resource deployments are changed less frequently. As the discrepancy widens between changes in structures or assets and the contents of crisis management plans, the ability to respond effectively diminishes.

Better deployment strategies begin with regular monitoring of the changes in organizations and communities, and consequent adjustment of plans and resource deployments to cover these changes. Crisis managers need to consider sophisticated approaches to deployment management, including response priority profiles, operational management triage and dynamic reserve strategies.

Get there faster

Crisis management respondents train and exercise to:

- familiarize themselves with what may happen and what they need to do;
- decrease the time taken to deploy for response action.

Planning and problem-solving sessions can also help identify:

- core processes and sites that need protection so that the organization continues to function (*see* risk and business impact analysis in Chapters 2 and 3);
- areas or sites presenting the greatest risk to people and resources;
- likely access routes for response deployment and establishing how to reopen, substitute and maintain these access routes for that deployment.

These three features increase speed of response by focusing attention on accessing likely 'hot spots' that are vulnerable to crisis or which are critical to organizational survival or performance. Other 'get there faster' approaches include better evacuation (for example, ACCCE) and onset management training.

Event delay strategies

These strategies involve actions designed to delay the impact(s) of the crisis situation so that more information can be gained, resources can be saved and better deployment and action decisions can be made. Consequently, most strategies focus on:

- deferring impact(s); or
- retarding such impact(s).

Combined with improved deployment, deferral and retardation strategies can help minimize impacts.

Impact deferral

Probably the most obvious and visible crisis response strategies are those that defer or detour impending impact(s) of a crisis. These are called 'wall' strategies. When flooding occurs, for example, pre-event levees act as flood barricades that prevent or defer flooding inside the levee-protected area. Dams are constructed to alleviate and control flooding. Storage facilities for dangerous chemicals are mostly screened by seepage and leak constraining bunds or walls. Firebreaks are used to stop or slow a wildfire. Wall strategies are useful in coping with impacts from earthquakes – stopping or deferring fires, chemical spills and floods from destroyed reservoirs or tsunamis. Tokyo, for example, has the highly visible Shirahige-higashi apartment complex that is designed to act as a fire wall should a major earthquake occur (*see* Hadfield, 1991).

Detour strategies adopt approaches that use walls to redirect impact(s). Avalanche shields and volcano 'channels' are examples of these (*see* Robinson, 1993). In 1973, at Heimaey in Iceland, respondents used water hoses for six months to cool over five million cubic yards (four million cubic metres) of lava in an effort to deflect it from homes and prevent the flow from closing the harbour entrance (Robinson, 1993). Similarly, use of explosives detoured lava flows from Mt Etna in 1992, saving the town of Zafferana (Robinson, 1993).

One problem with wall strategies is that once a part of a wall is breached the remaining wall acts as a containment wall, and this constraint increases impact damage on the assets being protected. Use of permanent walls is risky in natural disasters. Once the walls (or river levees) are breached – as happened in the Mississippi river valley in 1992 – the initial flood surge causes more damage than naturally spreading water and the flood is prevented from flowing back into the river as water levels decrease.

Wall and detour strategies have many forms in non-physical crisis situations. Businesses may use legal injunctions, asset acquisition, asset stripping, shareholder meetings, cessation of share trading, change of legal company structure, product recall, product replacement, downsizing or suspension of trading to defer or reroute business-type crisis situations – takeovers, sudden loss of operations, strikes, product problems and cash-flow deficiencies.

Event retardation

Event retardation strategies involve strengthening structures, developing impediments and reducing the exposure of resources and people to the source of crisis situations. Strategies include building away from sites of high risk, building better resistant structures and building structures that are congruent to both use and likely threat (the ABC building strategy for mitigation, as outlined in Chapter 4).

Retardation can also be promoted through pre-emptive strike strategies. These strategies work to retard the crisis onset or impact(s) from a crisis by actively meeting the threat away from the site of the likely crisis situation. Water and chemical bombing of wildfires, for example, is used to slow the progress of those fires. The 'scorched earth' strategies used by the Russians against the French invasion under Napoleon and against the German invasion under Hitler, and by the Chinese against the Japanese invasion, are retardation strategies aimed at slowing the success of the invasion by removing or destroying food and shelter assets. The MAD (mutually assured destruction) policies of the Cold War were strategies aimed at retarding any use of nuclear weapons.

Businesses can operate retardation strategies against specific threats and situations. Stock market raids on the shares of companies making hostile takeover moves can slow down takeover activity. Counter-litigation slows down legal proceedings by increasing the onus on the original litigators to establish their case (*see* the McLibel Reality Bite in Chapter 8) and through making the process more time-consuming and costly.

Gaining more information

One means of increasing predictability and familiarity with a crisis situation is to increase the concrete information about the situation. Without information, action choices are unlikely to be optimal. When action choices are sub-optimal, then time and resources may be wasted and lost. Crisis managers need strategies that enhance information gathering and assessment. These strategies use as many sources of available information as possible, ensure that information is as concrete and certain as possible and speed up the transmission of information within the crisis. Two fundamental strategies are *siphon* and *fact-talk*.

Siphon strategies

Siphon strategies are like a siphon system used to drain liquid from a container. The approach needs to be:

- simple to use;
- used on as many sources as possible;
- capable of continuing on its own once started; and
- designed to direct data into a single central collating pool of information.

Two such approaches are *tapping* and *vacuum strategies*. Both work to extract information from inside and outside the crisis or disaster environment.

Tapping strategies

Tapping strategies are common yet poorly used approaches that involve tapping into community communication systems for information. The systems can include television programmes, radio programmes, newspaper articles and Internet sites. By tapping into community communications, executives, managers and crisis managers can gain insight into the concerns, perceptions and beliefs held by members of the community surrounding the crisis site. These insights can include the perceived impact(s) and threats of the crisis on the community and the perception by community members of the management of the crisis.

Tapping strategies need to be co-ordinated and systematic. Eyewitness information and external visual coverage of a situation can often provide important and immediate information for crisis managers. Television current affairs and radio talkback programmes may indicate trends of opinion and perception, and can identify issues and concerns that need attention and management from members of the crisis-struck organization. Stakeholder opinions (especially from users, staff and shareholders) need to be regularly tapped for satisfaction with the crisis management and for problems that the stakeholders may be encountering.

Vacuum strategies

These strategies involve 'sweeping up' or vacuuming available information, just like a vacuum cleaner. By creating a vacuum, information gets 'sucked' into the collation and assessment system. Such strategies gain information while dealing with bystander and victim concerns in a way that helps an organization appear friendly and helpful.

Business organizations may conduct vacuum strategies through call-centres. By having a semi-formatted directed information questionnaire available on paper or computer screens, operators can gain information from those who call the organization by telephone or e-mail. Other vacuum tactics may include person-to-person on-site information interviews (rather like street or in-store opinion polls) and service delivery or service follow-up calls. The twin goals are to reassure stakeholders and the general public (thus promoting a positive organizational image) and to gather all available pieces of information and opinion.

Fact-talk strategies

These strategies gain information from victims and witnesses. Fact-talk approaches may also be used to debrief respondents during (and after) involvement in a crisis situation. The emphasis is on hard or concrete pieces of information (the 'facts') that are gained by an exchange ('talk'). Two basic techniques involve receiving *patterned responses* (from respondents on site) and developing *patterned recording styles* that enable people to gain information from non-respondent contacts. Those receiving the information need to be trained to a more than adequate standard in dealing with emotional communications from upset and stressed informants. The recipients of information also need skills in helping people shape information into simple and concrete statements with little or no emotional embellishments.

Patterned response styles

Patterned response styles (PRS) are sequentially structured approaches to information transmission that crisis respondents need to use. The emphasis is on presenting hard information in an agreed pattern as outlined in more detail in Chapter 6. PRS provides concrete information on who is reporting, what information they have to impart and what they will do next.

A report may take the following form: 'Red Team Leader speaking. We are at the computer rooms on Level 5. The time is 10.45 am. Damage on this level is mixed. The computers have been heat, dust and water affected. Power is off. Light fittings and wall sections have collapsed. Damage seems to increase toward the front of the building. We will check fittings and structure, moving along the main corridor, moving north.'

Patterned recording styles

Recording styles can be based on PRS formats. A good patterned recording style is user-friendly, sequential and easy to fill in. Approaches to dealing with informants from outside the organization are suggested in Chapter 5.

Patterned recording styles provide four benefits for information management:

- Identical recording styles mean that data evaluation and cross-checking can be done faster as assessors can quickly check the source of the information.
- Use of a semi-structured approach ensures most of the possible information is recorded.
- The style can be learned by those likely to use that style, and thus reduce information exchange times.
- Appropriate use can calm people down and assist in maintaining a calmer and more fact-directed approach to managing the event.

Remember to start with very structured identifier statements when developing a fact-talk approach. Get the information the informant wants to give before checking for the concreteness of the information. Although the patterned recording style is written down and can be used by anyone, users need to be trained in assisting people to be more concrete. Information can be hardened and cross-checked by requesting 'tell me more about ... how many did you see exactly?'

Resource conservation

The third component of *CrisisThink* keeps a crisis manager's attention on the conservation and deployment of resources. This divides into three issues:

- saving resources threatened by the crisis or crisis impacts;
- conserving those resources used to resolve the crisis and crisis impacts;
- deploying resources to resolve the crisis and crisis impacts.

Saving resources threatened by a crisis

Sterile ground approaches are the key strategies for evacuation and protection of resources. This strategy involves removing threatened resources from the threat. Consequently this approach is used in various crisis situations – floods, fires, terrorist sieges, wind storms and volcanic eruptions. A sterile zone strategy echoes the meaning of the words. Movable resources are conserved by shifting these out of the path of harm, creating a zone in which people and vulnerable resources have been removed.

Sterile ground strategies are used by law enforcement agencies in sieges because the strategies reduce the number of people exposed to harm. Those being besieged are denied any further assets with which to strengthen their position. Sterile zones also act as buffers between parties in conflict, allowing some rest and redeployment of resources.

For business organizations, sterile zone strategies may include:

- developing more precise evacuation strategies for stakeholders (such as outlined in ACCCE – *see* Chapter 4);
- creating buffer sterile zones around sites of dangerous activities (rather like adding noise-proofing features);
- removing all products that are threatened with contamination or failure so that no further damage may be caused.

Conserving resources used in resolving the crisis

The basic balancing of resource cost with gain can be seen in *positive gain* strategies. These strategies fix managerial attention on balancing positive goal outcomes against the costs such goal achievement may generate. Positive gain strategies are usually implemented after sterile ground strategies have been enacted.

Focus on outcome profit

One positive gain strategy is simply to balance gain against effort, seeking a positive gain when the gains outweigh the costs. Where time and conditions permit, resource costs may be assessed in a cost-benefit analysis, or even by accounting procedures that balance actual financial outlays against expected returns or gains.

Conservation of resources through optimal deployment

Two focal approaches are suggested by Sun Tzu and Clausewitz. Sun Tzu (*see* Tao, 1993, p. 113) argued that victory comes to those who oppose weakness with strength. Crisis managers may identify sites or activities at which the crisis situation is most vulnerable and concentrate resources at those points so that local resource strength is greater than the crisis threat. For example, community crisis managers may determine specific weak spots in a river flood levee system or low lying areas most prone to flooding and concentrate wall-building and evacuation resources at those sites.

Businesses may also identify aspects of a crisis situation that may reduce the threat and the damage with concentrated deployment of resources. Acquisition of shares in an organization itself conducting a hostile takeover may spoil that takeover. Concentrating resources on developing contamination-resistant products can reduce the threat of product contamination. A concentration of resources to resolve differences between pressure groups and an organization can deflate image assaults on an organization.

For Clausewitz, one key to victory on a battlefield lay in determining where the centre of gravity of an opposing force existed, and then concentrating one's own forces in demolishing the enemy at that point. The surrounding engagements become 'mopping up' operations of lesser importance.

For organizations, this search for the centre of gravity and subsequent deployment to 'knock the crisis situation off-balance' can take several forms. Stopping a leak, for example, can be more effective than deploying resources to clean up a larger area of spillage. Concentrating resources on resolving issues with unions or pressure groups may resolve industrial disputes or defuse image assaults on an organization.

Some other useful crisis management strategies

The following four strategies help improve crisis management by using situation variables to create resource strength. Managers can maximize their deployment by utilizing dynamic rather than static reserve strategies, and by using response priority profiles to determine quickly where resources may be best deployed. Decision aids can help smooth escalation of response (by removing personal self-esteem issues) and may improve deployment of resources on a local level by determining which of a number of competing tasks gains the limited resources available.

Dynamic reserves strategy

Crisis managers often have a real problem in holding resources for contingencies that emerge as more information is gained or as impacts from the crisis become apparent. Managers can get caught between deploying all the resources before all the requirements are known and failure to use all the resources optimally because the reserve of resources was not used. Pressures to fully commit resources increase with the amount of media attention placed on the crisis situation. Uncommitted resources are often seen as signs of poor management, particularly in large and visible crisis situations.

Conventionally, management of reserves has been static. This means a portion of the available resources is held as a reserve and is often committed in bits and pieces or as an entire force. The obvious problem with this approach is that the reserves are slowly reduced, and the major decision becomes simply when and where to use them. This problem is increased by the fear that any unused reserves may lead to angry inquiries from media, politicians, public and the response manager's own organization.

Dynamic reserve strategies recognize that a crisis situation is dynamic and changing and thus the response will also undergo change. As one aspect is brought under control, another aspect may flare up. Given this fluid nature of a crisis, reserves need to be fluid in nature as well.

A basic approach to dynamic reserve strategies follows the following pattern. Crisis managers:

1 Determine a desired level of reserve resources for the crisis response situations that could arise within their area of responsibility. Scenario exercises and training may help managers assess this level.
2 Determine the likely outcomes of the crisis impact(s) as outcomes create demand for quick response and reinforcement from reserved resources.
3 Develop conservative estimates of when reinforcements can be assembled, including any agreed dispatch of fresh resources from outside the organization or region.
4 Determine the turnaround times for resources returning to base and replenishing their needs.
5 Adjust the standing reserve to reflect the dynamic situation that includes resources coming from elsewhere and deployed resources returning and resupplying.

The combined total of flow-through, turnabout and standing reserve resources provide a dynamic reserve that allows frequent deployment of reserve units while maintaining a level of reserved resources.

Another technique is to work from the 80–20 cubed rule that suggests planning for initial use of 52 per cent of the available resources as the other elements will breakdown, get lost or lose their capacity to respond. In many cases the loss of resources may be temporary. Resources get mended, eventually find their way to a designated location or replenish their capacity to operate. Moreover, there will be cases where more than 52 per cent of available resources are ready for deployment from the start. These can be held in reserve or deployed to the next set of priorities that are either part of the crisis plan or emerge as management responds to the crisis.

Do consider maintaining reserves at a crisis site rather than at a remote base.

By assigning support and temporary resources to sites that might need their contribution, yet clearly establishing with the site crisis manager and the temporarily assigned personnel that these resources may be reassigned, two objectives can be achieved:

- closer proximity to a site that may suddenly need reinforcements; and
- a higher chance that the temporarily assigned resources will redeploy.

Remember that reinforcements from outside and any resources returning to base are used as central resources to be deployed from the base or headquarters location.

As an example of the dynamic reserve concept, consider a crisis management response facility that has 100 units: 93 effective and seven decommissioned or used in training. A major crisis occurs that entails a deployment of 65 units. Pre-crisis assessment determined that a reserve of 30 units is required. The decommissioned and training units can be readied and placed in reserve within a certain period of time. Of the deployed 65 units, eight are on notice for temporary redeployment and 15 are replenishing their resources or returning for reassignment. Pre-crisis arrangements mean that seven units can be brought into reserve within a set period of time from outside the organization or region.

Under dynamic reserve management, 65 units are initially deployed. A further 65 may be seen as a changing pool of reserves (seven training units being readied, seven outside units being sent to base or headquarter locations, 15 units returning for replenishment or reassignment, eight units on temporary site assignments and 28 units that were already on reserve). Given the calculated need for 30 units on standby at any one time, a crisis manager still has an excess of 35 units that may be deployed and redeployed over time while still maintaining the 30 unit reserve.

Once respondents adjust to the mobility of their deployment and are convinced that assignment-reassignment deployment makes best use of their skills and time, use of a dynamic reserve policy is one tool that assists in rapidly regaining control over the effects of the impact of a disaster or crisis.

Response priority profiles

One major reason for problems in managing reserve resources is the lack of knowledge about the impact a crisis is having on the surrounding environment. In examining aspects of the response to the Kobe earthquake, Heath (1995) found that a rapid assessment was needed (a) of the initial dimensions of the crisis impact, and (b) of a site-by-site demand for resources and personnel over the claims of other sites for those resources. One means of reducing the time lag between crisis onset and a relatively clear picture of response requirements is to develop proactively likely response profiles for the structures within a set area. By identifying the possible needs – including seasonal or even hourly variations therein – crisis managers may then use response units to check quickly through assigned set areas to assess damage and relative need for resource assignment. In this way a quick picture of likely overall need is developed.

As with dynamic reserve strategies, single-site organizations and industrial or business organizations can adapt these strategies to quickly assess situations within their responsibility. Office-by-office reconnaissance or a check-through of core operating facilities follow the same procedures.

Response priority profiling (RPP) is one such rapid assessment procedure that incorporates a risk-based evaluation of a given environment. This evaluation identifies varying levels of impact damage by time and source of risk. Time relevance is necessary to establish whether the levels of priority may vary according to time of day or time of year. Schools or work sites, for example, may operate only in daylight hours and sports or mass entertainment activities may occur infrequently. There are peak times for use of organizational catering areas, and there are times when retail or service areas are barely occupied.

Three areas of response management are included in any RPP:

- sources and sites of likely priority resource demand;
- tasks that facilitate and enhance response operations; and
- containment of sub-event threats to life and property.

Once the various risks and priorities have been determined, response managers develop priority-based site checklists for use by designated units. There are two means of checking the sites. The first approach involves planning logical paths for each designated response unit so that damage and response assessment is made in transit to (and in between) high priority focus points. By covering a specified area quickly, a rapid picture of impact damage is gained. Once the pre-set areas have been checked, the units can be deployed either to an identified impact management point or placed on dynamic reserve. The second approach is to use specialized assessment units to assess areas using pre-set routes that ensure all likely sources of demand for response resources are checked.

The RPP acts as a 'map' of sites, activities, and tasks that enable response managers to handle systematically major calls on resources. By developing interlinked RPPs for local or departmental, area or site, and overall or multiple site situations, managers can increase the speed with which near-optimal deployment is made and potentially reduce losses, costs and time spent in response management. RPPs are flexible and adaptive. Once unaffected higher priority items are checked off, resources can be quickly deployed to the next level of priorities that do need the available resources.

An example of a possible RPP-type approach is found in the Earthquake Emergency Operational Plan (EEOP) developed by the Los Angeles Fire Department. After conducting communication and organizational status checks, the EEOP requires area commands (battalions) to conduct rapid inspections by driving through pre-established routes of assigned areas or districts without stopping. These drives help gather information on the presence of fires, structural damage, needs for physical rescue and/or medical attention, the presence of threats from hazardous materials, the condition of water supply and access routes, the availability of infrastructure utilities and any other situations (Mittendorf, 1994).

Escalation triggers

To enable an adequate response, crisis managers need a quick means by which the response can be upgraded or escalated. Clear escalation processes are critical for any integrated response management that unites a number of response agencies. Many professional response agencies have established internal escalation processes. Fire departments, for example, use a system of upgraded alarms. With each upgrade, more resources and a more senior crisis manager are made available.

Too often escalation decisions depend on the subjective and objective decision-making capacity of a crisis manager. Managerial concern over loss of face and lack of clear escalation processes can impede rapid escalation to meet the crisis situation. Careful studies of the Chernobyl nuclear accident (*see* Read, 1994) or the *Exxon Valdez* oil spill (*see* Sherman, 1989) provide similar signs of lack of quick escalation to enable appropriate response to the event.

In 1983, Southern Victoria and southern South Australia faced one of the worst wildfire situations ever recorded. A number of out-of-control wildfires (called bushfires in Australia) encircled Melbourne and Adelaide. As the fires merged and winds from the south arose, the integrated response system became confused. Baxter (1984) reported that:

Many people feel that decisive action might have averted disaster and saved lives. But no such action was taken. Ash Wednesday was regarded until seven-thirty that night as strictly a series of local problems to be dealt with by those on the spot. (p. 90)

Reserves were not called up in Victoria. Off-duty Metropolitan fire personnel were not requested for assistance, nor were the armed services called upon for aid. According to their perception of the Victorian Disaster Plan, the two controlling authorities saw the fires as minor to serious (Stage 1 to Stage 2) but not perilous (Stage 3). By nightfall the Forestry Commission saw the fires as being Stage 3, while the Country Fire Authority continued to class the situation as a Stage 2. The realization that control had been lost emerged when a fresh fire began in rugged forest country only 80 kilometres (50 miles) from Melbourne city centre. There were no resources or personnel left to attend that blaze.

Crisis managers need a means of assessing the need for escalation that does not put at risk their self-perception nor indicate any lack of ability to manage. This means that the evaluation needs to be based on externally assessed measures. Two basic approaches exist. The first uses deployment of resources as a trigger for escalation, while the second uses a five-factor evaluation model to indicate whether an appropriate level of response is being made.

In the deployment approach, a deployed-to-reserves ratio is used as an escalation trigger. Once resource deployment reaches 80 per cent of the resources available at a particular site or area, then the next level of management and resources is called into action. This allows higher levels of management to begin their co-ordination and facilitation roles, while freeing subordinate managers to focus on the tactical and strategic-tactical handling of their parts of a crisis situation. Staged escalation triggers allow potential crisis managers time to come to grips with the strategic and tactical requirements.

The other approach assesses external measures of a crisis situation. As an example, the *crisis resources and event scale triggers (CREST)* approach uses five measures to formulate a score. The measures cover:

- size of the crisis (major [3], moderate [2], minor [1]);
- degree of threat (major [3], moderate [2], minor [1]);
- resources needed (major [3], moderate [2], minor [1]);
- area exposed to the crisis (major [3], moderate [2], minor [1]); and
- assessed capacity to cope (beyond [3], adequate [2], easily [1]).

Managers quickly make an assessment, combine the scores and check the outcomes against a pre-determined escalation table. The combined score indicates the likely level of response management and amount of resources that may be needed. Note that this approach may still be overly influenced by poor subjective assessment. Without regular training, using of scenarios and real crisis situations as a means of establishing major, moderate or minor assessments and the range of capacity to cope, managers may incorrectly assess a crisis situation.

Operational management triage

Operational management triage (OMT) mirrors human casualty triage in making decisions about task priorities and resource allocations at the crisis site or sites.

Traditionally, medical triage consisted of three classes of victim: those that are moribund or will take too much resource with little chance of long-term survival, those that have a high chance of survival provided resources are used immediately, and those that have a high chance of survival and can wait for resources. Modern triage actually uses four classifications (Grant, Murray and Bergeron, 1989):

- *Class 1: Highest Priority:* immediate treatment and evacuation; severe injuries requiring urgent attention; often colour-coded red;
- *Class 2: High Priority:* secondary treatment; moderate injuries requiring attention; often colour-coded yellow;
- *Class 3: Low Priority:* tertiary treatment (including first aid); lightly injured; often colour-coded green;
- *Class 4: The Dead:* no treatment beyond mortality check; often colour-coded grey or black.

OMT is used to help decide an order of priority of tasks within a given area using the amount of resources needed, the benefit in doing the task and the degree of threat to the resources at each task location. While these three factors can be applied to business and commercial or industrial organization settings, the process is pertinent for large-scale accidents or natural disaster settings. In these situations, the focus is paired with human casualties and humans at risk, so the three factors can be described as:

- level of demand for resources (amount of resources needed);
- the number of people at risk (benefit of doing task);
- level of risk to those on site if the task is not undertaken (threat to resource).

Those establishing the model need to check that the values assigned reflect the optimal outcome. As the model is combinative (the scores can be added or multiplied together to produce a single combined score) and people tend to select a high score, care needs to be taken to get the assigned values reflecting the best options. The smaller the amount of resources required by a specific task, the more resources can be used by other tasks. So the demand for few resources scores high (say 3), moderate demand scores next (2) and high demand for resources scores least (1).

The number of people requiring rescue and treatment is easier to assess. The more people rescued and saved the better the outcome. So large numbers score high (3), moderate numbers score next (2) and small numbers of people score low (1). This can imbalance a model so that large numbers of uninjured people who are exposed to little threat get more attention than smaller numbers facing serious threat. The third variable thus assesses the amount of threat facing those people in each location. Likelihood of crisis impact threat or ripple-effect threat and loss of health are assessed, so that high threat to safety and health scores high (3), moderate threat scores next (2) and low threat scores low (1). Users can determine their own precision of values by defining a large number of levels.

A passenger aircraft accident illustrates how OMT is conducted. Disabled by catastrophic engine disintegration, an aircraft crashes onto an industrial and urban area that is near a waterfront. Four major crisis response points exist in this situation:

- an engine has crashed and is burning on a chemical storage facility near an office building;
- the tail and part of the right wing lie shattered in a timber mill complex;
- the main body of the aircraft fuselage and the attached left wing lie in a street;
- the front cockpit and the section forward of the wings has partly demolished a factory on the other side of the road.

Given limited immediate resources and personnel to deploy, a crisis manager uses her or his own visual impressions and more detailed reports from other acceptable observers to develop a plan of action. Traditionally such plans depend upon the experience and skills of the planners, the experienced interpretation of the users and the non-systematic appraisal of a large number of situational variables and impressions.

Using OMT, a manager can determine a rational and potentially more systematic deployment. In this example the crisis manager may make the following OMT assessment. There are some people in the chemical storage area and the adjacent office block (value = 2). The level of life risk is likely to be moderate – those who can will evacuate to safety (value = 2). An unspecified chemical storage fire means using specialist resources and may require many support resources (value = 1 – remember the object is to deploy the resources as widely as possible). The total equals 5.

The timber mill site has few people present (value = 1). Given the current lack of fire and limited numbers of people, the level of life risk may be moderate (value = 2). Resource need could be mixed with a need for complex resources (foam tenders) and specialist personnel (value = 2). The total equals 5.

The street site is more complicated. There are trapped aircraft passengers, people trapped in crushed or damaged vehicles and victims from those in the street at the time. Hence there may be many people involved – say 100 to 200 on the aircraft, 10 to 20 in trapped vehicles and may be 20 scattered casualties on the street (value = 3). The level of life risk due to impact injuries may be high (value = 3). The trapped people are likely to need some highly complex equipment and many support resources (value = 1). The total equals 7.

From the factory site the crisis manager has a report that there are unknown dead, 20 injured and a further 30 trapped by the loss of the structural integrity of the building. Combined with the possible victims from the front of the aircraft, the site has a moderate number of people (value = 2). The level of life risk is mixed due to structural uncertainty over the building (value = 2) and there is a likely mixed demand for resources (complex for buried victims, simple for those unable to open doors (value = 2). The total equals 6.

The result is a priority list that begins with the street site (7 points), then leads to the factory site (6 points) with the lumber storage and mill area and the storage tank fire equal last (5 points each). This tends to fit the 'book answer' of many professional crisis response agencies where emphasis is first placed on saving lives.

Problems exist with the 'book response strategy'. While the 'save the people and then resources' principle of response management is not at issue, there is an increasing likelihood that without justification the 'book' response may be non-optimal and may not satisfy a post-crisis inquiry.

The first problem is that this assessment treats the situation as a static rather than dynamic incident. In reality, threats and risks change over the time taken to manage a crisis and the impacts of that crisis. In the aircraft crash example, the real threat of the storage facility fire may be under-assessed in a one-shot assessment that may be biased by the possibility of people trapped in and under the aircraft fuselage. Over time, however, the situation at the storage facility is likely to worsen unless effective action is taken. The smoke plume may be toxic and, according to prevailing wind direction, threaten the surrounding urban population. Likewise, an explosion from the facility may trigger surrounding fires including aviation gas explosions at the street and lumber storage sites. The spread of fire to the chemical storage site and of chemical pollution of the harbour water could add further threats and risks. Managers need to incorporate future risk into response actions that span hours or days of time.

A second problem is that the number of people thought to be at risk is often overestimated in a high-impact accident like this aircraft crash. In high-speed and poorly controlled landing crashes on flat surfaces, a surprising number may survive (as in the Sioux City accident – *see* Chapter 4). Crashes with a high angle 'dive' to the ground, as in this example, have few survivors. Many victims are likely to be dead or so moribund that resources are wasted on trying to retrieve and revive them while others are at greater risk elsewhere. Whether victims have survived the impacts of the crisis situation needs to be incorporated into the risk assessment.

A third problem resides in a belief that the responding force needs to attend each task site. In many cases, survivors will not only save themselves but also assist others to survive. In the Northridge earthquake, for example, a government inquiry determined that surviving victims and bystanders undertook 95 per cent of the rescues. An assessment on the likelihood that trained response management, personnel and resources are needed to manage the situation could be added to a risk-based priority assessment.

These three added dimensions change the response picture. The new combined scores will equal the old scores plus the assigned values for:

- survivability given the type of crisis (many survive = 3, some survive = 2, few survive = 1);
- potential increased threat over time (high increase = 3, moderate increase = 2, little increase = 1);
- need for highly trained response personnel (many highly trained personnel = 1, several = 2, few = 3 – remember the more sites covered by trained personnel, the faster and better the outcomes).

At the chemical storage site, the threat of increased risk from the facility exploding is high as is the unknown threat to the other sites and surrounding community (value = 3). Most victims are likely to be saved if treated (value = 3). The need for trained response personnel is high given the fire (value = 1). The new total equals 12.

At the timber mill site, the increased threat to the site and surrounding community is low – if the gas ignites, the timber may burn (value = 1). The likelihood of there being survivors is high (value = 3) and the need for some trained personnel is moderate – to place foam on spilt gas (value = 2). The modified total is 11.

For the street site, high-impact aircraft accidents in urban areas usually have few survivors on board or under the aircraft (value = 1). The threat of increased risk is moderate, given the fuel from the cars and the left wing (value = 2). The need for specialized personnel is moderate given the fire risk and the possible need to use specialized extraction equipment (value = 2). The modified total is 12.

The factory site has a limited threat to the surrounding community but may structurally disintegrate and thus place those inside at greater risk (value = 1). Unless the structure further disintegrates, those simply trapped or injured are quite likely to be survivors (value = 3). The need for specially trained personnel is high to moderate depending on the number trapped and the difficulty in getting to those people (value = 1). The modified total is 11.

The new order of priority has the chemical storage site (12) and street site (12) as equal first priority and the others as equal – the timber mill (11) and the factory site (11).

At first sight the OMT model seems to be indeterminate. In applying estimated values to these four task sites, however, most crisis managers will realize that the two first priority sites need different types of resources. The chemical storage fire needs foam tenders and firefighting units as a primary resource, with some paramedic and other support service units as secondary resource units. The reverse is virtually true for the street site. At this site, volunteers, paramedics and specialist units to lift and extract wreckage to free people are the needed primary resources, with some foam and firefighting tenders monitoring the potential threat of a fire from the spilt aviation fuel. Consequently, a crisis manager can make two separate deployments that meet the needs of both priority sites.

As can be seen by the above example, crisis managers need to select carefully the criteria on which they build their OMT tools. The above variables may not be appropriate for all situations. Other variables may need to be added. OMT tools can be built for other multi-site crisis situations and many multi-feature non-accident or disaster situations in business and geopolitical settings.

Businesses may also find OMT-type approaches worthwhile when confronted by multi-site or multiple demands for resources during a crisis situation. By defining criteria (cash flow, profit, demand on available personnel, effect on share value, impact on stakeholders), a set of tasks can be assessed for the 'return on the investment' of the crisis management.

Three obvious benefits emerge with OMT:

- increased rational efficiency of resource and personnel deployment;
- a reduction in mental pressure and stress on users;
- a rational process that can be produced and argued in inquiry and courtroom situations.

One further benefit is that use of such an approach enables managers to quickly identify the necessary soft and hard information they need to undertake the OMT assessments and will lead to faster and more informed decision making.

Some business crisis management strategies

The fundamental mission of a business is to create wealth for all of the stakeholders (clients, staff, creditors, debtors, owners and shareholders). The primary crisis management mission for business managers is consequently simple – get the business back to creating wealth for the stakeholders. In many cases, the primary mission becomes distorted by a more immediate concern such as the survival of the business. The change of mission emphasis from wealth creation to survival can compel an unconscious and possibly fatal change in decision-task selection. A focus on survival can ignore decisions and tasks that can continue creating wealth for the business.

Examples of the effects of this mission change can readily be seen. A business that focuses too rigidly on regathering its resources and rebuilding its structures after a major disaster may fail because the customers of that business are not attended to and move to a competing business. The subsequent loss of cash flow drains the business to death.

The stock market provides another example of how quickly a change in goal focus alters the actions of the decision makers and managers involved. Stock markets are about wealth creation through investing money in shares to create more future wealth. When confidence is eroded, investors may trigger a fall in share prices. In most cases, the assets and income-producing values of the organization have not changed. What has changed is that investors have shifted their focus from investment for wealth creation to divestment for perceived survival.

One final example shows the value of considering the points of view held by stakeholders. On 28 September 1982, Johnson & Johnson (J&J) had a 35 per cent market share in over-the-counter pain relief medication in the USA worth approximately $450 million. Between 29 September and 1 October in 1979, seven people died in the Chicago area after taking Tylenol Extra Strength capsules that were contaminated with cyanide. Public reports that cyanide was inserted in these capsules led to an 87 per cent drop in sales. Moreover, the effect of the Tylenol poisoning on J&J was a fall of around 20 per cent (around US$1.9 billion) in the value of Johnson & Johnson on the Wall Street market. J&J recalled and destroyed 22 million bottles of Tylenol.

The company reintroduced the product with triple tamper-proof sealed capsules. After a copycat incident, J&J reintroduced the product as a solid form caplet and promoted its safety features. Within five months, J&J recovered 70 per cent of their share of the market. The management did the two most effective crisis management steps in a product failure or product contamination incident: recalled the entire product and ensured potential players or users were quickly informed. By working from the points of view held by their consumers (fear of risk to life) and then by promoting diminished risk to life and health as a positive part of the re-engineered product, the business was able to keep solvent and regain market share.

Planners, executives and managers often plan poorly for involving those stakeholders who are not part of a response or recovery effort. As a result, organizations risk:

- losing their mission focus (for example, by redirecting effort totally away from maintaining wealth creation to system survival);
- reduced morale as those with no activity begin to feel unnecessary and aimless (and those involved feel stressed and overworked);
- loss of commitment from stakeholders as staff lose their sense of purpose and clients remove their custom and support.

By involving as many stakeholders as possible in response–recovery actions managers can gain higher levels of effort and commitment than ordinarily experienced. As argued in Chapter 15, this effort may actually improve the value and image of the organization.

In particular, executives and managers need to give more thought to using their non-response and non-recovery staff. These people are often marginalized by being kept on the sidelines or given recovery tasks that may be better done by specialist non-organization employees. The non-response and non-recovery staff may be better employed in making personal contact with the outside stakeholders (clients, customers, creditors, insurance agents, debtors and suppliers) to find out what these people need. By involving staff in seeking to continue the wealth-creating services and by involving the other stakeholders in the recovery and continuity process, managers may find that greater cash flows and fewer losses in staff and clients happen during the recovery period and beyond.

Planners and managers tend to ignore or trivialize the need for adjustment by everyone involved or affected by a crisis, including themselves. Setting aside arguments for or against trauma and crisis counselling, response and recovery task performance can drop as those involved are distracted by their own needs to assess and assimilate the stimuli they received during the crisis situation. Managers need to incorporate procedures for allowing for adjustment and for making available adjustment 'counselling' when and wherever needed.

REALITY BITE

The Bank of Melbourne, Australia, July 1990

Background
The Bank of Melbourne had converted from a building society, RESI-Statewide, into a bank. RESI-Statewide was Australia's second largest building society and had been floated on the stock market as a fully fledged bank, with branches in

most cities and towns in the State of Victoria. By the end of its first year as a bank, however, rumours suggested the bank was critically short of funds.

Incident

From early July 1990, rumours about the viability of the Bank of Melbourne were circulating Melbourne, and given the previous collapse of a large building society, the Pyramid Building Society, depositors became uneasy and began removing funds. Investors sold shares in the bank on advice from stock market brokers and share value slumped by 15 per cent. Rumours included:

- the Bank of Melbourne would close on Friday and not reopen (a repeat of the Pyramid Building Society situation);
- the Bank of Melbourne was in liquidity trouble (speculative sources may have included some rival bank managers and a former senior employee);
- 'over 150 depositors [were] already queuing at the doors at [...] branch, and you'd better get your money out quick';
- the Bank was limiting withdrawals to AUS$1000.

Response

The Chief Executive Officer and Bank Chairman, Christopher Stewart, began daily briefings for Reserve Bank officials from the time he became aware of the rumours. These briefings were continued during the crisis.

Stewart also released a bulletin to staff and customers pointing out that the bank had an A1 Rating from Australian ratings, had a strong asset quality and had a high capital adequacy ratio.

On Monday, 16 July Stewart called an informal board meeting and spoke to the Australian Reserve Bank Governor, Bernie Fraser, about the rumours. The Reserve Bank monitors the actions of banks in Australia and officials had contacted Stewart over the rumours, particularly over customers queuing and cash limitations. Stewart reassured the officials that these were not true. On Monday afternoon the Reserve Bank and Bank of Melbourne released formal statements about the bank's financial solidity.

Tuesday, 17 July began at 6.30 am with telephone calls from the media. By early morning queues at branches were stretching into the street. Withdrawals were three times higher than normal, with customers refusing any form of payment other than cash. The withdrawals continued over the next few days until Friday, 20 July when trading returned to normal.

Share values returned to the value prior the run on the bank.

Statistics

The bank had over one million customers and assets of approximately AUS$3.7 billion.

Comment

Perhaps the first point illustrated by this case is to keep in contact with regulators and key players as soon as a problem occurs. By regularly briefing officials from the Reserve Bank, positive support was available. However, the reassurance by major participants (CEO of the Bank of Melbourne and the Governor of the

Reserve Bank) did not reduce alarm among some depositors. An organization is most likely to need at least two further actions:

- an ability to meet the peak demand in an active and positive manner; and
- visible support from ordinary people and businesses.

The active and positive strategy includes staff reassuring customers about the solidity of the organization (and this information has to be the truth as the staff perceive it) and happily helping customers get what they want (even if this is a full withdrawal). Quick satisfaction of complaints reduces further complaints. In the case of financial institutions, truthful reassurance and happy helpfulness from the counter-level staff is one of the strategies best able to stop withdrawal of funds.

On a positive note, the crisis helped build an *esprit de corps* among Bank of Melbourne staff. By getting the bank through the crisis (and saving their own jobs) the staff were more cohesive and unified.

Management perspective

Reassurance from authoritative sources is a necessary step because absence of such support makes the situation worse. Formal statements of support alone do not reassure small depositors because of continuing suspicion of a cover-up. Moreover, formal authority seems remote and is often careful in the language used to express support. Senior executives are seen as relatively unaffected by any potential loss.

In the Bank of Melbourne case, for example, several people interviewed while waiting in queues stated that statements of financial solidity had been made by government ministers about the Pyramid Building Society, yet that business had failed. The attempt to help by the Premier of Victoria seemed out of touch. The Premier suggested people should consult their investment advisers. Most of those affected did not use investment advisers and had simply opened savings accounts with the bank.

Executives and managers need to use a two-step strategy for issue communications. When policy is being discussed or presented, the presenters need to be very senior – managing directors, CEOs, presidents of organizations. The central reason for this is that these people are seen as policy makers and enforcers. Should statements about what action was being done be required, then these need to be presented by 'working' personnel – senior staff or line-level workers. This gives a 'street level' or 'coal face' feel to the presentation where listeners and viewers identify with someone like themselves rather than a senior executive. Had the Bank of Melbourne used counter staff to present the 'sound financial status' message as well as the policy-level personnel, the financial crisis may have finished more quickly.

Strategies for dealing with four less tangible business crisis situations

Business organizations are exposed to natural disasters and accidents that are mostly tangible. In these situations, the organization is often a partial manager of the response effort. Less tangible and more business-specific crisis situations confront businesses as well. Four common situations include:

- hostile takeover;
- product contamination;
- industrial action; and
- assault on an organization's image.

Hostile takeover

Hostile takeover is increasing as businesses respond to economic and organizational pressures. While some early warning signs may be gained from transactions in shares and volatile movements in stock markets, less clear operations may entail a *co-operative acquisition technique (CAT)*. In a CAT one or more organizations acquire shares in a target organization with the intent of co-operating in boosting the share portfolio of one of the organizations once that organization declares an offer for shares in the target organization.

Warning signs of potential hostile takeovers include:

- stationary or diminishing earnings;
- below expected ROI (return on investment);
- poor cash management;
- overly high gearing ratios;
- cash cows (high-revenue generators) in subsidiaries or divisions;
- poor communications with shareholders and financial organizations;
- major shareholders selling shares;
- interest from organizations that would benefit from absorbing the organization;
- competitors removing competition while increasing their own market share;
- asset magnets (resources, managers or activities which attract interest from other organizations).

While holding some of these 'signal' elements may be beneficial (even vital) to an organization, the accent is on the perception held by likely predators of these elements.

Action steps

- *Take immediate action.* Remember *CrisisThink* – work to gain time by refusing access to the organization and by refusing to meet with the takeover organization.
- *Assemble the response team.* Inform senior people of the position and get specialists (legal, financial and public relations) into action as quickly as possible.
- *Involve specialists.* Get assistance from outside specialists (bankers, legal

representatives and PR firms) and determine strategies to cover the first working week (five days) on a day-by-day basis.

- *Look carefully at the offer.* After establishing a defence strategy, explore the offer. Should the offer appear a good one at the right price, change the strategy from determined defence to working for the best possible offer.
- *Reject offer.* Should the offer be inadequate and not in the best interests of the shareholders, clearly reject the offer.
- *Inform stakeholders and the public.* Notify all parties and explain the attack and the management's considered response.
- *Use legal and business wall and deferral strategies.* Using internal and external advisory teams, consider defensive options (including legal and technical challenges, counter-offers, share acquisition or takeover offers from 'friendly' organizations, organizational changes and getting rid of the attractions for takeover).
- *Outlast the attacker.* Use the time available to drain the resources and patience of the attacking organization, as prolonged battles add costs to the attacker.
- *Eliminate the attraction.* Change whatever aspects or elements appear to have attracted the attack in the first place, thus building market value.

Threats to products or customers

These threats can include:

- extortion (and sweetmail);
- consumer terrorism (ranging from active boycotts to attacks on sources and users);
- sabotage and grudge-directed activities (by internal employees);
- fraudulent claims made for compensation.

Non-criminal parallels to these situations include:

- product contamination (due to machine or system failure);
- product deterioration (due to incorrect handling, storage or inventory control);
- product failure (wherein a product failure occurs in a design element).

These situations can be reduced by use of quality control and quality assurance approaches. Such situations may also be monitored by reputation risk management activities (*see* Chapter 8).

Action steps

- *Implement sterile zone immediately.* Prevent customer access to the suspect product and remove it. Do not let further damage be caused.
- *Inform everyone.* This includes stakeholders, the public, the authorities and any likely response agencies (e.g. paramedic services, medical practitioners and hospitals).

- *Provide easy information access points.* Set up convenient websites and cheap or freefone telephone numbers.
- *Resolve the problem.* Given deliberate sweetmail contamination, an important decision may be whether to contact authorities and whether to meet any extortion demands. Such decisions need to be taken in the context of the situation and the legal onus on your organization in a given country. Expert and experienced advice may be needed in this situation.
- *Get rid of the problem.* If necessary, redesign the package or the operating process that produces the problem.
- *Inform public when all is safe.* Use special re-entry programmes and emphasize the safer aspects of the product. Arnott's (Australia, 1997) suffered a contamination threat to its products that caused the total withdrawal of the products along the Australian east coast. After the situation was resolved, Arnott's ensured sparkling clean trucks were publicly pictured leaving its factories to redeliver the freshly made and thus uncontaminated products.
- *Always emphasize customer safety.* By emphasizing safety and making an effort to meet customer needs, organizations gain support and reduce loss of customers.

Industrial disputes

Industrial disputes are the result of long-term problems. Disputation becomes heated, reaching a point at which employees or union members remove their labour. Organizations often attempt to outlast strikes but can find that cash flows begin to dry up and resources (from raw materials to finished product inventories) run low.

Action steps

- *Evaluate the situation.* Get as much detail as possible from all sides to gain a clear perception of the mood and positions of all involved. Move to defuse anger where possible.
- *Focus on perceptions (POV analysis).* Isolate the issues causing division and find out how each party views them. Seek common ground and areas in which agreement may be achieved.
- *Generate an offer.* Keep to the common agreement areas and reduce the number of issues causing conflict. Get agreement that the issues in conflict will be dealt with at a given later date.
- *Settle.* Work toward agreement and commitment to the agreement from all parties involved.
- *Do not rest on the current success.* Continue developing good relations with stakeholders and ensure that hard work toward eliminating or reducing issues in conflict is seen to be done.

Assaults on organizational image

Many of the techniques supporting the following strategy are discussed in Chapter 8.

Action steps

- *Analyze the perception problem.* Use POV analysis to find out:
  - what happened;
  - who is involved;
  - who gains from damaging the organization;
  - what is the issue;
  - what specific organizational operation is targeted;
  - what brought this operation and this issue into prominence.
- *Get outside POV assessment.* Check the POV analysis by getting an outside organization to evaluate the assault.
- *Keep all stakeholders informed.* Ensure that they know what the issues are and the organization's version and POV. Involve stakeholders in the resolution process.
- *Defuse the interactions.* Remember to listen calmly and use the interaction approaches outlined in Chapter 8.
- *Avoid litigation.* Get legal advice on the danger points and the organization's exposure to litigation. Do not overreact to legal concerns as the public's perception becomes negative when lawyers start legal quibbling over admissions of guilt or responsibility.
- *Maintain interactive communications.* Keep talking with stakeholders and encourage them to communicate their fears or any information they have with the crisis manager or team members.
- *Tell the organization's story.* State the organization's story regularly, remain consistent, avoid speculation and stating 'no comment' and avoid personality clashes with those assaulting the organization's image.
- *Work in the public gaze.* Avoid closed-door interactions as these may later be denied or distorted. Use the public gaze to work toward workable solutions.
- *Involve the critics in resolving the issues.* Remember that critics have difficulty remaining critical when they have no alternative to offer or become part of the solution process.

REALITY BITE

Perrier Water contamination, France/USA, 1990

Background

Perrier Water has bottled water containing naturally forming carbon dioxide from the same area for over 40 years. The product was introduced to the USA in 1977. By 1989, Perrier Water had around 52 per cent of the USA mineral water market (worth nearly $650 million). Many of the sales were through upmarket restaurants. The product was distributed across the USA from New York and Phoenix.

Incident

Between August 1989 and February 1990 consistently high levels of benzene were found in samples of Perrier Water, indicating a product contamination problem. The fact that traces of benzene naturally occur in mineral water did not help identify the source. While the benzene contamination levels were not sufficient to cause illness or deaths, the continuing high levels were of concern given the clean and healthy image of the product.

Response

Perrier recalled 70 000 000 bottles of its water from within the USA alone. The company also quickly set up a free telephone contact (an 800 number) for consumer concerns.

The global product withdrawal strategy lead to a rowdy shareholder meeting in Paris. There arose conflicting statements as to the likely source and cause of the benzene contamination.

The main objective of the withdrawal was to protect consumer trust and market presence while the product was absent. A well funded campaign to remind consumers that the product would be back as soon as possible was launched.

The investigation and correction took three months to complete. A faulty filtering system was identified and replaced.

The reintroduction of Perrier included offers of free bottles for loyal customers and cost an estimated $25 million. The reintroduction strategy included advertisements conveying the message that the real product (complete with a 'New Production' label) was worth the wait.

Statistics

In the USA alone the recall cost an estimated $40 million in sales. In one day (12 February) the global recall strategy prompted a slump of over 11 per cent on Perrier's share value in Paris (a fall of just over 200 Francs). The number of sell orders on the Paris stock market led to a temporary cessation in trading in Perrier shares.

Comment

The quick recall and ready co-operation with the relevant authorities gained praise from a number of sources. Perrier tried to reduce their market erosion with advertisements in the media.

Management perspective

The recall was an inopportune time for Perrier which had just completed a massive expansion in production capacity. Given a decreased market share (due in large part to the recall and to aggressive marketing by other mineral water bottling companies) production did not exceed 40 per cent capacity. This low output may well have caused Perrier to lose its corporate independence.

Note the impact of international market placements on management. Four important points need to be considered in any global crisis management strategy:

- round-the-clock surveillance and response capability;
- adaptation of response strategies to different cultural conditions and ways of behaving;
- awareness of time-critical delays in reshipping non-locally produced goods

(shipping Perrier took 14 days to New York and 21 days to Houston); and

● continued presence in the marketplace.

To some extent, the presence of other Perrier-produced brands (Poland Springs, Calistoga and Arrowhead) may have cushioned the loss by joining the active promotion of competitor brands in the three-month period.

Hints and tips on managing crisis situations

● *Use psychological stoppers such as PBR to calm down and focus on the crisis.*
● *Learn to counter distorted decision making.* These pressures can be offset by using relaxation techniques (to lower physiological stress) and by using cognitive guides such as *CrisisThink*.
● *Develop the means to protect information management from information discounting due to insider–outsider differences in familiarity and trust.* Discounting information from sources outside an organization is particularly found within professional response agencies, even when the information is supplied by other professional response agencies. There is a difference between checking the nature, content and validity of information and not heeding the information at all. Information discounting leads to four potential problems:
  – non-discounted information is unduly weighted;
  – the consequent lack of information generates more decisional uncertainty;
  – costs in time and resources increase as crisis managers seek information that was already available;
  – co-operation and trust decreases (and frustration increases) when the outside sources of information realize their information is being discounted.
● *'Black holes' often attract too much attention.* Just as black holes in space attract all surrounding energy, black hole-type features appear in crisis situations. Black holes are specific sites or issues that gain more resources and attention than can be optimally used. Most large crises produce at least one black hole, often due to media attention. Without balanced evaluation, crisis managers may find themselves directing more resources to the black hole at the expense of other issues or locations.
● *Avoid mindsets.* Mindsets occur when stereotypic thinking is present. Stereotypic thinking can come from improperly evaluated past experience or through over-preoccupation with the likely onset of a specific situation.
● *Avoid groupthink.* This occurs when all of a group think the same way or when members of a group fear to disagree with senior members.
● *Managers who become involved in doing crisis response tasks are no longer managing.* Crisis managers have the job of looking after the big picture while others concentrate on the local details. Once managers 'lend a hand' or become involved in 'showing how to do a particular job', they lose their

grasp of the big picture. This risks worsening the crisis impact and can endanger the manager's subordinates. When fatigue sets in, or a unit becomes directionless and inactive, a crisis manager may feel the need to lead by example. At best this needs to be done in a short burst until the team members regain a higher work rate.

- *Create a sterile zone around the crisis situation or environment.* One of the first tasks of crisis management is to prevent further losses. In a physical crisis situation, crisis managers need to secure the surrounding area as soon as possible, evacuating people and resources where necessary.

- *Understand that the 80–20 rule often applies to evacuations.* In most cases, evacuation of people from an endangered location rarely exceeds 80 per cent effectiveness. People stay on to protect property or to experience the crisis, or are simply overlooked in an evacuation process. People also return to the location to check that family members are safe, to pick up further property or even to satisfy a need for psychological security.

- *Understand that the 80–20 rule applies when specific instructions are given.* If people are instructed to evacuate, then a minority will refuse to do so. If people are instructed to stay inside and shut all doors and windows, then a minority will try to evacuate or go outside to see what is going on.

- *Separate decision making from communication and control sites.* When decision-making groups and communication and control groups are not separated, each distracts the other. Decision makers can become distracted by task problems experienced by the control and communication personnel instead of concentrating on evaluating information and options. Ongoing managerial discussions distract communication and control personnel. Separation leads to a quieter and more efficient process of management.

- *Separate internal (inside the crisis response) information flows from external (outside the crisis response) communication flows.* As outlined in the CMSS section, internal information flows need to be deliberately kept separate from external information flows. This helps maintain the image of the crisis response. Separation of information flows also makes the crisis response more secure in certain situations (war, sieges, hostage situations and terrorist alerts) and reduces rumours.

- *Credible and authoritative information needs to be made available to those affected by the crisis.* Information is a prime element in crisis management. Lack of information creates voids in which rumour and frustration increase the chances of conflict and the chances of further damage in a crisis situation.

- *Monitor and record the latest locations and status of all response units.* One common feature of crisis management is the lack of attention paid to the crisis respondents. Managers need to track the deployment and status of respondents so that both the welfare and effective use of those units can be maximized.

- *Keep plans and operations as simple as possible.* Once response efforts become complex, error and ripple-effect crisis situations are likely to affect the operations.

- *Ensure that managers know their role in the response operation.* Barton (1993) cites statistics from a sample of 120 crisis cases that show that subordinate managers:
  - speak to outsiders without authorization – often without understanding the norms and procedures of their organization (43 per cent of cases);
  - present incorrect data or give faulty information (27 per cent of cases);
  - take action(s) that complicate a crisis (22 per cent of cases).
- *Remember that crisis situations have noisy and confused environments.* One major difference between training exercises or simulations and a crisis situation is that the crisis not only generates a lot of sound and confusing stimuli, but takes place amid the normal distractions of everyday life. Family members try to speak to respondents. Normal operations continue among those unaffected by the situation, and non-affected personnel often need actions from, and information exchanges with, those caught up in a crisis situation.
- *Remember response effort is highest in the first three to six hours.* Most respondents and associated personnel may first show significant effort, but this will fade over time as the unusual situation becomes mundane and adrenalin fatigue sets in.
- *Those removed from their normal environments and daily work will wish to return.* In the field, people start pressing to go home or return to normal duties and lifestyles sometime between six and 72 hours after a crisis situation. Businesses will wish to return to their sites (pressure will be brought to bear on local government for this to happen) and residents will wish to return to their homes (even when these no longer exist).
- *Crisis management may not be the sole domain of an organization's crisis management.* Many crisis situations are integrated response efforts involving a number of separate organizations. For business organizations, physical crisis situations (natural disasters, major accidents, structural failure or fire, terrorist attack) lead to a partial management situation. Partial management usually means a dual role of supporting the outside response agencies and maintaining a positive image for the organization.
- *Remember that multiple-agency crisis management often means poor communication and differences in terminology.* This sometimes happens between separate units, groups or divisions in business organizations. Where possible standardize the positions, terms and communication equipment across probable crisis respondents.
- *Be prepared for ripple-effects.* Most crisis situations generate impacts that can become distracting crisis situations. Have specialist managers prepared to cover any emerging situations that may affect the crisis situation.
- *Take care to develop effective information management operations.* Decision making can be distorted by:
  - over-dependency on a few sources of information;
  - having too much information, particularly unsorted and non-evaluated information; and

– operating with too little information.

- *Maintain good image management.* Crisis management needs to be as concerned with how the crisis response is perceived as with the actual management of the crisis situation. This is particularly true for business organizations. Remember that image needs to match performance – espoused or stated actions and beliefs need to match actual or undertaken actions and policy decisions.

- *Argue for appropriate crisis response funding.* There are a number of ways to do this. One way is to take 6.5 per cent of asset value plus turnover (based on fire and insurance risk and debt protection) to provide a total potential estimate. This estimate may need to cover insurance and associated image/reputation control elements as well as a crisis management structure and response capability.

- *Crisis management personnel need to have first-aid training.* Given the stress involved and prospective encounters with dangerous physical situations, personnel need a basic ability to provide first aid to themselves and each other. Everyone needs to have at least the 'ABC' (Airway, Breathing, Circulation) training and an understanding of treatment for shock and stress management.

- *Remember legal responsibilities (before, during and after a crisis situation).* These responsibilities may include duty of care, corporate legal requirements and safety regulations.

- *Look after and obtain feedback from the stakeholders of the organization.* Stakeholders can help or hinder response and recovery if their needs are overlooked or their situation is taken for granted.

- *Ensure costs, resource use and personnel deployment is monitored.* At some point the costs of response will become part of the assessment of performance.

- *Ensure that the whole organization supports and accepts the crisis manager.* Too often senior executives try to take over the operation or countermand action choices. Similarly, without strong support from the leaders of an organization, other members of staff can ignore a crisis manager.

Crisis management lessons learned in the 1989
Loma Prieta earthquake

The West Coast of America (particularly the Californian coastline) is well known for frequent earthquakes. At 5.04 pm on 17 October, an earthquake that measured 7.1 ML on the Richter scale struck San Francisco. This was the strongest earthquake since the Great Earthquake of 1906, was felt over a region of some 1 000 000 square kilometres (400 000 square miles) and had an epicentre about 96 km (60 miles) southeast of San Francisco. Over 11 000 recorded aftershocks (from 1.0 to 5.4 ML) were recorded between 17 October 1989, and 12 October 1994.

The earthquake killed 63, injured 3757, and left 12 000 without homes. Around 23 400 dwellings and 3500 businesses were damaged, and 1100 dwellings and

360 businesses were destroyed by the impact of this earthquake. Overall estimated losses were assessed at $5.9 billion (£4.5 billion).

By June 1994, over $760 million (£570 million) financial assistance was given to
families, individuals and businesses from US federal government sources, and $4
million (£3 million) of state and federal money was spent in crisis counselling programmes. The California State Board of Control issued $72 million (£54 million) in
compensation for death, injury and property losses for the collapse of Cypress
structures and the Bay Bridge. Over $660 million (£495 million) was spent via
county, state and federal repair and restoration projects, and $44 million (£33 mil-
lion) was spent on specific earthquake mitigation projects.

Most of the 107 state law enforcement agencies in the affected region (90
municipal, ten county sheriff and seven university departments) reported that
between 80 and 90 per cent of their personnel reported for duty within four
hours. Many were sent home to ensure that those currently on duty could be
relieved. Some departments noted that communication personnel needed to be
told to make calling in off-duty personnel a priority.

Personnel undertook 12-hour shifts of emergency duty. These shifts continued
for 14 days after the earthquake, and led to days off, vacations and court appearances being cancelled. Note the ripple effect a crisis situation may have – families
and court cases become adversely affected.

Most professional response agencies have a standard operational procedure for
handling an earthquake event. In sequence these are as follows:

- Check the capability of the agency (and the stations) to continue operations.
- Assist in drive-by damage assessment of region.
- Screen emergency calls.
- Activate the emergency operations centre.
- Give aid to the injured.
- Undertake early search and rescue.
- Reassure citizens.
- Assist in evacuation of endangered sites.
- Check reports of hazards (gas leaks, alarms, power outages, failure of traffic
  signals).

After-action reports from these agencies noted the following:

- Personnel need more training in providing aid to the injured.
- More resources and skills need to be acquired to provide broader public safety
  (such as fighting fires, helping trapped and injured to safety and reducing local
  hazards where possible).
- Crimes against persons deceased and property theft (looting) did happen but
  mostly in unpatrolled areas or in locations with pre-existing high levels of
  crime.
- Increased criminal activities included fraud over repairs, fraudulent applications for emergency and earthquake financial assistance and fraudulent solici-
  tations for donations toward earthquake relief.
- Evacuated people were prepared to enter restricted areas to return to their
  homes or business sites despite potential charges of trespass.

Law enforcement departments noted a number of issues in their report printed in May 1990, including the following:

- There was a loss of emergency communications. The 911 emergency telephone call system was out of action for up to six hours, mostly due to overload.
- There was a need to ensure reliable alternative electric power generation.
- More planning was needed to outline how outside assistance may best be used.
- More and better training in managing under crisis conditions was needed.
- Departments and units needed pre-crisis prepared lists of specialist skills, including language and task skills.
- Management teams needed to improve their documentation of resource use and expenditure and of tasks undertaken.

Use of mobile telephones

Three aspects about mobile telephone use need to be remembered:

- Telephones may not work because the responder transmitters are damaged or inaccessible due to blind spots.
- The battery life for mobile telephones is quite limited, especially when these are left in an active transmission–reception mode for long periods of time. Extra batteries and charging equipment not dependent upon mains electricity need to be acquired.
- Mobile telephone services tend to overload as other users begin to use their telephones, particularly media personnel.

Electric power

Evidence from the Loma Prieta earthquake and other recent crises suggests that alternative sources of power needs reassessment. This includes:

- checking that the alternative sources of electric power work;
- checking that the alternative sources of electric power can handle the load requirements for the site over time;
- ensuring that adequate maintenance personnel are available to repair failed alternative power sources;
- ensuring that sufficient coolant and fuel is available.

Switching to alternative sources of power will often have to be force-tested as building managers and work supervisors dislike disruptions. Many alternative power sources have failed when needed, often due to failure to switch on automatically when the mains power is disrupted.

References

Barton, L. (1993) *Crisis in Organizations: Managing and Communicating in the Heat of Chaos*. Cincinnati, Ohio: South-Western.

Baxter, J. (1984) *Who Burned Australia? The Ash Wednesday Fires*. London: New English Library.

Grant, H. D., Murray, R. H. and Bergeron, J. D. (1989) *Emergency Care*, 4th edn. Englewood Cliffs, NJ: Prentice Hall.

Hadfield, P. (1991) *Sixty Seconds That Will Change the World: The Coming Tokyo Earthquake*.

London: Sidgwick & Jackson.

Heath, R. J. (1995) 'The Kobe earthquake: some realities of strategic management of crises and disasters', *Disaster Prevention and Management*, 4(5), 11–24.

Mittendorf, J. W. (1994) 'LAFD earthquake preplanning', *Fire Engineering*, 147(8), 14–21.

Read, P. P. (1994) *Ablaze: The Story of Chernobyl*. London: Mandarin Books.

Robinson, A. (1993) *Earth Shock: Climate, Complexity and the Forces of Nature*. London: Thames & Hudson.

Sherman, S. P. (1989) 'Smart ways to handle the press', *Fortune*, 19 June, 57–62.

Tao, H. (1993) *Sun Tzu: The Art of War*. Ware, Hertfordshire: Wordsworth Reference.

chapter 13

EXERCISE

The key objective of this exercise is to enable participants to experiment with complex response management activities as discussed in this and preceding chapters.

Note that the exercise provides a chance to practise information management approaches and skills (see Chapter 6), media or 'pressure group' management (see Chapter 7) and image shaping of responses to questions from these groups (see Chapters 7 and 8). Do spend time discussing and working on these areas as well as on planning and making game-turn moves (described below).

When you have finished the exercise, critically consider the strategies and actions you made and the consequent outcomes. Should you be doing this exercise in a small group, discuss your impressions and criticisms. Remember to acknowledge the positive aspects as well as analyze any 'what went wrong' aspects. You may wish to consider the brief comments made on this exercise on pp. 451–4 in Appendix 2 to help generate your analysis and discussion.

Beginning the exercise

Find the simulation map in the Appendix 1 and follow the preparation instructions.

Map descriptions

The map shows part of the city of Rage. There is a harbour running east to west at the top of the map. There is a school [T17, T18, U17, U18], hospital [T1, T2, U1, U2] and a high-volume dangerous chemical loading facility (from oil and gas to complex industrial gases and liquids [F7, F8, G7, G8]).

On the harbour coastline on the left-hand half of the map (columns 1 to 12) are industrial manufacturing facilities and dangerous chemical storage facilities (the grey rings are protective walls or bunds surrounding the tank). These are objects numbered 1, 2, 9, 10, 11, 12, 13, 14, 15 and 16. On the harbour coastline on the right-hand half of the map (columns 13 to 24) exist commercial premises and luxury residential premises. These are objects numbered 3, 4, 5, 6, 7, 8, 17, 18, 19 and 20.

Rivers and creeks drain the area, entering the harbour at F7, G10 and G15. High-density residential blocks (hatched squares at the bottom of the map) border the business and industrial areas.

Piece descriptions

All pieces may be moved up to four squares horizontally or vertically, or any combination of horizontal and vertical movement – but not diagonally. No more than four pieces can be placed on any square at the same time, and any piece can move through a square regardless of the number of pieces placed on that square.

HQ	Crisis Field Command: manages all units within a 12 square radius; supplies water, foam and other logistics to up to six units within a six-square path to the HQ unit (using vertical and horizontal pathway squares in the total).
S	Heavy Support Unit: provides effective support in own square (where it is worth two response units) and in any vertical or adjacent square (where it is worth the equivalent of one response unit).
P1, P2	Paramedic Units: these help reduce casualties within up to two squares in any vertical and horizontal direction from their own square.
TL, UL	Group Command Units for Group T and Group U: these pieces can elect to be team command and co-ordination pieces in which case they work as managers for the rest of the group but do not undertake response work, *or* they can elect to act as a fifth response unit, in which case the other units may or may not follow instructions (*see* Game Instructions below).
T2, T3, T4, T5; U2, U3, U4, U5	These response units work in their own square and can move to work any vertical or horizontal square adjacent to the square they occupy (but not diagonal squares). The even numbered units for both groups are firefighting and foam-carrying units while the odd numbered units are heavy-rescue units with metal-lifting and cutting equipment and some small firefighting capacity. Each piece only operates within the square it is placed.
X1	The nose, cockpit and passenger section of the aircraft back to the front of the wings.
X2	The middle passenger section of the aircraft back toward the tail including the left-hand wing.
X3	The tail passenger section of the aircraft and the right-hand wing.
FIRE	The missing engine that has already started a fire.

Scenario

Flight 1111, a Boeing 737 passenger aircraft from the premier airline of the nation of Angst, AngU Airlines, with ten crew and 190 passengers has crashed on the harbourside of the city of Rage. Witnesses claim that an explosion occurred shortly before the aircraft crashed and a large burning object fell from the aircraft shortly before impact. There is a fire at a chemical storage plant (currently believed to contain 4 000 000 litres of benzene) which is next to a high-pressure chemical converter facility.

The wind direction is blowing south (from top to bottom of the map).

The aircraft has disintegrated into four parts (FIRE, X1, X2 and X3). Roll the dice and place FIRE on the square indicated: 1 = E5, 2 = H5, 3 = K5, 4 = I8, 5 = L8, 6 = I12. This roll of the dice also indicates the direction of the wreckage trail: 1, 3 and 5 mean that the trail moves vertically south; 2, 4 and 6 mean the trail moves horizontally east.

Roll the dice again. Counting from the FIRE token, place the X3 token on the square from the FIRE token equal to the number showing on the dice. Remember to move in the horizontal or vertical direction indicated by the previous roll of the dice (see above). Remember the number on this dice.

Role the dice again. Counting from the X3 token, place the X1 token on the square from the X3 token equal to the number showing on the dice. Remember to move in the same direction as previously. Add the score from the roll of the dice with the score on the previous dice roll and divide the combined total by two. Count this number of squares from the X3 token then place the X2 token on the square to the right of this square.

Reports suggest that there may be 17 casualties and 14 people trapped at the FIRE site, possibly 37 persons trapped, injured or dead at X3, 130 persons trapped, injured or dead at X2, and possibly 90 persons trapped, injured or dead at X1. These figures include aircraft and ground impact estimates. There are no clear figures of dead and injured.

This exercise has two parts – a response component (turns 1 to 6) and a recovery component (turns 7 to 12).

For the response component (turns 1 to 6), the field response command team consists of a site commander (the operational commander of the Rage firefighting service – the CM), a response commander (field commander of one of the two response groups – the FC), a senior Rage law enforcement officer, the mayor of Rage, a senior executive or manager of AngU Airlines, and the senior work-site executive or manager of Storage International (the location of the initial fire).

The mission is to resolve the situation.

Take some time to consider and discuss strategies. Ensure someone keeps track of these discussions, decisions, actions and outcomes so that the exercise can be evaluated and discussed afterwards.

General game instructions
The first six turns cover the response process, then the last six turns focus on recovery management. The turns can be tracked on the timetrack line found at the bottom of the joined maps, using the piece with the 💣 symbol.

To introduce a sense of time pressure found in crisis situations, set a time limit for each game turn. A suggested limit would be somewhere between 15 and 20 minutes per turn.

The CM (in consultation with the FC) starts the HQ, S, P1, TL and T-group pieces on any of the starting points (the dark hatched squares covering F7, F8, G7, G8 and T1, T2, U1, U2 and T17, T18, U17, U18). The P2, UL and U-group pieces are available from the beginning of turn 3 (entering from the school or hospital sites – T1, T2, U1, U2 and T17, T18, U17, U18).

In each turn

1 Move one, some or all pieces up to four squares up, down or sideways on the map in any combination of those moves. Pieces cannot be moved diagonally across the map.

  (a) Note that when pieces are not in contact with their command pieces (within 12 squares of the HQ piece, or four squares of the TL or UL pieces, then the response to orders changes as outlined in (b).

  (b) Roll a dice for each piece not in contact with its HQ (12 square radius from the HQ piece) or group leader (4 square radius from the TL or UL piece) and which is moving or under orders that require movement: 1 = still in contact and follows existing or new orders; 2 = shift one square north; 3 = shift one square south; 4 = shift one square east; 5 = shift one square west; 6 = still in contact and follows existing or new orders. If units were under a prior movement order, then pieces continue toward the previous objective but along the verticals and horizontals (no mixture of these) from the new position. For static or stationary units (or those ordered to remain on one square) which also are out of contact with HQ or UL or TL, the roll of the dice means: 1, 6 = still in contact; 2, 3, 4, 5 = remain on the square but do not respond to new orders.

2 Roll a dice to determine whether you receive a report from the 'Situation' or the 'Incident' Module. The Situation Module contains reports on what is happening while the Incident Module contains reports about incidents or crisis-sourced changes in the environment. Situation = 1, 3, 5; Incident = 2, 4, 6.

3 Once you have found whether you are dealing with the Situation or Incident Module, roll a dice to see which of the six Situation or Incident reports your crisis committee receives.

4 Respond to the information in the report from the Situation or Incident Module. You may only move those pieces that are directly indicated in the report you receive and only in terms of the instructions presented in that report.

5 Roll a dice to determine whether you receive a message from the 'Information' Module or a question from the 'Public Comment' Module. The Information Module contains messages that give soft or hard information about the situation while the Public Comment Module contains questions from the media, from pressure groups or from groups affected by the situation. Information = 1, 3, 5; Public Comment = 2, 4, 6.

6 Once you have found whether you are dealing with the Information or Public Comment Module, roll a dice to see which of the six messages or questions from the Information or Public Comment Modules your crisis committee receives.

7 Verbally respond to any questions from the Information or Public Comment Modules. You may decide to divide your committee into sub-groups to handle

the game moves and information management. You may only move those pieces that are directly indicated in the report you receive and only in terms of the instructions presented in that report.

8 Assess any response impacts on the situation, either from the Situation or Incident Modules or because a response unit has remained on a square for four turns. Should two or more units stay on the same square for two turns then that site is declared safe. This assessment overrules any subsequent casualty sustained in any Situation or Incident Report although fire may restart and destroy the site unless again extinguished by the presence of the response units.

Begin the next turn
Once the sixth turn is completed, proceed to the next part of the activity (below).

Modules for the six response turns
Situation Module (from a dice roll of 1, 3, 5): roll the dice
1 Heavy plume of toxic smoke is now blowing (roll dice: 1 = still south; 2 = southeast; 3 = east; 4 = west; 5 = southwest; 6 = north).
2 Communications failure in HQ facility. No new orders or new moves can be made next turn.
3 Transport accident has immobilized one of the field units. Roll a dice twice and add the scores to determine which unit cannot move for the rest of the exercise: 2 = report is found to be false; 3 = UL; 4 = U2; 5 = U3; 6 = U4; 7 = U5; 8 = TL; 9 = T2; 10 = T3; 11 = T4; 12 = T5.
4 While at least ten ground impact casualties have been found at X1, there are no aircraft survivors at X2.
5 Any square with two response units on it will have any fire extinguished in this turn.
6 Supplies of foam are running dangerously short. No fuel fire can be contained or extinguished for the next two turns.

Incident Module (from a dice roll of 2, 4, 6): roll the dice
Remember that any unit sustaining casualties has the casualty figures halved if within two vertical or horizontal squares of a P1 or P2 unit.

1 People using unprotected cutting and lifting equipment at X3 in an attempt to save 23 people in the aircraft section and seven ground impact victims cause sparks that ignite a fire. Roll a dice to see if this fire worsens (1, 3, 5 = fire is extinguished with no casualties; 2, 4, 6 = fire engulfs site). If the fire engulfs the site then remove one response unit of any description if any response units are on or adjacent to this site. Roll a dice. Total casualties among response personnel stand at: dead = roll of dice multiplied by 2; injured = roll of the dice multiplied by 5. The ground impact victims are saved but the possible aircraft survivors are believed to have died in the fire (although reports suggest that [roll a dice: survivors = roll of dice multiplied by 3] were rescued).
2 A sudden explosion at the FIRE square ignites fires in any adjacent structures within a three-square radius of the FIRE square. If there are any crisis response units within this radius then the equivalent of one unit is destroyed. Remove the unit (if only one is involved) or one response unit (T2 to T5, U2 to U5) from

the map for the duration of the game. Roll a dice: dead = casualty dice number; wounded = casualty dice number multiplied by 3.

3 Provided one paramedic and one response unit is on or adjacent to the [roll a dice: X1 = 1, 2; X2 = 3, 4; X3 = 5, 6] site, all survivors and bodies are quickly removed from this site. This report overrules any subsequent report on casualties sustained due to an incident at this site. Survivors (from aircraft and from the ground) = [roll a dice: survivors = roll of dice multiplied by 6].

4 Group of at least 12 aircraft survivors (including children) reported trapped in X2. Very high fire danger exists given fuel leaking from the wing.

5 A group of 15 survivors (at least four critically injured) are reported trapped in either a collapsed building or a bus at the site of X1.

6 Units on or adjacent to the [roll a dice: X1 = 1, 2; X2 = 3, 4; X3 = 5, 6] site become over-committed to their tasks. They ignore any new orders or assignment of tasks for the next three turns.

Information Module (from a dice roll of 1, 3, 5): roll the dice

1 Chemicals and fuel (and any waste products from firefighting) are leaking into the harbour water.

2 Fuel is leaking onto the ground at the X2 and X3 sites.

3 Complaints are being received from the headquarters of the response agencies and at the field command site over the graphic footage of the accident shown by International News Incorporated, a world-wide cable news service.

4 The forcible evacuation of a nearby business premises has led to a US$20 000 000 legal compensation claim against the crisis management team and the response agencies from the multinational company on restraint of trade and deprivation of liberty.

5 The burning chemicals stored at the FIRE site turn out to include dangerous cyanide-based liquids and methyl isocyanate which appear not to have been reported to the on-site field commander.

6 A multiple vehicle accident between two paramedic ambulances near the hospital blocks the key access route to the hospital and leaves all ten occupants injured (drivers, paramedics and crash-site casualties).

Public Comment Module (from a dice roll of 2, 4, 6): roll the dice

1 Media representatives want to know why any information on the passengers on board is still not available from AngU Airlines and why such information appears not yet available to the response and investigating agencies.

2 Media reporter: 'Is it true that a number of VIPs, including some company owners and business leaders, were on this flight?'

3 Television crew at one of the sites: 'Is that smoke likely to kill people? Why have you not undertaken better evacuation of those in the path of the smoke?'

4 Speculation on a special edition of the International News Incorporated programme, *This Day Tonight*, from a former fire commissioner from South Angst claims that the field commander got the priorities for action wrong.

5 Reporter near field headquarters: 'Is it true that response management activities actually caused an explosive fire to kill and injure many survivors and response persons on site?'

6 Reporter to Storage International manager: 'Why were the firefighters not told

what was stored on site? How come your stored product is leaking into the harbour water?'

Recovery component – turns 7 to 12

Spend some time evaluating the performance in the response section before moving onto the recovery component.

The recovery component runs from turn 7 to turn 12. This activity does not involve placement or movement of pieces and thus cycles through the Modules only. Try to assess the situation, develop priorities and address the issues raised.

Simulate the time pressures involved by restricting discussion and decision making to a 15- or 20-minute period per turn.

Divide the previous group of participants into two. One group represents AngU Airlines while the other group represents Storage International. Before you begin, decide on the roles of those forming the recovery management team for each business, then commence the recovery management process.

Determine a strategy for recovery. You may wish to consider recovery priorities, image management, information management, dealing with public and media issues and looking after the stakeholders.

Immediate post-response situation

AngU Airlines situation

The airline has a fleet of aircraft, including 20 Boeing 737 passenger jets. The cause of the crash is unknown, but speculation includes structural failure and a bomb. The large falling object was an engine from the right wing. No one survived the crash (any survivors subsequently died of their injuries) and possibly 23 people are missing from the impacts of the aircraft on the ground. Air traffic recordings have messages that suggest there was an explosion near an engine shortly before the crash. The 'black boxes' have not been recovered. While 190 bodies have been recovered, 31 have been formally identified and have had autopsies performed. There were no suspicious wounds to these 31 bodies. There were 11 AngU Airline staff on board as well as the ten crew. People checking on relatives have gridlocked the AngU Airlines call-centres and sales offices. Ticket sales have decreased by 15 per cent, and a further 8 per cent of tickets have been cancelled.

Storage International situation

The site is substantially destroyed. Four bodies of employees have been recovered and four more are missing. Toxic chemical waste is mostly contained in the bunds, although there are reports of chemical pollution in the harbour. Storage International owns a further two sites in the city, both of which are at two-thirds capacity. The estimated costs for decontamination, salvage and reconstruction run into $100 000 000. Estimates of recovery times are between 12 months and three years. Decisions need to be made about what to do with staff, how to deal with customer services (many forward bookings for storing chemicals), and whether to fully recover the site or simply decontaminate, salvage any useable and recyclable material, and sell to a developer. While the Rage operation is a semi-independent company, there are pressures from international and national shareholders and creditors over the future of the Rage operations.

The mission of this component is to identify broad priorities of action, strategies to speed up recovery, and factors that may impede or inhibit recovery. Having done so, consider how the factors impeding recovery may be overcome or minimized. With these four 'lists' of management choices, begin the six turns.

In each turn

1 Roll a dice to determine whether you receive a report from the 'Recovery Situation' or the 'Internal Pressure' Module: Recovery Situation = 1, 3, 5; Internal Pressure = 2, 4, 6.

2 Once you have found whether you are dealing with the 'Recovery Situation' or the 'Internal Pressure' Module, roll a dice to see which of the six reports your recovery committees receive – one each for the airline and the storage recovery management teams.

3 Consider the information from the report.

4 Roll a dice to determine whether you receive a message from the 'External Pressure' or a question from the 'Media' Module: External Pressure = 1, 3, 5; Media = 2, 4, 6.

5 Once you have found whether you are dealing with the 'External Pressure' or the 'Media' Module, roll a dice to see which of the six messages or questions your recovery committees receive.

6 Respond to any issue raised by the 'External Pressure' Module or question from the 'Media' Module.

7 Reassess the recovery management strategies you have selected.

Begin the next turn

The exercise stops on the completion of turn 12.

Modules for the six recovery turns

Recovery Situation Module (from a dice roll of 1, 3, 5): roll the dice

1 *AngU Airlines* – Staff report poor morale since the crisis as well as continued customer suspicion and lack of confidence in the airline.
Storage International – Staff report poor morale since the crisis and increased restlessness from those made idle by the loss of the storage facility.

2 *AngU Airlines* – Maintenance workers call for industrial strike action over rumours that they are to blame for the accident.
Storage International – Some employees are reporting symptoms that may indicate toxic exposure from working on the site.

3 *AngU Airlines* – Aircraft accident investigators find readings from the 'black box' data recorder that support the theory of catastrophic loss of an engine.
Storage International – Government inspectors wish to know why the site still had an above-ground fire suppression system and why the bunds around some of the storage sites failed to prevent leakage of the chemicals.

4 *AngU Airlines* – The leased aircraft replacement for the lost Boeing 737 has to postpone takeoff (coincidentally on the Flight 1111 route) three times due to temporary inability to close a cargo door, failure of key cockpit wireless equipment and smoke coming from an engine. Several of the half-filled aircraft's passengers elect not to fly with the replacement aircraft and speak to media

representatives at the airport. Requests are made for a response from AngU Airlines management.

Storage International – A television news programme runs a story claiming that employees have suggested that panic by on-site managers and supervisors led to failure to protect the facility adequately as pumping operations were continued after the impact of the burning engine.

5 *AngU Airlines* – The *Rage Times* newspaper reveals that preliminary inspection of the engine pylons suggests that a stress fracture may have led to loss of the engine.

Storage International – An independent engineering specialist has uncovered faulty bund construction that was commissioned by the previous facility owner and undertaken by Constructions Are Us. The foundations were not compacted properly and were too shallow, allowing subsurface erosion and microscopic cracking to occur.

6 *AngU Airlines* – The operations manager resigns to take up a better paying position with an overseas airline and the maintenance manager requests early retirement. Media speculation suggests these are either admissions of guilt or 'rats deserting the sinking ship' of a company with increasing financial difficulties.

Storage International – Two of the site decontamination management team are rushed to hospital, one with a heart attack, the other with a severe asthma attack. Media speculation suggests they have been affected by the chemical pollution still on the site.

Internal Pressures Module (from a dice roll of 2, 4, 6): roll the dice

1 *AngU Airlines* – Sick leave taken by those brought under added work pressures at call-centres, sales points and information locations has increased 100 per cent since the crash happened.

Storage International – Employees seem to be under pressure to join a series of industry-wide strikes for a 15 per cent increase in wages and reduced working hours.

2 *AngU Airlines* – Profit has fallen for the third year in a row.

Storage International – Partner companies add pressure for a review of the decision made on the rebuilding of the facility.

3 *AngU Airlines* – A recent survey shows a continued decline in public support for AngU Airlines, with many still unconvinced about the safety of flying with the airline.

Storage International – Speedy certification by local and national government agencies halves the cost and time taken for any rebuilding decision taken up to this turn and before this report.

4 *AngU Airlines* – Recent strikes by the air crew of competing airlines increases demand for services by AngU Airlines by 30 per cent.

Storage International – Delays in certification by local and national government agencies doubles the cost and time taken given any rebuilding decision taken up to this turn and before this report.

5 *AngU Airlines* – A replacement aircraft is permanently acquired from Boeing.

Storage International – Any reconstruction is halted for two turns as defects have been found in recently bought tanks and pumping systems. This increases costs by $8 000 000 and recovery time by seven months.

6 *AngU Airlines* – Air traffic management agrees to change the Flight 1111 designation to Flight 1100.
Storage International – Insurance payouts and parent-company support provides guaranteed backing of $150 000 000 for any rebuilding effort.

External Pressures Module (from a dice roll of 1, 3, 5): roll the dice

1 *AngU Airlines* – Families of victims begin a compensation class action for $2 000 000 000.
Storage International – The harbour authority claims costs of $10 000 000 for clean-up and water decontamination.

2 *AngU Airlines* – Key stockholders request reassurance about the safety situation and about the financial position of the company.
Storage International – Health and safety inspectors demand access to all other company work-sites in Angst.

3 *AngU Airlines* – Internal auditors find $4 000 000 unaccounted for in the crisis management (response and recovery operations) fund.
Storage International – Cost overruns for decontamination work increase by $15 000 000.

4 *AngU Airlines* – Local pressure groups have increased their campaign to prevent airlines from increasing the number of flights over Rage. They cite the Flight 1111 crash in favour of a reduction of flights. AngU Airlines flies twice the flights of any other airline over Rage.
Storage International – Community pressure groups are calling for the removal of any storage sites from the regions around the harbour.

5 *AngU Airlines* – A rival airline launches an advertisement heavily focused on their own safety record.
Storage International – A legal claim for compensation for damage to health on behalf of 2500 citizens of Rage is filed against the company and local and international management of the company (and the local government of Rage) for failing to protect the claimants from the effects of toxic smoke.

6 *AngU Airlines* – An inquiry into the aircraft crash and the operations of the airline is being discussed in the media and in the Angstian parliament.
Storage International – An inquiry into the storage facility and the operations of the company is being discussed in the media and in the Angstian parliament.

Media Module (from a dice roll of 2, 4, 6): roll the dice

1 *AngU Airlines* – 'Why did the aircraft crash?'
Storage International – 'Why did the safety features fail?'

2 *AngU Airlines* – 'Is it true that cost-cutting led to poor maintenance, and this poor maintenance caused the accident?'
Storage International – 'Should facilities like yours be operating where they are?'

3 *AngU Airlines* – 'Why did no one from the airline appear on site while the rescue operations were being conducted?'
Storage International – 'Has the site really been decontaminated?'

4 *AngU Airlines* – 'What assurance can you give that this accident will not happen again?'

Storage International – 'What new safety features would your company place in any of its facilities?'

5 *AngU Airlines* – 'Why haven't you compensated the families of the victims yet?'

Storage International – 'Do you think the possible compensation claim against your company for causing ill-health due to the smoke plume is justified?'

6 *AngU Airlines* – 'Why are your senior staff quitting the company?'

Storage International – 'Why are health and safety inspectors going to examine all your company's work sites in Angst?'

Managing in a crisis situation

Two elements critical to managing crisis situations are information and people management. This chapter considers some of the issues specifically raised about people management, looking at reactions of people encountering crisis situations and at the crisis manager's own need to cope emotionally and cognitively with that situation.

Human involvement – participants

The one certain fact about encountering a crisis is that people will react in physical and psychological ways to that crisis. Different chemicals are released into the system to prepare muscles for action and to narrow the range of sensory perception to those senses that may help cope with the crisis. Muscles tense, breathing changes, blood flows increase and change in distribution, and psychological changes parallel these physical and physiological responses. One of the problems with the release of such chemicals is that the body's ability to cope with the stresses and survive increases, but the capacity to solve relatively complex problems decreases.

The prime essential is to remain calm – neither reacting aggressively nor defensively to the crisis, but seeking how best to escape or deal with it by limiting damage and resolving the situation. Calmness, as Green (1992) points out, is the most important consideration if effective functioning in a crisis is to be achieved. How this calmness can be achieved and what psychological reactions and responses may arise in a crisis situation are the subject matter for this chapter.

Psychological effects on those at the site of the crisis

Every person encountering a crisis situation (victims, bystanders and respondents) experiences feelings and beliefs about the crisis, themselves and others that are shaped by their own experience of that situation. Sometimes these experiences lead to extreme behaviours. For some the experience of a crisis may be so overwhelming that they mentally draw a line between themselves and those who were not at that crisis. This is the war veteran's sharp experience of a specific locality at a specific time and action that leads to the exclusion of those who were not there (even other war veterans) from his or her experience of war. When the behaviours last long after the crisis is over – and those behaviours cause damage to the person or those around them – then some form of psychological dysfunction is likely (*see* Chapter 16) and some help to recover a more normal POV and set of behaviours may be needed.

Sometimes the extreme behaviours emerge upon contact with the crisis. These behaviours are called *crisis impact reactions (CIR)*. The CIRs can include particular fight and flight responses and physical or psychological withdrawal.

One 'flight' response is the 'abandon ship' reaction. Here, the behaviour of a person is focused on getting out of the crisis situation and away from the crisis site as quickly and directly as possible. Those undergoing the reaction tend to close out the surrounding environment and focus specifically on self-survival. The response may not be panic as is often expected – agitated, hysterical, jerky movements, or unco-ordinated or undirected movements. The 'abandon ship' reactant determinedly gets out of the situation in the most direct (or quickest path) possible. They may trample on or over other people in their way. They may appear to move purposefully and even calmly. Some victims undergoing such a reaction have been found up to 5 or 10 kilometres away from the scene of a major accident, when they then begin to behave in vague and disoriented ways.

Signs of an 'abandon ship' reaction include:

- rapid but directed movement;
- fixed facial expression;
- an out-of-focus gaze;
- a lack of awareness of the reactant's state of appearance or well-being.

People in such a reaction will ignore (or actually shut out) orders or instructions, and will continue – at times quite determinedly and forcefully – to move away from the situation.

Another CIR is a 'negative panic' reaction. 'Negative panic' may happen in less physical but cognitively overwhelming situations or in life-threatening circumstances. When comments that 'everyone was wonderful – everyone stayed quiet' or 'no one panicked' are made, 'negative panic' may equally have been present. This reaction involves being cognitively and physically frozen – incapable of thought or action. There are recorded accounts of situations in which passengers on crashed aircraft did not react to their situation. In one case, passengers watched a burning trail of kerosene move down the aisle but did not move.

'Negative panic' appears to be a reaction against the impact of a crisis. Signs of 'negative panic' include:

- unnatural quietness;
- fixed or locked limbs;
- an apparent fugue-like state;
- a rigid (sometimes unblinking) gaze.

The reactant will often be breathing lightly, seem listless and often present minimal to no movement or reaction to stimuli. Anxious people are likely to freeze in this sort of reaction.

A reaction sometimes presented when people emerge from 'negative panic' or are momentarily stunned by the crisis is to revert to basic 'normal' behaviours. People retrieve luggage, get fully dressed, go out the way they came in. This reversion to routine behaviours absorbs time, which is probably part of the explanation for the reaction – the mind finds time to adjust to the situation by putting the behavioural actions on automatic for a short period of time. One experienced crisis manager experienced the jolting of the Northridge earthquake (Los Angeles, USA, 1994) and within minutes was called to come into his office and activate his organization's crisis plan. He found a considerable number of minutes had elapsed from when the earthquake and telephone call happened and when he actually set out to report into his office. He cannot recall what exactly he did, but remembers spending some time carefully shaving.

A third CIR can be seen when people manoeuvre or fight their way back into the crisis situation in order to retrieve or find some object or some other person. This is the 'retriever reaction', where people are driven by a belief that they must retrieve something or rescue another person after they have initially escaped the crisis situation. In some cases, retrievers will aggressively place themselves at great risk and seem oblivious to this risk to themselves. As a result, they put other people at risk who are trying to ensure the safety of people in the situation. Retriever reactants move directly toward the place where they believe the other person or object will be found. This reaction particularly happens among family members once one member realizes another member is missing.

Dealing with those in a retriever reaction can be quite time-consuming, distracting and wasteful of resources at moments when attention directed toward reducing or controlling the crisis is vital. Non-respondents need to be moved from physical presence and awareness of the situation as quickly as possible, while ensuring that their well-being and concerns are registered and attended. This strategy reduces retriever reactions.

One CIR that emerges among respondents is the 'rescuer mode' reaction. This can emerge in any crisis situation, although the symptoms are most visible in natural disaster situations and at sites of major accidents. People displaying 'rescuer mode' reactions appear overly committed to their (often selfselected) task in hand. Their faces are often described as 'closed' and 'fixed' while their speech and interactions can be described as brief to terse and impersonal. They often have a stiff posture and a gaze that is fixed on the 'targeted' task or that drifts continuously back to that task if compelled to take a break or attend someone else. 'Rescuer' reactants often have reduced eye contact.

Probably the best way to establish whether 'rescuer mode' is present is to use the following check. Are there:

- Rigid or fixed interests or attention targets?
- Emotional 'highs' in action and commitment?
- Shuttered perceptions about the surrounding environment?
- Critical attitudes towards 'outsiders'?
- Urgency beliefs about the task in hand?
- Exaggerated beliefs about their endurance (or need to endure)?
- Resistance to stoppages or pauses?

If most of these are present then a 'rescuer' reaction is present.

What is wrong with 'rescuer mode' behaviour? Probably little provided that the crisis situation:

- can be resolved in less than six hours;
- is limited in size and tactically simple;
- the behaviour is the best option (or can be treated as such).

'Rescuer mode' reactions enable people to work in dirty and dangerous situations for longer than their normal capacity while ignoring fatigue and much of the disturbing impact of a crisis. The intensity of the focus can enable people to perform acts that would not be possible in more normal situations.

Every person responding to a crisis will emit 'rescuer mode' behaviours to some degree. Problems emerge when these behaviours lead to excessive commitment or exhaustion. 'Rescuer mode' reactions are inappropriate when the crisis exceeds six hours, when the crisis is large and complex, and where response requirements may change (thus meaning that respondents may be redeployed before they complete their tasks). People who are in 'rescuer mode' resist stopping their task, refuse to redeploy, and can become too fatigued for use in future operations. Crisis managers need to monitor levels of behaviour, enforce rest and encourage a healthy POV where possible.

Effects of crisis situations on humans

During (and after) a crisis event, bystanders, victims and respondents are likely to feel stress. Symptoms of this include tiredness, irritability, lack of concentration and sometimes vivid dreams based upon (or reflecting) significant emotional moments from the crisis situation and the impacts of that situation. Symptoms of acute and long-term stress are described in Chapter 16.

For most people, these stresses are transitory and slowly fade as time passes. Each person can work to reduce the effects of stress during and after a crisis. On encountering a crisis, people can use psychological stoppers to reduce the sense of being overwhelmed by stimulus–reaction effects. During a crisis, and after leaving the crisis, people can try to relax. Sleep and relaxation help detoxify the body.

Other strategies to reduce stress include the following:

- Minimize the use of stimulants (including coffee) and have food and water at regular intervals.
- Ensure a proper diet and reduce drug and alcohol consumption.
- Get involved in a hobby or special interest that is different to the tasks and focus of working in crisis situations.
- Get regular exercise.
- Become familiar with likely conditions and stimuli that may arise in crisis situations.
- Talk to others who have experienced the crisis, allowing exchanges of experiences and feelings.
- Learn to accept that crisis situations are stressful and can be upsetting.

The PBR technique

People can use a psychological stopper whenever stimuli tend to overwhelm the alert state of their bodies. The Pause, Breathe, Relax technique (PBR) is one such stopper. By pausing, users stop the normal reaction to cause-and-effect stimuli that accelerate physiological responses to the situation. Users next slowly breathe in, then slowly breathe out' silently saying to themselves 'relax'. Psychological stoppers help produce a number of important effects. The stimulus–behavioural reaction cycle that otherwise can generate increasing feelings of being out of control is slowed. Proper use of PBR impedes the flight or fight physiological responses from fully happening, thus increasing the ability to problem solve. Using the PBR approach also helps people concentrate on the immediate set of tasks they need to undertake.

Psychological stoppers are designed to reduce panic and stop impetuous and reactive actions, which is why they are called stoppers. Incidentally, appropriate use of PBR improves a user's performance in any focus sport (golf, baseball, cricket or tennis, for example). Similarly, PBR can be effectively used in many work situations, by public speakers, when responding to interviews and when undertaking school and university examinations.

Relaxation

Learning to relax the body is another means of reducing stress. Relaxation and rest help detoxify the body and remove the feelings of heavy limbs and stiffness that are by-products of the stimulant chemicals used in making our bodies more alert. The benefits of rest, relaxation and periods of quiet are part of the rationale of having a quiet room or retreat in any established crisis management facility.

Undertaking self-guided relaxation

Find a quiet environment with few distractions. Where possible, remove or filter out radios, telephones, television, conversations, industrial sounds and harsh light or vivid colour schemes. With practice and experience, relaxation can be induced in more distracting environments.

Loosen any tight clothing such as coats, ties, shoes or belts. This avoids interruptions to relaxation due to the body sending signals about discomfort or restrictions.

After ensuring a quiet environment, find a comfortable position in which you can relax for some time. Most therapeutic forms of relaxation are done with the client lying down. However, a lying down position often leads to sleeping, which does not provide the same effects as proper relaxation. When relaxing in a group, lie down or sit down facing away from each other to reduce visible distractions. Perhaps the best positions are in a comfortable chair or by adopting a Zen yoga position – provided that the position is already learned and comfortable to the user.

The approach to relaxing muscles is quite easy. Work from the feet up in body clusters. Often, people do not realize the amount of tension in their bodies and cannot tell tensed states from relaxed states. To re-educate the brain and consciousness, clench a fist as tightly as possible. Explore the feeling of tightness and pressure. Keep the fist tense while slowly counting from one to twenty, then release the pressure and open the fist. Notice the difference between the tensed and 'relaxed' states.

As most people cannot relax the left foot or leg without the tension from the right foot and leg re-alerting the left side, relax by right and left pairings.

Silently tell the feet to relax. Try to find the same feeling that came from the relaxation of the hand after holding a tight fist for some time. Slowly and silently move up the body – legs, stomach, torso and back, arms, neck and finishing with the head. As focus shifts from one part of the body to the next, the relaxed parts may retense. This can happen to most people. Simply return to the earliest part that returned to being tense and proceed through the relaxation process from that point. Do this until the total body feels relaxed.

Once the entire body feels relaxed, focus on making the body breathe as gently and as deeply as possible, without straining or tensing the lungs and

▶

▶

surrounding muscles. Breathe through the nose where possible. Try to establish a slow and even inhalation and exhalation.

When the body feels relaxed and the breathing is even and slow, instruct
the brain and body to relax by silently pairing the command 'relax' with both
the state of feeling relaxed and each slow and even exhalation of the air
breathed into the lungs.

Some approaches then direct users to focus gently on an object or mantra.
Zen meditation may ask practitioners to focus on a leaf (or even a drop of
water upon a leaf). Another approach is to envision a tranquil scene. In this
approach, the practitioner relaxes the muscle groups, slows the breathing
and then builds a mental vision of a desirable and calming environment, such
as a quiet beach or a green peaceful field. Use any of these approaches to
deepen the effect of relaxation.

Continue relaxing for between 10 and 20 minutes. Without moving, gently
check from time to time that the body is relaxed and the breathing is even,
comfortably deep and slow.

Should the feeling of a need to check the time arise, gently do so – with as
little disturbance as possible. Do not set alarms or let someone abruptly end
the relaxation session.

A good practice is to develop a natural end-time sequence that gently tells
the mind and body that the relaxation session will end. State the instructions
silently – for example, 'In a few minutes, I shall allow this session to end. I will
feel quieter and more refreshed.' If this sounds a little like a hypnotic trance
suggestion, it is. Hypnosis fundamentally uses states of compliant relaxation
and induced autosuggestion. Another way to signal closure to the brain and
the body is to naturally allow the mental vision to change – let the image
recede or the wind freshen.

Should an interruption or disturbance happen, absorb the interruption
rather than try to ignore or reject it. Gently check that everything is as it
should be (or even respond to a message), then return to the comfortable
position, relax the body, focus on calming the breathing and return to the
state of relaxation.

Most people find it difficult to let their minds relax and focus at the same
time. If thoughts, feelings or body signals intrude, quietly and silently
acknowledge and accept these rather than try to ignore or reject them. Contemplate whether the intrusive thoughts or feelings need attention or immediate response and act accordingly. Should no response appear necessary,
return to relaxing the body and the relaxed easy breathing and allow the
points to fade from attention.

- Try to practise relaxation twice a day (at least two hours after any meal).
- Avoid performance measures. Achieve better and deeper relaxation at a
  natural and unpressured rate.
- Avoid rushing from the relaxed to the moving state for a few minutes,
  unless really necessary.

Note the connections between relaxation and the PBR stopper. By rehearsing relaxation, effective use of the PBR stopper is increased.

REALITY BITE

Tylenol product contamination, USA, 1982

Much has been written on the Tylenol (1982) product contamination scare. While some readers may feel that this case is old and too well known, the lapse of time has meant that the cause-and-effect of the crisis, the crisis response and the crisis recovery efforts can be better assessed than situations of a more recent nature. Crisis respondents, managers and executives can learn from crisis management examples from any time and covering any situation.

Background
Prior to 28 September 1982, Johnson & Johnson (J&J) had a market share in over-the-counter pain reliever medication of 35 per cent. This had a value of $450 million.

Incident
Between 29 September and 1 October in 1982, seven people died in the Chicago area from taking Tylenol Extra Strength. Media reports that cyanide had contaminated these capsules led to an 87 per cent drop in sales. Public alarm made every suspicious death a potential Tylenol poisoning (leading to a total of 250 suspected deaths and illnesses). The effect of the reports and deaths led to a fall of around 20 per cent (around $1.9 billion) in the value of Johnson & Johnson shares.

Response
J&J did not have a crisis plan, but had a company policy which was that 'the first concern was for customers and public'. J&J recalled, sample tested and destroyed 22 million bottles of Tylenol. They quickly made available a toll-free 800 telephone number for inquiries and widely advertised the number.

A seven-member crisis management team met twice daily in the CEO's office. At one stage, a '60 minutes' current affairs crew filmed the team in a strategy session. The CEO personally appeared on major national TV shows.

Eventually, J&J reintroduced the product in triple tamper-proof sealed bottles. After a copy cat murder, the company reintroduced the product in a solid form caplet (a solid capsule-shaped tablet). Within five months, J&J recovered 70 per cent of their pre-crisis share of the market.

Statistics
Over 2500 media inquiries were made and 125 000 press clippings on the topic were cut (Barton, 1993). J&J tested around eight million tablets and found only 75 contained cyanide – all from the same batch from the South Chicago area. Barton (1993) reports that the cost of testing and destroying the 22 000 000 bottles exceeded $100 million (with a total likely crisis management cost of $500 million).

Comment
Note the ripple effect of the crisis in terms of the cost to Johnson & Johnson.

Dealing with the poisoned pills meant clearing stocks, warning the public and conducting a number of public relations programmes. Clearing and checking stock (and the public fears of product contamination) led to a fall in their market share in analgesics. The loss of public confidence and market eroded the price of shares of Johnson & Johnson by around 20 per cent ($1.9 billion).

While the company did not have a crisis plan, the principle of concern for customers and public was a key for successful response management. This concern was espoused and acted upon – warnings were sent out to all medical locations (hospitals, medical surgeries and pharmacists), staff checked that shelves were cleared, a public free telephone number was quickly established and the CEO made personal appearances on television shows. This image of caring was enhanced by letting a current affairs programme film the crisis team's strategy sessions.

Management perspective

The most notable point from this case was the speed with which J&J reacted, given they had no fully formed crisis management plan at this time. The management did the two most effective crisis management steps in a product failure or product contamination situation:

1 recalled all of the product (a sterile zone strategy); and
2 ensured all potential players or users were quickly informed.

These moves contained the damage and covered a worst-case scenario for the crisis. By adopting a sterile zone strategy (remove all accessible units of the product) and making a massive communication effort (warning about the possible contamination of the product), J&J reduced any further growth of the problem. A quick response is likely to reflect favourably in any subsequent litigation.

Note the classic risk management action in this case. The capsules contained the poison, so J&J designed the crisis out of the product. When tamper-proofing failed, the organization redesigned the capsule into a solid-form or caplet. This is also a good example of one of the bouncing-back strategies of recovery management (see Chapter 16). By looking for opportunities to gain from the situation, J&J were able to link the safer design into a campaign that made J&J appear as a public protector, thereby improving the corporate image.

Personality characteristics of responders

One of the first decisions in setting up a crisis management structure is selecting the crisis manager. Some executives and managers believe that crisis managers can be identified and selected using problem-solving tests and personality attribute inventories.

Flin (1996) finds that personality characteristics of incident commanders include:

● willingness to lead;
● emotional stability;
● stress resistance;

- decisiveness;
- controlled risk taking;
- self-confidence;
- self awareness.

A skills profile for incident commanders (Flin, 1996, p. 44) includes:

- leadership;
- communication skills (briefing and listening);
- delegating;
- team management;
- decision making (under time pressure and stress);
- situation evaluation;
- planning and implementing courses of action;
- remaining calm;
- pre-planning.

Flin favours (with a few qualifications) use of the occupational personality questionnaire (OPQ) for selection purposes. She finds that the OPQ is useful when used with trainer-rated assessments on simulation test performances of candidates.

There are areas where such selection is useful – armed services, professional response agencies and permanent crisis room command centres. However, management ultimately has to depend on whoever is present. Ideal candidates may not be available or may fail due to the real pressures exerted in actual crisis situations. Ultimately, executives and managers need to emphasize reality training, skills acquisition and performance assessment for all likely respondents and response managers.

Another possible selection strategy could be to examine how potential incident commanders cope with the stresses inherent in crisis situations. Some of these stresses may include:

- a serious threat to life, values and goals;
- responsibility;
- fear of failure;
- loss of control;
- rapid changes in situation;
- time pressures;
- information uncertainty;
- information overload;
- team/group pressure.

Reactions to stress may vary over time, over duration of exposure to the crisis situation and due to accumulation of bad experiences. A respondent who appeared to cope well in one crisis situation may not do so well in the next. Providing people with skills and knowledge can reduce stress. By increasing familiarity and understanding (thus predictability) of what may happen in crisis situations, and by linking acquired skills to working within such situations, respondents and their managers become better prepared to cope with stress. Reference to the FPC model consequently helps managers and executives devise appropriate training programmes and exercise activities.

In a review of existing research on personality selection and response to stress, Driskell and Salas (1991) concluded that the research did not reveal any personality variables that predicted response to stress.

Managerial reactions to crisis events

In assuming the role or duty of a crisis manager (or a crisis response task manager), people may experience some interesting effects. These are mostly due to managerial reaction to three cues from the surrounding environment:

- the lack of specific, applicable or certain information;
- the apparent need to make a decision or action choice instantly;
- the responsibility for people and resources in the manager's area of command.

Managers also react differently according to:

- their own personalities;
- their own concerns; and
- the tugs and pulls of what they believe is their role and what they actually do.

Managers are likely to react to information, responsibility and decisional cues in different ways. Some reactions can be defined by the behaviour involved. For example, managers may simply deal with the first bundle of information with which they are presented ('first cab off the rank'). Equally, managers may feel pulled or distracted by missing or uncertain information (the 'TUG' effect), or may feel that time is so limited that they will be too late if they do not make an immediate decision (the 'LATE' effect – *see* below). On site, managers may be influenced by the 'rescuer' effect.

'First cab off the rank' decision making arises partly due to the pressure of needing to do something as soon as possible and partly from the sometimes undue importance that can be given to the first information a decision maker hears. This effect can be reduced by using PBR and by over-learning *CrisisThink*-type approaches which encourage a search for more information.

'The uncertainty gap (or TUG) effect' can occur when decision processes are distorted (or 'tugged') by distractions over the amount and nature of information made available to the decision maker. When a crisis manager becomes over-preoccupied with the nature of the available information, two outcomes emerge. The first is one of extreme conservatism (or risk aversion). In this outcome, response decision making can be frozen or extremely limited to a specific set of data (or data sources). This results in an ostrich reaction (not recognizing the situation by 'burying the head in the sand'), or a blinkered reaction (ignoring all information save a chosen or selected 'tunnelled' vision), or even a catatonic reaction (staring at the information in a frozen and unheeding state).

The second outcome of a 'TUG' effect is seen when a decision maker acts in the opposite direction: extreme risk acceptance. Here, a decision maker becomes over-preoccupied by the size and/or immediacy of available information. Common outcome reactions are:

- the 'fool's gold' reaction (in which information 'nuggets' are sought and acted upon haphazardly);
- the 'fast and furious' reaction (each packet of information leads to rapid and high-energy decisions being made as each packet of information appears, often giving rise to conflicting orders);
- the 'long-shot' reaction (taking the riskiest course of action as the quickest way of handling the situation).

'TUG' effects can be mitigated by training and by increasing both information-gathering and evaluation practices. The more information that can be gathered, and the more that information can be hardened by trained evaluators, the more confidence a crisis manager may have in the value of that information.

The 'limited action time environment (LATE)' effect can occur when a crisis manager is over-preoccupied with the constraints and pressures of the amount of time available to analyze, decide, act and recycle such processes. Crisis managers caught in this reaction start making decisions on little information and with little apparent consideration because they are over-conscious that time is passing and that a decision must therefore be made now. Outcomes of LATE include the 'first cab' reaction (going with the first idea or option that is seen), 'frozen moments' (paralysis in mental and possibly physical responses to the situation), and the 'doomsday' reaction (resignation to being beaten by the situation). Training and practice in operating under crisis conditions are needed.

R E A L I T Y   B I T E

Bhopal, India, 1984

Background
In 1980, an Indian subsidiary of Union Carbide (a US multinational) established a chemical plant in Bhopal. That produced a pesticide called Carbaryl used by Indian farmers and fruit growers. The plant provided hundreds of new jobs for the region, although some community criticism arose over the location of such a plant actually within Bhopal.

Incident
At midnight on 2 December 1984, the plant contained 42 tonnes of liquid methyl isocyanate in small underground tanks. On the previous day, engineers used

water to flush out piping above the storage tanks but much of this water had not drained away as at least two valves were blocked and others were partly blocked. The engineer in charge told the operators to flush the system again. A leaky valve apparently let 2000 tonnes of water into the methyl isocyanate stored in Tank 610.

In the early morning of 2 December 1984, poison gas from the methyl isocyanate began to form. The gas was a yellow-white cloud and covered an area of approximately 64 square kilometres (25 square miles). The gas suffocated many sleeping people and over 1200 were dead by the morning. By 7.00 am, the local hospital had received 20 000 affected people.

Response

At 12.00 am, workers noticed dirty water at the foot of a methyl isocyanate structure and their eyes felt irritated. At 12.15 am, leaks were confirmed in the control room and the first line of defence was activated. Caustic soda was used to neutralize the gas, a mechanism designed to deal with small leaks, but inadequate to cope with the size of leak that was taking place. A second defence – burning the leaking gas through a flare tower – was unavailable as the flare tower was closed for maintenance.

By 1.00 am, workers were attempting to reduce the gas by spraying water on the structure, but the water could not reach the top of the structure from which the gas was leaking. Gas continued to form and leak from midnight till 3.00 am, forming ground hugging clouds as the cold air condensed the vapour.

Once the alert was confirmed, executives at Union Carbide called for an immediate world-wide stop to the production and shipment of methyl isocyanate. They dispatched a doctor who was an expert in treating the gas-related injuries and four technicians to Bhopal. At the first media conference in a local hotel, Union Carbide management revealed that they had sent medical supplies, respirators and a doctor and technical specialists to Bhopal.

On 4 December, Warren Anderson (Chairperson of Union Carbide) flew to India, despite a threat that he may be arrested. He was, and then released.

A few days after the accident, the plant was reopened to neutralize the remaining chemicals. Over 200 000 people evacuated themselves from the vicinity in case the leaks reoccurred.

Statistics

Over 3000 people died, and 40 000 were injured by the gas leak. Initial reports estimated 1750 dead and 200 000 injured.

Comment

This case presents a number of interesting points. With corporate headquarters in Danburg (USA) and the incident in Bhopal (India) the crisis stretched both the company's ability to manage and the speed with which accurate information could be exchanged. Lack of information and access led to many speculative rumours that were poorly handled by the management of Union Carbide.

The departure of Anderson to the site underscores an important process element in crisis management. Not only would he see first-hand the nature and content of the crisis and its impact, but also the effort demonstrated to the onlooking public and media reporters concern by the organization. Under Indian law, Anderson was arrested (and released a short time later), and this could have generated a positive image for Union Carbide.

One point worth noting was the apparent lack of concern that the local employees of the plant showed for the surrounding community. Few tried to warn those threatened downwind as the staff on the plant retreated upwind. This issue masks the larger issue surrounding the local government allowing people to build next to the Bhopal facility.

Moreover, on-site crisis management appeared rudimentary and unable to offer elementary levels of preparedness. The surrounding community seemed to lack basic warning on what to do. Many would not have died or have been injured had they simply moved slowly, breathed shallowly, sealed themselves inside their dwellings and, most importantly, *used damp towels as effective yet primitive filters through which to breathe*. No one had bothered to formulate such policies and inform the surrounding community at risk. Likewise, little effort at alerting the community by siren or public announcement appears to be in place at the time.

After the event, some Union Carbide officials tried to downplay their involvement by discounting the effect of the gas. The Union Carbide medical officer claimed that the gas was not poisonous. Fifteen days after the leak (when the death toll had apparently passed 2000), the Bhopal plant manager was still claiming that the gas was not lethal (but only had an effect like teargas). He pointed to the fact that no one from the plant had died.

Management perspective

Managers and executives need to consider carefully the issues that arise with international operations. Some key matters include the following:

- The need to have a 24-hour response capability.
- The need to understand cultural differences. This is important not only on an individual and community level, but in terms of how political and bureaucratic processes of government are conducted in different countries.
- Economic lifestyles are different across the world. While senior managers and executives may be aware of this, most Western media and pressures groups do not attempt to relate the domestic standards and cost of living to the situation, but rather use their own experience as the measurement baseline. This does not mean that management should seek cheap compensation because of a possible developing nation's situation, but rather that costs and compensation need to be assessed from an internal and regional perspective.

The cross-cultural perspective underscores a number of discrete differences between nationals from different countries. For this case study, note the differences between the USA and India on the three dimensions illustrated in Chapter 9. Where people from the USA are generally likely to be more individualistic and less distant, Indian managers may be more group-focused and formal.

The ability to manage can be further weakened by the effects of cross-cultural perceptions. Involvement by management from a USA-based company (no matter how independent the subsidiary) can lead to an inference about greedy Western capitalists. There are likely to be differences in management styles, values and ethics that do not reflect the prevailing beliefs in the other country.

One rule of thumb to note is that cultural differences in business really only emerge when problems arise and crisis situations occur. This rule is relevant even in single-cultural cases as differences between companies, response agencies, departments and even organizational specialization emerge. What is important and vital for an accountant, a marketing manager, a production manager or a personnel manager will differ in content and priority.

References

Barton, L. (1993) *Crisis in Organizations: Managing and Communicating in the Heat of Chaos*. Cincinnati, Ohio: South-Western.

Driskell, J. and Salas, E. (1991) 'Overcoming the effects of stress on military performance: human factors, training and selection strategies', in Gal, R. and Mangelsdorf, A. (eds), *Handbook of Military Psychology*. Chichester: Wiley.

Flin, R. (1996) *Sitting in the Hot Seat: Leaders and Teams for Critical Incident Management*. Chichester, England: Wiley.

Green, P. S. (1992) *Reputation Risk Management*. London: Pitman/Financial Times.

15

Recovery management – managing event and impact recovery

The focus of attention now shifts to the fourth R of the RRRR model – recovery. Once the crisis situation has been brought under control, executives and managers need to begin to focus the effort of the organization on recovering the assets, facilities, processes and people to normal functioning. Given the impacts and experiences from encountering and dealing with the crisis situation, pre-crisis situation normality is unlikely to be regained. Some crisis situations allow recipients to refocus their activities and improve their organizational outcomes in terms of process efficiency, product delivery, market share and stakeholder loyalty. This chapter presents seven strategies that help harness these 'bouncing-back bigger and better' outcomes.

The process of recovery involves two streams – people management (*see* Chapter 16) and material or system recovery. This chapter significantly focuses on material and system recovery.

Recovery

Recovery management can be based on two dimensions:

- desired speed of recovery; and
- actual impact damage.

Executives and managers can determine the desired speed of recovery, which is then modified by the size of the crisis and the amount of damage caused by the impacts from the crisis situation. Actual impact damage can equally be modified by the amount of response and recovery resources and capabilities available when the crisis situation occurs.

Some key factors that may determine the speed with which recovery takes place include:

- available cash;
- available resource replenishment;
- access to resupply and rebuilding materials and labour;
- the amount of damage to the organization;
- the amount of recovery planning done before the crisis situation;
- the degree of involvement and information exchanged with stakeholders;
- whether the situation is local (sole organization) or regional (multiple organization); and
- the demand for return of services and supply from stakeholders.

These factors usually interact to dictate the pace of recovery.

Basic terms

A number of terms are used in recovery management, sometimes loosely used to mean the same concept. The broadest term is that of 'recovery management'. Most business and industrial organizations use the term 'business continuity' to address the processes for recovering an organization to the point of continuing its business activities.

Other terms include:

- resumption planning or management;
- rebuilding;
- restoration planning or management;
- seamless continuity (continuity based on non-interruption of production or service supply).

These terms are related to the time taken to return a disrupted situation to one that functions normally. Generally, three approaches are discussed – immediate or seamless continuity (in which the business returns to normal operations with little disruption), restoration (in which some hours or days elapse before resuming normal operations) and reconstruction or rebuilding (in which weeks or months elapse before resumption of normal operations takes place). These three approaches are depicted in Figure 15.1.

Continuity

Three fundamental levels of continuity exist for an organization or community. These levels are:

- *Continuity of structure.* Continuity of structure has physical and psychological elements. While structures may need to be repaired and rebuilt, groups that live and/or work in such structures need to be kept together

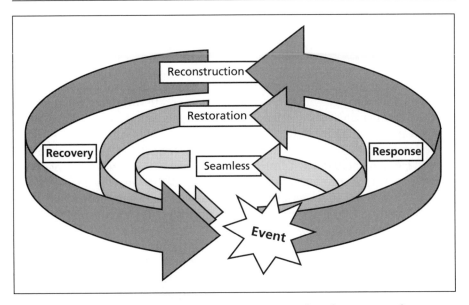

Fig. 15.1 The three main continuity approaches in terms of increasing time taken to resolve the event

and given tasks to undertake. The facilitation and repair of group structures – of families and of work-groups – needs equal priority and support from recovery management.

- *Continuity of function.* This level involves repairing and maintaining the functions performed by systems and people within an organization or community. Attention is initially focused on the most important activities covering the security and survival of organization or community members. Emphasis then shifts to repairing and maintaining the systems and activities that define the organization or community.
- *Continuity of existence.* This level often involves the financial operations of an organization or community. Survival depends upon maintaining links with those who support and interact with the organization or community agencies. An organization's structure and functions are not always completely damaged. Units and activities based elsewhere may be functioning normally. Likewise, many communities that have been badly impacted by a crisis or disaster have areas that continue to function normally. In both cases, managers need to remain aware that much of the cost of recovery may be borne by those business units or areas that were unaffected by the crisis or disaster. Consequently, the needs of those living and working in unaffected areas ought to be promptly satisfied, so that these people continue to support the organization or community and not go elsewhere.

363

Business continuity

In general, business continuity involves eight stages:

- *React.* Activate recovery team when response team is activated. Undertake preliminary assessment of areas of impact damage and likely degree of asset and facility damage within those areas. Co-operate with response management team and with any outside response agencies. Place specialist recovery teams on standby alert.
- *Declare.* Declare likely size and type of recovery action. Activate recovery management personnel. Confirm the activation (remember the need for confirmatory information – *see* Chapter 5). Call a recovery management strategy meeting to undertake an initial assessment of the impact on business functions and determine action priorities. Inform team leaders of strategy and priorities.
- *Prepare.* Prepare recovery location(s) for operations (if needed). Recovery site teams move to the location(s) to check the availability and readiness of the facilities. Collect and distribute appropriate recovery documentation and commence processing any priority requests from on-site recovery teams.
- *Commence.* Begin the recovery system operations at the designated off-site location(s) or the on-site working area. Check configurations, restore back-ups, and initiate user tests to verify systems. Implement process modifications (or workarounds) which allow departments to recommence core and then desired operations. Ensure contact with stakeholders and initiate strategies towards meeting the needs of stakeholders – including customers and suppliers.
- *Continue.* Transfer the conduct of IT operations, call centres and temporary department operations (e.g. administration, servicing, storage and possibly production lines) to users at the recovery location(s). This work then continues for the duration of the recovery period.
- *Rebuild.* Recover or rebuild damaged assets and facilities. Attend to stakeholder needs (with emphasis on staff and shareholders). Plan for return of operations to organization's restored site.
- *Return.* Move operations and any associated facilities and material back to the restored or rebuilt site. Continue the temporary (recovery) site operations until all restored site processes and equipment have been tested and made fully operational.
- *Close.* Close down recovery site operations once the restored site has established fully functioning and fully effective operations. Do deconfigure and clean any IT recovery systems and check security of closure and transfer. Undertake extensive debriefing and problem-solving activities to ensure a better response and recovery operation for the next crisis situation. Undertake group closure activities for recovery personnel and users (*see* ceremonies and celebrations, later in this chapter).

Starting recovery – from regional disasters to single-site crisis situations

Major natural disasters are a very visible example of the lack of integration and information exchange that often happens once response management is completed. While wealthy and heavily industrialized countries can recover infrastructure (roads, rail traffic, bridges, water and gas mains, electricity supply) surprisingly fast, recovery of businesses, families and individuals living within the affected area is a great deal slower. After the earthquakes in Kobe and Loma Prieta, for example, most infrastructural lifelines were restored in half the estimated time to recover. Both events happened in highly industrialized countries and yet both cities had vacant and untenanted sites long after the infrastructure recovery. These vacant business and residential sites reduce the available local revenue that businesses and local governments need to maintain recovery and return to effective 'normal' levels of functioning.

Parts of Mexico City were still being rebuilt 11 years after a major earthquake in 1985. Since a major wildfire in 1982, the city of Oakland (California) has struggled to recover. Much of the recovery problem stems from the reduction in revenue – from response costs and then rebuilding costs, and then from lack of revenue as people and businesses fail to return to the affected area. Businesses can also find recovery difficult. For some organizations, economic losses may be spread over the unaffected business units. The costs are still present, however, and can contribute to changes in numbers of people employed and locations of businesses. Coopers & Lybrand, for example, are said to have lost millions of dollars in client accounts after losing access to their premises when the World Trade Center in New York was bombed. Stuart (1993) finds that only 29 per cent of small businesses will exist two years after a major disaster.

Many small and medium-sized businesses suffer due to five main adverse influences:

- direct damage;
- loss of access;
- loss of lifeline (or infrastructural) support;
- loss of workforce;
- loss of clients.

Direct damage to premises, facilities, hardware and equipment means that goods cannot be produced or sold. Recovery costs will erode cash reserves unless insurance or government assistance is quickly provided. Even when the structure and contents of a site are intact, lack of access and lifeline amenities can lead to a period of non-operation which can close businesses. Loss of water, electricity, gas and access routes means that organizations cannot maintain cash flows.

Loss of a workforce through death, disablement, loss of residency and lack

365

of access to places of work means that production, sales and product servicing ceases to function. Dislocations and the need for time for personal recovery diminish output from staff. Even when workforce and operations are relatively intact, businesses may find lack of clients reduces income that in turn inhibits or closes the business. Loss of clients can arise through three main outcomes:

- inability to service client needs immediately (as happened to Coopers & Lybrand after the World Trade Center bombing);
- inability to service client needs in the future;
- lack of client demand due to the crisis or disaster.

Executives and managers need to have a plan for recovery that is based upon a blend of:

- the needs of those likely to be affected;
- the likely ability to fund recovery;
- the likely ability to improve any damaged or destroyed facilities and operations.

These plans need to operate from three core perspectives:

1 Managers need to pre-plan strategically for major crises or disasters. This planning involves identifying possible options for redesigning or replanning large areas of destroyed structures. There can be economic and personal resistance to replanning. For example, after the 1931 Hawkes Bay earthquake in New Zealand, the narrow street width and street plan of the nearly totally destroyed town of Hastings was not altered. This was apparently due to the insistence of a town councillor who owned the only shop with any structure still standing and who wanted to save money by not having to fully rebuild the shop. Strategic replanning needs to develop a plan to meet current and future needs, and which enables:
    - a better lifestyle or operation within the affected area;
    - more resilient and disaster-resistant organization or community.
2 Recovery management needs to run parallel with response management. People likely to be managing the recovery programme need to be included in the briefings that are given to response managers. Recovery managers also need to know what respondents did. This knowledge can reduce costs by avoiding replication of work and information gathering and can make recovery managers aware of potential dangers in the environment (toxic and chemical hazards, infrastructure and lifeline failures).
3 Managers need to involve those who experienced the disaster as well as those implementing recovery programmes. Involvement can emerge on three levels – communication, decision making and action.

    By involving people in exchanging information, they can be involved in some decision making or decision shaping. People then tend to resist change less and commit more to the programme that involves them in the process. Similarly, resistance and loss of self-esteem can be reduced by involving affected people in the recovery programme. Whether those affected or impacted by the crisis situation help run and maintain their temporary shelters or offices, assist in clean-up or work in reconstruction programmes, involvement in decision making and in the recovery process reduces inertia and resistance and increases feelings of self-worth. Executives and managers need to monitor their stakeholders for any signs of learned helplessness, as this reduces self-image, lessens loyalty and can lead to disassociation and loss of support and business. Recovery will not be effective unless people feel their needs and concerns are being met. After the Three Mile Island nuclear accident, for example, the surrounding community still shows signs of ongoing unease with the way in which the local nuclear power plant is managed (Flynn and Chalmers, 1980).

Recovering from intangible crisis situations

So far recovery strategies have focused on very visible and physical or tangible crisis situations. These strategies can be adapted for the less tangible crisis situations like assaults on image and cash flow or stock market incidents. The response for these less tangible crisis situations is to increase efforts in image management (*see* Chapter 8) and to stop the situation from increasing the impact and ripple-effect damage (*see* Action Steps in Chapter 13). Recovery strategies build on these response actions and work to protect or restore image credibility and to defuse the pressures and perceptions generated by the visible upheaval caused by the less visible crisis situation.

Recovery from intangible crisis situations has two key advantages and two key disadvantages. The two advantages are that:

- the less visible situation may mean less cost in physical recovery;
- people tend to regard outcomes from intangible crisis situations as more important than the management process used to achieve those outcomes (mostly because the details involved in intangible crisis situations are often not seen or not sufficiently understood).

The disadvantages of recovering from intangible crisis situations are that:

- if people cannot see physical damage and 'blood on the floor' they quickly forget there was a crisis and become impatient for normal working interactions to take place;
- any concentrated focus on the outcome rather than the managed process means that the product or service provided needs to be of high quality, be prompt in delivery and be supported by efficient and customer-friendly after-sales service. Failure to meet these criteria commonly leads to erosion of market share and a rapidly developed corporate image of being inefficient, unreliable and non-competitive.

Executives and managers consequently need to ensure that product quality, service delivery and product support are given increased emphasis when recovering from intangible crisis, and that any agreed delivery dates are met. For tangible and non-tangible situations, executives and managers can improve the level of recovery by ensuring that information exchanges, involvement of stakeholders and core business processes are emphasized in their plans. These emphases can be incorporated using meta-strategies similar to the PICPIC approach (*see* below).

The PICPIC strategies

So far a basic outline for recovery has been presented. Executives and managers need to work toward a recovery that is quick, effective and beneficial to the business processes and for the stakeholders. One approach that helps focus managerial effort in accomplishing these dual tasks is the PICPIC set of recovery strategies.

For PICPIC strategies to fully work, plans need to be constructed so that recovery can be implemented for all stakeholders (government, business, residential owners, inhabitants and victims). Plans need to outline how recovery information will be made available before a crisis and after a crisis is resolved. Such information dissemination is important because plans and actions need to be explained in detail and much care needs to be placed upon facilitating flows of information in and around a crisis environment during response and recovery activities.

The central intention of PICPIC strategies is to get people involved in a recovery programme through actively participating in planning, information exchange, identifying and restoring core activities, and in recovering the infrastructure of the organization or community. PICPIC thus interweaves physical and tangible aspects (such as *p*lanning, *i*nformation exchange and identifying the '*c*ore' needs for recovery) with the psychological and less tangible elements (that include *p*eople, *i*nvolvement and *c*ontinuity).

Planning

Recovery management, as does response management, relies heavily upon strategic planning. Planning needs to cover all possible risks, regardless of the estimated likelihood of each risk. On the other hand, recovery managers will get bogged down in an overload of planning for all possible risks and are thus unlikely to produce any usable directions. This overload can be reduced by identifying and emphasizing common activities and by weighting the planning focus in favour of more likely risks and situations (*see* Chapters 2, 3 and 4). Preservation of vital records, safe evacuation of people (where required) and replacement of damaged or lost resources are examples of common activities that can be developed in detail because these activities will apply in most events. Loss of resources and structures from fire is more likely in most locations than from earthquakes, so recovery planning emphasizes activities related to structure fires. Note, however, that the impact of an earthquake (or flood or bomb) is likely to require similar activities.

One benefit of including area or regional risks is that back-ups of vital information may be placed outside a region (beyond earthquake effects) and can thus be protected by less common events such as widespread flooding or bomb damage. Serious damage from the Oklahoma City bombing was found up to six blocks away from the detonation site. Similarly, at least one back-up centre for computer information in the 1995 Canary Wharf bombing failed because the back-up site was only two buildings away from the organization's site and was also damaged.

Managers need to identify a set of programme priorities that meet organizational or community needs *and* which meet the concerns and needs of those affected by the crisis or disaster. To do so, pre-event identification of risks and recovery activities needs to be made and disseminated among those affected. When a recovery plan is developed into an actual programme to meet the consequences of an event, the details need to be communicated (loudly and often). Information exchange thus becomes an important element in any recovery plan and recovery programme.

Information

Information needs to flow from those affected by a crisis or disaster so that managers can establish the nature and severity of damage from impact(s) from that event. Information also needs to flow out to those affected by the crisis or disaster from those managing the recovery so that they know what is being done and what they may do for themselves. In many cases, media outlets and telephone contacts (as well as fax and Internet bulletin boards) can be used. This is one means by which the media presence can be made useful and positive.

Information management is vitally important in recovery from a crisis or disaster, and cannot be overstressed. Supplying appropriate information not only keeps people aware of what is happening, but also allows those managing the recovery to understand (or at least hear) how people feel and perceive the recovery process.

Particular attention consequently needs to be placed upon four aspects of disseminated information. These aspects are:

- what is being done *now*;
- how such action fits within the big picture (the overall plan);
- what those gaining such information can do; and
- what is likely to happen in the near future.

In major crises or disasters, such as earthquakes and floods, managers need to remember that those displaced or in other ways affected by that crisis often will demonstrate a strong psychological need to return to familiar and normal environments within a period of between 24 and 72 hours. Should these needs not be met, increased frustration, stress and conflict may emerge. This is another strong motivating reason for emphasizing information management in response and recovery planning. When people have greater knowledge about what is happening, they feel more in control of their own lives and more familiar with what may happen to them. As a consequence, levels of frustration and conflict may fall, and acceptance of restrictions on lifestyles may increase.

The quality and credibility of information management depends upon whether subsequent actions support the words used. Decisions and actions need to be congruent and support the information being disseminated. Should any group of people realize that some proposed action has not happened within the time stated in disseminated information, the readiness with which these people will listen to and act on future information will be reduced. Managers need to remember that information should be made available as quickly and as often as possible. Without ongoing flows of information, victims and respondents can feel more isolated and become more worried that nothing is being done, and their sense of privation and futility is increased. At best, rumours will begin to spread; at worst, friction between people will escalate into conflict.

One way to maintain appropriate word-to-action congruence is to have performed organization-wide or community-wide analyses that establish the essential or core activities vital to the survival of that organization or community. This needs to be done before any event happens, and needs to be regularly updated.

Core

Core activities are those most needed to keep an organization or community functioning. Mitroff and Pearson (1993) use the concept of 'identification of basic services and procedures necessary to conduct minimal business and assignment of related business resumption accountability' to cover core activity planning and management. After a major fire on its premises in central Los Angeles, the First Interstate Bank quickly resumed its primary services because the organization had identified preservation of customer and operational data and customer service as core activities. Having identified these core activities, the recovery plan emphasized the use of off-site computer back-up of data and readily designated alternative work sites for customer convenience.

Managers of ARCO Oil and Gas identified a core activity (personnel information) and a possible event (earthquake) which prompted them to incorporate a relocation agreement with Employee Information Service (EIS) of Pasadena, California, a company that undertakes these activities for ARCO. In the event of an earthquake, EIS has key members of staff ready to relocate to Plano, Texas, where computer data is backed-up (Barton, 1993). This is an example of geophysical separation of site and back-up site contingency management.

For a community, core activities may start from lifeline systems or infrastructure elements (water, electricity, gas and roads) through to support elements (hospitals, law-enforcement stations, paramedical agencies and government agencies). Organizations are likely to identify information records, specialist equipment and key organizational facilities and operations as being the 'core' of the existence and survival of that organization. Business organizations and local government authorities are likely to identify income-producing activities as being those essential for keeping the organization functioning and able to pay for recovery. As a result, core activities include income-producing activities, information recording activities and lifeline support functions that are vital to maintain business and community systems.

A recovery programme can be divided into three simple activity clusters: core, support and expanded. As core activities are fully serviced, support activities can be restarted. Again, when support activities are fully operational, then the rest of the organizational or community activities (those that expand out to make the community or organization feel fulfilled and unique) can be recommenced. The speed of transition between each cluster depends on resources being available to repair or replace the damaged components.

After a major disaster, for example, a community may focus on restoring and maintaining core activities such as lifelines (electricity, water gas, access roads), emergency offices and buildings (shelters and processing centres) and cash-flow operations. As resources become available, the recovery programme can begin to work on the support activities such as connecting roads and reopening schools and hospitals. When the core and support clusters are recovered (or seem to be well on the way to recovery), attention turns to the expanded cluster – libraries, parks, sports centres and public meeting places.

Organizations can perform similar actions – contracting to core activities, then recovering support and expanded activities as resources and demand requires. A bank, for example, may contract to what the managers see as essential or core activities (customer account transactions and arrangements for loans), then slowly recover support activities (more customer-convenient branches) and then expanded activities (whatever extra financial services a particular bank offers).

In essence, recovery management depends upon dealing with people, and thus integrates tangible and physical activities (plans, information exchanges, identifying and recovering core activities) with the less tangible and more psychological aspects of people, involvement and the sense of continuity.

People

A crisis is rarely deemed to be a crisis unless the impacts from that crisis or disaster affect people. Response and recovery management consequently entails a heavy involvement in people management. People in this sense covers victims, those affected materially by a crisis or disaster and those responding to or supporting the recovery process.

Managers need to be aware that the term 'people' also includes those viewing or watching the response and recovery process unfold but who are not directly involved in the situation. Media organizations transmit images, narrative descriptions and interviews around the world, often as the situation is happening. In contemporary situations (Chernobyl, the Oklahoma City bombing, the Northridge and Kobe earthquakes, Hurricane Andrew, the volcanic explosions of Mt St Helens and Mt Pinatubo, the Sydney and California wildfires and the *Exxon Valdez* oil spillage, to name a few), the media transmit graphic footage of the situations and the responses to those situations. The media often return to record the recovery from those crisis situations. What people are shown and told becomes the perceived reality of the response and recovery management. This perceived reality could influence the amount of aid, support, investigative inquiries and scapegoating.

During the onset of a crisis or disaster, the major interest in 'people' held by crisis managers is usually about those who have (or are likely to) become victims. 'People' in this perception are the casualties and those evacuated or displaced from the site of the crisis or disaster. Affected people, however, also include bystanders, respondents and those assisting with any response. When the Cairo (Egypt, 1992) earthquake happened, many of the 552 dead were schoolchildren trampled in their efforts to flee the school buildings (Davis, 1993). Affected people included those who survived or witnessed the trampling panics, as well as those who responded to those school sites. Affected people can be forced to watch the effects of a crisis or disaster. During the King's Cross Underground Railway fire (1987, London), commuters travelling on trains that passed through the burning station were entrapped witnesses to the fire and the effects of the fire on those victims trapped on the platforms. These entrapped witnesses also become affected people.

As response shifts to recovery, affected people can include those supporting and affected by the recovery programme, as well as those undertaking recovery activities. After a major disaster, for example, those not directly affected by any impact from that event may become affected by the impact of the recovery. They often have to accept diminished services and pay directly or indirectly for the costs of recovery. Moreover, emotional upset due to feelings of guilt (from not being as affected as others), lack of attention due to recovery efforts and loss of service choices due to recovery processes can develop conflict and divisions within groups in an organization or community. In business organizations, for example, personnel are affected by having to work elsewhere or even being stood down until operations can restart. These actions also place strains upon family and community relationships, which in turn can impact on the quality and quantity of effort being placed in recovery or ongoing work activities.

People are a fundamental component in any response and recovery programme. Executives and managers need to maintain flows of information and involvement with all that are affected in some way by the situation, by the impact(s) from that situation and by the processes needed to recover from the impact(s) and situation. Working without information exchanges and involvement of those directly and indirectly affected by the crisis or disaster impact(s) can lead to criticism, resistance and loss of attention and time. By using approaches that enable people to feel involved in the information exchange, decision making and effort involved in recovery, criticism and resistance is reduced.

Involvement

In the stress and urgency of response and recovery management, information exchange and decision making tends to become centralized and limited to management. This limitation may even tighten to those at the response or recovery command centre. Shortly after the event has ceased, people tend rapidly to desire to return to their homes and places of work (Heath, 1994). This adds to the pressure on recovery management. Pressure increases when three strong desires lead to conflicting action choices and desires:

- The option to change and improve a site clashes with a strong desire for a return to pre-event normalcy.
- The desire to keep recovery costs to a minimum can block chances to implement complete change or completely restore a site.
- The pressures and needs of specific groups of people within an organization or community can clash with any attempt at fair and equal response and recovery management.

Resentment and conflict appears to increase as competing needs and desires become compromised. Effective recovery management needs to *be seen* to be open and sensitive to the desires of all groups involved and needs to show a detailed and sequential recovery programme that is aimed at achieving the optimal outcomes for as many of those affected as possible. In many cases, recovery management also becomes a dialectically driven process that alternates between short-term and long-term goals and is influenced by the need for speed of decision and action and the need to include all affected.

By involving people within the process of management and recovery activities, more commitment and acceptance of the goals which are consequently developed can emerge. Involvement can be achieved on any or all of three levels by:

- pre-crisis and pre-disaster consultation and information exchange;
- distributing information through as many media outlets as possible;
- getting people involved in doing things that enable those people to participate in the response and recovery process.

For optimal co-operation and support, involvement needs to have been introduced before any crisis situation arises. Essentially, involvement can be seen as a two-process strategy in which people are involved in information access and exchange and in doing some physical action for themselves.

By using as many outlets as possible (public notices, newspapers, television, radio and even electronic communication) people get involved in understanding and exchanging information. When people feel such information is current and credible, they also begin to feel they are part of the process. Information presented regularly and directly is more acceptable than the traditional use of media conferences.

People far beyond the crisis or disaster environment may be made to feel better, more co-operative and more supportive by involving them in actions they believe can affect the outcome in that crisis or disaster. When nations go to war, for example, governments may involve communities through volunteer or conscription campaigns, in making donations (war bonds) and in undertaking such involvement activities as civil preparedness and community health programmes. Many governments even conduct public campaigns for the donation of resources (such as saucepans and similar metal material, or gold and valuables) which need not actually be used. In crisis and disaster events, public involvement often emerges in public appeals for donations of money, food, clothing and toys for those who have materially lost from the impact of the crisis or disaster.

One approach often overlooked by managers is to involve respondents in some recovery processes, especially when response management is in transition to recovery management. In the Northridge earthquake, for example, a number of fire service and specialized units were allowed to help displaced people quickly recover essential valuables from their destroyed residences and workplaces (Warford, 1994). The positive emotional increase to morale that such permission gave these respondents is worth noting. Many involved in helping people retrieve valuables and personal items found that this was a positive activity after having spent many hours associated with search and rescue efforts and in recovering the dead.

Involvement of people, careful management of information, identification of core activities and effective strategic planning assist managers to maintain the essential focus of recovery management upon establishing *continuity*.

Continuity

Perhaps the most important support strategy involves providing a sense of normalcy and continuity. Continuity emerges from the plans that people have been involved in producing. These plans need to outline how the core processes will be continued and how and when support and adjunct processes are likely to be restarted.

Many people impacted by a crisis need to be able to predict outcomes and be familiar with their surrounding environment (*see* the FPC model in Chapter 12). This leads to a desire for a return to a pre-crisis state of normalcy that is unattainable. Executives and managers need to use their planning, communication and involvement strategies to create predictability and familiarity through the recovery programme. Through constant exposure to what to expect, insight into current and future operations, and pre- and post-crisis involvement in response and recovery issues, people develop familiarity and ownership of the processes. They develop some ability to predict correctly what will happen. This increases their comfort zone and encourages co-operativeness and a sense of continuity.

Ultimately, continuity becomes a goal of the recovery process. When people are convinced that effort is being made to recover from the situation and return the environment to an acceptable state of normal familiarity and predictability, they then sense continuity – and place greater effort in attaining that sense of continuity.

REALITY BITE

Altasteel, Edmonton, Canada, 1987

Background
Altasteel is a mini-steel mill using two electric arc-furnaces to produce 250 000 tons per year of steel bar products for gas, oil and agricultural uses. The mill employs 400 people with annual revenues of $104 000 000 (£65 000 000) and monthly profits of $1 600 000 (around £1 000 000).

Incident
On 31 July 1987, a tornado struck Edmonton, killing 27 people. The tornado path was approximately three blocks wide and around twenty blocks long, passing through a mostly industrial area that included the Altasteel site. Over 50 businesses were destroyed.

At Altasteel, the tornado injured one person and virtually destroyed the plant. Key damage involved:

- electricity transformers;
- a cooling tower;
- fume control ducts and the baghouse (a vacuum cleaner type structure for filtering out precipitates and noxious emissions from the furnaces that weighs 300 tons and was shifted 45 feet);
- two overhead 60-ton cranes; and
- equipment and office blocks.

The cost of the damage was expected to total somewhere in the hundreds of millions of dollars.

Response
The company had no pre-defined plan.

Post-tornado estimates for recovery were not good. Estimates included a six to nine month reconstruction period that meant a potential a loss of work for most employees and loss of these employees and their skills as they went elsewhere for work. Financial projections were for a loss of $9 600 000 to $14 400 000 (£3 000 000 to £9 000 000) of the profit.

The recovery management team had to decide on a number of action choices and determine a workable priority list. The key priorities became (in descending order):

1 Make the site safe. This is standard for most recovery operations.
2 Ship out existing inventory. This would create some revenue and help meet immediate customer needs.
3 Get the rolling mill (the value-adding component or profit maker) back into operation. This would use existing steel outputs and generate cash flow and continuity of employment.
4 Establish some level of steel-*making* capacity so that orders could be taken and met. This would emphasize to customers that the company was intending to continue operating and thus reduce loss of market share.
5 Bring the furnaces back into operation.

The latter two priorities depended upon on whether the baghouse could be put in place. The baghouse is a custom-designed facility that then costed around $2 400 000 (£1 500 000) to construct. Altasteel engineers estimated that the baghouse could be repaired and put in partial operation for around $640 000 (£400 000).

Management chose the costly repair-and-replace option, figuring that the temporary structure should pay for the repair costs by providing earlier steel production capability. The choice to repair the damaged baghouse and build a new baghouse at the same time led to a decision to run the two activities in tandem, using relatively independent teams. To facilitate this decision and manage the recovery operation, five teams were formed. These were:

● Management and Communication (to centralize internal and external communications);
● Salvage and Restoration (to undertake initial damage assessment, co-ordinate site clean-up and determine what could be repaired);
● two Reconstruction Teams (to repair and rebuild facilities and structures); and
● Purchasing and Accounting (to run budget and track contract and service suppliers).

Statistics

Within eight hours the Salvage and Restoration team was working on site. The clean-up was completed within a week, when inventory shipments were restarted. The rolling mill was partly back in operation within two weeks, with a jury-rigged cooling system but no cranes.

Within seven weeks the temporary baghouse was in place and interim repairs to the transformers were completed. One furnace could begin operating. The Ministry of Environment accepted a request for permission for a short term of sub-performance for the baghouse.

By the thirteenth week the new baghouse was in place. By the twentieth week the transformers were fully functioning. Altasteel moved toward full operations by 20 weeks, less than the estimated 24–36-week disruption.

Comment

Note the need for making the site safe and the emphasis given to site security. Few response and recovery plans place sufficient attention on these two important activities. Disaster sites are dangerous – so employees need to be kept off-site until trained personnel and specialists have assessed the site and made it safe. Security personnel can help make a site safe by keeping people out.

As noted elsewhere in this book, by demonstrating to the appropriate government and response agencies that you are security and safety minded, there is a strong chance that the agencies involved may let you look after your site. This decision, after all, saves the agencies costs in personnel and resources. Consent may be more likely if an organization:

- can quickly set up adequate site security first;
- conducts these activities as part of the regular crisis test exercises;
- undertakes such exercises while involving the appropriate response agencies (so that the response agencies build a relationship of trust with the organization by finding that the organization will perform its tasks properly).

One important feature of site security is to be able to admit the appropriate personnel. To do so effectively, admission processes need to be set up and ways developed in which identity permits may be supplied and controlled.

The ability to keep inventory rolling out meant that Altasteel preserved much of its market share. This was accomplished by looking beyond their reserves of steel – Altasteel purchased 3500 tons of steel from another company. Organizations may find that short-term product purchase and supply to customers (even at no profit to the organization) can maintain cash flow and retain market share.

Altasteel now has a pre-defined plan.

Management perspective

This Reality Bite again emphasizes the need for pre-planning and training. From a manager's perspective, the above response and recovery operation involved close attention to priority setting and co-ordination. Communications needed to be accurate and quick. These aspects can be predetermined in plans and in training exercises, which can then further speed up the response and recovery processes.

Pre-event planning includes two specific components:

- to identify available skills from inside and outside the organization that may be needed;
- to determine the personnel management details – such as what rates of pay and compensation cover a potential round-the-clock operation, and what conditions (from on-site meals and rest centres to hours of work and recreation leave) and support services (from clothing and transportation to provision of child-minding and entertainment) need to be offered.

These issues need also to be considered for internal employees and outside contractors. By determining these in advance, time can be saved, confusion minimized and potential disputes and fraud can be reduced.

Managers also need to pre-define control measures, authorization, documentation requirements, credit limits and financing arrangements, and procedures for quick placement of orders by telephone and facsimile (and by the Internet, if so desired). All of these need a clear assignment of accountability and a good set of monitoring and reporting procedures.

Finally, managers need to assess carefully how to manage any impaired supply of services and products to customers. Two basic and complementary processes help to achieve this. First, look at ways of mirroring the business outputs. This mirroring may be accomplished by acquiring the finished inventory or half-finished resources from other departments or businesses within the organization or corporation, or by acquiring the products from competitors. The latter action may appear costly (and may well lead to short-term losses) but can retain clients and market share. The second process is to identify the key customers. Many managers may find that around 20 per cent of their clients acquire around 80 per cent of the services or goods offered by the organization. The rest may be regarded as less essential or one-off clients. These less essential or one-off clients should be cancelled or refused. Make arrangements for these to be serviced by other suppliers, then focus resources and effort on the key customers (those 20 per cent that give 80 per cent of the business).

Doing better – bouncing back bigger and better

Surviving a crisis is not enough for many organizations and communities. Survival is not sufficient if this means the organization achieves a level just short of extinction and suffers from reduced energy and resources. Without quick injections of resources and energy, just surviving means a slow lingering death.

Even when organizational recovery and reconstruction takes place, the time lost and lowered service or production outputs often mean loss of stakeholder confidence and support and lost market share. Executives and managers need to seek to do more than consider survival and conventional recovery strategies. They need to seek ways in which the organization may bounce back bigger and better than before the crisis situation.

Towards a bounce-back strategy

'Bounce-back' strategies need to be overlaid upon a solid response and recovery programme. These strategies will not work if the fundamental response and recovery tasks and decisions are not effectively undertaken. The basic response and recovery actions involved in response and recovery programmes need to be so well learned that key team members can focus on the three goals beyond survival:

- reducing any loss of client base or market share;
- maintaining or asserting a positive organizational image;
- seeking ways in which the organization can use the current crisis experience to improve the organizational situation (in terms of market share, image and/or performance.

The goal of market share or client base protection is ideally that of 'no loss whatsoever'. Similarly, the goal for continuity or recovery is ideally that of a seamless and imperceptible response and recovery action. Most crisis recovery situations, however, are more likely to involve loss of customers (no matter how temporarily) and market share. A withdrawal from operation for some days may permanently lose clients. A disruption of a few minutes or hours may convince high-volume users to change suppliers of electronic information-based services. Less physical crisis situations may precipitate a sudden and seemingly unstoppable loss of business. The bank that has the first really publicly known raid on its electronic banking services via a computer hacker is likely to suffer a severe loss of client-base.

Managers need to look for ways in which positive outcomes and visible improvement can be presented to those within the response and recovery environment, and more particularly to those looking at the response and recovery management from outside. As is done with conventional strategic management and marketing analysis (such as SWOT), managers need to look at how to turn threats into opportunities and weaknesses into strengths.

A conceptual picture of bouncing back

Take, for example, the room within which you currently sit.

- *First*, there is the public image of the organization. Make that the wall behind you.
- *Second*, there are the activities and tasks that directly achieve the goals or objectives of the organization, which for most profit-centred organizations are the cash flow generators or value-adding activities. Let these be represented by the wall in front of you.
- *Third*, there are those activities that support the achievement of goals and objectives, but do not necessarily provide value to the organization on their own – administration, customer services and so on. Let these be represented by the wall to your right.
- *Finally*, there are all the people (the stakeholders) who have an involvement with the organization – staff, users, clients, customers, suppliers, creditors, shareholders, mandatory government agencies, insurers and so on. Let these be represented by the wall on your left.

The four walls form a room. Just as each wall represents the status of the organization's image, work and profitability, efficiency and service support, and stakeholder satisfaction, the floor of this room represents the current overall performance of the organization. At this moment the floor (the white surface of the rectangle in Figure 15.2) represents the 'normal' pre-crisis performance of the organization. Should a crisis situation occur, one or more of the four walls is likely to be damaged.

Suppose an organization suffers a crisis situation. A structural failure due to fire or a bomb, for example, may disrupt the value-adding and support services (the two sides in the foreground of Figure 15.3).

In conventional response and recovery management, the members of the organization react to reduce the damage and recover the damaged 'walls'. The sagging floor is made secure, alternative facilities are put into action, and the

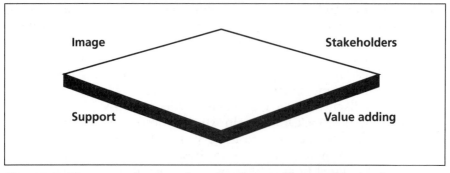

Fig. 15.2 The organizational performance floor with the four 'walls' of image, value adding, support and stakeholders

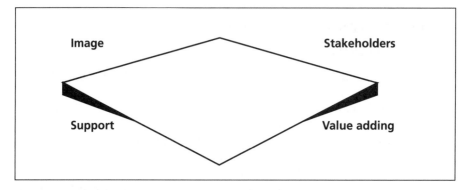

Fig. 15.3 The slope of the performance floor due to damage or cessation of activities in the value-adding and support functions of an organization caused by a crisis situation

appropriate continuity or recovery plan to return each wall to its pre-crisis state is activated. In some cases, this effort may take only a few minutes and the staff of the organization may congratulate themselves on a seamless recovery or continuity effort. In some other cases, the switch to alternative facilities may need to continue for some time while the damaged facilities are repaired or replaced, and the reduction in available facilities may cause a gradual decline in performance. In most other cases, the time taken between the crisis situation and the ability to operate normally may take so long that there is a loss of cash flow, a decline in user and customer base, and a loss of market share.

To do more than just survive, executives and managers need to speed up the recovery process and seek ways in which such losses of resources and market share may be minimized. Conceptually, the question becomes *how can the 'floor' be lifted or raised to the performance level that was present before the onset of the crisis situation.* The term 'lift' indicates the course of action. By lifting the overall floor (that is, lifting the performance of the organization during crisis response and recovery operations), the slumped area is lifted to an approximate pre-crisis level (*see* Figure 15.4). This is done by lifting the height of the floor at the non-damaged walls.

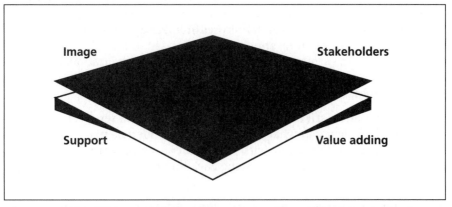

Fig. 15.4 The lifting of the performance floor (black rectangular surface) through increased effort in the image and stakeholder components

In the current example, the organization increases efforts in image management and concern for stakeholders. This can be done in many ways. Using staff to keep contact with users, clients and suppliers so that these people feel able to continue a working relationship is one approach. Being more efficient in recovering debts, in paying debts and in servicing existing contracts also helps. Another approach may mean being innovative in how cash flows are maintained, even if the ways temporarily produce little profit or value. Usually, 'bounce-back' strategies are likely to use combinations of all such approaches.

The 'lifting' of the floor or performance is thus done by increasing the effort in the undamaged areas while recovering those that are damaged. By placing more effort and resources in maintaining an organizational presence, managers can reduce loss of market share and cash flow. The same conceptual argument can be made for damage caused by a crisis situation that arises at any of the other walls. Should the organizational image come under assault from pressure groups, for example, the organization needs to put more effort into image management and try to become more efficient and close to the customer in its support functions.

To do more than survive, executives and managers need to:

- protect the market share of the organization;
- maintain and assert a positive organizational image;
- seek ways in which the crisis may be turned into an advantage.

Staying close to users and customers and going out of the way to continue supplying goods or services to them will reduce loss of customer and client base. Increased efforts in maintaining and asserting a positive image can lead to a reduction in the loss of reputation and increased visibility among external stakeholders and the general public. Efforts to improve unaffected operations and functions and to find ways in which the crisis situation can be turned into opportunities mean that losses in image and market share may be further reduced, and even reversed into gains.

The effort to lift or raise the level of the floor (or organizational performance) focuses on the undamaged 'walls' – organizational image and stakeholder activities. Such efforts include:

- searches for alternative means of supplying goods and services;
- improved efficiency in what functions can be undertaken;
- combining stakeholder care with stakeholder involvement;
- continuously updating and bringing back into operation those repaired or replaced functions.

A key bounce-back strategy is to invest effort and resources in the undamaged elements of an organization as well as repairing the damaged elements.

Note that the intense efforts made during the period of the crisis situation are unlikely to be sustained when the organization returns to normal operations. When recovery operations are complete, the floor is likely to settle as the increased effort is reduced. Done correctly, however, the performance (or floor level) may remain higher than the level prior to the onset of the crisis situation (*see* Figure 15.5).

In the example of the disrupted value-adding and support areas, any improved focus on stakeholders and organizational image and the extra effort placed in delivering services and support may leave the organization with a better than pre-crisis performance level. The amount of raised performance depends on how much of the extra effort and improved organizational image is not discarded on resuming normal, post-recovery operations. If the

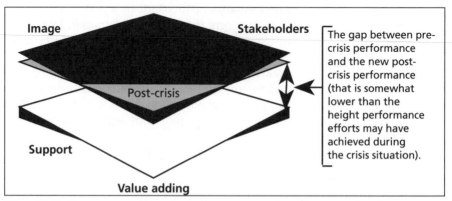

Fig. 15.5 The new normal performance after bounce-back strategies have been used, showing a lower height due to return to normal operations

improvements become part of the 'normal' operations of the organization, the organization may gain an added benefit of bouncing back bigger and better with an improved level of performance.

Bounce-back strategies offer organizations improved chances of doing more than just surviving and can add further benefits through improving the on-going performance of an organization in the post-crisis period. This latter benefit is even more likely should the management of the organization take the opportunity to make structural and operational changes leading to a more efficient organization.

Basic strategies for bouncing back

While each organization may find and develop unique bounce-back strategies that suit its culture, performance criteria and surrounding environment, seven basic strategies are common for all organizations.

Develop and maintain wishlists

Wishlists are lists of things members of an organization would like to change should an opportunity arise. These wishlists may include new designs for facilities or products, different staffing procedures, changes to operational processes or new equipment and locations. Wishlists need to be developed before any crisis situation arises so that:

- time is not wasted in trying to determine what improvements can be made when replacing facilities, equipment or operations;
- some consensus on what changes are worth doing and on the priorities involved can be gained;
- crisis managers and senior managers within the organization can immediately assess the damage caused by the crisis in terms of implementing the wishlists.

An important key to developing useful wishlists is that a measurable or clearly identifiable benefit needs to be offered and not some vague 'it would be nice if we ...' statement.

Two constraints may act upon using wishlists. The first is that organization members may not agree on the priorities or benefits of the items on the wishlist. This is one reason for developing such lists well before a crisis arises. The second constraint may arise through insurance contracts and legal requirements. Existing insurance contracts need to be checked as these may not fund changes to facilities and lost resources. Likewise, check for any legal and regulatory constraints upon making specific changes that may otherwise have been placed on a wishlist.

Increase the skills of organizational members

As indicated in the FPC model, a key construct for effectively coping with, and operating in, crisis environments is to have the skill capability to do so. Currently, few organizations appear to seriously improve the crisis management skills of their members even though many of these skills can be used in the day-to-day operations of the organization. Basic and necessary skills would include first aid, time management, communication, information management, image management, self-presentation, people management and stress management.

Improve communication activities

Perhaps the major key in surviving – and in doing better than surviving – comes from effective communication practices. While many organizations provide some communications skills training (from doing presentations through to answering media-type questions) few organizations provide adequate communication structures and facilities.

Two main communication channels need to be kept separate – those connecting personnel dealing with the crisis and those connecting the organization to its stakeholders and the outside general public. Even the outside channel needs to be separated into special (often dedicated) channels supplying specific information to staff, suppliers, shareholders and creditors, as well as to the public and the media. Without such specialized channels managers will not be able to assert even reasonable control over flows of information, rumours and organizational image.

Two major constraints emerge when communication channels are examined in organizations. The first is that organizations do not provide sufficient communication resources. Communication channels tend to breakdown or gridlock when most needed (such as in a crisis). The second constraint is the need to counter the increasing likelihood that major users of communication channels will not register new messages as time goes by. This failure arises because most signals appear to have the same content so minor changes do not get noticed. Given that communication needs to be accurate, readily available and frequently broadcast, messages using the same or similar structure and presentation lose impact and appear the same, with the resulting loss of attention and absorption. Significant changes in message structures need to be made on a regular basis so that information is appropriately and fully noticed.

Develop an effective image management programme

Image management is as important as actually managing the crisis situation. Organizations need to develop effective images that suit their self-perception and objectives and which match the perceptions held by the outside world. This area involves a number of complementary skills that range from careful selection of words through to the body language of representatives and the images that an organization purposefully and accidentally emits to onlookers.

Image management includes reputation risk management and thus needs to be proactive and commenced well before any crisis arises. Members of organizations need to be able to present confidently a range of behaviours that create the espoused image of an organization. This is a skill area that needs high levels of understanding and hours of experiential training for effective use.

As outlined in Chapter 8, some simple principles of image management during a crisis situation include the following:

- The image presented must be seen to be consistent with pre-crisis attitudes and actions (so if the organization has a poor image prior to a crisis then that organization will have trouble in communicating a better image during and after the crisis).
- The image presented has to reflect the real attitudes and actions of the organization (which means that any uncovered inconsistencies will worsen an image).
- Image management needs to be outward in direction (concern needs to focus upon those hurt by the crisis and upon rectifying any damage caused).
- The image has to be maintained after the heat of the crisis is gone (otherwise this will be seen as inconsistent and therefore fraudulent and manipulative).

Note that image management involves presenting accurate pictures of the organization in the most positive fashion, wherein espoused or claimed attitudes and actions need to match enacted or undertaken attitudes or actions.

A major constraint in image management is the tendency to select inappropriate personnel to represent the organization. In most cases avoid using known public relations personnel directly in public view, as many people hold suspicions about their credibility and accuracy. Ensure that senior managers (particularly CEOs) have limited but sufficient exposure so that they are seen to be involved and caring yet are not perceived to be patronizing or even misleading the audience. As a rule of thumb, use appropriate junior staff or junior managers to tell the public what is being done, and use senior managers and CEOs to state the policy and future plans for the organization.

Get closer to and involve stakeholders

Many organizations concentrate response and recovery plans upon equipment and electronic information systems and fail to attend equally to the human or stakeholder areas. *Effective crisis management places a high degree of attention on the human interface as the interactions of clients, staff, users, regulators, suppliers, creditors, debtors and even owners or shareholders create the goal-achieving environment.*

With the onset of a crisis, managers need to move immediately to inform and assist stakeholders in coping with the effects of the crisis. This is what is meant by 'getting closer' to the stakeholder.

When an organization suffering a crisis tries hard to maintain service and supply, clients and users are less likely to take the extra effort to move to another organization. Left alone, however, clients and users soon turn to other sources to satisfy their needs. Those unaffected by a crisis will continue operating as normal. Many will make some allowances for obstructions and problems but will look elsewhere for goods and services should their own needs go unmet. By continuing to inform stakeholders about what is going on as far as their needs are concerned, and by trying to meet those needs through temporary and innovative means, organizations may effectively reduce loss of cash flow and clients.

Organizations need to do more than provide information and a rough supply of services in order to hold on to stakeholders. Managers need to involve the stakeholder in dealing with the effects of the crisis. This involvement need not be direct and significant (such as cleaning up damaged facilities or supplying alternative facilities), but can be smaller and indirect (such as suggesting what needs the stakeholder desires to be met, or making a little more effort to satisfy their needs). Involvement is dependent on accurate communications and on genuine appreciation of the help those involved may contribute.

The psychological secret of involvement is that those encouraged to be involved feel part-ownership of the process, the solution and the problem. By identifying with the process and solution, they come to feel more bound to work and stay with the processes and thus with the organization.

Note that the major constraint in dealing with stakeholders resides in the willingness and ability of the members of the affected organization to keep in contact and involve those stakeholders outside the organization. Morale and motivation of staff is thus an important aspect needing management, as well as monitoring how the stakeholder interactions are being managed as the newness and stimulation of the crisis situation fades.

Many members of organizations will at first respond well to the novelty of crisis situations in the short term. However, these members are likely to tire of doing unfamiliar tasks as time goes by, and eventually lose energy and press for a return to pre-crisis levels of operation. Remember that organizational members are both stakeholders and people who will influence the thoughts and behaviours of other stakeholders outside the organization – so invest time and effort in looking after organizational members. Staff left feeling used or uncared for have a habit of losing interest in their work, communicating disinterest or even anger to those around them (including members of the outside public), and, at times, becoming unwanted sources of rumour, adverse speculation and critical comments in the media.

Focus on resolving the situation soon and positively

As noted earlier, response and recovery activities need to be understood and so well learned that senior managers and appropriate organization members become more free to seek ways in which recovery can be achieved faster and with a chance of avoiding loss of performance. Two areas thus need to be kept continuously in focus by those managing the response and recovery process:

- active updating of the status of recovery;
- the search for ways of turning the impacts of the crisis into opportunities for positive organizational image and growth.

These twin interests help managers identify the speed and direction of actions that foster recovery and which can promote a bigger and better performance for the organization.

The demands and distractions of managing a recovery process in a dynamic environment often seem to leave little time for full assimilation of the status of all the organization's activities, functions, divisions, processes and groups. Managers are usually confronted with issues to resolve and decisions to make and thus lose track of where the recovery process is at the current moment. Conventional updates are often slow in release, get overlooked or do not provide the information required.

The solution is to improve information collation skills and to ensure that a continuous update of organizational status is provided. Response and recovery specialist units need to be trained to report status frequently, even if that status is unchanged, so that managers stay aware of where everything is and how everything is going. Without an almost continuous updating process, managers will make decisions based either on hope or on doubt, and either way slow the likely speed of recovery down and lose momentum and credibility with the stakeholders of the organization.

Note that stakeholders and the public outside the crisis environment need the information made available to them to be regularly updated as well.

The other focus of interest is that of looking for ways in which the crisis produces positive outcomes for the organization. Such searches often work on three levels:

- improvements to offered products or services;
- improvements to operations and facilities;
- improvements to organizational image.

Obviously each of these areas is somewhat interdependent with the others. An improved product or service can improve the image the organization has with its stakeholders and the surrounding general public.

Undertake ceremonies and celebrations

When the crisis situation draws to a close and recovery processes are in place, managers need to consider again the psychological impacts of the crisis. While being sensitive to the wishes of those affected by the crisis, use of ceremonial acts and celebrations can help signal an end to a particular stage or a state of being, and thus help people to recover.

Ceremonies are usually quiet and somewhat sombre and are often used to remember those who died or were catastrophically affected by the crisis situation. Other ceremonies include award presentations and victim support activities. Appropriate use of these initiatives allows all who attend to draw strength from the presence of each other. *Ceremonies are thus often used to mark an end to the resolution of a crisis and the impacts caused by that crisis.* While most visible ceremonials tend to revolve around significantly public crisis events (the ceremonies after the Hillsborough soccer stadium crowd-crushing crisis, Amsterdam after the El Al aircraft crash), smaller more local efforts can also be used. The concept of having a wake after a funeral, for example, is a smaller and more private activity that has the same effect.

Celebrations are positive moments that are used to signal a positive outcome that is usually at the end of a particular stage of recovery. Moments that may be celebrated can include a return to premises and facilities, opening of new premises and facilities, a return to the organization of those affected by the crisis, and even a thank you to staff and stakeholders for efforts made during response or recovery activities. Four key principles for conducting recovery celebrations are that the celebrations need to:

- be inclusive and not divisive;
- be held as soon as possible to the moment being celebrated;
- have a clear and unambiguous focus;
- have a definitive conclusive moment.

For improved morale and organizational image, the celebrations need to be public and visible. Do not be shy about celebrating a real achievement in the recovery process.

R E A L I T Y   B I T E

Heathrow Terminal One fire, UK, 1997

This case illustrates two elements of crisis management – partial management and how soft information may create additional decision problems.

Background

Heathrow Airport is one of the busiest in the world. The airport handles over 1000 flights per day flying to over 200 destinations. Aircraft take off or land every 90 seconds during peak periods. The four terminals handle around 170 000 travellers a day and over 50 000 people are permanently employed in aircraft and passenger management or in running shops and other service centres. Terminal One handles around 70 000 of the daily passenger flow.

British Airways (BA) is a prime tenant at Heathrow, with half of the airline's mainline operations passing through this airport. Two key centres are set up as part of BA's crisis response management. One is their Operations Control Incident Centre (OCIC). This is the equivalent of an EOC with staff making strategic and tactical crisis response decisions, co-ordinating the effort, and shaping internal and external communication strategies. OCIC personnel work to ensure the protection of the people involved, the corporate reputation and confidence in BA products. The other centre is the Emergency Procedures Information Centre (EPIC) which is an external communications facility set up to handle inquiries and requests. EPIC is designed to handle a 1000-person incident and has 64 telephones that are routed through two telephone exchanges. The facility can be used as a staff contact point for information or deployment instructions.

Incident
At 4.38 am on 12 December 1997, a fire began in the ventilation ducting above a Burger King outlet in Terminal One. By 5.10 am the whole roof of Terminal One was ablaze.

Response
Two brief pictures of the response can be outlined – the emergency response and the partial management response by BA.

Emergency response
From 5.50 am road access to Heathrow was limited to emergency vehicles. This limitation quickly led to gridlock on all main and minor roads by 7.20 am. London Underground suspended commuter train services at 6.30 am which were not restarted until 10.20 am. The fire was deemed out by 9.15 am and inspections inside Terminal One began around 10.05 am. The building was reopened for use at 2.10 pm.

Around 100 firefighters responded to the fire. Flames were reported as high as 50 feet (15 metres). The fire jumped a 50-foot (15-metre) space to ignite a fire in an adjacent building. Around 5 per cent of the terminal building was affected – and most of this was water and smoke damage.

BA response
As a partial manager – in fact a partial partial manager, as BA and the airport authorities were not the lead response agency to handle the fire – BA had to organize around the situation. The OCIC was activated at 5.05 am (just over half an hour from the start of the fire and as the fire was sweeping along the full length of the Terminal One roof). By 6.15 am the OCIC and EPIC were fully operational and had transmitted a global warning about the situation. Within 15 minutes a full evaluation of the possible operational impact was underway, resulting in an operational order to stop all European/domestic flights at 6.45 am.

By 7.30 am a decision was taken to cancel all Terminal One departures until 3.00 pm. As the roads were gridlocked aircraft crews were unable to reach the airport. At 8.40 am statements were issued requesting all customers to rebook and not travel to Heathrow. Flights to Tokyo, San Francisco and Los Angeles were cancelled at 9.05 am due to crew shortages. Terminal Four became congested with passengers, and an outage in Terminal Four check-in systems occurred at 9.50 am.

By 10.15 am evaluation of Terminal One suggested that damage was limited. At 10.45 am, BA agreed with the airport operators to restart at 3.00 pm. Traffic was still gridlocked and there was no restored fire alarm system in Terminal One by 11.30 am so a statement about the restart time was deferred. All inbound European and domestic flights were released by 12.15 pm, and 30 minutes later BA committed to operating all services in the 3.00 pm to 7.00 pm schedules. Check-in at Terminal One recommenced at 3.10 pm.

Statistics

Around 45 000 customers suffered cancelled, diverted or delayed flights. For BA, 14 000 transfer passengers (those moving from one flight to another without leaving the departure flight lounges) suffered disrupted itineraries. The airport operators cancelled 307 flights. Operations were consequentially impacted. The backlog of bookings or rebookings took three days to clear, aircraft crew schedules were disrupted for five days, and integrated flight schedules were disrupted for 48 hours.

All hotels within a 15-mile (24-kilometre) radius from Heathrow were filled by 11.00 am. BA telesales figures rose from 20 283 to 53 264. This meant delays in responding to the telephone calls as the service factor halved (48 per cent answered within 20 seconds, as opposed to 96 per cent in normal conditions).

Comment

This turned out to be a small crisis as the fire did not destroy the whole building and the response management effectively ensured a discontinuity of only 10 hours. While there was still a cost (£5 000 000 or $9 000 000 in revenue loss for the airport operators and airlines involved), the impact fell short of what may have been the case had Terminal One been destroyed.

The fire attracted a degree of media and public attention. This attention was based on the visible impact of the incident upon airport operations and users, the gridlocked roads in the suburbs surrounding the airport, and in the concerns raised by pressure groups over whether the planned fifth terminal at Heathrow would further add to the disruption. One spokesperson noted that the fifth terminal would probably have improved operational continuity.

The Heathrow 1997 fire illustrated the ripple effect in action. Because of the closed access, traffic feeding into Heathrow banked up, gridlocking access points for normal commuter traffic. No one can know what small crisis situations such gridlocks may inflict. Paramedics may be unable to reach ill or dying people. Law enforcement personnel may fail to apprehend criminals. Firefighters may have been unable to respond effectively to calls for help. One effect of the traffic gridlock was that further response personnel, airport staff and BA personnel were unable to reach the airport. While little can be done for those quickly caught in major traffic gridlocks, organizations like BA and the airport operators may need to look for creative solutions – such as getting personnel to nearby helipads and airports and flying the personnel into Heathrow.

The limitations of partial management are illustrated in the corporate response to the fire. While BA personnel had no control over the response to the fire and a return to operations of the airport facilities, the company was able to influence and motivate the airport operators by being a prime user of the facility and through previous productive and co-operative interactions. At the same time, BA as a major user and proponent for construction of a fifth terminal building, was in the firing line from aggrieved pressure groups, unhappy passengers and media interest. Consequently BA executives and managers needed to make timely decisions about restarting services and dealing with pressure groups, passengers and media interest. Note that these three groups have influence over how the reputation and image of BA may be affected.

Management perspective

This focus on ripple effects is salutary for executives and managers. Crisis managers need to look at the knock-on effects or impacts of a crisis event to see how these effects can be reduced or eliminated. Take a few minutes and jot down some of the possible issues you think may need to be considered by an organization like BA. Think of a working airport situation, with passengers coming and going, with storekeepers and service agents operating their businesses, and the myriad of speciality jobs (from ticketing and issuing boarding passes to baggage handling).

One of the reasons for establishing strategic management advisory groups like the PAG outlined in the CMS structure (*see* Chapter 10) is that members of these groups can help identify possible issues and solution options. This enables the crisis manager and operations staff to concentrate on their immediate response activities caused by the crisis.

Executives and managers need to ensure that good relationships can exist with the major response agencies for various situations, and that any contribution to the publicly visible crisis response by their organization appears to be timely and appropriate. In many cases, this consists of reassuring stakeholders (including passengers) of corporate assistance, and in developing temporary strategies to work around crisis-impact blockages (with the agreement of the major crisis managers, where appropriate).

Some of the knock-on or ripple issues that may have been identified by the BA crisis management team included:

- determining whether BA aircraft parked against the building needed protection or removal;
- deciding whether future incoming flights should be prevented from leaving their airports;
- considering what may be done with passengers already at (or arriving at) the airport – BA had around 3000 customers in Terminals Two and Three;
- finding out what could be done for in-flight transit passengers who would be passing from an arrival hall to a departure hall without leaving the airport – BA expected 14 000 transit passengers;
- assessing options for the complete loss of Terminal One – remember crisis management decisions are dynamic and uncertain in nature, and managers need to plan for worst-case and unexpected problems as the crisis is being resolved;
- evaluating how baggage handling could best be done should the baggage system be lost;
- determining the best way of communicating future operational activities with stakeholders (especially staff and passengers). Ideally, the internal communications should be part of an already established policy. Staff should be trained to check in electronically at a given telephone number or e-mail address to find out what they need to do;

- deciding policy on safety issues – such as working in an environment that has no activated fire alarm.

This is a sample of the issues that needed to be considered. Note that some of these issues are 'now' crisis response concerns and others are 'subsequent' crisis recovery decisions. Some organizations may try to combine response and recovery operations. While some personnel may well operate under either structure, the focal concerns and management issues can be quite different. Best policy is to operate response and recovery teams as separate entities – at least in terms of core staffing. Both need to be activated when a physical crisis situation is evident.

In all crisis situations managers need to remember that information is often uncertain and even misleading. This is why emphasis is given to collation and evaluation of information in management structures like CMSS. Take a moment to think about the issues identified above and any other issues from the list you made. What potential information uncertainties or distractions may be deduced?

Four common distractions and uncertainties are as follows:

1 *Speculative statements from the media reporting different return-to-service times.* Once any variation arises or wrong estimates have been reported, any 'correct' information is less likely to be noted by any target audiences.
2 *Internal and external speculation about the cause of the crisis.* Managers need to be able to respond appropriately to different causes when these bear direct threats to those involved in the crisis situation. At the same time, managers need to remain focused on actual response or recovery actions that are within their current control and refuse to be unduly distracted by speculative comments on the causes of the situation.
3 *Speculation about actual damage.* Reports about destroyed property could cause unnecessary communication contacts from passengers on site. Similarly, ongoing speculation about lost equipment and facilities can distract from a co-ordinated response. A preferred process would be to work with early estimates of possible worst-case damage and hone the response and recovery process as these early estimates become refined and firmed by more hard information.
4 *Speculation about health and safety issues.* Such speculation may include:
   - the presence of asbestos – so check building plans and alteration records;
   - lack of safe running water – check existing health and safety regulations: in some countries regulations state that lack of suitable water means no staff may work on the premises; or
   - fears of flash backs or reignition of fire – these can arise especially when fire warning systems are restored and tested.

Three points are worth noting from this sample. First, inaccurate and misleading information is received all the time. Second, information from sources within an organization is more likely to be believed than information from outsiders, thus inaccurate internal information is more likely to cause decision hiatus or decision and action misdirection. Third, unconfirmed reports are likely to become public-domain rumours. Any incorrect or inaccurate information needs to be logged as such and considered in terms of clarification and correction before the information becomes internal or external 'fact'.

Speculation can lead to greater uncertainty and distract managers from focusing on the actual current crisis management issues. This is one reason why crisis management structures need an information processing system (as shown in the INCO and scouts roles in the CMS structure in Chapter 10). Similarly, those being interviewed by media representatives or interacting with members of the public are advised not to speculate or respond to speculative questions (see Chapter 7).

Because of the partial management circumstances for BA, crisis response management was a mix of here-and-now response decisions and recovery programming. Running response and recovery operations using exactly the same team seems attractive. Yet consider other circumstances. Had Terminal One been totally destroyed the operation would have widened to two different processes – one aimed at resolving the here-and-now problems, the other focused upon re-establishing long-term operations until a permanent replacement was constructed. Similarly, had a BA aircraft crashed then the physical recovery operation seems relatively straightforward – acquire a replacement. Crisis management activities, on the other hand, require a high level of stakeholder communication and inter-agency co-operation. Consequently, response and recovery need to be seen as fundamentally different clusters of activities.

References

Barton, L. (1993) *Crisis in Organizations: Managing and Communicating in the Heat of Chaos*. Cincinnati, Ohio: South-Western.

Davis, L. (1993) *Encyclopedia of Natural Disasters*. London: Headline Books.

Flynn, C. and Chalmers, W. (1980) *The Social and Economic Effects of the Accident at Three Mile Island*. Washington, DC: Nuclear Regulatory Commission.

Heath, R. J. (1994) 'Integrating crisis management: some principles and practices', *Abstracts from the First International Congress of Local Authorities Confronting Disasters and Emergencies*. Tel Aviv: IULA, pp. 45–53.

Mitroff, I. I. and Pearson, C. M. (1993) *Crisis Management: A Diagnostic Guide for Improving Your Organization's Crisis-Preparedness*. San Francisco: Jossey-Bass.

Stuart, H. (1993) 'The Newcastle earthquake: local government response', *Macedon Digest*, 7(4), 17–21.

Warford, R. (1994) 'LA quake: Los Angeles City', *Rescue*, 7(3), 36–46.

chapter 15
EXERCISE

Now that you have covered aspects of recovery management and the reaction of people in crisis situations (Chapter 14), return to the Exercise outlined at the end of Chapter 13. Try this exercise using the concepts and knowledge you have gained.

When you have finished the exercise, critically consider the strategies and actions you made and the consequent outcomes. Should you be doing this exercise in a small group, discuss your impressions and criticisms. Remember to acknowledge the positive aspects as well as analyze any 'what went wrong' aspects. If you have already performed the exercise in Chapter 13 and have kept records of what you did and your post-exercise analysis of what was effectively and ineffectively accomplished, compare the outcomes and feelings held then with the outcomes and feelings after doing this exercise. What was done better or worse? Were the outcomes better? Where? How? What led to this difference? Once again you may wish to consider the brief comments made on this exercise on pp. 451–4 in Appendix 2 to help generate your analysis and discussion.

chapter 16

The psychology of recovery

In the previous chapter, great emphasis was placed on involving people in the process of recovery. Such involvement increases the speed with which recovery is made, and increases the quality and quantity of recovery. Involvement is also one of the best ways in which people affected by a crisis can be helped to recover. This chapter, then, focuses on psychological recovery.

Everyone is affected to some degree by the pressures and uncertainties of a crisis situation. Given severe threat, close proximity to death and severe casualties or actual injury from the situation, many may be psychologically displaced. This means that their beliefs about themselves and about the surrounding world are severely shaken or even erased. The mind goes numb and often closes down because of the sharp loss of belief – and because of the overwhelming impact of the crisis situation on the senses of the body and on the ability of the brain to process these stimuli and their associated mental constructs. At the extreme, people in this state may physically shut down and appear in a trance or even physically freeze into rigid shapes.

Most people can recover over time with little assistance. The mind appears to distance the events, and almost allows the events to be forgotten should the exposure have been moderate to light. As an example, most people would suffer a light exposure to crisis distress when passing a car accident in which a person was later reported to be killed. This distress would be a little stronger if they saw a person being treated as they passed, and could become moderate if they were a little involved in the response operation. The distress can become moderate to severe if they were heavily involved in the treatment of the dying person. Finally, the distress may be severe if they were the single person involved in that treatment, if they were directly involved in the accident that caused the death, or that person was a family member or close friend.

Becoming a victim

In Chapter 1, a victim was defined as being anyone who directly or indirectly comes into contact with a crisis situation. This definition did not automatically mean that victims were 'patients' needing 'to be cured'. The broad definition is used to remind executives and managers that everyone is affected to some degree by the pressures, stresses and perceptions encountered during a crisis situation.

Reactions to a crisis

Aftershock

During a crisis, respondents, onlookers and bystanders, and victims encounter experiences that are sharp and painful (in both physical and mental senses). *Aftershock* is the potential reaction a person undergoing a crisis may experience *after the crisis*. In many cases, aftershock emerges as a distancing process, a kind of 'time-out' that allows the brain to come to terms with what has happened. At the extreme, aftershock can produce a complete psychological withdrawal (called a fugue).

Symptoms and indicators of aftershock include:

- periodic or persistent trembling or shivering;
- appearing persistently distracted or absent-minded;
- excessive restlessness or a trance-like lack of motion;
- mental confusion.

Blame

Another major reaction to a crisis or disaster is *blame*. Some victims blame themselves for making a choice of action that went wrong. Others simply blame themselves for being present at the disaster. Thoughts and comments take the form of 'Why did I ...' Behaviours include internalization of guilt that leads to psychological distancing – even catatonic displays – and possibly self-punishment and self-directed anger.

Many blame others. In community situations, an obvious source of blame will be the local government or authority which 'should have protected its members from the disaster or crisis'. Staff from business organizations may similarly blame management for lack of protection and being greedy for profit. Sometimes witch-hunts arise, wherein some person or persons must be found to be responsible, thus purging the rest of an organization or community of blame and allowing them to feel closer to being 'innocent victims'.

Guilt

Some time after a crisis situation, some bystanders and victims will express guilt at being luckier (or more fortunate) than others who were badly affected (even killed) by the crisis. This is termed *survivor guilt*. Survivors often wonder why they and not others survived, and can uneasily recall moments or actions they took that could have been at the expense of those who were not so lucky. Some survivors of recent sea-ferry disasters recalled moving past and stepping over others who seemed unable to save themselves. In storms and wildfires, people who survived and who find that their residences are habitable (or unscathed) often find difficulty in coping with the guilt of being less damaged than those around them. Such guilt can cause isolation and even permanent departure from the site where the disaster happened.

Flashbacks

For many victims, one immediate effect of a crisis is that involuntary *flashbacks* of perceptions of the crisis repeatedly occur. These flashbacks can take the form of exact replays of particular moments or of transplanted flashbacks that apply to a current setting. Thus survivors from the Piper Alpha explosion or the King's Cross Station fire may recall vivid moments at the crisis scene, or may find such recollections are 'updated' to the hospital or home they currently occupy. These latter hallucinations lead to disturbed sleep and increasing anxiety attacks.

Flashbacks and hallucinatory transfers are one way in which the human mind tries to come to terms with intense overloads on its sensory records. While we understand this is so, the result of any persistent flashback and hallucination activity is a victim who becomes increasingly confused, tense, stressed and frustrated. Sleep is disturbed and tempers fracture more easily. Victims become irritable and quick to react to their anxieties. Note that victims in these conditions can include bystanders and volunteer and professional respondents.

When confronted with distressed victims, most people tend to try to console them and stop the victims from crying. Others adopt an abrasive 'pull yourself together' approach. Either approach may not only fail, but can increase feelings of isolation among the recipients and provoke a tendency to withdraw or lash out in frustration. Victims become further locked into a point of view that determines an *us* (those who lived the experience) and *them* (the rest of the world) position. When this position is adopted and affirmed over time, victims are unlikely to deal properly with the surrounding world (because it is a *them* representative).

A preferable approach is simply to listen to what the victims wish to say, imposing no judgemental attitude on their current (or recalled) behaviour. In fact, affirming that feeling upset and disturbed is natural, given the experience of the crisis, actually helps a victim sort out their feelings and beliefs.

397

Ultimately, people need to realize that return to normalcy does not mean a return to the pre-crisis event state. The goal is to get those affected by a crisis situation to be able to accommodate their experiences and be able to cope effectively with the world *in which they now exist.*

Changed beliefs

Beliefs about the world may also be challenged. People can lose confidence in the stability of land when they experience a damaging earthquake where earthquakes rarely happen. Others who experience flood situations take a very long time to forget and become apprehensive when heavy rains fall. Workers caught in a business crisis can find that their basic assumptions about workplace existence are changed. Being made redundant, for an example, can lead to anger over perceived injustices and guilt over failure to hold on to a job, regardless of the precipitating event.

Stress

Aftershock is a product of stress. A crisis generates a number of temporary changes in the physiological and neurophysiological processes within an individual experiencing a crisis.

At the onset of a crisis, the release of adrenalin in the body enables a higher heart rate that delivers more oxygen to muscles for greater muscular output. Other biochemicals released during periods of stress are prolactin and ACT. These hormones or chemicals may be excreted by emotional crying. Release from stress through crying may be one natural way we restore our bodies to normalcy. Some qualitative surveys indicate that 77 per cent of people surveyed (83 per cent females; 73 per cent males) feel better after crying. Females may be more prone to cry simply because of the presence of higher levels of these hormones than males. Some psychiatrists and psychotherapists support any form of crying as a stress release; others warn that crying in public (unless found in acceptable circumstances) may indicate an individual who has lost control and thus could endanger the safety of themselves or others.

Prolonged exposure to stress (or overstress) eventually affects the human body and mind. Physical symptoms associated with overstress include:

- headaches;
- high blood pressure;
- increased aches and pains (particularly aches to the neck and back);
- gastrointestinal upsets (ulcers, colitis, diarrhoea);
- weight loss or weight gain.

The more severe and persistent such symptoms are, the more likely the stress reaction needs to be alleviated.

Overstressed individuals display less ability to function normally. As overstress increases, temper control decreases, restlessness increases and sudden changes in mood can become apparent. Psychological symptoms of overstress may thus include:

- inability to sleep;
- increased loss of temper (irritability, sudden strong outbursts of anger);
- increasing dependence on, or use (abuse) of drugs, alcohol and tobacco;
- problems in making and maintaining relationships;
- sexual problems (impotence and premature ejaculation);
- non-typical behaviour (depression, withdrawal, apathy, hyperexcitability).

Should changes in behaviour persist and begin to disrupt the life of the overstressed individual, or the lives of those around that individual, then a mental health intervention is needed.

Prolonged experience of overstress leads to subtle changes in ability to cope with the surrounding environment. One eventual outcome is a decline in overall health. Long-term declines in health may include:

- decreased immunity (increase in colds, flu, communicable diseases);
- increased vulnerability to heart attacks, strokes, cancer and diabetes;
- increased allergic reactions, including asthma and skin irritations;
- increase in arthritis.

Research studies show responders suffer from stress reactions (Andersen et al., 1991; Taylor and Frazer, 1982). In most cases, this overstress is accretional in that it emerges over a number of response incidents including responses to crisis situations.

Factors that can modify and reduce the impacts and effects of stress include the following:

- the amount of training and experience held by the person – however, familiarity and ability to cope with crisis situations may be offset by cumulative stress that leads to burnout;
- the degree to which the situation may be objectively managed – this is less likely if the crisis situation has a real overwhelming nature;
- the life status held by the person – this status includes their current perceptions and beliefs about their work pressure and personal life situation, as well as the residual or left-over stress that they bring into the crisis situation;
- the psychological traits and states held by the person – this includes their underlying psychopathology, coping mechanisms and tolerance of stress;
- the availability and degree of support available to a person – this support may be a combination of formal and informal support from the organization, colleagues and family and friends.

Executives and managers need to establish appropriate programmes for counselling and stress reduction, as this can improve the morale and loyalty of the workforce and reduce loss of work effort due to ill-health or resignations. Equally, availability of these programmes may have a positive impact in any subsequent claims for compensation.

Crisis-induced and post-crisis stress may increase when:

- children are involved;
- respondents and victims are not mentally prepared;
- informational certainty is low;
- respondents and victims perceive their own safety and lives are under threat;
- colleagues are injured or dead;
- long periods of waiting before acting are present;
- the site provides strong tactile or cognitive impressions of threat and destruction;
- the size and scale of the event appears overwhelming;
- vital equipment fails and adds to the damage or impedes response action;
- co-ordination between people and organizations is impaired;
- executives, managers and even on-site team leaders show little support.

On looking through the above list, executives and managers can reduce stress by:

- providing pre-crisis mental preparation and instruction in stress reduction (from relaxation training to improving lifestyles);
- ensuring as much hard information is available as possible;
- by employing a range of post-crisis stress reduction strategies – from informal peer interaction to more formal programmes run by properly qualified and capable professionals.

However, with or without outside assistance, most people employ instinctive and often non-optimal coping strategies.

How people cope

Many people who experience crisis-induced stress try to sort themselves out on their own. Many instinctively choose informal debriefing approaches. They usually talk about their experiences with colleagues – especially with those that were involved in the same crisis and in the same response effort. Less frequently, they talk through the experiences with family members, other relations or with friends. This latter strategy is less likely to be used, partly because of perception of *us* versus *them* (those who were there versus those who were not there) and partly because people often believe that they should be able to cope with the stress without showing such weakness to others. As a result, instinctive stress-reduction discussions are restricted to colleagues. This tacit rejection of family and friends can add to the stress of the overstressed individual, leading to withdrawal, separation and estrangement. Similarly the rejection estranges family and friends who may feel unwanted. Long-term, the fall in communication of experiences and feelings can lead to friendships ceasing and divorce, and this further isolates an increasingly stressed individual.

In coping with stress, people may move toward substance dependency. They may drink more alcohol, smoke more tobacco or consume more prescription and non-prescription drugs. Those that do seek medical help often are treated with prescription relaxants or 'downers' to help them sleep or with stimulants or 'uppers' to help them concentrate. None of these approaches are particularly optimal in terms of reducing stress – they simply mask the effects and can even increase the problems faced by those using such strategies.

Generally, the root cause of stress is psychological. Respondents, witnesses, victims and survivors have trouble fitting their experience back into a big picture of the situation. Experiences get relived, often in great and sharply painful detail, as the mind tries to come to terms with the experience. People experiencing such inability to let go of one or more sharp experiences of a crisis event tend to develop behaviour that reflects both the trauma and the stress involved.

Two central problems emerge in this condition. The first problem is that the recollections distract the person from what they subsequently are doing. This not only has safety concerns but also creates some distancing and watchfulness among those around them that, in turn, irritates the stressed person.

Second, the distracting recollections can become quite intrusive. The seemingly continuous cycle of intrusive thoughts can erode confidence in beliefs that an individual holds about themselves, how they interact with the world and their ability to cope with the situations they are in. This is covered by a term called *self-efficacy*. The erosion of pre-crisis beliefs leads to the person adopting new beliefs based on the potentially distorted information gained from the crisis experiences. This change can happen due to the fact that people tend to seek information and evidence that supports and confirms their judgement. They rarely seek evidence that disconfirms their judgement. This is called *confirmatory bias*. As a result, they confirm the weak or ineffective state suggested by their perceptions and recollections of the crisis and by the physically distracted and disturbed state in which they may find themselves.

Those suffering from stress can be placed into three categories according to the duration of interference to their lifestyles. These are:

- acute stress (symptoms last up to three months from event);
- chronic stress (symptoms are present beyond three months);
- delayed onset (wherein symptoms begin to appear six months after the event).

The latter two cases often produce symptoms that define post-traumatic stress disorder (PTSD – *see* below) that may require professional help over a lengthy period. Early intervention that prevents the onset of PTSD is socially, economically and personally desirable.

Critical incident stress debriefing

Critical incident stress debriefing (CISD) is one way of counselling emergency service personnel and crisis respondents (Mitchell, 1983; Mitchell and Dyregrov, 1993). In this sense 'debriefing' is focused on the feelings of those undertaking the process, as opposed to the conventional use of debriefing in which people are interviewed to gain all possible facts of a situation. The approach is also used with victims and bystanders and generally involves four possible interventions in which people unpack their remembered experiences under guidance from a properly trained facilitator. The four interventions are:

- on-site
- defusing
- formal CISD
- follow-up CISD.

On-site debriefing has participants sorting and sifting through their thoughts and feelings while the associated stimuli from the site are present. Primary focus is on developing a less distorted 'perspective' by identifying the stimuli, the consequent feelings and thoughts, and seeking to place actions, thoughts, feelings and events within a bigger picture. This helps participants normalize their experiences and distance their consequent reactions to subsequent recollections and intrusive thoughts.

Defusing is done in an informal setting and conducted within a group. Group members tell each other their personal 'war stories', taking the opportunity to release emotional and cognitive insights in the process. Effective defusing depends on the amount of trust members of the group hold in each other and in the facilitator. The facilitator is often a senior and experienced group member. Defusing has a number of potential problems. New members to a group are less likely to participate, for example, or may filter their expressions of thoughts and feelings. Should senior group members be responsible for performance and promotion evaluations, then other group members are less likely to reveal all their thoughts and feelings. Defusing sessions can generate other organizational problems, ranging from substance abuse to growth of group cohesion to a level at which aggressive elitism against non-members of that group is practised.

Formal debriefing is best facilitated by a trained and empathic mental health professional. The process generally has seven stages:

- an initiating stage in which the process is explained and rules of participation are developed;
- recreating the actualities or facts of the event (where participants were and what each participant saw, heard, smelled, touched, did);
- outlining first thoughts;
- describing the consequent feelings and reactions;
- an assessment of the event in which group and individual support and

understanding enables a more 'normal' and adjusted perception of the experience of the event;

- some education in stress response indicators and stress management;
- re-entry to likely demands and POVs of the outside world.

The process is usually conducted in small groups around a table in a quiet room. The facilitators sit as far from the door as possible to allow those involved to feel they can quickly leave the room without passing authority. Emotionally, participants are likely to feel a slump in their morale and emotional states as they relive their own experiences and listen to the experiences of the other participants. Morale and emotional states increase, however, as participants uncover three important 'facts' for themselves:

- that feeling hurt and angry is acceptable;
- that they are not alone in their experiences (as they find common ground in perceptions and feelings);
- that their post-crisis feelings of separateness and estrangement from the world around them are normal and to be expected, given the sharp experiences of the crisis situation.

The process starts with a cognitive level of introduction and facts. People are asked to express their thoughts and the decisions they took during the event. They may feel upset and confused as they react to what they just experienced. Other members of the group are likely to verbally identify with these feelings and with the experiences. This sharing and support leads participants to realize that others feel the same way – they are not alone. As people come to terms with their experience, facilitators begin to prepare them for re-entry into the outside world.

Follow-up debriefing begins at least two days (48 hours) after an event, and is used either to work with those previously not debriefed or as a post-debrief process for those needing further help. While the process is very much the same, greater effort is needed to move past rationalized fact to real fact, as participants have had time to interpret and filter the original stimuli of the actual event.

Problems

There are a number of concerns about CISD. First, the process itself is less than systematically evaluated (Silove, 1992). Brom, Kleber and Hofman (1993) reported the results of a randomized treatment control study on preventing post-traumatic stress disorder. They found no significant differences between the treatment group of 68 people (who underwent three sessions of counselling) and a non-treated control group of 83 people. One problem with this study (and with many similar findings) is that the treatment started one month after the incident, and not from the 24-hour to 72-hour initial intervention recommended by most CISD and PTSD practitioners. On the other hand, Hytten and Hasle (1989) found high levels of competence and access to debriefing are favourable factors in coping with stress. They sampled 58 volunteer and 57 professional firefighters who participated in rescues of 114 people in a 12-storey hotel in which 14 people died.

A second concern is how CISD should be performed in an organizational setting. Should the facilitators come from the organization, then those undergoing debriefing may worry whether the facilitators and debriefed materials may be used in future evaluation and promotion of those being debriefed. Facilitators from the same organization may be seen as outsiders should their experience and conditions of work differ from those being debriefed. On the other hand, should the facilitators come from another (outside) organization, then trust may be low as the facilitators may be seen as outsiders. Current best practice is to develop a relationship with an outside group of professional facilitators so that trust is established and those who may need debriefing in the future may perceive the process is independent from management and personnel systems.

Perhaps the most important concern is whether the emphasis on access to debriefing and crisis counselling (especially in the Western world) makes any difference. Opponents see the rush to provide crisis counselling as costly and often ineffective. High-profile American opponents have suggested that millions of people and hundreds of thousands of soldiers from the First and Second World Wars received no counselling and coped successfully, and that people surviving crisis situations in less developed countries appear to recover without extensive counselling facilities.

The problem with these superficially appealing claims is that the claims are equally untested. In the argument about the world wars we need to reduce the large vague numbers down to those that actually saw combat and civilian populations that encountered acts of war. Three observations may correct this POV:

1 Combat personnel did suffer psychological impairment. Look at the 'lack of moral fibre' questions or the American Armed Service psychiatric treatment records. Speak with veterans, and many of them show remnants of thought disturbance about experiences from fifty years ago.
2 Counselling services were not broadly available at the time.
3 Given the larger rural population and the stronger sense of community prevailing before the fast transport and cities promoted a depersonalized living environment, people from the wars may have coped better with critical natural disasters and combat situations.

Similar arguments can be made for the coping skills of large populations in less developed countries. In either case, the argument is far too general. Where many cope, some will not.

The real problem is the quality of the counselling. Too many situations have well-meaning but poorly trained and inexperienced people offering help. In the TWA 800 aircraft accident off New York, variable advice given to passengers flying out from the airport after the accident probably increased stress among some passengers rather than allaying fears brought on by the proximity of the accident. Likewise counsellors sometimes forget the basic tenet of good counselling which is to leave the client feeling better or at least no worse for the experience. Any counselling and debriefing effort needs to convey four significant cognitive points to any recipient:

1 It is okay to feel hurt and anger and to express these feelings.
2 It is quite natural to feel temporarily estranged or separate from the surrounding world due to the experiences.
3 They are not alone in their feelings – others have similar hurt and anger.
4 They will get better. No matter how bad they currently feel, or even if they feel worse later on, they will get better.

This last point is important. People who believe they are going to get better have a far greater chance of actually becoming physically and mentally better.

Executives and managers of communities need to make every effort to obtain properly qualified and experienced professionals for intervention strategies and guidance. On a fundamental level, organizations can improve stress management through situational awareness programmes that focus on likely experiences in given crisis situations, improving coping skills through skill training, providing training in stress management skills and by developing fundamental debriefing skills among their own personnel.

Post-traumatic stress disorder

Traumatic experiences reshape the beliefs and behaviours of those unable to renormalize their experiences. Many accept that their experience deviates from the normal and gradually release the memory of the experienced stimuli. Others use religious and philosophical belief systems to explain or avoid the outcomes of the crisis experience. Some find themselves haunted by their experience. They persistently relive moments from it and are reminded about conditions or events by normal everyday stimuli. As a result, these people feel less able to cope with their changed existence and increasingly feel:

● frustrated by repeated replays of events;
● unable to control their post-crisis state of being;
● isolated and alone as the rest of the world moves on seemingly unchanged and uncaring;
● lacking in self-worth due to what happened in the crisis event or due to changed beliefs about themselves in their post-crisis world.

These feelings combine to promote increasing levels of self-doubt and can lead to sudden eruptions of anger. These sudden eruptions also show the sufferers that they are not in control of their lives, leading to ever tightening closed-circuits of anger, self-doubt and questions within themselves about why they cannot come to terms with the experiences and return to their pre-crisis state of being.

Individuals experiencing post-event trauma display a number of symptoms and report further symptomatic cognitive activities. These include:

- recurrent and intrusive recollections of the event or moments from that event;
- recurrent and distressing dreams in which the event is replayed and even exacerbated;
- intense distress or physiological reactions to trigger stimuli that evoke the crisis experience;
- persistence in avoiding stimuli that trigger recollections or potential reliving of the crisis experience;
- attempts to avoid thoughts, feelings or talking about the crisis event and their experiences within that event;
- reported amnesia about the crisis event and experiences associated with it;
- diminished responses to the outside world (often termed *psychic numbing* or *emotional amnesia*);
- lack of participation in or enjoyment of pre-crisis activities and pre-crisis beliefs;
- feelings of emotional detachment or foreshortened existence;
- marked reduction in emotional interactions with those close to the sufferer.

Further specific details can be found in the *Diagnostic and Statistical Manual of Mental Disorders* – DSM–IV (American Psychiatric Association, 1994). One means of identifying PTSD can be via the Hopkins Symptom Checklist (HSCL). This checklist includes most of the DSM–III criteria for PTSD. Other psychological tests that can prove useful include the Horowitz Impact Event Scale (HIES) and the Diagnostic Interview Schedule (DIS). Properly qualified personnel need to perform this testing and evaluation.

Planning psychological recovery

Kristoffersen (1992) claims that support services need to be integrated into the organization rather than come from the outside. He finds that the advantages for doing this include:

- better accessibility;
- more effective follow-up;
- reduction in stigmatization;
- increased confidence of employees;
- effective signal of care from management;
- positive effect on the working environment.

The obvious advantages are those of better accessibility and more effective follow-up as the internal availability means an ongoing, less public process of stress counselling can be undertaken. A major disadvantage may arise from placing stress counsellors within management positions – a consequent suspicion that these managers may base future promotion and employment decisions upon advice or information about an individual's 'weakness'.

Three approaches to providing stress management need to be integrated in order to provide effective stress management. These are:

- education;
- peer support;
- crisis intervention teams.

Educating people to become aware of the stresses involved in their work and in ways they can reduce their stress is important. Education means that people can be ready for a crisis and the impacts of that crisis, and thus may prove more resilient and be less affected by these impacts.

Peer support involves a close to hand yet approachable person who can help reduce stress. Durlack (1979) finds that this is a proven way of establishing support for response personnel. The peer supporters need to be carefully selected and well trained. Alongside peer support strategies there needs to be some formal debriefing processes (Dyregrov, 1989; Mitchell, 1983). Where the peer support personnel may feel (or be) inadequate, professional crisis intervention teams with psychologists and psychiatrists can provide expert knowledge and help.

Stress management programmes

These programmes need to be based on principles of confidentiality, independence and impartiality. The actual processes used need to become part of the SOP (standard operating procedure) and not something novel and awkwardly produced. Any programmes have to apply to all personnel, otherwise the people most needing help can avoid such assistance and the process will fold through lack of employee commitment. Any programme needs to make early contact when a crisis situation has occurred, and be available as soon as possible after the stress-inducing event. Counselling support personnel need to be different people to those controlling or managing the situation or the routine operations of the organization – otherwise employees will see any real use of the counselling process as a threat to their security within the organization. While not functioning as active support providers, managers need to be educated in identifying stress symptoms and in providing secondary support for their staff.

Any provision of support programmes needs to be extended to the families of staff involved in the incident, as the families will also receive stress from contact with the stressed person. These programmes may include support meetings, peer support and provision of information.

Some basic approaches to dealing with traumatized and overstressed people

In the field:

- Give water.
- Do not use victimizing statements.
- Talk clearly and simply.
- Do not lie to the person.
- Talk in the language level of the victim.
- Touch the person only with permission.
- Shield from onlookers.
- Do not nag.
- Ask them how they feel and think.
- Do not take on their pain.
- Allow them to be silent if this is what they wish.

Dealing with stressed people

Look out for:

- Change of normal behaviour.
- Blank expression.
- Mood swings.
- Inability to concentrate.
- Overactivity.
- Trance-like withdrawal
- Inability to sleep.
- Emotionality.
- Apathy.

Basic response steps include:

- Remain calm.
- Do not ridicule the feelings or POV of the person.
- Calm the person.
- Show understanding.
- Reassure them that 'they will get better'.
- Provide warm drinks.
- Enlist peer support.
- Find a suitable job for them to do.

Severe stress reactions can include:

- Repeated nausea/vomiting.
- Loss of bodily control (especially motor extremities).
- Failure to do job.

- Guilt.
- Excessive use of comforters or compensators (alcohol, tobacco, drugs).

Basic response for severe cases may include:

- Keep with team but away from actions that may cause further stress.
- Try to get person to rest (sleep).
- Treat as a person not as a patient.
- Enlist peer support.

References

American Psychiatric Association (1994) *Diagnostic and Statistical Manual of Mental Disorders: DSM–IV*, 4th edn. Washington DC: American Psychiatric Association.

Andersen, H. S., Christensen, A. K. and Petersen, G. O. (1991) 'Post-traumatic stress reactions amongst rescue workers after a railway accident', *Anxiety Research*, 4, 245–51.

Brom, D., Kleber, R. and Hofman, M. (1993) 'Victims of traffic accidents: incidence and prevention of post-traumatic stress disorder', *Journal of Clinical Psychology*, 49, 131–40.

Durlack, J. A. (1979) 'Comparative effectiveness of paraprofessional and professional helpers', *Psychological Bulletin*, 88, 80–90.

Dyregrov, A. (1989) 'Caring for helpers in disaster situations: psychological debriefing', *Disaster Management*, 2, 25–30.

Hytten, K. and Hasle, A. (1989) 'Firefighters: a study of stress and coping', *Acta Psychologica* (Scandanavian Supplement), 80(355), 50–5.

Kristoffersen, J. I. (1992) *Caring for Emergency Personnel – Organizational Challenges*. Paper presented at the World Conference on Trauma and Tragedy: International Society for Traumatic Stress Studies, Amsterdam, 21–26 June.

Mitchell, J. T. (1983) 'When disaster strikes ... the critical incident stress debriefing process', *Journal of Emergency Medical Services*, 8, 36–9.

Mitchell, J. and Dyregrov, A. (1993) 'Traumatic stress in disaster workers and emergency personnel', in Wilson, J. P. and Raphael, B. (eds), *International Handbook of Traumatic Stress Syndromes*. New York: Plenum Press, pp. 905–14.

Silove, D. (1992) 'Psychotherapy and trauma', *Current Opinion in Psychiatry*, 5, 470–4.

Taylor, A. J. and Frazer, A. G. (1982) 'The stress of post disaster body handling and victim identification work', *Journal of Human Stress*, 8, 4–12.

17

Assessing and evaluating crisis management

This chapter looks at one of the most important aspects of crisis manage-ment that executives and managers need to fully endorse. Evaluation and assessment of what happened and what was done to resolve the situation is important because such efforts:

- help identify what happened – a cognitive and a culpability goal;
- look for what can be done to prevent the crisis from happening again – a reduction goal; and
- consider what can be done to improve the response and recovery activities and management – a readiness, response and recovery goal.

Evaluation helps people learn from the experience. If done carefully and ob-jectively, evaluation produces positive conclusions that can lead to better struc-tures, better systems and more effective response and recovery management.

Assessing and evaluating crisis management

Improvements in crisis avoidance or reduction, readiness, response and recov-ery are not the only motivations for executives and managers to support effec-tive evaluation practices. Governments and legal systems are placing increasing attention on issues of due diligence (Albrecht, 1996; Schreider, 1996), organizational liability (Allinson, 1993; Cohen, 1991; Schreider, 1996) and duty of care responsibilities. This increased attention means that organ-ization executives and managers need to establish more clearly and in more detail what happened, what was done and what evidence negates any organ-izational liability or negligence.

Up till now, however, evaluation methods have been sporadic and unevenly applied. Two central approaches are usually applied – those of accident investigators and those of criminal investigators. Few investigations are as rigorous as the aircraft crash investigations conducted by many Western countries – particularly Britain, the United States, Canada and Australia. Many evaluations tend to be *ad hoc* managerial-level actions until a public inquiry is forced upon the post-crisis situation. Once a public inquiry is undertaken, however, attention tends to shift from objectively determining what happened and what was done (in an effort to improve these aspects) toward a search for wrong-doing and guilty people. This is particularly true when inquiries are given scope for identifying guilt, are conducted by senior members of the legal profession or are supported by law enforcement personnel as investigators.

For maximum benefit, executives and managers need to separate an inquiry that has the goals of reducing crisis situations and improving on crisis management from any activity aimed at identifying guilty people and delivering punishment or censure.

Existing literature appears unhelpful, with few attempts to establish principles of evaluation beyond summary checklists (Albrecht, 1996; Barton, 1993). There are four reasons for the lack of theory and practice in establishing rigorous evaluation procedures:

1 Most effort is still placed on developing crisis management.
2 The objectives of evaluation become blurred.
3 Evaluation is used to find a scapegoat.
4 Organizational management encourages secrecy.

Each of these reflects an underlying concern that a thorough evaluation may produce knowledge that managers and executives do not want to have and which they certainly do not want people outside the organization to have.

Most effort is still placed on developing crisis management

The argument here is that crisis management is:

- too poorly established to permit methodical evaluation;
- too recent to expect appropriate evaluation practices; or
- too important and urgent to waste time on non-contributory efforts such as conducting detailed evaluation.

There probably is a fourth factor that emerges from the physical and mental effects of being involved in a crisis situation. Once the crisis is over and the consequential impact damage seems to be getting fixed, those involved become physically tired and mentally want to return quickly to a pre-crisis type of normalcy.

These arguments appear weak on inspection. Skills and procedures are not developed without conscious or unconscious evaluation of cause-and-effect consequences. None of us learn to walk without assessing what worked and

411

what did not work too well as we develop from passive wriggling to crawling to being able to walk. Successful sportspeople do not achieve success from unthinking training. Evaluation assists in learning effective skills that improve performance. Similarly, evaluation is undertaken – no matter how simply – from the moment actions are being performed. So the relative recency of modern crisis management should not be used to excuse poor evaluation practices, and effort placed in post-situation evaluation can improve response and recovery performance.

The objectives of evaluation become blurred

Evaluation can be used for two central objectives:

- to establish what happened to improve resilience;
- to establish what was handled poorly or done incorrectly and so identify and punish the guilty.

While these objectives seem to involve the same process, once people perceive that a scapegoat is being sought or that a legitimate search for wrong-doers is underway, they refuse to talk or reduce the detail they give to protect themselves. Executives and managers need to separate the two objectives if they wish to gain detailed information that can be used to reduce the risk of future crisis situations and improve the handling of those situations when they occur. Punishment and blaming do not encourage people to evaluate and inform honestly and openly on what happened.

Evaluation is used to find a scapegoat

Allinson (1993) states that the search for a scapegoat to blame for the crisis can distract from a full investigation, particularly in non-natural disaster crisis situations. Other factors that may have produced the crisis may be left unsought once a scapegoat is successfully identified. Allinson finds that 'whenever a scapegoat is searched for or cited as the cause of any catastrophe, one may be duly suspicious whether the true culprit or culprits have been found' (p. 11). Seeking a scapegoat also lowers the amount of help and information an inquiry receives. As noted previously, once a search for guilty people is seen to be taking place, people become wary and self-protective, and maintain a low profile to avoid any chance of being the scapegoat.

Organizational management encourages secrecy

Most attempts at secrecy by members of organizations probably arise because they feel that people outside the organization may not tolerate error or misjudgement. People seem secretive about their actions when they feel threatened by criticism or vulnerable to blame. Part of the explanation for this reticence is the growing perception by organizations involved in crisis situations that admission of error or being blamed may lead to criminal charges such as corporate manslaughter or costly litigation. There is also some need for delays in releasing information. The validity of information needs to be checked and often executives and managers need to assess whether the release of particular information harms the crisis management or those involved in the crisis. Business and government organizations also need to respect issues of confidentiality and protect corporate assets and customised processes from indiscriminate access.

Evaluating crisis situations and crisis management

Any evaluation of a crisis situation and its management is shaped by how carefully investigators pay attention to three characteristics that define the evaluation. These characteristics are:

- the scope of the evaluation;
- the ability to understand the situation;
- the reliability of the evidence.

Investigators who lose sight of one or more of these characteristics can find that their investigation changes shape, loses objectivity and becomes enmeshed in confused detail.

The scope

As noted earlier, two basic types of investigation exist. These are a search for:

- improving crisis management and reducing the chances of future crisis through better design, maintenance and training;
- the guilty (or even a scapegoat) and the initiation of legal proceedings against them.

As both types of evaluation use the same or a parallel path of identifying the cause of the crisis and assessing the effectiveness of the response (and recovery) management, the missions of making the situation safer and establishing guilt can easily blur together. Drabek and Quarantelli (1967) consider that assignment of blame fosters an illusion that corrective action is taking place.

Once people perceive that an inquiry into cause and effect is being used to identify the guilty, at least two behavioural reactions take place. First, people who feel they could be guilty (or know they are guilty) will avoid implicating themselves. They will do this by editing or distorting any information they may give to protect themselves. Second, staff and management of organizations may protect the image of those organizations by omitting information that is prejudicial or perceived as potentially damaging to the image of their organization.

Executives and managers need to it make clear that judgements about guilt will not be made in the evaluation process set up to improve crisis management. By clearly communicating and continually demonstrating the non-judgemental process involved in a search for improvement, people *may* give more information about what happened and what was done. Consequently, managers and executives need to clearly and publicly outline the precise scope and objectives of an inquiry and ensure that these are met.

The situation

Having defined the scope of the evaluation, those involved in the inquiry need help in understanding the limitations and pressures that exist in a crisis situation. The quiet of air-conditioned court rooms and the long periods of time investigations can take when compared with the duration of a crisis situation can mislead investigators and observers into believing that objective and balanced management could have existed in the situation. By definition, crisis situations are situations in which:

- demand for resources exceeds the available resources;
- time to resolve the situation is very limited or appears to be very limited;
- information is limited and potentially unreliable; and
- a threat to the safety of people and their resources exists or appears to exist.

None of these criteria are likely to promote cool and calm environments in which to make and enact crisis-managing decisions. To these pressures may be added distracting noise, extraneous and non-pertinent communication exchanges, smells, movement and even flashing lights.

While investigators are unlikely to be able to recreate the environment in which a crisis resolution was attempted, they can try to establish aspects of the environments for themselves and others. These attempts can include:

- audio-visual recording of crisis management as that management performs;
- audio-visual recording of the post-crisis environment and management;
- ensuring that investigators or evaluators arrive at the crisis situation as soon as the crisis response or recovery management is activated;
- having those assessing the findings of the investigation visit the site or sites so that they can develop some physical and mental picture of the situation.

Some of these actions raise issues of health and safety, confidentiality and the 'compresence' effect on those involved when audio-visual recordings are made of their interactions, decisions, actions and behaviours. *A compresence effect* arises when people are so conscious of being observed that the observation inhibits or changes their behaviours and actions.

Some law enforcement agencies use dedicated audio-visual units to record major incidents. Many firefighting agencies try to get experienced evaluators to the scene of a fire, although these people tend to fully focus on establishing the source and cause of a fire and not on how the firefighting is managed.

The evidence

Investigators need to be very aware of the fallibility of eyewitness testimony. Research into eyewitness reliability and the effects of biases on memory and judgement suggests that people are unreliable witnesses and their memories are likely to be influenced by a number of biases.

Eyewitness fallibility

Humans are poor eyewitnesses. As a result, investigators try to gain a picture from a large number of eyewitnesses whenever possible. Even this may not be a safe practice. Of the thousands of witnesses interviewed after an aircraft accident at a Farnborough Airshow in the UK, only around one per cent had the correct sequence of the accident. In an experiment in the USA, an aircraft flew twice over several hundred conference delegates, most of whom were incorrect in their reports on the direction the aircraft had flown and the simple aerial manoeuvres it had performed. The delegates were participants in a conference on aircraft accidents.

Unreliability in testimony may arise from a number of sources, including:

- *lack of preparedness* – the event happens without warning;
- *uncertain memory* – the event is too quick or too unimportant for the witness to remember;
- *misdirection* – the witness confuses compass directions and even right or left handedness;
- *incorrect terminology* – a witness causes confusion through trying to use correct technical terms rather than simple language (confusion of port and starboard, specialist terminologies used incorrectly);
- *rationalization* – a witness creates an acceptable story that fits the facts, even if the sequence of the facts is changed or some facts are changed or omitted;
- *convergence* – a witness accepts the version of others (for example, broadcast interviews overheard) and realigns her or his testimony;
- *suggestibility* – a witness changes the facts to agree with the statements of a significant person;
- *recall consolidation* – a witness recalls a number of points or facts so often that other points or facts become omitted or forgotten;
- *heuristic or stereotypic recall* – a witness recalls facts according to most-likely stereotypes or common rules of thumb (for example, red-haired people are violent therefore the red-head made the threat; young people drive too fast therefore the young driver must have been driving too fast);
- *memory decay* – facts change in importance and clarity of recall over time.

This list assumes that the eyewitness is normal and has no deficiency in any of her or his senses. Field investigators have generally found that males want to be seen as expert in what they witnessed and thus over-interpret their facts. Females are traditionally uncertain over technical details and seem more ready to converge or change their opinions. The best but legally questionable witnesses appear to be boys aged between 11 and 13. These boys have sufficient command of language to be coherent but have not yet started to wish to be seen as expert in what they witness.

Biases

Biases in human memory and judgement include primacy effects, recency and hindsight (Hogarth, 1981). *Primacy effects* stem from reception of strong and vivid images and signals. Graphic pictures of victims from aircraft crashes, for example, make most people more fearful about their chances of injury or death when using aircraft than of injury and death from domestic accidents, yet many more deaths and injuries result from domestic accidents than from aircraft crashes. *Recency effects* stem from the weight and easier recall of recent experiences when compared with experiences from some time ago. *Hindsight biases* (*see* further below) can influence the evidence of witnesses *and* the judgements of those evaluating the crisis incident and crisis management. This is because the witnesses, investigators and evaluators know causal outcome consequences involved.

Hindsight biases

Fischhoff (1975) is one of several researchers who find that given the historic information on an event, people tend to revise their beliefs about that event. People thus become 'wise' after an event and this wisdom may lead to failure to work with only the information available to managers and respondents *during* a crisis situation. Hindsight biases can be seen at work when information about the subsequent cause-and-consequence chain of a situation is used to evaluate the information, choices or actions made at some earlier point in that chain.

Hindsight effects can be seen in many critical commentaries on crisis situations. In the *Challenger* and Flight 103 disasters, for example, trails of warnings and danger signals were present, but *only when the outcome of events beyond a given incident or action is consulted.* Anger over the trail of memoranda warning about potential failure of the O-rings on the engines of *Challenger* seems justified. Indeed, concerns were raised over the information sifting that took place as decisional information was passed up the management chain. In reality, many of these actions are lost in a system and often emerge as part of either guilty confessions or position protection *only after a crisis situation happens.* Allison (1993) argues that this lack of open disclosure is a root cause of people-induced problems. This argument, however, does not really take into account the current realities of organizational psychology and community cultures. The facts that people do not like to hear bad news, and their personal status and even their employment may be endangered through adopting a contrary stance suggest that messages may be delayed, changed or lost.

In hindsight, warnings about a pending terrorist attack on an aircraft from the USA made prior to the terrorist bombing of Pan American Flight 103 in 1988 seem to have been ignored or undervalued. Given the information available at that time, however, could a real threat be distinguished from a false threat? In 1988, the number of terrorist threats exceeded 1500 in the United States alone. How much validity can we give a signal that *something may happen* when many such signals are found to be false? Had Pan Am cancelled all flights because of a *potential* threat, no Pan Am aircraft would have been destroyed. Many of the people making the hindsight judgement that Pan Am should not have flown their passenger aircraft may then have declared this action to have been an over-reaction as no aircraft were bombed. Of course, once Pan Am resumed flying aircraft the bombing may still have happened at a later date.

The chairman of the inquiry into the Clapham rail disaster in England identified concerns over the effects of hindsight in post-crisis evaluation. He found that 'hindsight also possesses a lens that can distort and can therefore present a misleading picture: it has to be avoided if fairness and accuracy of judgement are to be sought.' (Hidden, 1989, p. 3). This concern is real. Too often people take post-situation knowledge of outcomes and postulate the presence of more insight into the real state of the situation than can actually exist given the uncertain and pressured exchanges of information taking place during a crisis. After analyzing seven human-connected disasters, Bignell, Peters and Pym (1977) find that hindsight information comes much easier to mind in assessing the cause and effect than *insight*. Insight requires more mental effort that continues past confirmation of intuitive or hindsight-based conclusions.

The effect of hindsight biases may be reduced by:

- establishing a sequential cause-and-effect chain that remains focused upon the situational facts at each cause-and-effect link;
- attempting to recreate the actual set of events or cause-and-effect links;
- attempting to establish the quantity and quality of information available at each significant decision and action point (or node) in the crisis cause-and-effect chain;
- separating intuitive findings from hard factual information;
- searching for other solutions beyond hindsight-induced and obvious findings.

The key process is to try to follow in the footsteps of those involved with the crisis situation, see what they saw and work with the 'facts' as these became apparent. Complex investigations often use cause-and-effect information to simulate the crisis situation. One example of this situation re-creation is the aircraft accident investigators who use black-box information to reproduce what was happening in the moments before a crash happened.

Crisis events and time distortion

Each person's sense of time may become warped or distorted by the intensity of a crisis experience. Sensations and happenings may appear to take longer than they do in reality – time forms an *expansionary distortion* experience for those people. Most people who experience the shaking of an earthquake exaggerate the duration of shaking by between four and ten times the real duration. Thus a quake lasting 5 to 10 seconds may *feel* like 20 to 100 seconds. Due to the motion sensitivity of the human body, people can report movements felt from earthquakes that are between five and 50 times the size of the actual motion.

Expansionary distortion may also emerge when adrenalin fatigue and tiredness sets in or when those experiencing intense events try to report sequentially all that happened. So much is recorded, felt, cognitively processed and reacted to that they have trouble relating recalled data to a time sequence. One historical example of this expansionary distortion was reported by Samuel Pepys when recalling the Great Fire of London (1666). He stated:

> And I lay down and slept a good night about midnight – though when I rose, I hear that there had been a great alarme of French and Dutch being risen – which proved nothing. But it is a strange thing to see how long this time did look since Sunday, having been always full of variety of actions, and little sleep, that it looked like a week or more. And I had forgot almost the day of the week. (Latham, 1990, p. 666)

This shows the distortion brought on by nervous stimulation, cognitive overloading and tiredness. Pepys reports feeling that the fire had been going for 'a week or more' instead of the four days. This is a common distortion when crises are serious and prolonged. Incidentally, another outcome of crisis situations and the confused and uncertain information these situations produce is rumour. This extract shows rumour was present in 'I hear there had been a great alarme of French and Dutch being risen'.

With the sensory impressions, thoughts and actions made during a crisis, time may become compressed, as if the whole experience was of a very short duration. This is *compressionary distortion*. Sudden change often freezes humans and animals and seconds appear as milliseconds in which to act. Crisis managers are likely to experience compressionary distortion.

The effect of time distortion may be reduced by:

- accepting that time frames may warp through expansion or compression;
- establishing more frequent recordings of events during a crisis situation;
- using easy and quick recording instruments (such as action maps and EOT records) during crisis situations;
- cross-checking time and activities across a number of separate records;
- undertaking debriefings soon after the period in which such experiences were had.

While those involved in dealing with crisis situations may feel that more frequent recording of their interactions and actions is overloading them, frequent EOT-type recordings improve post-event reports and aid memory when giving information or evidence at inquiries that may take place months or years into the future. The sooner information is gained the less likely will be the effects of rationalization, convergence and suggestibility. Evaluators are also more able to check the timescales and information received.

Towards a method of evaluating crisis management

A process is needed to gather objective detail while avoiding biases and easy solutions to the questions raised in the scope of the investigation or evaluation. Obvious solutions are not acceptable if an inquiry is trying to prevent future situations from arising, or trying to improve crisis response and recovery management. Far too often quick and apparently accurate solutions involve blaming a central operator or manager.

A number of crisis situations occur because of apparent poor judgement or error. The King's Cross Underground Railway fire was due to poor managerial supervision (not clearing the rubbish from under the escalators) and lack of training in coping with fire. Chernobyl showed an example of poor managerial judgement that precipitated the nuclear power plant meltdown then further poor judgement in handling the evacuation response. The decision by Shell managers to dump the Brent Spar in deep water was poor when the context of Western public opinion against further global pollution is considered. Further examination, however, suggests that such judgements are superficial and inaccurate. Management accountability, design of equipment, environmental influences, and training and support by others are factors that can influence the onset and shape of a crisis – and influence the effectiveness of response and recovery operations. Investigators and evaluators need to explore the background, the crisis situation and the management response from before the crisis happened to long after the crisis has been resolved.

Any evaluation begins with the crisis situation. This can be decomposed into the situation itself (which includes the surrounding environment within which the crisis happened) and the management (which includes operational activities) of that situation. The situation can also be divided into before, during and after components, with the during component divided further into onset and impact components.

Hence the crisis situation is divided into four situation components (*see* Figure 17.1) – before or pre-crisis situation, onset situation, impact situation and after or post-crisis situation. Each of these has a corresponding management grouping – pre-crisis management, onset management, impact management and post-crisis or recovery management.

Evaluators examine each component in turn for possible contributing factors. The pre-crisis situation and management aspects considered include how

419

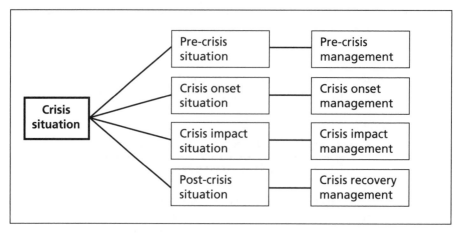

Fig. 17.1 The eight evaluation components

structures or systems were designed and built and how people worked in the structures. The onset situation and management include prevailing environmental conditions, how equipment and structures performed, why the crisis occurred and how people handled these aspects. Impact situation and management examine the situation when the crisis begins to affect the surrounding environment, what happened, what was done and how equipment, structures, systems and people coped (or did not cope) with the impacts of the crisis. Finally, evaluators examine how the situation was recovered and brought to a state approximating pre-crisis normalcy in the post-crisis situation and management.

The easiest way to see how this method works is to take a real example and show how the crisis situation can be decomposed into the eight evaluation components.

REALITY BITE

El Al Flight 1862 aircraft crash, Amsterdam, Holland, 4 October 1992

This case is drawn from reports including the Netherlands Aviation Safety Board Aircraft Accident Report 92-11. As a consequence, note the concrete language – more nouns and fewer emotive descriptions and opinions.

Background
El Al Flight 1862 took an intermediate stop at Schiphol airport on a flight from New York to Tel Aviv. The aircraft received a departure slot at 5.20 pm on 4 October 1992. The flight had a total of 72 metric tonnes of fuel, four people were on board (the captain, co-pilot, flight engineer and one non-revenue passenger), and 114.7 metric tonnes of cargo. The flight crew had had 20 hours rest prior to beginning their duty.

Incident

There were no extraordinary circumstances at takeoff according to air traffic control witnesses. No anomalies were evident during the initial climb until at 5.27 pm when the aircraft reached an altitude of 6500 feet (2000 metres). Subsequent analysis shows the flight data recorder information confirming that No. 3 and No. 4 engines and their pylons broke from the right wing at this time.

Response – onset management

The co-pilot transmitted an emergency call. The aircraft turned right and started dumping fuel according to witnesses on the ground. When the aircraft turned right two vapour trails were seen to emerge from the wing tips. The Amsterdam air traffic controller confirmed the emergency call and cleared the area of other traffic. At 5.28 pm, the controller, not knowing the reason for the emergency, asked the crew if they wanted to return to the airport. Witnesses heard one or more explosions and saw a dark plume of smoke from the aircraft. Some witnesses saw objects fall; others reported fire on the right wing that eventually disappeared.

At 5.28 pm the flight was informed that runway 06 was open for use and that the wind was blowing at 21 knots at an angle of 40 degrees. The flight crew requested runway 27 for landing. As the aircraft was only seven miles from the airport and still flying at 5000 feet, a straight approach was not feasible and the crew was instructed to turn right and descend to 2000 feet (615 metres). The crew was informed that the wind was blowing at an angle of 53 degrees and at 22 knots. During the turn to the right, the controller asked for the status of the aircraft and was informed that 'No. 3 and 4 are out and we have problems with the flaps'. At 5.35 pm the co-pilot added, 'we have a controlling problem'. Around 25 seconds later the co-pilot called 'going down 1862 going down ...'

Response – impact management

At 5.35 pm (just over eight minutes from crisis onset), Flight 1862 crashed onto an 11-floor apartment building in Bijlmermeer, a suburb of Amsterdam, 13 kilometres east of Schiphol airport. The aircraft struck the apex of two connected apartment blocks. All on board the aircraft died.

Four of the vehicles from the airport fire brigade units joined the units from the Amsterdam city fire brigade in firefighting activities. The response agencies were confronted with a complex situation. Wreckage and debris were strewn over an area 400 metres wide and 600 metres long with fires burning in several adjacent apartments and a number of locations on the ground. Access was limited by canals and by volunteers, onlookers and media representatives. A multi-agency response operated for four days, first extinguishing the fires and looking for survivors, then making safe the site and extracting the dead. The initial chaos of the scene, the intensity of some of the fire sites and the lack of information on who was living in some of the apartments led to uncertainties over the final death toll.

Post-crisis – recovery management

The buildings had to be torn down subsequently. Soil in the impact area was heavily contaminated with aircraft fuel and products from the aircraft and freight.

Besides relocating survivors, the Netherlands government approved an amnesty for survivors who were illegal residents (as large numbers of these people were

421

apparently living in the apartment blocks). Many who did not live in Bijlmermeer claimed amnesty and social service support, leading to a ripple-effect critical problem for the government.

The mayor of Amsterdam led a commemorative service some days after the event. As noted in the previous chapter, such services help those who are mentally hurting feel less alone and signal a transition point from response and loss to recovery and looking after the living.

Statistics
The four people on board the aircraft died, along with approximately seventy people in the apartment buildings.

Comment
This case illustrates the clear separation between onset and impact management. In onset management, the pilots and air traffic control personnel were involved in handling the response to the crisis onset – an aircraft needing to make an emergency landing. Response personnel, management and activities change once the crisis creates impact damage. Thus the crash of the aircraft upon the apartment complex led to impact management involving response agencies (firefighting, paramedic and law enforcement) and local and national government agencies. Note that another clear change of activities and personnel emerges when impact management is complete, and recovery or aftermath management requires different agencies (social services, builders and architects) to take over.

The case also highlights the very small period of time that is often available for onset management. In this case there was just over eight minutes between the appearance of the crisis and the crash of the aircraft.

Evaluation management

The four pairs of evaluation components covering pre-crisis, onset, impact and recovery can clearly be identified in the Reality Bite above. Pre-crisis examinations would include the status of the aircraft before takeoff and the prevailing conditions up to the onset of the crisis – weather, air traffic control actions, airport activity and aircraft proximity. This pair of situation and management components would also look at the aircraft in terms of design, maintenance and life history – and examine the profiles and background of the pilots involved.

Some aspects would suggest a non-connection. For example, the fact that something went wrong with the engines on the left wing would suggest there was no need to examine the training and skill levels of the pilots or the air traffic personnel. A thorough and effective investigation needs to reassure evaluators that there were no contributory causes – drug taking or alcohol absorption that may have affected response times and capabilities.

The aircraft involved in the El Al Flight 1862 crash had a Certificate of Air Worthiness, issued on 15 March 1992 and valid until 15 March 1993. Examination of the maintenance and history of this aircraft revealed an accumulation of 45 746 flight hours and 10 107 flight cycles.

Onset situation and management evaluation includes a close look at prevailing weather conditions, a search for the incident trigger (the cause of the crisis situation) and a careful consideration of the actions undertaken by the pilots and the air traffic controllers. In commercial aircraft accidents, this review is assisted by a look at the data stored in the 'black boxes' carried on most aircraft. These black boxes record aircraft performance parameters on a flight recorder and flight crew communications within the cockpit area on a cockpit voice recorder (CVR). Physical inspection of the crash site and of the remains of the aircraft is undertaken to form ideas about what happened in a cause-and-effect sequence.

The flight recorder was heavily damaged. The tape and the tape drive was slightly damaged by heat and water, with the tape broken in four places where it was not wound on the reels. A read-out was accomplished on all parameters. The cockpit voice recorder was not found.

At the scene of impact, the relatively small impact area among the high obstacles of the buildings and trees indicated a very steep aircraft descent. The scatter of fragments (particularly those of the left wing and the tail section) and the spread of damage from the building suggested that the aircraft had a bank angle of slightly over 90 degrees to the right and a nose down attitude of 70 degrees on impact. Engines 3 and 4 and their pylons were recovered from water around half a kilometre from the entrance to Naarden harbour.

The combination of flight recorder information and examination of the site and wreckage suggested that the No. 3 engine and pylon separated from the wing and collided with the No. 4 engine in an outward and rearward direction. The right wing would then have been damaged up to the front spar. Given the speed of the aircraft, aerodynamic distortion and turbulence probably removed some parts of the leading edge. When the engines broke away from the right wing, the fuel supply lines were ruptured. This information generally matched eyewitness testimony of fuel dumping, bits falling from the aircraft and smoke. This confirmation provided an each-way reinforcement of findings – the read-out was supported and eyewitness testimony was deemed reliable. Establishing grounds for reliability is important should the flight recorder data or some eyewitnesses provide more information that is not supported.

For the aircraft crash evaluation, the need to look into impact management and recovery did not fit the scope of their inquiry. Nonetheless some attention is paid to airport response and the speed with which impact damage was managed.

Testing and investigation revealed that a fatigue crack of the outboard midspar fuse pin on the pylon of engine No. 3 probably led to failure of that pin and loss of the engine and pylon. This probably should have been detected in the last inspection of the engine and pylon. The aircraft operators disputed this finding. They claimed that the redistribution of loads after initial failure would have increased the crack growth rate. There was no evidence of bird impact and no evidence of sabotage.

For the city of Amsterdam, the evaluation would take a different form. Pre-crisis evaluation may look at the ability and readiness of the professional response agencies to handle this crisis situation, at the availability and use of equipment and at potential political issues of airport proximity and access to suburban sites.

For the city, onset management was extremely short and unlikely. Once the wing damage took effect on the aircraft the crash was inevitable.

Evaluation of the local government response covers both the impact management and recovery operations. The firefighting authority (lead agency according to the Netherlands Calamity Act) assessed the response effort and concluded that a number of response actions and concerns needed improvement, including the following:

- The need for larger site control headquarters (at least facilities to handle visitors to the small control site).
- The need to clarify agency control, given the conflict of authority between the firefighting command and the disaster identification team during the initial 24 hours. This conflict of authority took three days to properly resolve.
- The need for more site control to handle onlookers and media representatives.
- The need for better co-ordination between likely response agencies rather than independent efforts that adversely affected operations. A police helicopter initially hovered overhead and used its spotlight to help light up the site but created a noise that prevented communications other than by car radio. A military helicopter landed on a major road crossing, forcing firefighting vehicles and ambulances to be rerouted. This cost response time.
- The need for clearer understanding of the different methods and terminologies used by the responding agencies, as lack of understanding led to communication failures and resulted in lost time and increased feelings of irritation.
- The need for better organization of multi-agency response efforts, particularly in terms of registering each agency that reports to the site.

These findings again illustrate the need to search beyond convenient issues of inter-agency rivalries or access difficulties so that improvements in performance can be suggested. The search for ways to reduce exposure to crisis situations and to improve response and recovery performance is the single most important reason for learning to conduct effectively post-exercise and post-crisis evaluation processes.

The El Al Flight 1862 case also helps identify the next level of evaluation – looking at human and structural factors. A number of these could include the following:

People

- preparation and training
- decision making
- strategic management
- tactical management
- effect on:
  - victims
  - bystanders
  - respondents
- concerned others (including meeters-and-greeters).

Processes

- alarms and warnings
- chains of command
- media
- management of:
  - victims
  - bystanders
  - respondents
  - concerned others (including meeters-and-greeters).

Systems

- information collection, collation, processing
- communication
- control
- site security.

Structures

- design and materials
- safety features
- risks or threats involved
- equipment.

These factors form four general groups – structures, systems, processes and people (*see* Figure 17.2) which allow evaluators to focus on specific issues yet see potential cause-and-effect links between them. Evaluators can then develop some insight into how a crisis may have arisen or how response performance may have been influenced.

In Figure 17.2 each of the eight evaluation components is separated into four lines of investigation (structure, system, process and people). Each line looks at a dynamic and interdependent aspect of the component and proceeds through three primary assessment considerations that may assist evaluators in identifying any causal link or links. These causal links may move across the lines of investigation to form a chain of causal links. This chain of

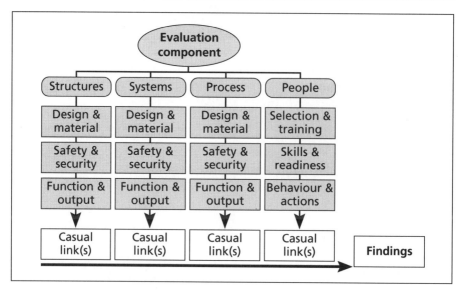

Fig. 17.2 Assessment methodology for each evaluation component

cause-and-effect links describes each moment of the crisis situation in terms of what, where, when, how and effect or consequence.

For the structure, system and process lines the three primary assessment considerations are:

- design and construction;
- safety and security;
- function and output or outcomes.

For the people line, the three primary assessment considerations involve:

- examining how the particular people or groups of people were selected (and/or were on site for the onset of the crisis situation);
- what levels of training they had at that time and what skills and levels of readiness to cope with the situation were held by each relevant group or groups of people;
- what behaviours were displayed and what actions were undertaken by each relevant group or groups of people.

By investigating each of these areas, evaluators can:

- identify the strengths and weaknesses in crisis preparedness;
- look for ways in which crisis situations may be prevented from arising;
- seek ways in which the effects or impacts of a crisis situation may be reduced;
- suggest ways in which management responses to a crisis situation may be improved.

Structures

Structures are human-made or natural formations within the crisis situation, particularly those in which the crisis event occurred. Volcanoes, earthquake faults, rivers and geological ground features are structures, as are vehicles, buildings, manufacturing plants and community constructions. For evaluation, structures may need separation into discrete types – engines, wings, fuselage and support or attachment structures in the case of Flight 1862.

Systems

Systems are the devices and mechanisms that help operate or monitor the structures and are particularly vulnerable to damage in crisis situations. In many cases, control systems form part of the primary source of crisis situations as loss of these precipitates crisis impact damage. Evaluation needs to examine those systems that provide warnings on changes of status in systems or structures, as well as those systems designed to regain control, minimize the situation or deliver response actions.

Some primary systems in the Flight 1862 crash that needed examination included warning systems, the capability of power and infrastructural systems to continue in adverse conditions, communications systems, outside response warning and communication systems, fire suppression systems used on site, and evacuation systems used to rescue passengers and staff.

Process

Process aspects are the people-based efforts to manage operations, deal with crisis situations and handle human interactions. If systems cover 'what' is used to do something, then processes cover 'how' people manage these systems. Investigation of the reliability and use of procedures is made during the line of investigation into the processes used to manage the systems.

For crisis response management, evaluation considers the organization of the crisis response effort (for each of the responding agencies) and the mechanisms used to re-exert control over other systems or structures. Evaluation covers:

- the established tactical and strategic response management structures;
- the strategic planning and management involved in preparing for crisis management;
- the contribution of chains of command;
- the effectiveness of information management (including data collection, validation, and exchange and communication interactions with people outside the crisis situation and media representatives);
- the management of victims (and of victim identification and public inquiries about potential victims).

People

The line of investigation that looks at how people behave and perform in crisis situations is most important. People can precipitate crisis situations and respond to crises. Among the categories of people to be examined are:

- victims (those physically or psychologically impaired when in immediate contact with the crisis situation);
- bystanders (those not impaired but who do not respond to the situation, which can include meeters-and-greeters in some situations);
- respondents.

The respondents category may be divided into first-on-scene, first-arrivers, professional response personnel, volunteers and logistical support groups, and can further be looked at in terms of function – strategic management, tactical or on-site management and response delivery personnel.

A simple yet comprehensive evaluation methodology thus separates a crisis situation into pre-crisis, onset, impact and recovery pairs of situation and management components, forming the eight evaluation components. Each component is examined in terms of four general lines of investigation – structures, systems, processes and people. By using this approach a sequential and detailed analysis can be presented from which post-crisis action recommendations for reduction, readiness, response and recovery can be made.

This sequence can be glimpsed in air accident reports. As an example, the report on the El Al accident produced a detailed summary of the investigation, conclusions and recommendations. The structure of the Netherlands Aviation Safety Board, Aircraft Accident Report 92-11 – El Al Flight 1862 included the following sections:

1 Factual information
1.1   History of the flight
1.2   Injuries to persons
1.3   Damage to aircraft
1.4   Other damage
1.5   Personnel information
1.6   Aircraft information
    1.6.1   General
    1.6.2   Pylons, fuse pins and nacelle attach fittings
    1.6.3   Aircraft design
        1.6.3.1   Pylon to wing attachment design
        1.6.3.2   Hydraulic systems
        1.6.3.3   Pneumatic system
        1.6.3.4   Electrical system
        1.6.3.5   Flight controls
        1.6.3.6   Fuel system
        1.6.3.7   Engine fire detection and extinguishing systems
    1.6.4   Service bulletins and airworthiness directives
        1.6.4.1   Service bulletins applicable to midspar fuse pins

This outline of the Aircraft Accident Report 92-11 shows how the examination of the different aspects of the crisis situation (factual information and analysis) can then lead to sequential findings that establish probable cause(s), contributory causes and improvements that could be made (conclusions and recommendations). Such evaluation processes are time consuming which means handling pressures for conclusions, probable causes and guilt attribution before the work is done.

REALITY BITE

TWA Flight 800 from New York, 1996

The storyline for this case study is not yet finished, although mid-term reports suggest a possible design problem. The central issue in this case is how evaluation can be slowed and distracted by the pressures for quick findings and judgements.

Background
Boeing jumbo jets are flown by nearly every major airline in the world, so any flaw in their design or operation can bring an unseen threat to travellers anywhere.

Incident
On Wednesday, 17 July 1996, at 8.20 pm a 25-year-old 747, Flight 800, took off from Kennedy Airport (New York) for Paris. The aircraft had been delayed for three hours due to a succession of problems – a faulty engine cable, a failed indicator light in the cockpit controls and problems with baggage handling equipment. Given the light load of passengers (230 people) and baggage (around four tons), the main fuel tank under the forward passenger section was left virtually empty while the wing fuel cells were full.

At 8.20 pm, the aircraft departed Kennedy Airport and flew along the southern edge of Long Island. The crew acknowledged clearance to climb to 15 000 feet (4800 metres) at 8.30 pm. Ninety seconds later the transponder cone identifying the aircraft went off air. The aircraft had catastrophically disintegrated at an altitude of 13 700 feet (4200 metres).

Eyewitnesses reported between one and three explosions. Some witnesses reported a flickering upward path that may have been a ground-to-air missile. The fire was described as a firework, a setting sun or a ball of fire approximately 100 feet (29 metres) wide and 200 feet (58 metres) high. A National Guard helicopter crew reported a streak of orange-red light like a shooting star with an explosion at about 8000 feet followed by a much larger second explosion.

Response

Given the explosion and height, the incident was non-survivable. Response activity quickly moved from search-and-rescue to search for bodies and for aircraft structures scattered on the bottom of the sea off Long Island. This was performed at times in adverse weather conditions and with reduced visibility on and near the sea-bed.

At 6.10 am, 18 July, a 26-member go-team of the National Transport Safety Board arrived on site. Media reports were already speculating on a terrorist bomb as the cause, given some parallel occurrences to the Pan Am Flight 103 (Locherbie) bomb in 1988. The safety record of the Boeing 747 aircraft was such that many commentators and media aviation experts claimed that a bomb must have been the cause.

Jack Kallstrom, Assistant Director of the Federal Bureau of Investigation (FBI) and head of the FBI New York office, launched an investigation into the possibility of a terrorist action.

Robert Francis, head of the NTSB go-team (which officially is the investigative agency) spent most of Thursday talking down media speculation over a terrorist bomb. He pointed out that the same speculation was made about a Lauda Air 767 that mysteriously exploded near Bangkok until later investigation showed that the aircraft was torn apart when a computer malfunction reversed two of its engines. He sought to establish that:

1 there was no current supporting evidence for a bomb;
2 the NTSB was running the investigation.

The volume of media reports suggested that he was not believed. This lack of belief may have been because he was not presenting an 'interesting' storyline.

On Saturday, Kallstrom indicated that he believed the probability of mechanical failure was slight ('1 per cent or 5 per cent') and a high explosive device was more probable. Forensic autopsies, however, did not establish the damage usual in bomb explosions – burns to mouth or windpipes and lungs, coarse amputations, deep puncture wounds, pellet injuries.

Experienced homicide detectives advised the coroner to restrain family members from viewing any of the recovered bodies. They felt that the damage to the bodies from sudden deceleration (including decapitation), explosive decompression, gravitational pressures and impact on the sea was too severe for many people to cope with. This constraint along with the slow performance of autopsies due to FBI insistence on scene-of-crime evidential procedures led to conflict with grieving relatives and friends. The media amplified the conflict as it was a good storyline charged with high human and emotional content. As TWA had housed many of the victim's families at the Ramada Hotel in New York (70 miles away), the forensic team was unable to visit them and explain what was happening.

Autopsies on the first 20 bodies lasted from 6.00 am to 8.00 pm. A further 80 bodies were retrieved from the sea surface and awaited identification and examination. No evidence for a bomb explosion was found in these 100 bodies, nor from the 115 bodies retrieved from the bottom of the sea over the next month. The forensic team had to withstand attacks from politicians and families that were emphatically presented by media outlets. The only projectile pieces found in the bodies of passengers seated in Rows 17 to 29 were from the cabin floor.

While the FBI maintained its belief in the criminal source of the crash and thus that the FBI was a legitimate lead-agency in investigating what happened, the NTSB was not included in the primary investigation. When traces of PETN explosive were confirmed, the NTSB investigators only found out through reading the *New York Times*, which had a report some two weeks after the discovery was made. The PETN traces were most likely due to an earlier test of bomb-sniffer dogs at St Louis Airport. Traces of RDX were also found toward the rear of the aircraft but this was probably due to flying military personnel and equipment into the Gulf War. The fuel tank, on the other hand, showed signs of having exploded.

Speculation that a bomb exploded in a forward cargo hold gained support. Supporters pointed to the parallels to the Locherbie bomb explosion on Pan Am Flight 103, conveniently ignoring the significant bomb-type damage to aircraft structure and passengers quickly found in the Locherbie case. The forward cargo holds of Flight 800 showed no evidence of an internal explosion. There were no high explosive signs – blistered and stretched aluminium skin, craters pock-marked with dust that burned with the 8000 degree Celsius temperatures of an explosion, nor petal-shaped projectile puncture holes (where the petals bend in the direction of the flight).

The favoured theories were:

1 bomb (FBI);
2 friendly fire (40 credible witnesses believe they saw an upward streak before the aircraft exploded – this was dismissed by FBI and NTSB, but favoured over the Internet. No recording of missile echoes was made on any of the radars operating at the time); or
3 explosion in the central (belly) fuel tank (NTSB).

By the end of November 1996, 98 per cent of the aircraft had been recovered. In July 1997, with no definite finding on the cause of the aircraft crash, a ceremony attended by thousands was held on the shores of Long Island.

Statistics
Flight 800 was a 25-year-old Boeing 747, possibly acquired from the Shah of Iran's fleet some time in its history. The death toll was 230. Two crash victims were not identified.

The NTSB has investigated 374 major airline accidents over 29 years (around an average of one a month).

The debris was found in three clusters strung along the southern edge of Long Island, some 4.5 miles (7.5 kilometres) and 1.5 miles (2.5 kilometres) apart. The first (furthest from the airport) contained the wings (and all four unexploded engines) and trunk of the aircraft. The second (1.5 miles from the first patch) contained the cockpit and the first-class and business-class section of the aircraft forward of the wings. The third (4.5 miles away from the second and closest to the airport) contained the cabin section forward of the wings, the landing gear and luggage from the forward hold.

At the peak of the search period, some 26 NTSB and 600 FBI and federal officials (including 500 Suffolk County Police at a cost of $3.98 million) were involved, as well as a small fleet of US Coastguard and Navy vessels. Divers made more than 3800 trips to the seabed areas of the crash site. At least eight terrorist groups claimed to have brought the aircraft down.

Comment

Boeing experts disagreed with the idea of a central fuel tank explosion, but may have a vested interest in so doing. They argue that the flashpoint of 100 degrees Fahrenheit could not be met given the ground temperature of 71 degrees Fahrenheit. Early makes of the 747, however, had an air-conditioning unit placed under the fuel tank that may indirectly heat the fuel. At the insistence of the NTSB, Boeing established that the flashpoint could be reached on a trial flight across the Mojave Desert in similar conditions. The central fuel tank temperature reached 115 degrees Fahrenheit.

There have been cases of central or belly fuel tank explosions. In 1990, a 737 at Manilla Airport had its empty centre tank explode as it was being pushed back from the terminal gate (eight dead, 30 injured). The engines were not running at the time. Latest indications from the NTSB (May 1998) were that exposed thermocouples might have conducted a surge of electric charge into the central fuel tank that was sufficient to cause the explosion. Most major users of 747 aircraft-types claim to have examined the structural and system environment surrounding the fuel tanks. This safety check was extended to 737 aircraft in May 1998.

From the TWA business perspective, two points emerge. First, TWA (the operating airline) was part of, but not a significant partner, in the search-and-investigation activities. This means that the TWA organization operated as a partial crisis manager, with all the consequent limitations. Partial management is a reality for most business-based crisis situations with a physical setting (bombs and fires). The organization cannot direct the immediate response activities.

Second, given the partial management role of business organizations in these situations, the central concern for the business is to maintain its image. For TWA, this would mean they needed to:

- quickly supply operational and storage details and an accurate passenger list (in accordance with lead-response agency requirements);
- assist investigating agencies with quick and accurate information, publicly demonstrating openness and willingness to help;
- reassure stakeholders (particularly staff and users) so that business would continue (where possible) and public confidence would be maintained. Reassurance is important particularly when members of the organization are directly affected. TWA management needed to focus on the feelings of their staff given the large number of TWA staff and their families who were on board Flight 800.

Quick supply of accurate details is pivotal to the immediate post-incident image of an efficient organization. This is rarely accomplished by airlines, often because of last minute changes and passengers travelling under different names. Regulations and legal requirements may prevent early dissemination of this information beyond the responding agencies. Any visible delay in providing this information, however, usually leads to negative images of confusion, or dilatoriness or attempts to hide organizational inefficiency and wrongdoing.

The Flight 800 crash highlighted concerns about stress counselling. As part of post-incident management, personnel were used to try to reassure passengers departing from Kennedy Airport. Given the variation in skill and experience, many of these people may have done more damage than good. Many left passengers focused on the possibility of accidents and feeling stressed and trapped. Even after experienced counsellors advised that this operation should stop; those offering refused to do so. Eventually a combination of management and union leaders convinced the would-be helpers to stop their work. Basic reassurance counselling involves telling people that regardless of how they may feel now they will feel better (as outlined in Chapter 16).

Management of evaluation perspective

To explore methodically all the aspects and features of a crisis situation requires time and much effort. To reduce the time taken and have people with appropriate expertise undertaking the lines of investigation, aircraft accident teams have grown from one or two to a large number. The number of members in the NTSB go-team, for example, does not count others brought in to reassemble pieces of the aircraft or evaluate specific systems or structural elements.

Note the summary of eyewitness accounts. There is disagreement between the number of explosions (one, two or three). Some claim to have seen a streak going up to the aircraft, suggesting that a rocket-propelled explosive brought down the aircraft. Depending upon proximity to the explosion and quality of eyesight, the explosion was a firework, a setting sun or a ball of fire. Eyewitness testimony rarely agrees in detail between the accounts. Some testimony will unconsciously change as the witnesses try to make sense of fleeting impressions. What is sought is consistency of report (rough height, explosion) and agreement with other sources (such as audio-visual records or 'black box' data).

The clash between investigation agencies was unusual but not uncommon. Each had a specific scope that gave legitimacy to their presence – the FBI seeking the guilty people and the NTSB seeking what happened, with the supplementary role of recommending how the situation may be eliminated or reduced. Both need to look at the same evidence. Most inquiries begin with the 'what happened' (NTSB-led) effort who hand over the evidence to the criminal action investigators (in this case, the FBI) if there is evidence of criminal cause. By precipitating action because of the need to find evidence quickly, the FBI delayed and distracted efforts by the appropriately qualified agency, the NTSB go-team. This was compounded by media pressure for exciting and interesting storylines and by the more general expectation of a quick solution. Properly considered answers that reflect probable cause-and-effect links in a crisis are not quickly produced. Evaluators are likely to need to resist pressures from within the organization and from outside it to identify why something happened, whether this was preventable and whether any guilty persons may be identified.

Those who set in motion an evaluation process need to define the scope of the process clearly and then support the people appointed to conduct it. Executives and managers need to be sensitive to the pressures that may be placed on the evaluators – from accusations about covering up for the organization to being made to feel part of a scapegoat process. For those undertaking a full and detailed evaluation, there are rewards in making the effort to determine what may actually have happened, to identify weaknesses and failings, and to suggest ways weaknesses may be eliminated and failings corrected. Just how satisfactory these conclusions and recommendations may be, however, depends on the degree to which the organization's managers and executives accept the findings and implement the appropriate changes.

References

Albrecht, S. (1996) *Crisis Management for Corporate Self-Defence*. New York: Amacon.

Allinson, R. E. (1993) *Global Disasters: Inquiries into Management Ethics*. New York: Prentice-Hall.

Barton, L. (1993) *Crisis in Organizations: Managing and Communicating in the Heat of Chaos*. Cincinnati, Ohio: South-Western.

Bignell, V., Peters, G. and Pym, C. (1977) *Catastrophic Failures*. Milton Keynes: Open University Press.

Cohen, D. (1991) *Aftershock: The Psychological and Political Consequences of Disaster*. London: Grafton Books.

Drabek, T. E. and Quarantelli, E. L. (1967) 'Scapegoats, villains, and disasters', *Transaction*, 4, 12–17.

Fischhoff, B. (1975) 'Hindsight ≠ foresight: the effect of outcome knowledge on judgment under uncertainty', *Journal of Experimental Psychology: Human Perception and Performance*, 1, 288-99.

Hidden, A. (1989) *Investigation into the Clapham Junction Railway Accident*. London: HMSO (Department of Transport).

Hogarth, R. M. (1981) 'Beyond discrete biases: functional and dysfunctional heuristics', *Psychological Bulletin*, 90(2), 197–217.

Latham, R. (1990) *The Shorter Pepys*. London: Unwin Hyman.

Schreider, T. (1996) 'The legal issues of disaster recovery planning', *Disaster Recovery Journal*, 9(2), 31-3.

The fifth R ...
developing resilience

At the beginning of this book we found that crisis management included information management and action management of response and recovery operations. Effective crisis management involved proactive planning and preparation that followed an RRRR model – Reduction, Readiness, Response and Recovery. In subsequent chapters components of this model were presented alongside suggested strategies and practices. In actively pursuing these strategies and issues, executives and managers improve the ability of their organizations to survive crisis situations.

Survival is fundamentally based on the capacity to deal with crisis situations held by executives, managers and staff of organizations. This capacity involves mental and physical preparation – understanding what may happen and what response efforts may be needed. The ability to effectively survive and respond is called *resilience*. Resilience is the fifth R of effective crisis management: developing and using resilient structures and people to diminish the effects of a crisis where possible and to recovery effectively when crisis situations impact on the structures and upon the members of the organization.

Towards resilience

The foundations of resilience consist of two parallel efforts:

- to reduce the exposure to crisis situations (and to the impacts from those situations; and
- to increase the psychological and organizational readiness to respond to crisis situations and to recover from those situations that cannot be removed, reduced or avoided.

To reduce exposure, executives and managers may use strategies like the ABC mitigation strategies outlined in Chapter 2. Whether dealing with physical threats, geographical threats or more intangible business threats, resilient people can avoid the crisis (build away) or be better prepared to respond to (and recover from) the crisis (build better). Alternatively, people can defuse and reduce the crisis by blending in with the environment or developing ways in which the crisis and crisis impacts may take place with minimal effect on the organization (build compatible).

People who understand the likely effects and consequences – who are thus familiar with and able to predict likely consequences – are more likely to respond appropriately. They are less likely to be inoperative due to aftershock and are more likely to make choices that increase their own chances of survival as well as increasing the chances of organizational survival. Given the capability to respond and recover effectively through skill acquisition, training and planning, the stakeholders of an organization may even be able to do better than survive. They may be able to bounce back in a better performing position than was the case before the crisis.

Familiarity, predictability and capability were discussed in the FPC model presented in Chapter 12. Anyone can quickly assess how they, their family or their community or organization currently rate according to the FPC model, and so can identify the area in which they can place their next effort for greatest benefit.

Being aware that crisis situations will happen need not mean that organizations should rely on reactive strategies. By investing in mitigation strategies, executives and managers can develop a resilient organization that can gain from a number of benefits, including:

- reduced insurance premiums;
- increased audit approval;
- safer organizational structures and facilities that reduce losses in profit and work hours through less downtime and workplace injuries;
- an improved market position when less-prepared organizations suffer crisis situations.

A similar emphasis on quality of output and correct practices can lead to better long-term profits and more satisfied organization members, while reducing crisis situations due to human error.

All these efforts lead to a resilient organization or community.

Developing resilience

Regardless of the strategies and approaches selected by the executives and managers of an organization, resilience is developed by satisfactorily addressing four stages:

- *Stage 1.* Determine the existing and future potential exposure to risks and hazards by doing risk and impact analyses (Chapters 2 and 3). Commence

437

risk management programmes for the risks and hazards (Chapter 4). This can *reduce* the number of crisis situations.

- *Stage 2.* Develop plans and management strategies that focus and guide response and recovery actions (Chapters 9, 10 and 11). Determine what warning and alert systems will be used (Chapter 5). This increases the *readiness* for crisis response and recovery.
- *Stage 3.* Build and train a crisis management team that flexibly covers response and recovery operations (Chapters 6, 7, 8, 12, 13, 14, 15, 16 and 17). This establishes a functional *response* and *recovery* management.
- *Stage 4.* Develop awareness and training programmes for all members of the community based on (and supporting) the skills and approaches developed for the crisis management team in Stage 3. This develops community-based and organization-wide *readiness* for *response* and *recovery* management, and enhances resilience.

The key transition points for developing resilience are the construction and testing of response and recovery plans or guides and the development of a crisis management team with specialist crisis response teams. Specialist teams need to have high FPC ratings and be well resourced if the teams are to provide definitive management. One outstanding development in this area is the development of urban search and rescue (USAR) teams undertaken in America at the instigation of the Federal Emergency Management Agency (FEMA). These teams specialize in responding to urban disaster situations (from bombed buildings to earthquake devastation).

These groups have specialists in medical trauma, construction (for shoring up structures), confined-space rescues, and search and rescue dog teams. These capabilities are available 24 hours a day and can be mobilized for inter-state and international crisis situations. There are currently 25 task forces in the USA. Each task force consists of 56 members and brings with it 18 tons of equipment and supplies. Members are required to be ready to move within six hours of activation and to be self-sufficient for ten days. The teams work two 12-hour shifts to provide continuous 24-hour response.

Preparing community-based and organization-wide readiness can reduce losses and improve the post-impact situation. By 1988, some 10 000 people had training in disaster preparedness in Los Angeles. This training proved useful in 1994 when bystanders and onlookers made most of the rescues after the Northridge earthquake had struck. When the water pipe burst outside premises occupied by Penton Publishing (*see* Chapter 11), members of staff had the awareness to shut down computer facilities. These actions reduced losses from water-sourced electrical faults and meant that the recovery teams were certain (hard information) about the status of these computers and were less likely to compound any damage.

Resilience and learning from experience

Experience can enhance resilience, provided executives and managers seek out the lessons. By conducting broad post-crisis debriefing and investigative activities, strategies can be refined and structures improved. Terrorist bombings, for example, have highlighted the need to keep people *away* from large areas of glass and to revise engineering approaches (such as changing from using square weight-supporting columns to using round weight-supporting columns as these deflect more of the explosive force).

Japanese community planners and engineers used the impacts of the Kobe earthquake (1995) to develop strategies to enhance structural and community resilience. Strategies included creating greenbelts along the Rokko Mountains to reduce slippage and slides, designing firebreak zones, adding water storage tanks to buildings, developing the Hanshin Canal project to increase assured water supplies and adding back-up systems to many of their community lifeline utilities.

Resilience is a psychological state

Resilience depends upon the psychological awareness and preparedness of people, and on the attitudes people hold about themselves and their relationships with the world around them. Resilience is reduced when people believe:

- all risk can be predicted and defined (particularly in numeric form) and is static;
- mistakes can be eliminated;
- stability and security comes from control and conformity;
- technology solves crisis management problems;
- others are responsible for response and recovery activity.

These factors illustrate a highly structured, tight and mechanistic approach that reinforces dependency on others. These attitudes also encourage learned helplessness when a crisis situation occurs.

Resilience is strengthened when people believe:

- risk is predicted and defined in limited ways, and changes over time;
- mistakes are likely to happen and thus need to be covered by planning response measures;
- stability and security is established through accepting diversity and co-operation;
- technology solves some problems but can create others;
- each person can have responsibility for themselves and their own actions.

These attitudes reflect tolerance and expected diversity, which means the holders are more likely to accept sudden changes that are inflicted by crisis

439

situations. They are more likely to seek adaptive solutions that resolve their specific problems.

By developing effective crisis management skills and practices, people can increase their resilience to the stresses, threats and problems that arise in crisis situations. By being more resilient, people can reduce the size and nature of many crisis situations. As the costs in resources and human health and well-being increase over time, and human technological development increases the number of complex threats and hazards to organizations and communities, then everyone needs to become more able to deal with crisis situations. To help manage this process, executives and managers need to become more skilled and trained in effective crisis management.

Appendix 1

Working with the case-based and simulation exercises

Preparation for the case-based exercises

Before reading and undertaking the case-based exercises in Chapters 7 and 8, consider some of the points outlined below.

The case study material should be self-sufficient yet concise. The participants (you) bring experience, beliefs and assumptions into play. If the cases are too detailed, time gets lost in absorbing the information and participants feel cramped and uncertain. The focus of case-based exercises is on the decisions and interactions that these exercises produce.

Two keys to the usefulness of simulated training lie in the ability of participants to:

- assess the situation and select effective management options; and
- assess the beliefs and assumptions that underlay your choices.

Real learning and insight comes from assessing the beliefs and assumptions used in making decisions in terms of their reality, validity to the situation and influence on option selection and subsequent behavioural interactions. A useful exercise would be to assess how decisions and actions would change if the beliefs and assumptions changed – a 'what if these were different' evaluation.

So what are beliefs and assumptions? Beliefs are interpreted sets of experience and knowledge and are being used when someone claims that 'This is how people would react in this situation ...' or 'This is how organizations like this would operate ...' Assumptions are attempts to fill in missing information by setting a parameter (limit of the exercise) or by deciding on a possible set of facts. Participants are making assumptions when they state something like 'Let's assume that all our senior managers make the meeting ...' or 'This time, let there be some dead and injured from that event ...' Obviously, assumptions sometimes emerge from beliefs.

Participants need to note all beliefs and assumptions made at the start of, and during, the simulation. When working in small groups, these assumptions may be noted by a member who records the action choices made, behaviours undertaken and the outcomes.

You should also record assumptions for later own use. Take a blank page and draw a line down the middle. On the left-hand side write down the beliefs and assumptions on which decisions are based, then write down the action choices and the assumptions and beliefs on which these were based. Note what beliefs, assumptions and action choices were from a specific member of the group or were generated by the group.

At the end of the exercise, return to the beginning of the list and begin to explore the effects of each noted belief and assumption. Ask (or discuss within the group) what if the assumptions were (a) not made, (b) were less than estimated, (c) were greater than estimated, or (d) were different to those expected. How could the beliefs and assumptions be better assessed before these were made the basis upon which action decisions were made?

By exploring what was done and what led to those actions participants improve their skills in:

- POV analysis;
- assessing beliefs and assumptions about how to handle events;
- flexibility in evaluating problems and action choices;
- the interaction skills necessary for future success.

If you are doing simulated exercises or workshops with a trainer or facilitator (someone who runs the exercise or workshop), gain approval for any new information (assumptions) you wish to add to the case material.

Preparation for the simulation exercises

The following map and playing pieces are for use in the simulation exercises in Chapters 5, 9, 13 and 15. The scale and features of the map will vary throughout the exercises as explained in the relevant text.

Photocopy and join the pages together, sticking the right-hand edge of the first page to the left-hand edge of the second page. You may find it useful to enlarge the map as you photocopy it. Make as many copies as you need. You may also like to stick some acetate (such as write-on overhead projector film) over the top and use soluble felt pens during the exercise to mark out actions and consequences.

Photocopy and cut out each square in the two strips of playing pieces. Before doing this you may wish to stick the photocopied strips on some tough cardboard to make the pieces more robust.

Obtain a dice. If a dice is not available then cut out 36 equal sized squares of paper and number these from 1 to 6 six times. Place these in a jar or box, shake the jar or box each time you use it, and draw out a slip of paper. Be sure to return the slip of paper to the jar or box after you have read the number on that piece of paper.

HQ	S	P1	P2	TL	T2	T3	T4	T5	UL	U2	U3	U4	U5

W	W	MINE	OIL WELL	VIP	FIRE	NOSE	BODY	TAIL	X1	X2	X3	💣	

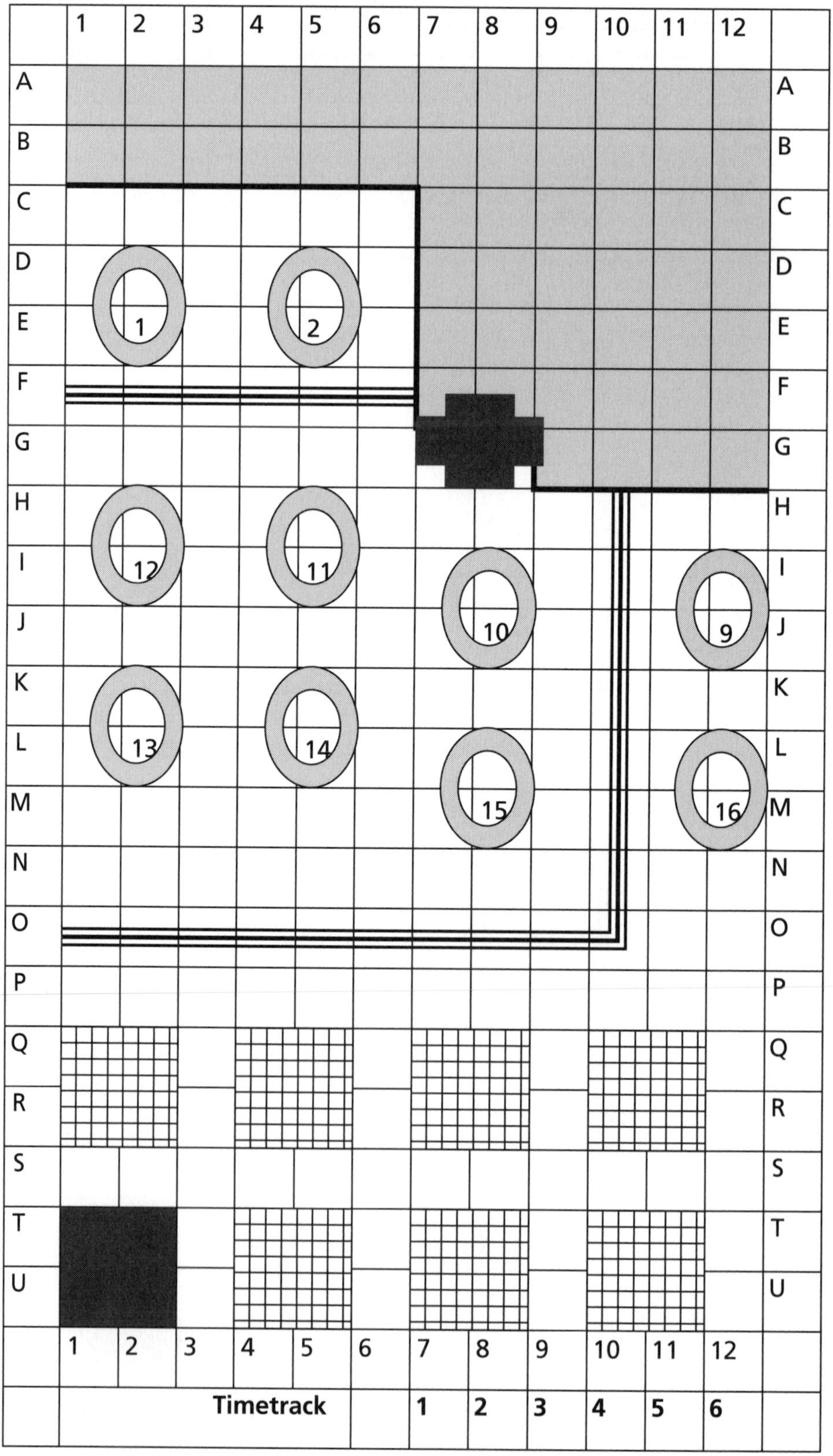
1 2 3 4 5 6 7 8 9 10 11 12
A B C D E F G H I J K L M N O P Q R S T U
1
2
12
11
10
9
13
14
15
16
Timetrack
1 2 3 4 5 6

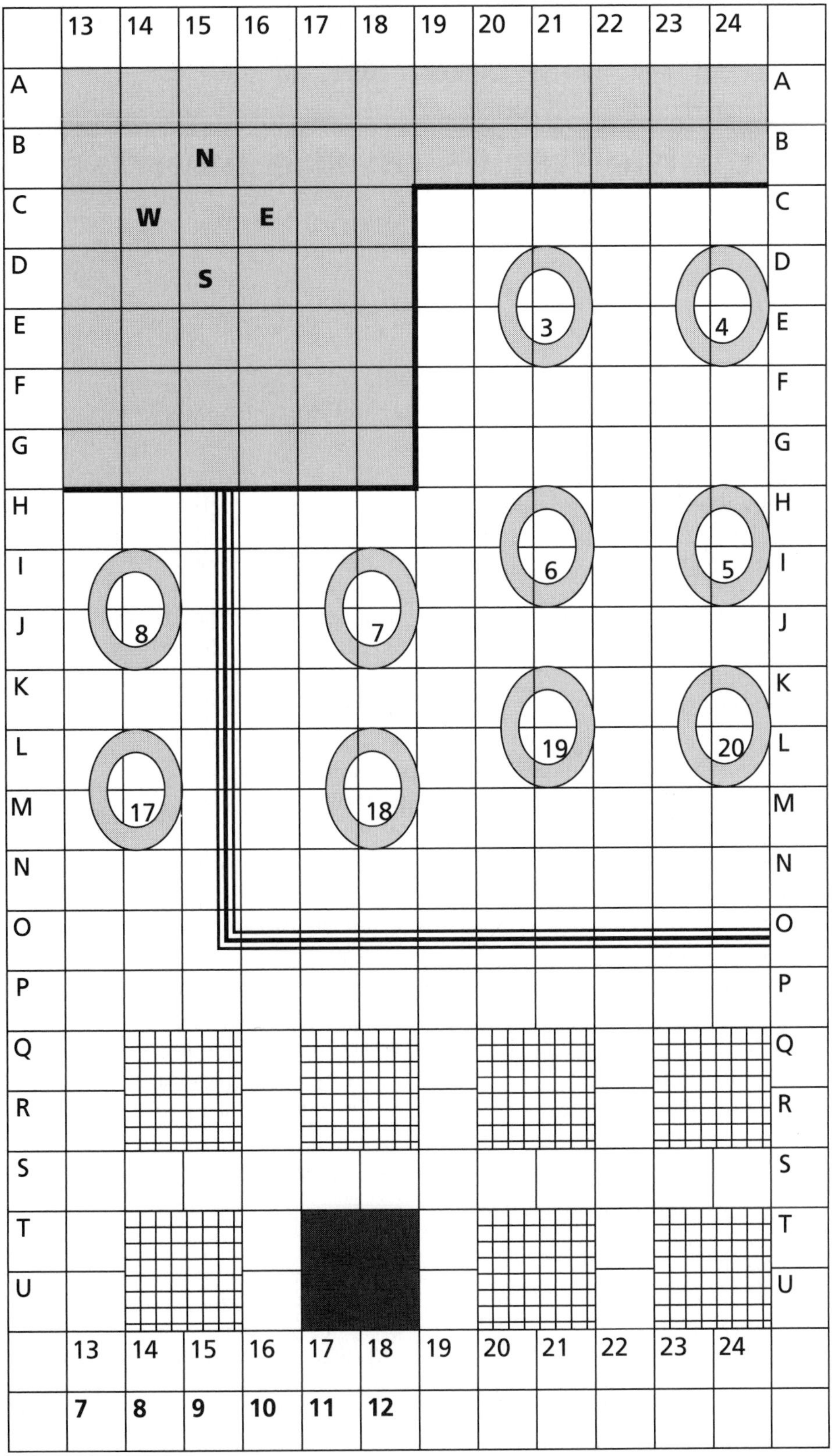
13 14 15 16 17 18 19 20 21 22 23 24
A B C D E F G H I J K L M N O P Q R S T U
N
W
E
S
3
4
6
5
8
7
19
20
17
18
13 14 15 16 17 18 19 20 21 22 23 24
7 8 9 10 11 12

Appendix 2

Commentaries on the exercises

Chapter 2

A fairly comprehensive list of threats (but not exhaustive) would include the following:

Internal (within the organization):

- Internal floods
- Internal fire
- Loss of facilities climate control
- Power failure
- Computer failure
- Production line failure
- Information systems failure (including all forms of electronic communication systems)
- Explosion
- Structural failure
- Chemical or gas leaks
- Chemical or gas storage failure
- Loss of data or records
- Computer system penetration (hacker or virus)
- Loss of key personnel (kidnap or competitor induced)
- Loss of information confidentiality
- Malicious damage to data, facilities or product
- Product defect and recall
- Extortion (product threat, kidnap)
- Fraud
- Theft
- Terrorist-type attacks (workplace violence, bomb threats)
- Strikes
- Pressure group actions (including picketing and product boycotts)
- Loss of reputation and corporate image (including loss of brand reputation)
- Environmental pollution (hazardous material spillage)
- Accidents (including transportation and site-based)
- Cash-flow failures

Adjacent or neighbouring facilities and environment:

- Transportation access loss
- Power failure
- Explosion
- Structural failure
- Loss of access to site(s)
- Terrorist-type attacks (workplace violence, bomb threats)
- Strikes
- Environmental pollution (hazardous material spillage)
- Accidents (including transportation and site-based)

External or regional sources:

- Fire
- Earthquake
- Landslide
- Wind (microburst, tornado, cyclone)
- Storm
- Snow
- Volcanic activity (direct or indirect including lava, laha and ash dispersal)
- Tsunamis (tidal waves)
- Epidemic
- Power failure
- Loss of resource supplies
- Transportation access loss
- Computer failure
- Information systems failure (including all forms of electronic systems)
- Explosion
- Loss of access to site(s)
- Loss of lifelines
- Chemical or gas leaks
- Chemical or gas storage failure
- Computer system penetration (hacker or virus)
- Malicious damage to data, facilities or product
- Terrorist-type attacks (workplace violence, bomb threats)
- Strikes
- Civil disorder
- Environmental pollution (hazardous material spillage)
- War
- Accidents (including transportation and site-based)
- Mass transport accidents (that happen on organization's site)
- Hostile takeover
- Share market failure
- Government regulations

Remote (national and international) sources:

- Fire
- Earthquake
- Landslide
- Wind (microburst, tornado, cyclone)
- Storm
- Snow
- Volcanic activity (direct or indirect including lava, laha and ash dispersal)
- Tsunamis (tidal waves)
- Epidemic
- Power failure
- Loss of resource supplies
- Computer failure
- Information systems failure (including all forms of electronic systems)
- Explosion
- Loss of access to site(s)
- Loss of lifelines
- Terrorist-type attacks (workplace violence, bomb threats)
- Strikes
- Civil disorder
- Environmental pollution (hazardous material spillage)
- War
- Accidents
- Hostile takeover
- Share market failure
- Government regulations

Chapters 5 and 9

The 14 units cannot protect all of North Angst. The crisis managers need to use a mixture of mobile and static warning and defence systems, knowing that any visible terrorist action has to strike at the cities or at the oil well, mine or VIP resort.

Note that as the crisis proceeds it is possible that meeting the various demands for protection can erode the combat power.

One possible strategy is to place one unit on each of the six sites (with the HQ, TL and UL units being based on the cities and a combat unit placed on each of the bases. This leaves eight units that can be divided into four mobile patrols of two units. Two of the patrols can move up to 12 squares from the HQ unit and still be under control and the other Leader pieces also control units up to four squares away. Try placing the HQ unit on T17 to see how that exerts control. Place each of the non-combatant P1 and P2 units with a combat unit to make up patrols in the bottom half of the map. Try keeping the S unit close to Rage.

Remember that a crisis consists of information management and image management (review Chapter 8). Sift through the sometimes conflicting information to see if a pattern emerges. Note that one or two units may get severely damaged in clashing with the Kalmist forces, so be ready with good storylines before that happens – 'actively seeking out those who would destroy our peace and prosperity', 'protected the civilians from the horrors of war as far as the unit(s) was (were) able', or 'fought valiantly against superior numbers of insurgents who use every unthinkable means to hurt our people.'

At the same time, placing units to defend the six sites reduces charges of favouritism or of leaving some key areas undefended.

As the incident, information and media questions begin to mount, you are likely to notice that some units fail for other than combat reasons and a latent hostility emerges from the population you are trying to protect. One reason for placing a combat unit stationary on each of the six sites is that immobility does not reduce a unit's ability to defend a square. Note that six out of ten stationary units means that any immobilization is less likely to upset the overall strategy.

Deal politely with appeals for help and accusations of cover-ups and military brutality.

Within your crisis management team you are likely to witness a natural divide between the three military and the three civilians, although the Minister of Police may move between these groups. This is not surprising as two different preoccupations emerge – finding and dealing with the Kalmists and managing the communications and information efforts. You may find that the unassigned Colonel and the Minister of Police would become spokespersons in any media arrangement. Have a look at how the CMSS approach would handle the team structure – each group role can adopt a key role in the CMSS structure and thus focus participants on their operational, image management or communications roles.

Chapter 7

While this exercise is primarily set to help practise responding to media questions, a number of useful insights may well have been uncovered as well, some of which may have included the following:

- Stop the problem from getting worse (*see* Chapter 13) by removing possible contaminated stock and closing the area down.
- Find out hard information about the situation.
- Get ready for media inquiries.
- Activate the crisis management team.
- Have someone visit the hospital(s) to check on the condition of any victims (even if it turns out the organization is not the source).
- Do not assume any of these actions have been done.

Of course many more assumptions and insights are likely to be generated. Take some time to think through the list you have. Try to identify ways these assumptions may be checked for accuracy and validity. Moreover, if bias seems present, look for ways of countering it.

Answering media questions

The best advice you can absorb in answering these questions is to follow the guidelines outlined in Chapter 7.

- Control where the media may go.
- When undertaking verbal interviews develop some short statements of between 10 and 30 seconds in length to convey important positional information.
- Appear open and honest when interviewed, and deal with concrete 'facts' and not with assumptions.
- Remain calm and open to questions, and speak as a person not as a mouthpiece.
- Personalize any comments or statements so long as this does not conflict with the aims and objectives of the organization and/or crisis management effort.

The four questions

- *Is it true that your company is already being investigated for other health and safety issues?* **Trap:** saying no comment, being aggressive with questioner.
- *How many deaths and injuries may result from this?* **Trap:** speculating, avoiding comment.
- *Are the companies supplying you with security most likely to be at fault?* **Trap:** blaming others, getting aggressive with questioner.
- *When are you going to come clean and really tell us what is going on?* **Trap:** getting aggressive with questioner, arguing.

Remember you can shape the answers to questions toward those areas that suit you and/or the organization:

- 'I think what you are trying to ask is ...'
- 'While I need more information to fully respond to that, I can point out that what we are doing at this moment is ...'

Avoid saying 'no comment'.

Avoid misrepresentation.

Avoid speculation. Refuse to be drawn into a speculative response:

- outline other speculative scenarios and then conclude that speculation is consequently not helpful; or
- acknowledge that the speculative question is interesting and worth considering given time, resources and a more predictable situation – none of which is currently available.

Avoid assigning blame to organizations or people. State that:

- such judgements are not useful at this point in time;
- all the facts are being examined by the appropriate authorities; or
- such speculation distracts from the current effort of managing and resolving the crisis.

Avoid clashes with the media.

Chapter 8

This pressure group interaction is best approached by using an open win–win strategy that gets the issues out into the public view and shows you and your organization to be thoughtful, respectful of the opinion of others, honestly trying to achieve a workable solution and prepared to listen to others.

This strategy can shift to a win–lose effort (disguised as a win–win) in which the effort of being open and honest and seeking a practical resolution is emphasized to the surrounding audience so that the other party looks bad. This may happen inadvertently, so work hard to keep the situation honest and open if you are really seeking a win–win outcome.

At the point the news is heard by you, you need to:

- find out hard information about the situation;
- get ready for media inquiries;
- activate the crisis management team;
- do not assume any of these actions have been done.

If the organization is connected to the problem via third-party arrangements, then some obvious steps may be considered:

- change the third party;
- encourage the third party to change the contracts to more suitable sources;
- improve the working environment in some way if the contracts cannot be changed.

Before any dramatic change, however, investigate the costs to your organization (customers may prefer lower prices) and remember that severing the unfair contract may put the 'slave labour' out of work.

Using a win–win approach, invite PAPPAW to assist in devising 'fair contract' definitions so that the industry (as well as your organization) may benefit. A third-party and independent assessment and research operation may be set up (involving all interested parties – PAPPAW and the unions included). This third-party effort would establish more clearly what may be fair and unfair practices in various regions of the world, and what positive changes may be encouraged within those regions (and within the industry). Remember, if you can get the industry group or market to change then you do not lose by changing your operations to conform with the changes.

Your organization may consider providing aid to the survivors and families of the victims as a benevolent gesture, or offer to match the financial and material assistance that PAPPAW and similar pressure groups may offer the victims and their families.

Chapters 13 and 15

This activity presents two parts of crisis management – response and recovery management.

Response management

All pieces are not immediately available, so those who deploy the initial units need to remember where the next 'Group' comes into the map and plan accordingly. Divide the map into northern and southern halves until all pieces have been deployed. Remember to read through the instructions carefully as useful information is placed throughout the response scenario.

Try to do an OMT on the soft information given in the introduction. You can use the model(s) outlined in Chapter 13 and see how the resulting priorities work. Look at the main contribution of each unit. Try dividing units into groups according specialization, then try pairing rescue and firefighting units. The latter strategy works well providing an early control is exerted on each site. Once a site is out of control (explodes or is well on fire), piecemeal strategies are unlikely to work. You could try a mix of specialist and mixed groupings.

Note what happens if you use 'management' units as 'workers'. Communications fail and co-ordinated effort becomes tenuous. Because direction and support is not present, units and non-response people can be placed at greater risk.

Recovery component

This component illustrates elements of recovery from intangible and partial-response management crisis situations. As a result, most recovery management groups may feel a little confused, vague about what is happening and at the mercy of 'outside' forces.

You were to draw up four 'lists' of actions. Check whether these choices hold during the six turns. Many recovery managers become immersed in the reconstruction to find that the rest of the organization and the outside world have moved on oblivious to the crisis. Note how outside events (stockholder concerns, financial strains, industrial action, competitor's advertising campaigns and pressure group campaigns) can distract or impede recovery. Were any of these noted in your list of impediments?

AngU Airlines This company appears to be in some financial trouble, with sales sliding before the accident. Recovery seems quite simple – acquire a replacement aircraft. The real problem resides in a deepening negative public image of the company. How could this be changed? Is this the province of crisis management? (Yes – otherwise a full-scale crisis could emerge. Remember crisis management is as much about stopping crisis situations from happening as it is about dealing with crisis situations when they arise.)

Effort needs to be placed in image management, in looking after all the stakeholders and in delivering the best product possible. Recovery management from the impacts of intangible crisis situations means long-term efforts in turning negative images into positive images while improving short-term service or product delivery. This is the time for AngU management to recover staff morale (a ceremony for the victims then later a party to say thank you for the hard work), reward loyalty, refurbish the aircraft and provide reasons for would-be customers to fly with the airline. If this was a rare accident, then begin to say so. Encourage staff to lift their game.

The real recovery effort consequently needs to focus on stakeholders. Have another look at your four 'lists' and determine whether sufficient emphasis was placed on this area (as opposed to material aspects – new equipment, new advertising campaign or even new uniforms and logos).

Storage International This situation may at first appear more tangible. The facility is destroyed so the core question is whether to rebuild or not. Note that the cost of decontamination and salvage may not be absorbed in any sale. On the other hand, note that the other storage facilities are only two-thirds used. Is this an over-supply situation? Is this a recovery management situation? (Yes – because rebuilding a mostly unused facility will prove costly over time.) Some careful research needs to be done before the decision is made. Was this noted in your 'lists' at all? In most cases, the answer would be 'not on my lists'. This is because many managers jump quickly into rebuilding before thinking all the aspects through. Note that if the two-thirds capacity is not a trend (and thus indicating lost markets or over-supply of the facilities in the industry), your company may be able to continue meeting around half the possible pre-set contracts for services.

The recovery may also be troubled by replacement material that is flawed, outside pressures for industrial action and a growing pressure to be moved from the area. Recovery management needs to help normal management come to decisions over the cost of rebuilding.

Note that until a safe and operational storage facility is constructed, there is no business for that site. Unlike other businesses which may have stored products, reconstructed assembly lines or strong after-sales service programmes to fall back on, Storage International has one line of business – storing industrial liquids and gases. As a result, recovery management shifts toward recovery management from an intangible crisis. The company needs to rebuild quickly yet very visibly with added safety features (outcomes, not processes achieving those outcomes). At the same time, it needs to take positive steps to stop any developing negative public image. This may be done by involving critics as well as stakeholders in the reconstruction process. Similarly, the company needs to be seen to be recovering, preferably with a bigger and better business effort. If the decision is to rebuild, then involve the public and media in seeing the safest facility in Angst being built. Keep prospective clients informed how the reconstruction is going and when they may be able to use the facility. If the decision is to vacate the site, then remember to 'sell' the ability to handle the work elsewhere. Find other providers for clients – do not just let clients move away on their own volition.

Post-crisis media management

After the response activities and associated excitement have diminished, media management needs to be continued at a quick and professional level. Three elements need to be noted:

- Other stories will be grabbing public (and media) attention, so it is more difficult to 'sell' a 'things are getting better' storyline. You may have to launch your own publicity campaign, but be sure you have something that is positive from the public's POV.
- With most interest coming from investigative and 'cover' stories, media representatives will generally have longer deadlines. This does not mean that they will not expect (even require) a fast response from your company's representatives, but that they may take longer to search for an attention-grabbing interesting slant.
- Questions are likely to be less direct and emotionally urgent, but more opinionated and deliberate. In many cases, questions change from information-seeking to information-confirming. Unless the person being interviewed is trained and on the alert, what is not said or what is confirmed by default or by grudging agreement establishes the storyline of the finished media product.

Do not make the mistake of relaxing into any form of hands-off media and public interest management. Pressure groups and media representatives may still target the four 'homecoming' dates:

- The weekend after the response management is finished – the storyline may focus on aftermath stories and try to 'get a handle on what happened'.
- Between 100 and 200 days – if no cause has been identified ('what if …' pro-

grammes), if recovery is still not visibly achieved ('when will this get back to normal ...'), or if 'new' evidence is beginning to emerge.

- The year anniversary – especially if the cause is still not established, there are still people mourning victims or recovery has still not been visibly achieved.
- The *n*-date kicker – when another similar crisis situation happens, the media and the public will recall and maybe inquire about your organization's situation and look for parallels and differences.

One other key difference in dealing with post-crisis media and public interest is that you no longer have the excuse of crisis-stress, lack of knowledge due to a confused and changing situation or a need to return to urgent response work. As a result those asking the questions are likely to ask them longer, louder and more often.

Have a look at your four 'lists', the bits of new information and questions asked, and see whether your strategies could be better tailored to ease recovery along and reduce associated negative images. Do not let the seeming lack of detailed recovery information (project schedules, activity timelines, exact costings and use of temporary facilities) distract you. Unless carefully planned, there will be problems in reconfiguring the rest of the organization and relocating staff and operations. Write the questions you want answered down and analyze them for patterns and their contribution to hard information and more certainty in decision making. You learn much more from clearly establishing what you need to know than you will learn from just working with facts someone else gives you. This is the quintessential fact you can learn from this exercise: learn to look for the questions, not just the answers.

Index